尾 田 栄 一 郎

I turned 30 this year. What's more,
I got married last year. There are days
when I worry that I still do nothing but
draw manga, and I wonder if I should
be a bit more serious about life. But
I'm healthy, and that's the important
thing. Volume 36 begins now.

-Eiichiro Oda, 2005

 iichiro Oda began his manga career at the age of
17, when his one-shot cowboy manga **Wanted!**
won second place in the coveted Tezuka manga
awards. Oda went on to work as an assistant to
some of the biggest manga artists in the industry,
including Nobuhiro Watsuki, before winning the
Hop Step Award for new artists. His pirate
adventure **One Piece**, which debuted in
Weekly Shonen Jump in 1997, quickly became
one of the most popular manga in Japan.

ONE PIECE VOL. 36
WATER SEVEN PART 5

SHONEN JUMP Manga Edition

STORY AND ART BY EIICHIRO ODA

English Adaptation/Jake Forbes
Translation/Taylor Eagle, HC Language Solutions, Inc.
Touch-up Art & Lettering/John Hunt
Design/Sean Lee
Supervising Editor/Yuki Murashige
Editor/Yuki Takagaki

VP, Production/Alvin Lu
VP, Sales & Product Marketing/Gonzalo Ferreyra
VP, Creative/Linda Espinosa
Publisher/Hyoe Narita

Printed in the U.S.A.

Published by VIZ Media, LLC
P.O. Box 77010
San Francisco, CA 94107

10 9 8 7 6 5 4 3 2 1
First printing, March 2010

www.viz.com

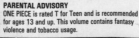

THE WORLD'S MOST POPULAR MANGA
SHONEN JUMP
www.shonenjump.com

SHONEN JUMP MANGA

Vol. 36
THE NINTH JUSTICE

STORY AND ART BY
EIICHIRO ODA

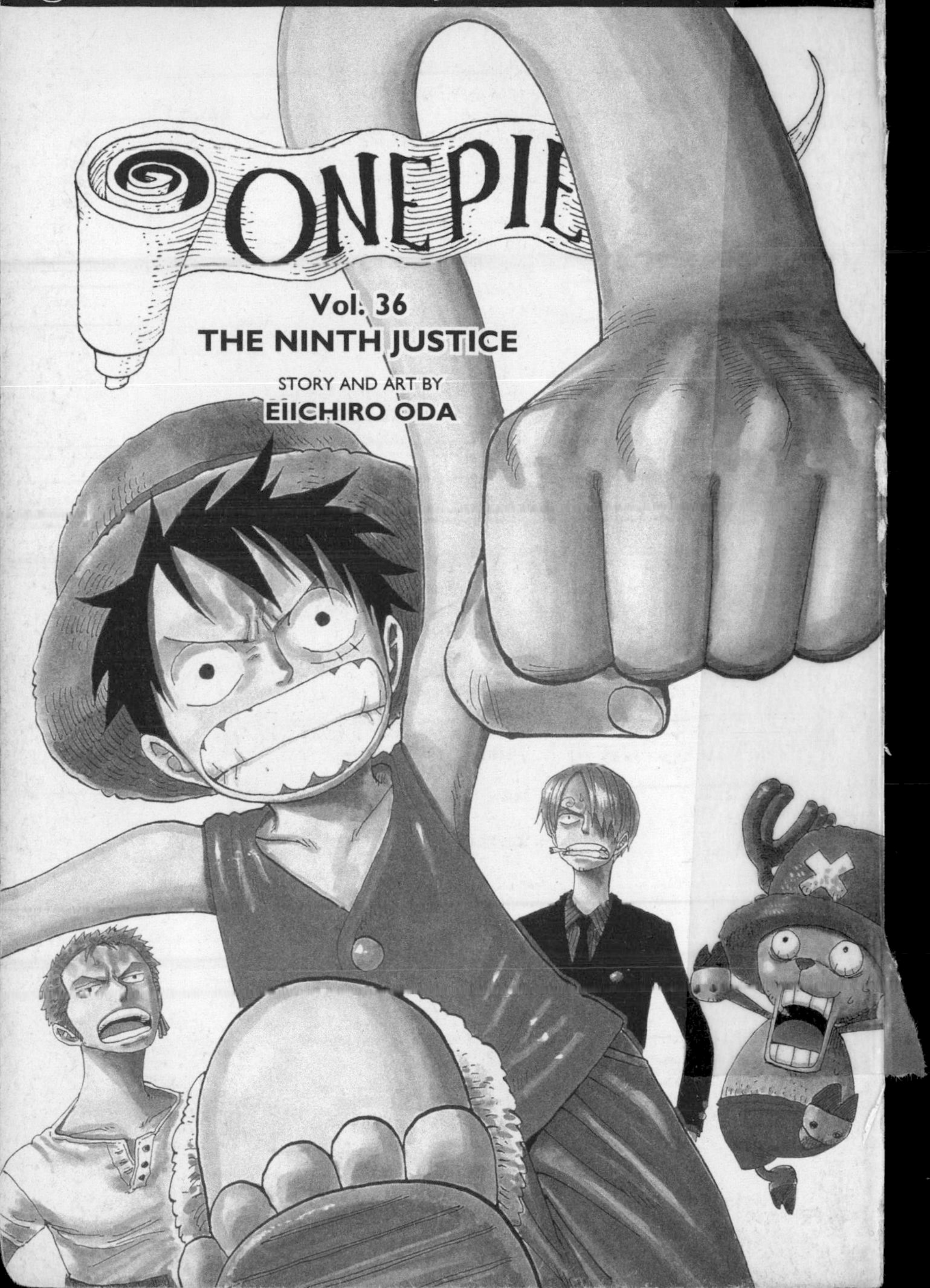

The Straw Hats

Boundlessly optimistic and able to stretch like rubber, he is determined to become King of the Pirates.

Monkey D. Luffy

A former bounty hunter and master of the "three-sword" style. He aspires to be the world's greatest swordsman.

Roronoa Zolo

A thief who specializes in robbing pirates. Nami hates pirates, but Luffy convinced her to be his navigator.

Nami

The bighearted cook (and ladies' man) whose dream is to find the legendary sea, the "All Blue."

Sanji

A blue-nosed man-reindeer and the ship's doctor.

Tony Tony Chopper

A mysterious woman in search of the Ponegliff on which true history is recorded.

Nico Robin

A village boy with a talent for telling tall tales. His father, Yasopp, is a member of Shanks's crew.

Usopp

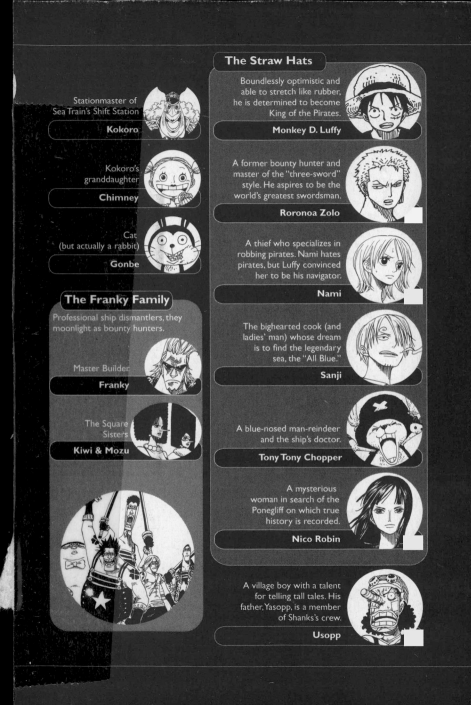

Stationmaster of Sea Train's Shift Station

Kokoro

Kokoro's granddaughter

Chimney

Cat (but actually a rabbit)

Gonbe

The Franky Family

Professional ship dismantlers, they moonlight as bounty hunters.

Master Builder

Franky

The Square Sisters

Kiwi & Mozu

THE STORY OF ONE PIECE

Volume 36

Monkey D. Luffy started out as just a kid with a dream—to become the greatest pirate in history! Stirred by the tales of pirate "Red-Haired" Shanks, Luffy vowed to become a pirate himself. That was before the enchanted Devil Fruit gave Luffy the power to stretch like rubber, at the cost of being unable to swim—a serious handicap for an aspiring sea dog. Undeterred, Luffy set out to sea and recruited some crewmates—master swordsman Zolo; treasure-hunting thief Nami; lying sharp-shooter Usopp; the high-kicking chef Sanji; Chopper, the walkin' talkin' reindeer doctor; and the mysterious archaeologist Robin.

Luffy's ship, the *Merry Go*, has taken a beating during the crew's adventures on Sky Island. To get it repaired, the Straw Hats head to the metropolis Water Seven, home to the world's best shipwrights. Using the gold from Sky Island, they hire the island's biggest shipbuilding outfit, the Galley-La Company, but they soon discover that the ship's keel is damaged beyond repair. The news troubles Luffy, but then, as captain, he makes a shocking decision. The crew will part with the *Merry Go* and find a new ship! Furious, Usopp resigns and leaves the crew. On top of that, Nico Robin is linked to a failed attempt to kill Mayor Iceberg, and suspicion falls on the crew! Robin then disappears after hearing the mysterious name "CP9." Then Franky shows up and declares war on the Straw Hats for destroying his hideout. The Galley-La Company joins in, too, to catch the criminal behind the attack on Mayor Iceberg. Is this the start of a three-way battle?!

Galley-La Company

A top shipbuilding company. They are purveyors to the World Government.

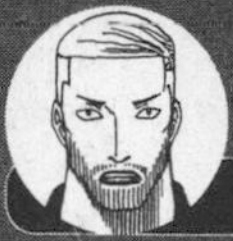

Mayor of Water Seven and president of Galley-La Company

Iceberg

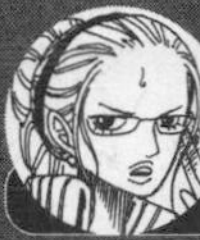

Beautiful secretary

Kalifa

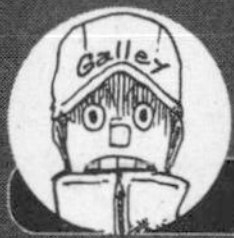
Galley

Carpentry Foreman

Kaku

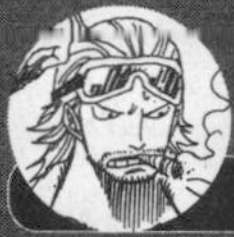

Rigging and Mast Foreman

Paulie

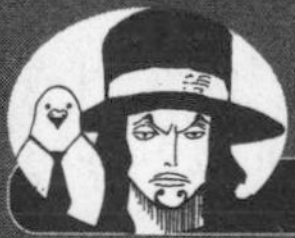

Sawyer and Treenail Foreman, with his pet pigeon

Rob Lucci & Hattori

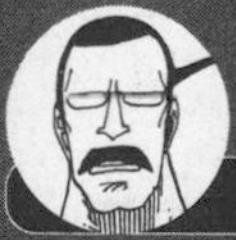

Pitch, Blacksmithing and Block-and-Tackle Foreman

Peepley Lulu

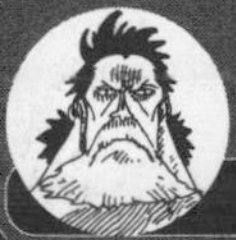

Cabinetry, Caulking and Flag-Making Foreman

Tilestone

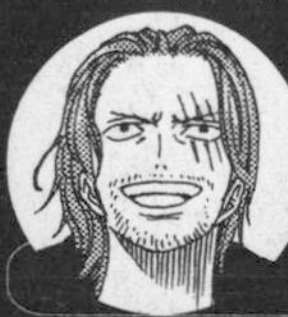

A pirate that Luffy idolizes. Shanks gave Luffy his trademark straw hat.

"Red-Haired" Shanks

WATER SEVEN
ONE PIECE

Vol. 36
The Ninth Justice

CONTENTS

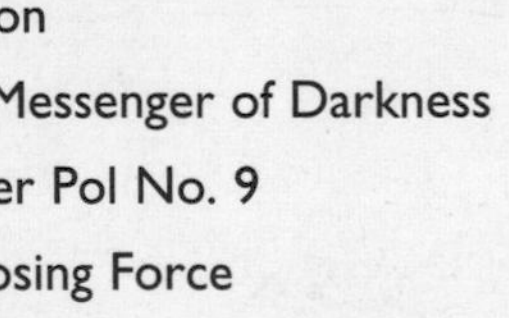

Chapter 337:
PROTECTORS OF THE CITY OF WATER

TEXT ON HELMET SAYS "BOSS"; ON T-SHIRT, "SAND"--ED.

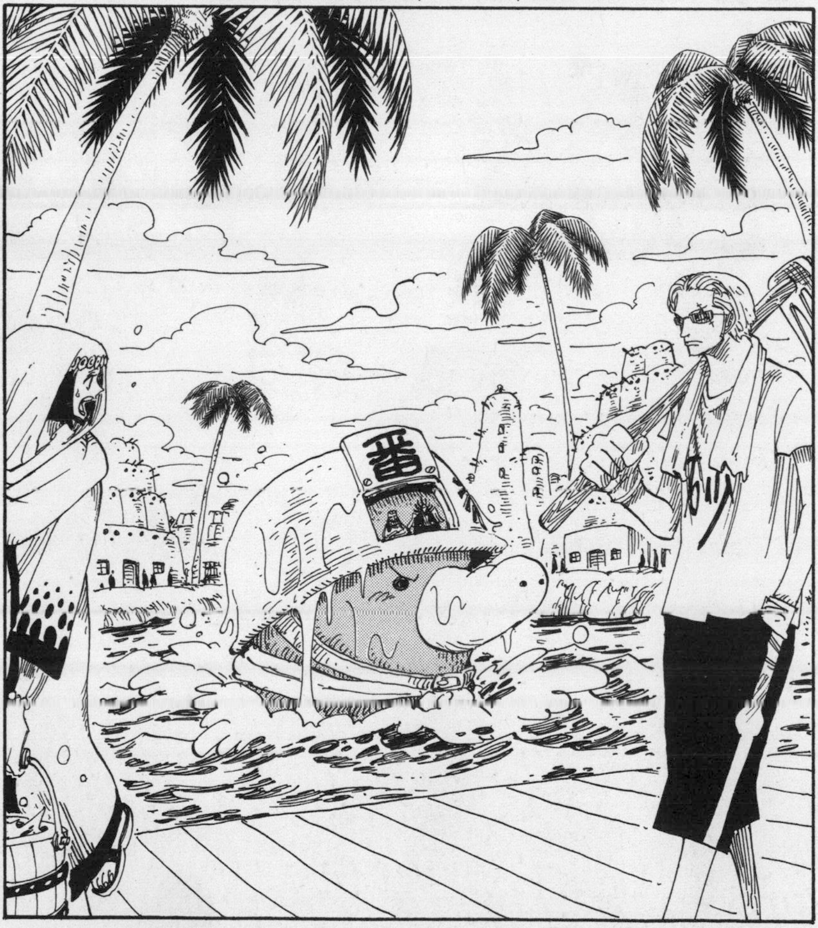
番

GEDATSU'S UNEXPECTED LIFE ON THE BLUE SEA, VOL. 21:
"THE UNEXPECTED ARRIVAL AT THE DESERT OASIS"

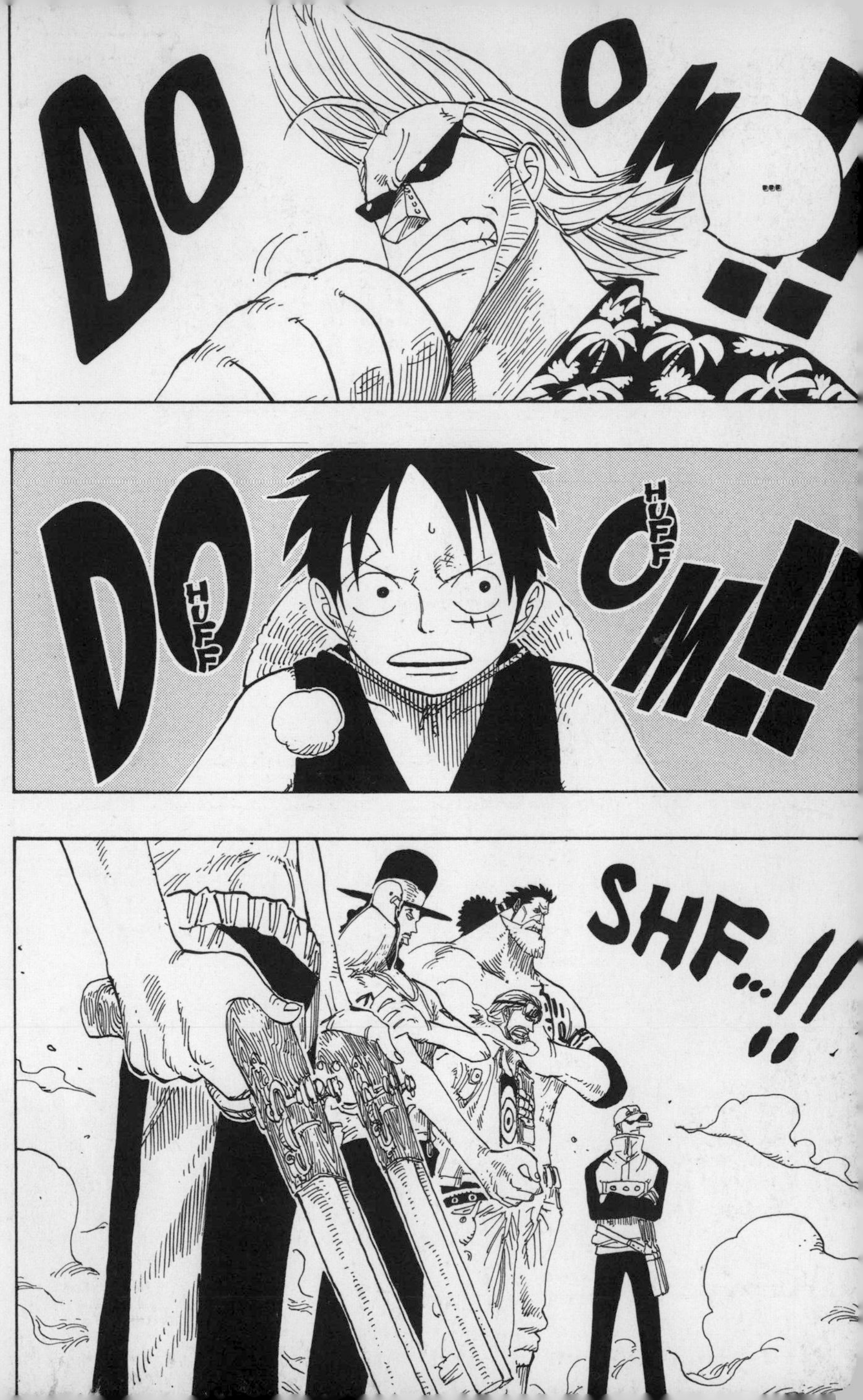
...
DO OM..!!
DO OM..!!
HUFF
HUFF
SHF...!!

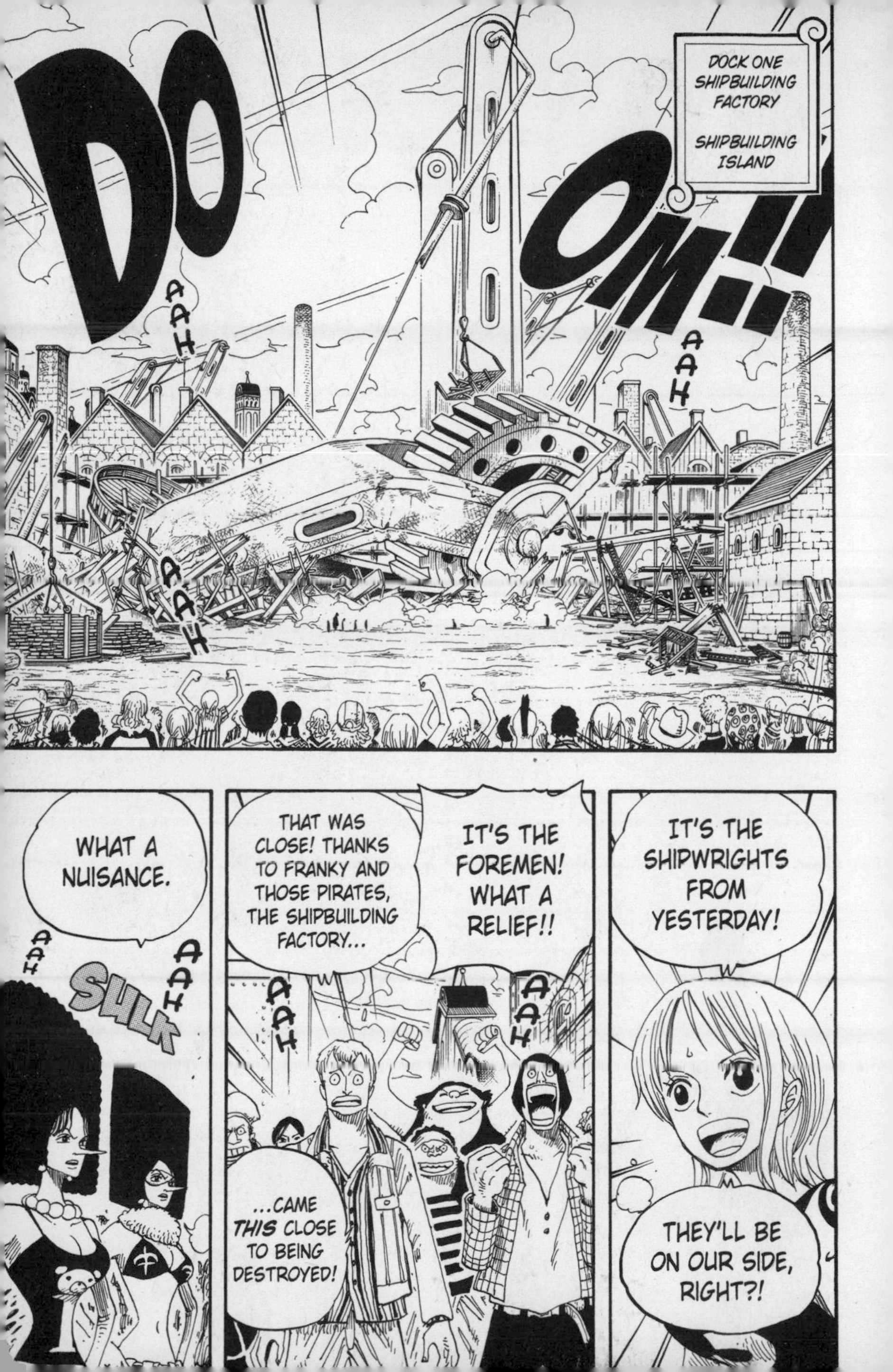
DOCK ONE SHIPBUILDING FACTORY
SHIPBUILDING ISLAND
DOOM!!
AAH
AAH
AAH
IT'S THE SHIPWRIGHTS FROM YESTERDAY!
THEY'LL BE ON OUR SIDE, RIGHT?!
IT'S THE FOREMEN! WHAT A RELIEF!!
AAH
THAT WAS CLOSE! THANKS TO FRANKY AND THOSE PIRATES, THE SHIPBUILDING FACTORY...
AAH
...CAME THIS CLOSE TO BEING DESTROYED!
WHAT A NUISANCE.
AAH
SULK
AAH

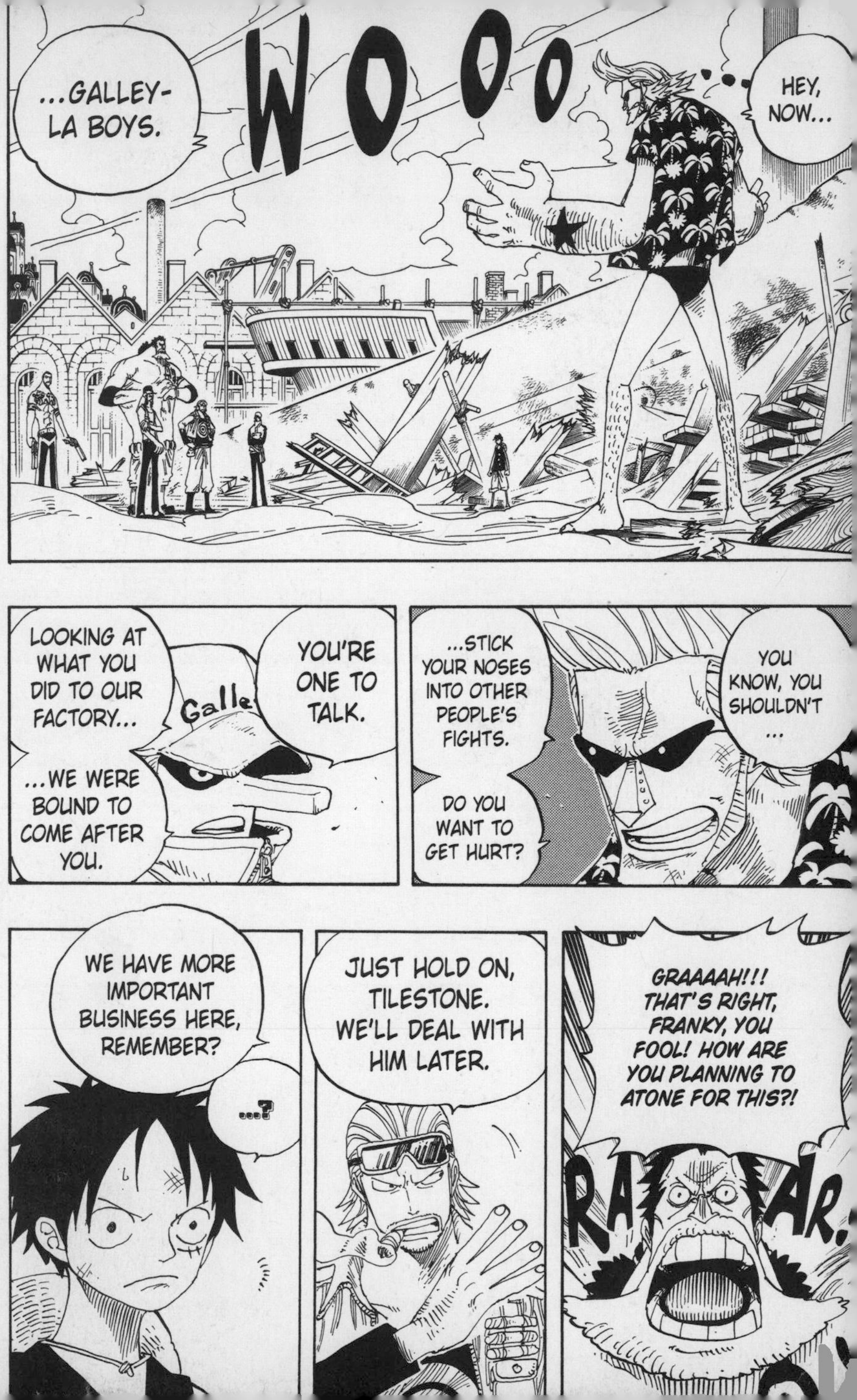
HEY, NOW...
WOOO
...GALLEY-LA BOYS.
YOU KNOW, YOU SHOULDN'T ...
...STICK YOUR NOSES INTO OTHER PEOPLE'S FIGHTS.
DO YOU WANT TO GET HURT?
YOU'RE ONE TO TALK.
Galle
LOOKING AT WHAT YOU DID TO OUR FACTORY...
...WE WERE BOUND TO COME AFTER YOU.
GRAAAAH!!! THAT'S RIGHT, FRANKY, YOU FOOL! HOW ARE YOU PLANNING TO ATONE FOR THIS?!
RA
AR.
JUST HOLD ON, TILESTONE. WE'LL DEAL WITH HIM LATER.
WE HAVE MORE IMPORTANT BUSINESS HERE, REMEMBER?
...?

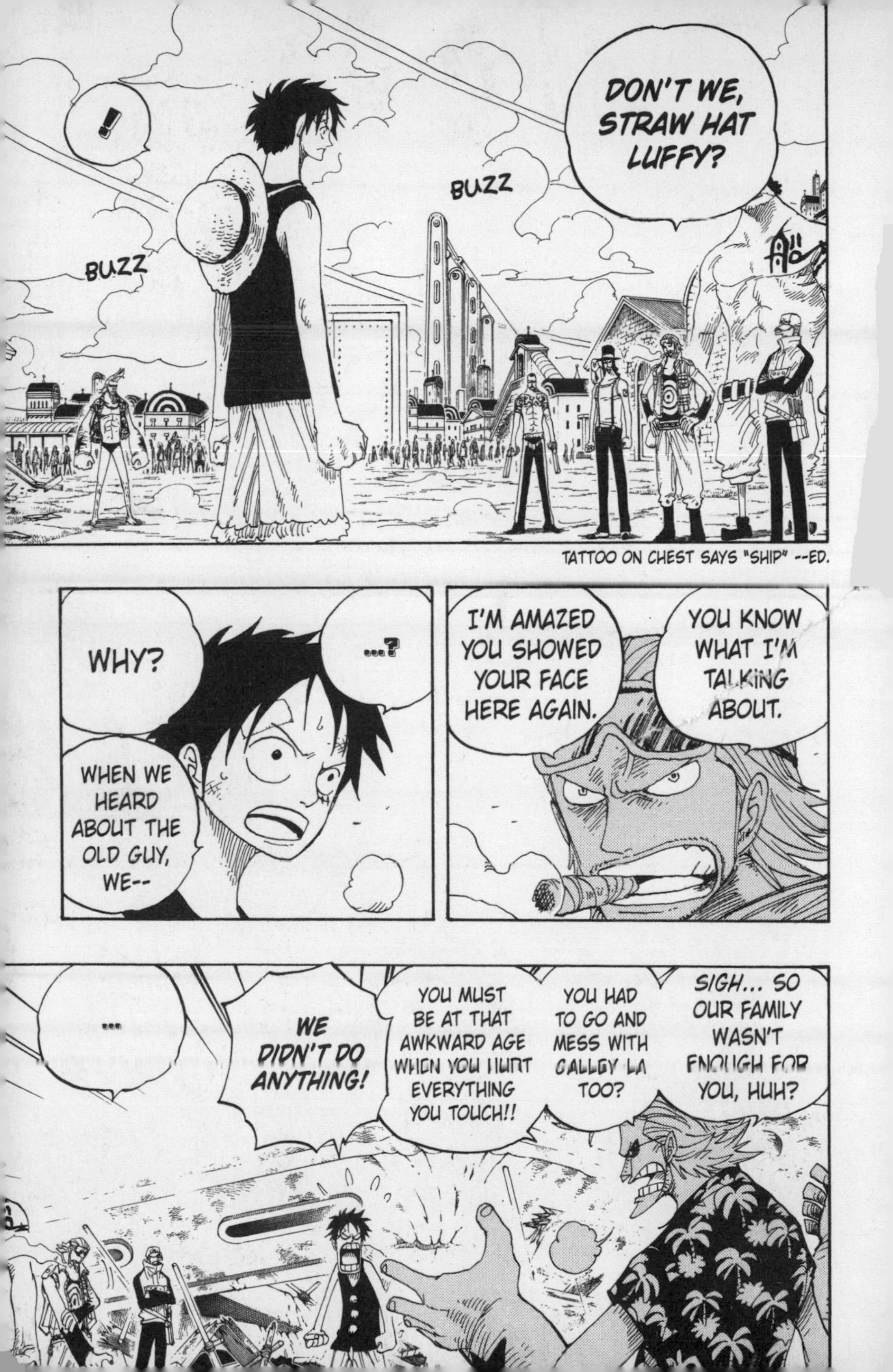
DON'T WE, STRAW HAT LUFFY?
BUZZ
!
BUZZ
YOU KNOW WHAT I'M TALKING ABOUT.
I'M AMAZED YOU SHOWED YOUR FACE HERE AGAIN.
...?
WHY?
WHEN WE HEARD ABOUT THE OLD GUY, WE--
SIGH... SO OUR FAMILY WASN'T ENOUGH FOR YOU, HUH?
YOU HAD TO GO AND MESS WITH GALLEY LA TOO?
YOU MUST BE AT THAT AWKWARD AGE WHEN YOU HURT EVERYTHING YOU TOUCH!!
WE DIDN'T DO ANYTHING!
...
TATTOO ON CHEST SAYS "SHIP" --ED.

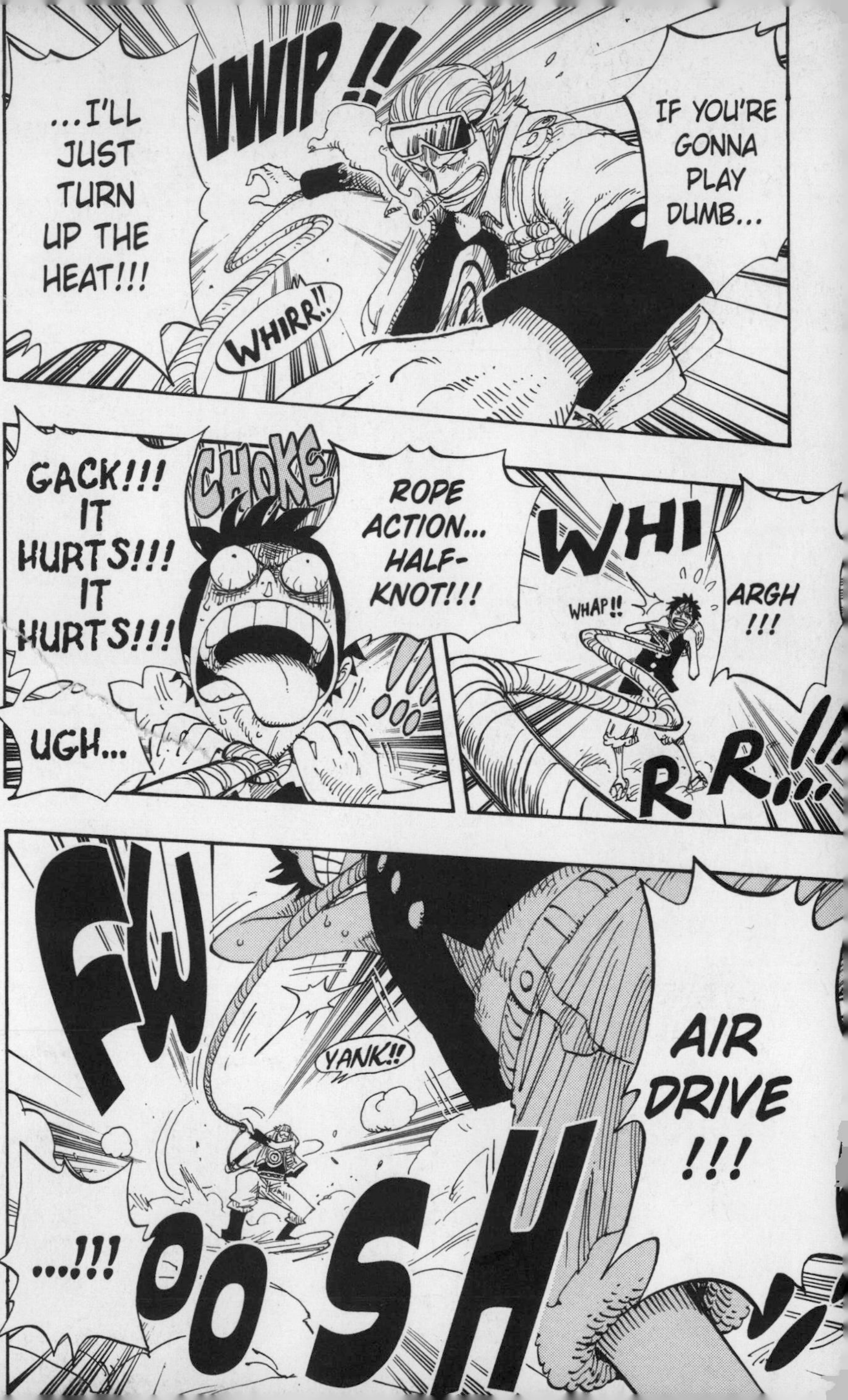

IF YOU'RE GONNA PLAY DUMB...
VWIP!!
...I'LL JUST TURN UP THE HEAT!!!
WHIRR!!
WHI
ARGH!!!
WHAP!!
RR!!!
ROPE ACTION... HALF-KNOT!!!
CHOKE
GACK!!! IT HURTS!!! IT HURTS!!!
UGH...
AIR DRIVE!!!
FW
YANK!!
OOSH
...!!!

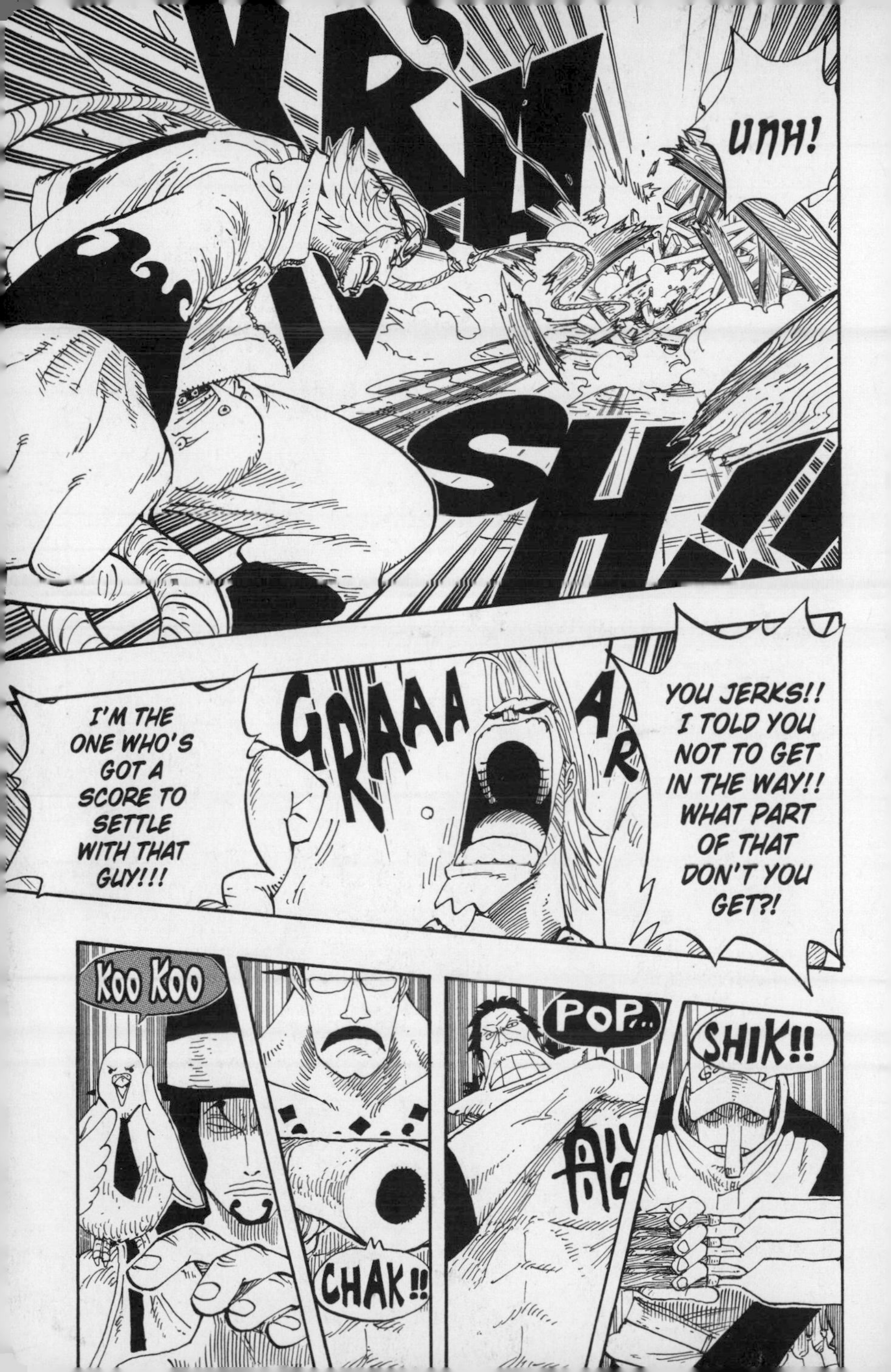
UNH!
YOU JERKS!! I TOLD YOU NOT TO GET IN THE WAY!! WHAT PART OF THAT DON'T YOU GET?!
GRAAAAR
I'M THE ONE WHO'S GOT A SCORE TO SETTLE WITH THAT GUY!!!
SHIK!!
POP...
CHAK!!
Koo Koo

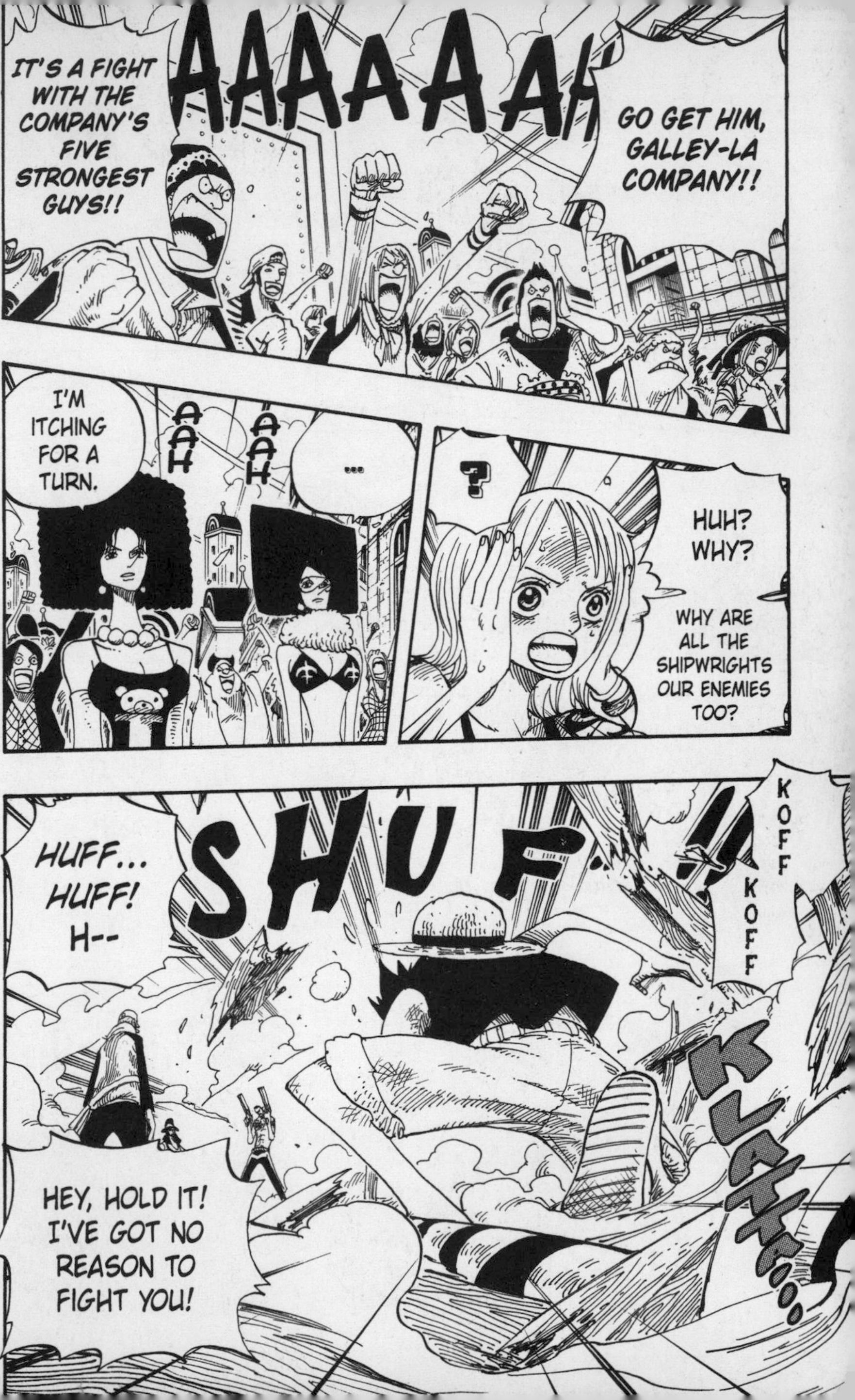
AAAAAAH
GO GET HIM, GALLEY-LA COMPANY!!
IT'S A FIGHT WITH THE COMPANY'S FIVE STRONGEST GUYS!!
?
HUH? WHY?
WHY ARE ALL THE SHIPWRIGHTS OUR ENEMIES TOO?
...
AAH
AAH
I'M ITCHING FOR A TURN.
KOFF KOFF KOFF
SHUF!!
HUFF... HUFF! H--
KLAK...
HEY, HOLD IT! I'VE GOT NO REASON TO FIGHT YOU!

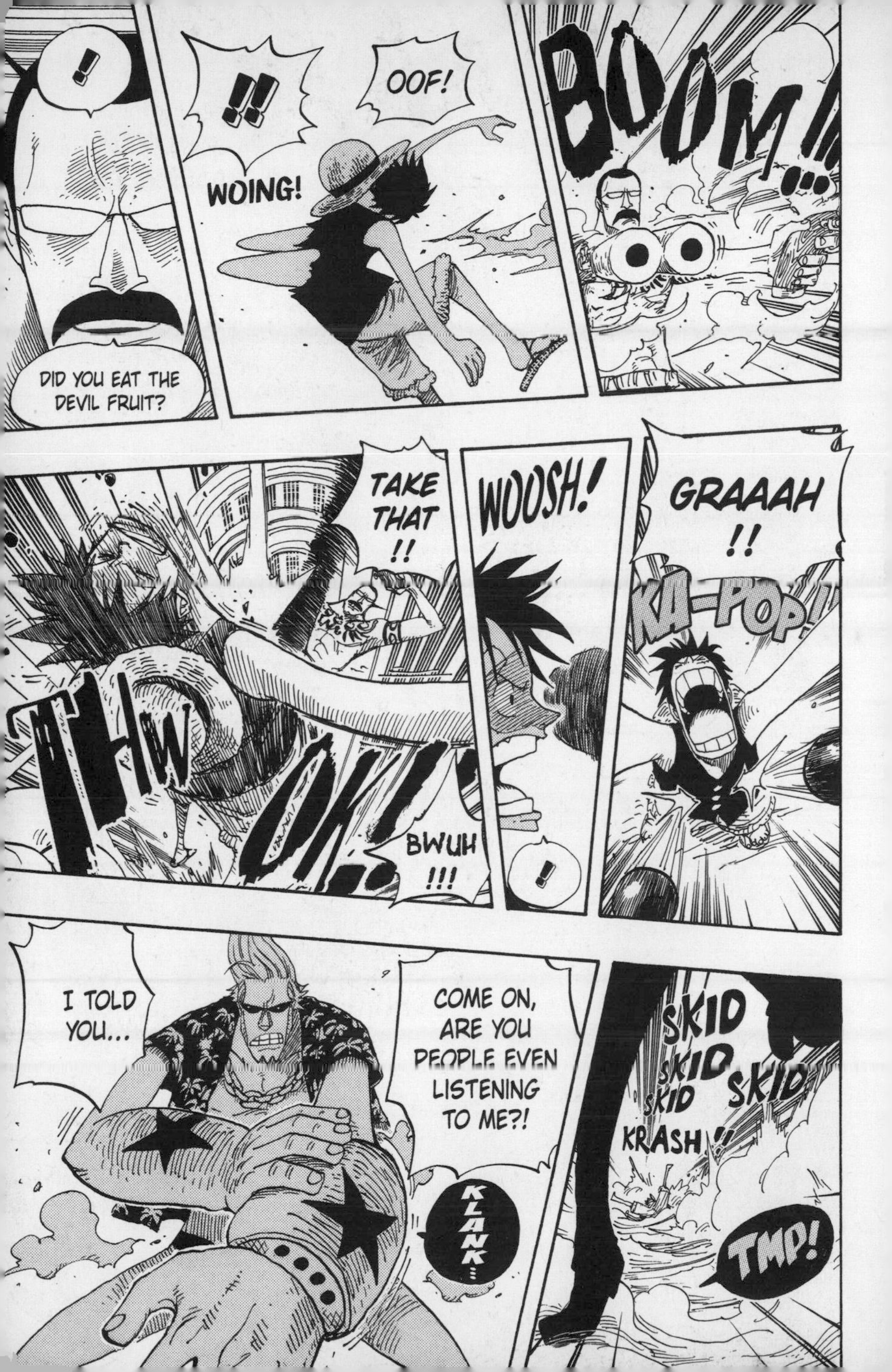
BOOM!!
OOF!
!!
WOING!
!
DID YOU EAT THE DEVIL FRUIT?
GRAAAH !!
KA-POP!!
WOOSH!
!
TAKE THAT !!
THWOK!!
BWUH !!!
SKID
SKID
SKID
SKID
KRASH!!
TMP!
COME ON, ARE YOU PEOPLE EVEN LISTENING TO ME?!
I TOLD YOU...
KLANK...

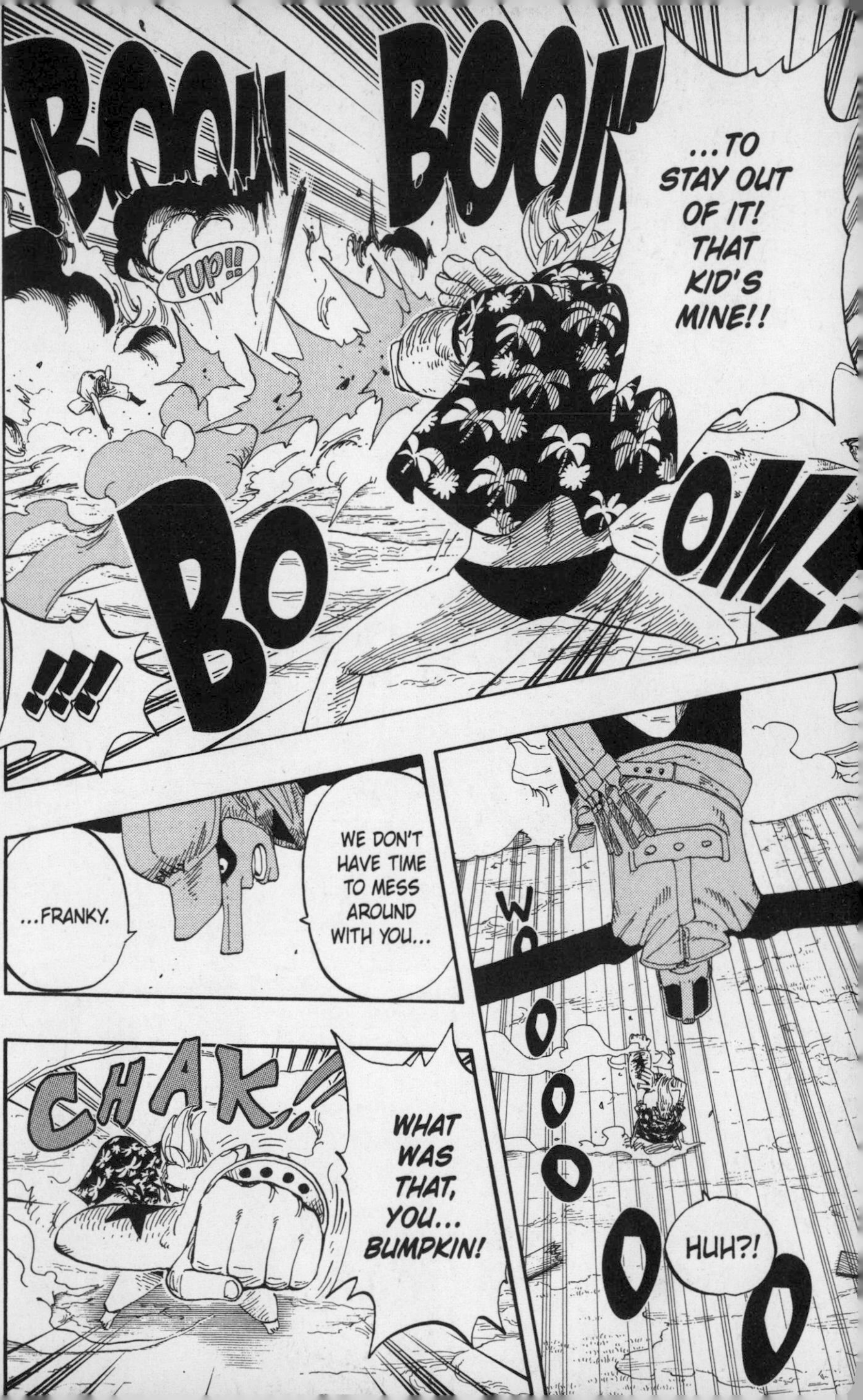

...TO STAY OUT OF IT! THAT KID'S MINE!!
BOOM
BOOM
TUP!!
BOOOM!!
!!!!
WOOOOOOOO
HUH?!
WE DON'T HAVE TIME TO MESS AROUND WITH YOU...
...FRANKY.
WHAT WAS THAT, YOU... BUMPKIN!
CHAK!!

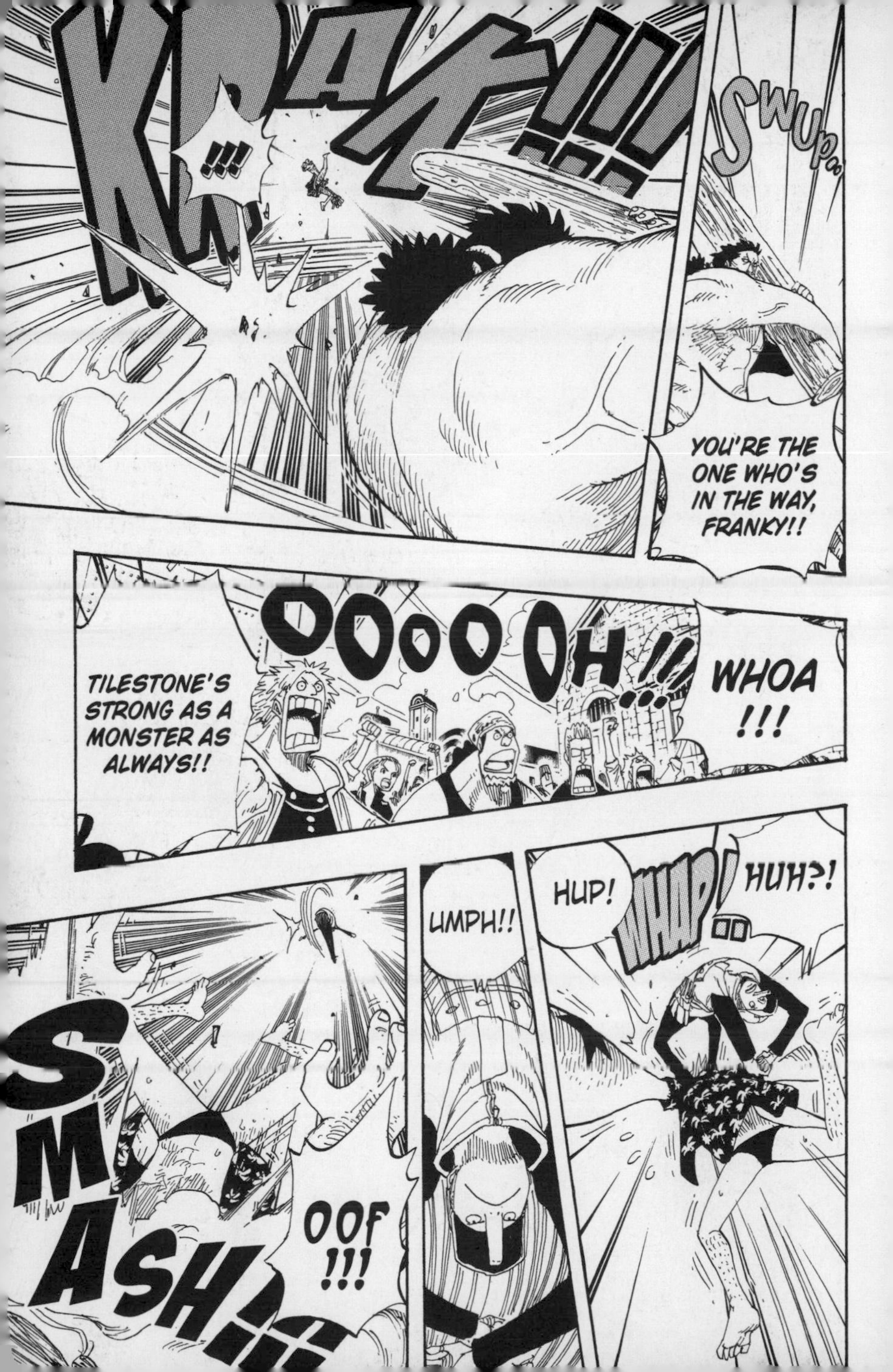
SWUP
YOU'RE THE ONE WHO'S IN THE WAY, FRANKY!!
WHOA !!!
OOOOOH!!!
TILESTONE'S STRONG AS A MONSTER AS ALWAYS!!
HUH?!
WHAP!
HUP!
UMPH!!
SMASH!!!
OOF !!!

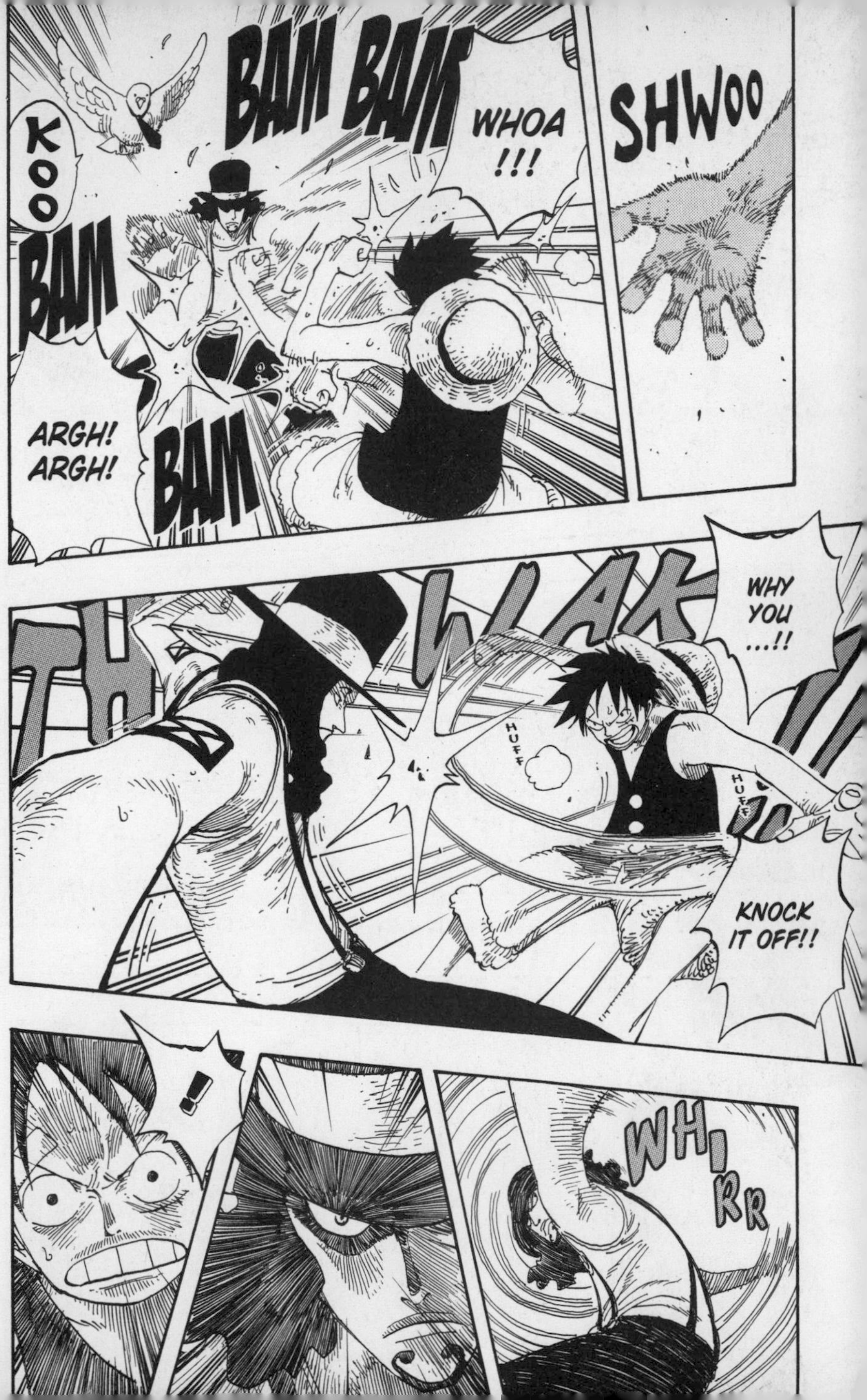

SHWOO
WHOA !!!
BAM BAM
KOO
BAM
ARGH! ARGH!
BAM
WHY YOU ...!!
WAK
HUFF
HUFF
KNOCK IT OFF!!
TH
WHIRR
!

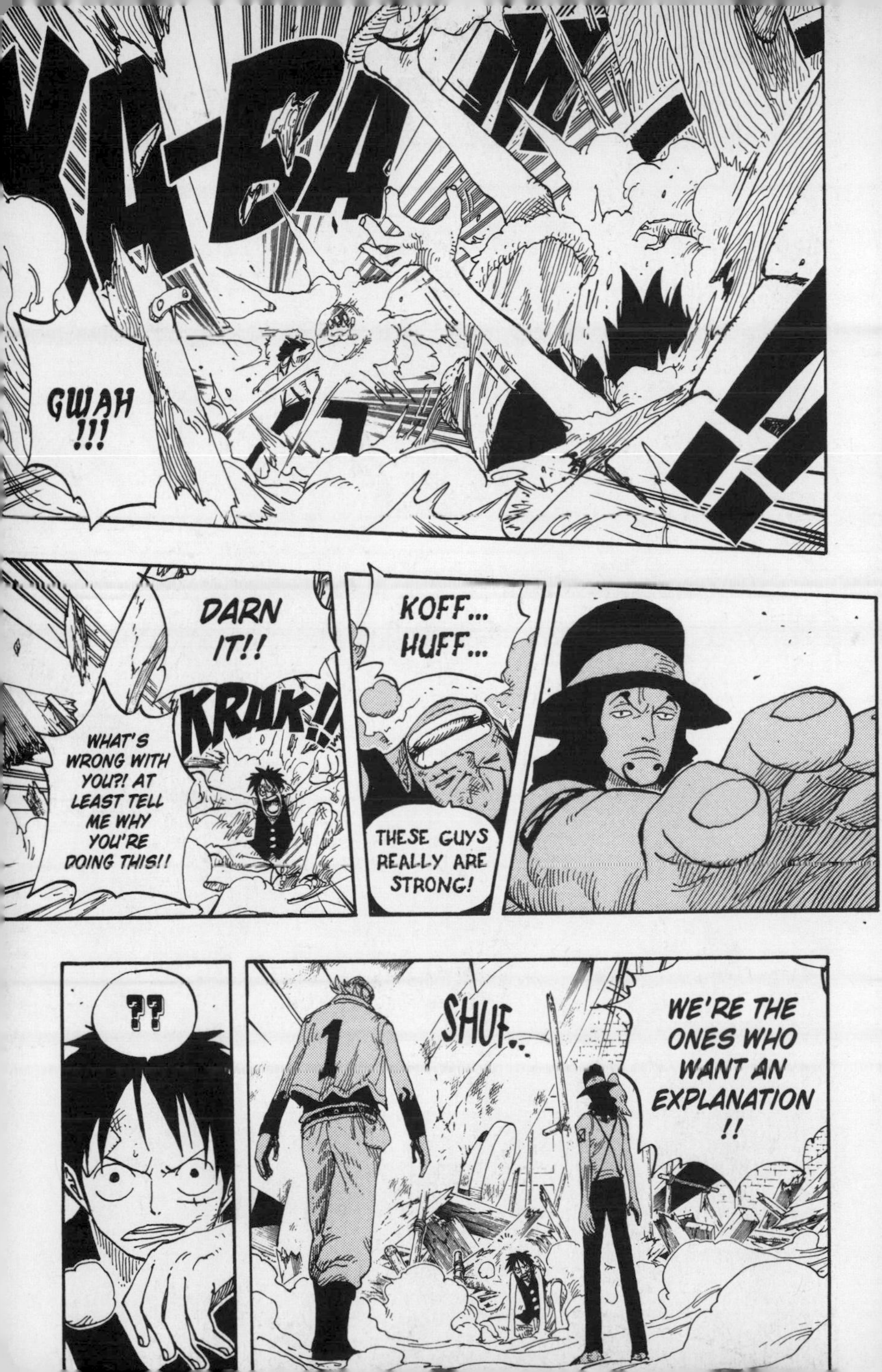
GWAH !!!
KOFF... HUFF...
THESE GUYS REALLY ARE STRONG!
DARN IT!!
KRAK!!
WHAT'S WRONG WITH YOU?! AT LEAST TELL ME WHY YOU'RE DOING THIS!!
SHUF...
WE'RE THE ONES WHO WANT AN EXPLANATION !!
??

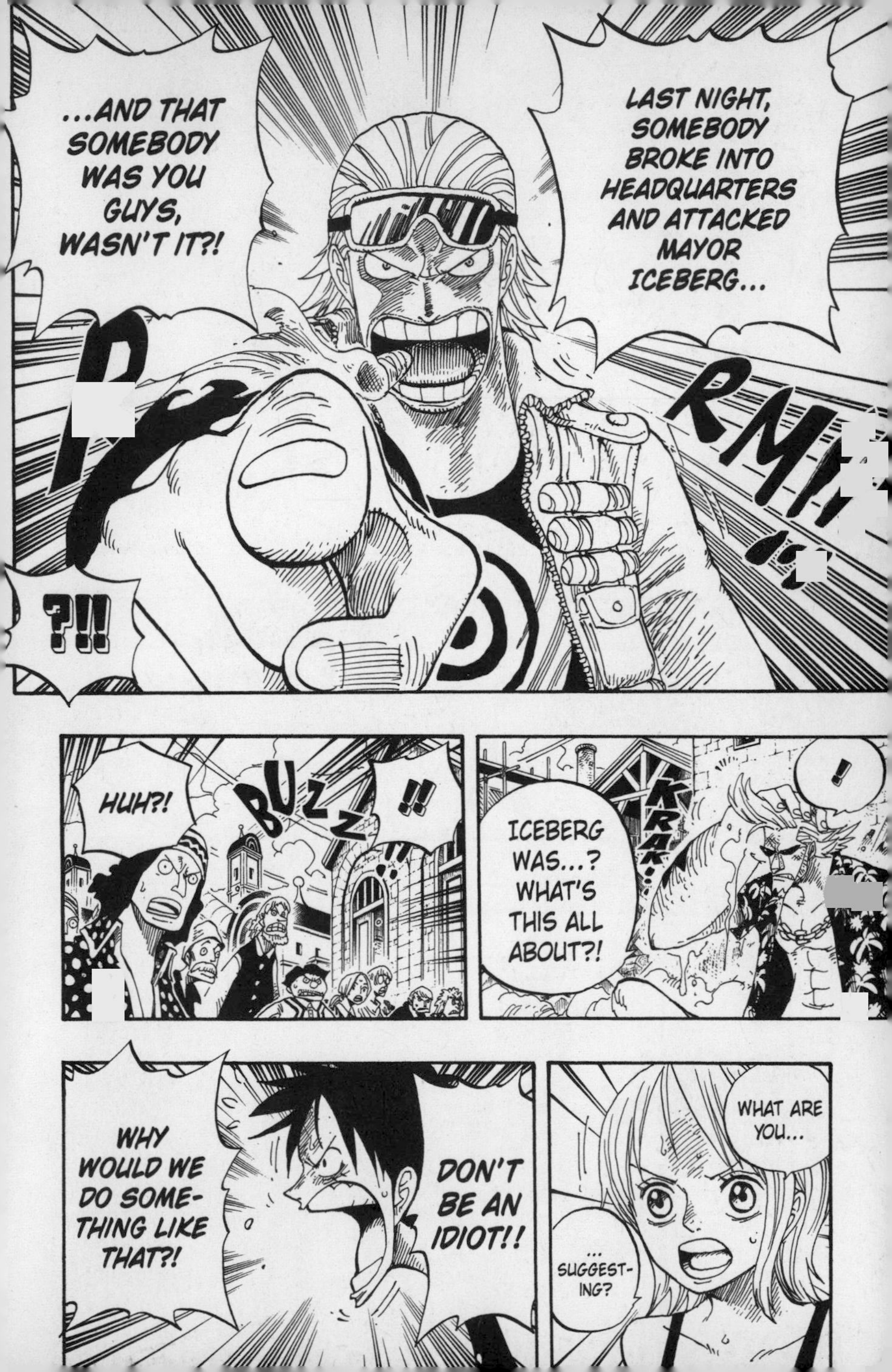

LAST NIGHT, SOMEBODY BROKE INTO HEADQUARTERS AND ATTACKED MAYOR ICEBERG...
...AND THAT SOMEBODY WAS YOU GUYS, WASN'T IT?!
?!!
!
KRAK!
ICEBERG WAS...? WHAT'S THIS ALL ABOUT?!
!!
BUZZ
HUH?!
WHAT ARE YOU...
...SUGGEST-ING?
DON'T BE AN IDIOT!!
WHY WOULD WE DO SOME-THING LIKE THAT?!

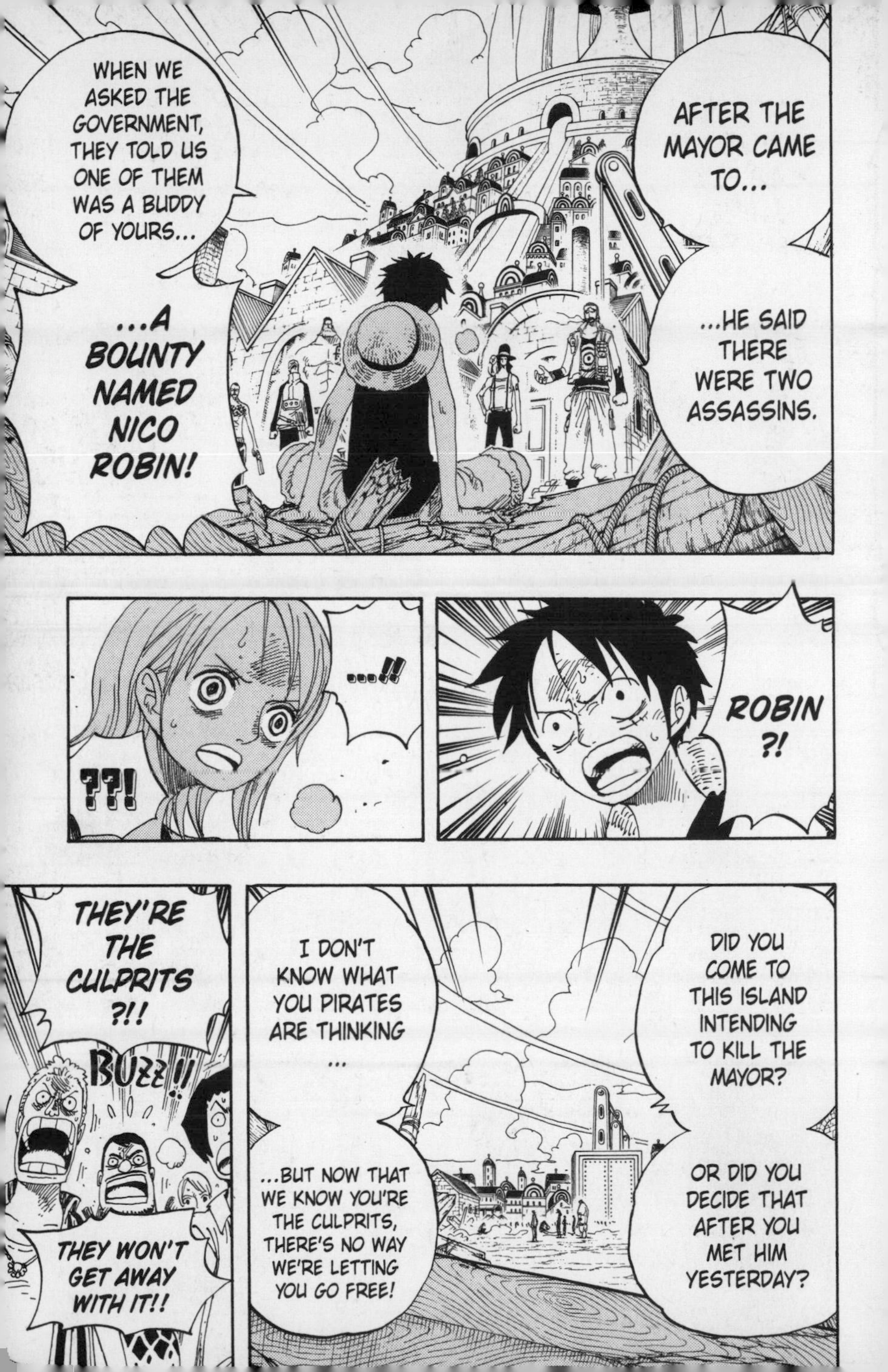
AFTER THE MAYOR CAME TO...
...HE SAID THERE WERE TWO ASSASSINS.
WHEN WE ASKED THE GOVERNMENT, THEY TOLD US ONE OF THEM WAS A BUDDY OF YOURS...
...A BOUNTY NAMED NICO ROBIN!
ROBIN ?!
...!!
??!
DID YOU COME TO THIS ISLAND INTENDING TO KILL THE MAYOR?
OR DID YOU DECIDE THAT AFTER YOU MET HIM YESTERDAY?
I DON'T KNOW WHAT YOU PIRATES ARE THINKING ...
...BUT NOW THAT WE KNOW YOU'RE THE CULPRITS, THERE'S NO WAY WE'RE LETTING YOU GO FREE!
THEY'RE THE CULPRITS ?!!
BUZZ!!
THEY WON'T GET AWAY WITH IT!!

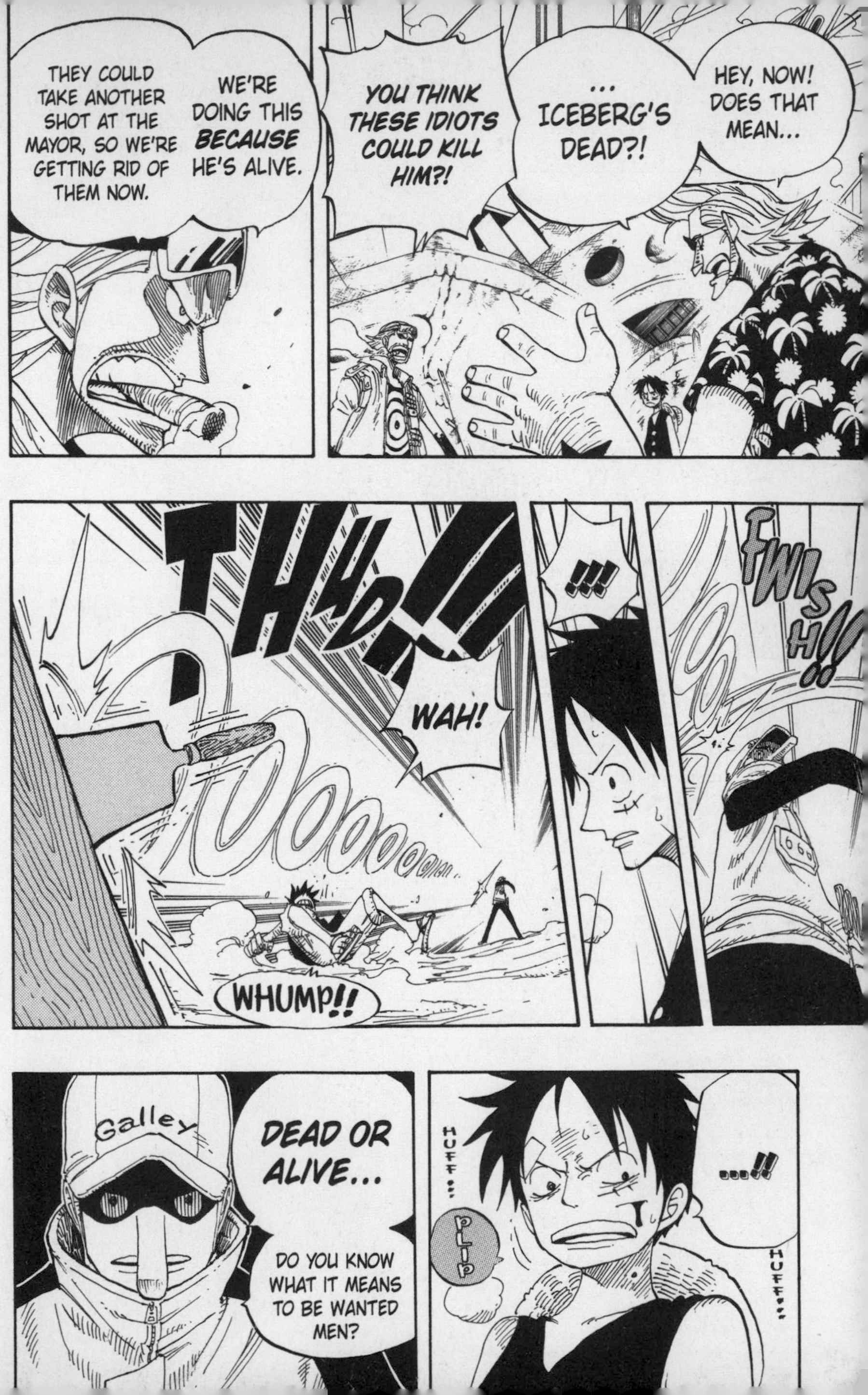
HEY, NOW! DOES THAT MEAN...
... ICEBERG'S DEAD?!
YOU THINK THESE IDIOTS COULD KILL HIM?!
WE'RE DOING THIS BECAUSE HE'S ALIVE.
THEY COULD TAKE ANOTHER SHOT AT THE MAYOR, SO WE'RE GETTING RID OF THEM NOW.
FWISH!!
!!!
THUD!!
WAH!
WHUMP!!
...!!
HUFF...
PLIP
HUFF...
Galley
DEAD OR ALIVE...
DO YOU KNOW WHAT IT MEANS TO BE WANTED MEN?

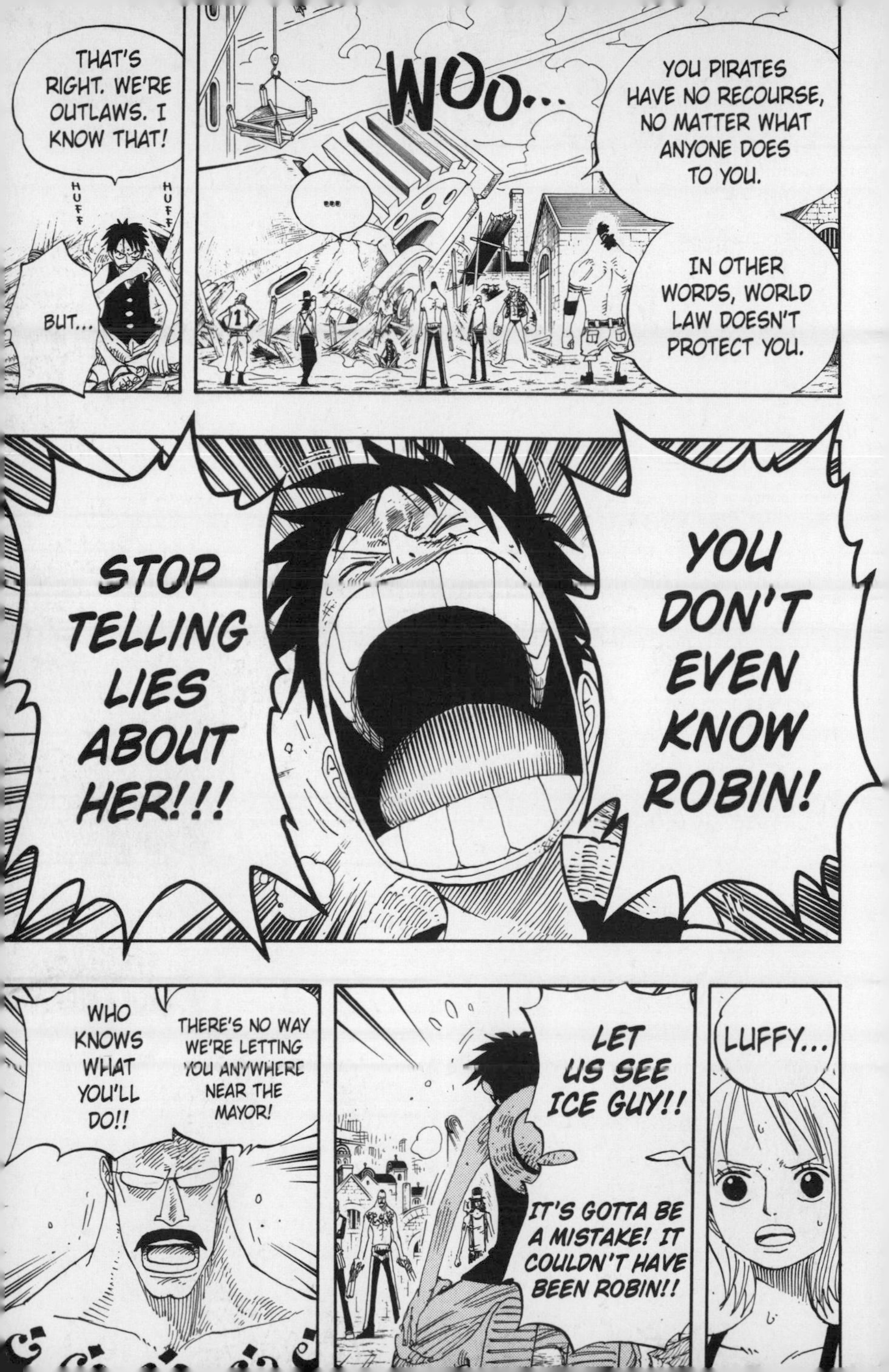
YOU PIRATES HAVE NO RECOURSE, NO MATTER WHAT ANYONE DOES TO YOU.
WOO...
...
IN OTHER WORDS, WORLD LAW DOESN'T PROTECT YOU.
THAT'S RIGHT. WE'RE OUTLAWS. I KNOW THAT!
HUFF
HUFF
BUT...
YOU DON'T EVEN KNOW ROBIN!
STOP TELLING LIES ABOUT HER!!!
LUFFY...
LET US SEE ICE GUY!!
IT'S GOTTA BE A MISTAKE! IT COULDN'T HAVE BEEN ROBIN!!
THERE'S NO WAY WE'RE LETTING YOU ANYWHERE NEAR THE MAYOR!
WHO KNOWS WHAT YOU'LL DO!!

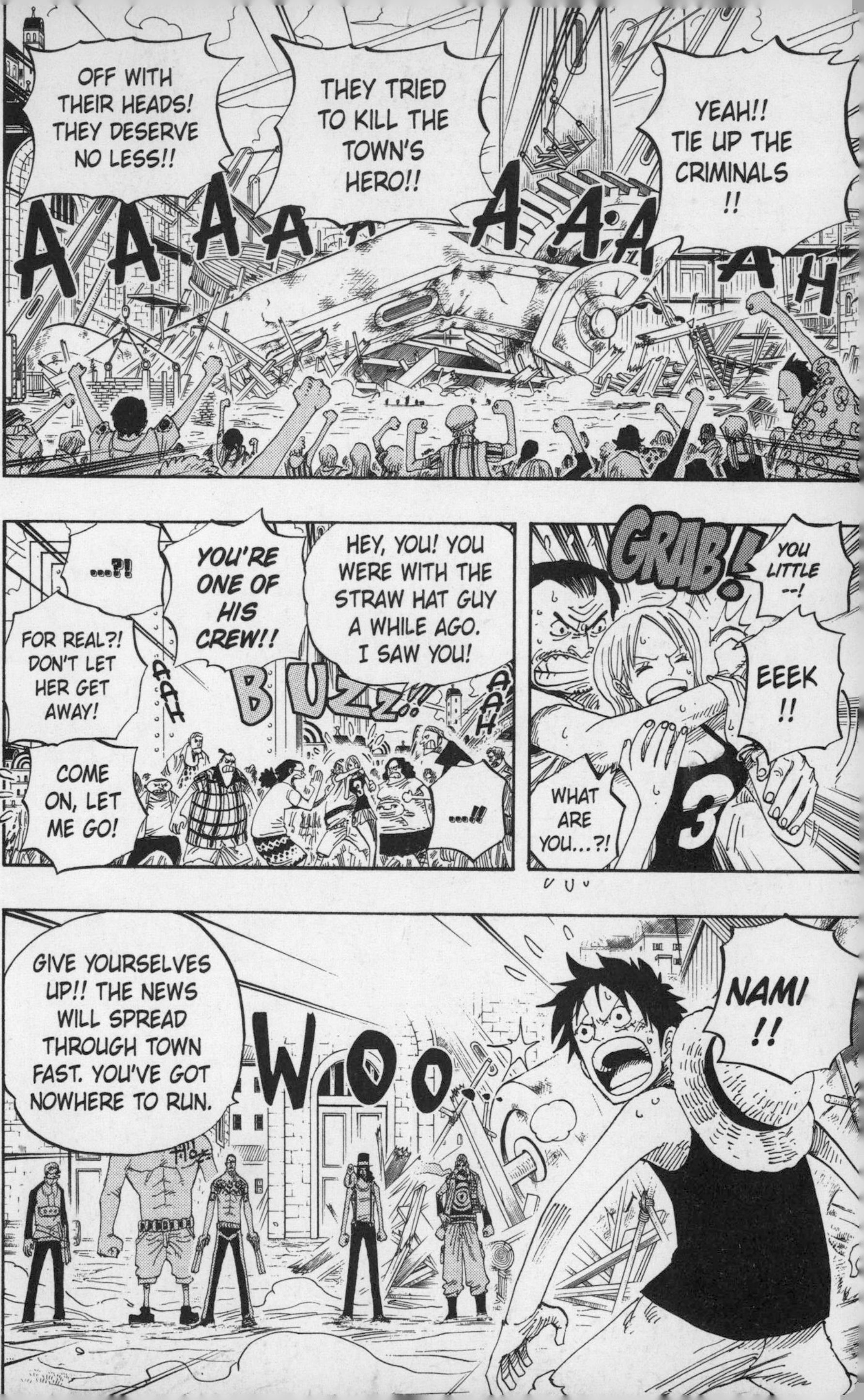
YEAH!! TIE UP THE CRIMINALS !!
THEY TRIED TO KILL THE TOWN'S HERO!!
OFF WITH THEIR HEADS! THEY DESERVE NO LESS!!
AAAAAAAH
GRAB!
YOU LITTLE --!
EEEK !!
WHAT ARE YOU...?!
HEY, YOU! YOU WERE WITH THE STRAW HAT GUY A WHILE AGO. I SAW YOU!
YOU'RE ONE OF HIS CREW!!
...?!
FOR REAL?! DON'T LET HER GET AWAY!
AAH
AAH
BUZZ
...!!
COME ON, LET ME GO!
NAMI !!
WOO
GIVE YOURSELVES UP!! THE NEWS WILL SPREAD THROUGH TOWN FAST. YOU'VE GOT NOWHERE TO RUN.

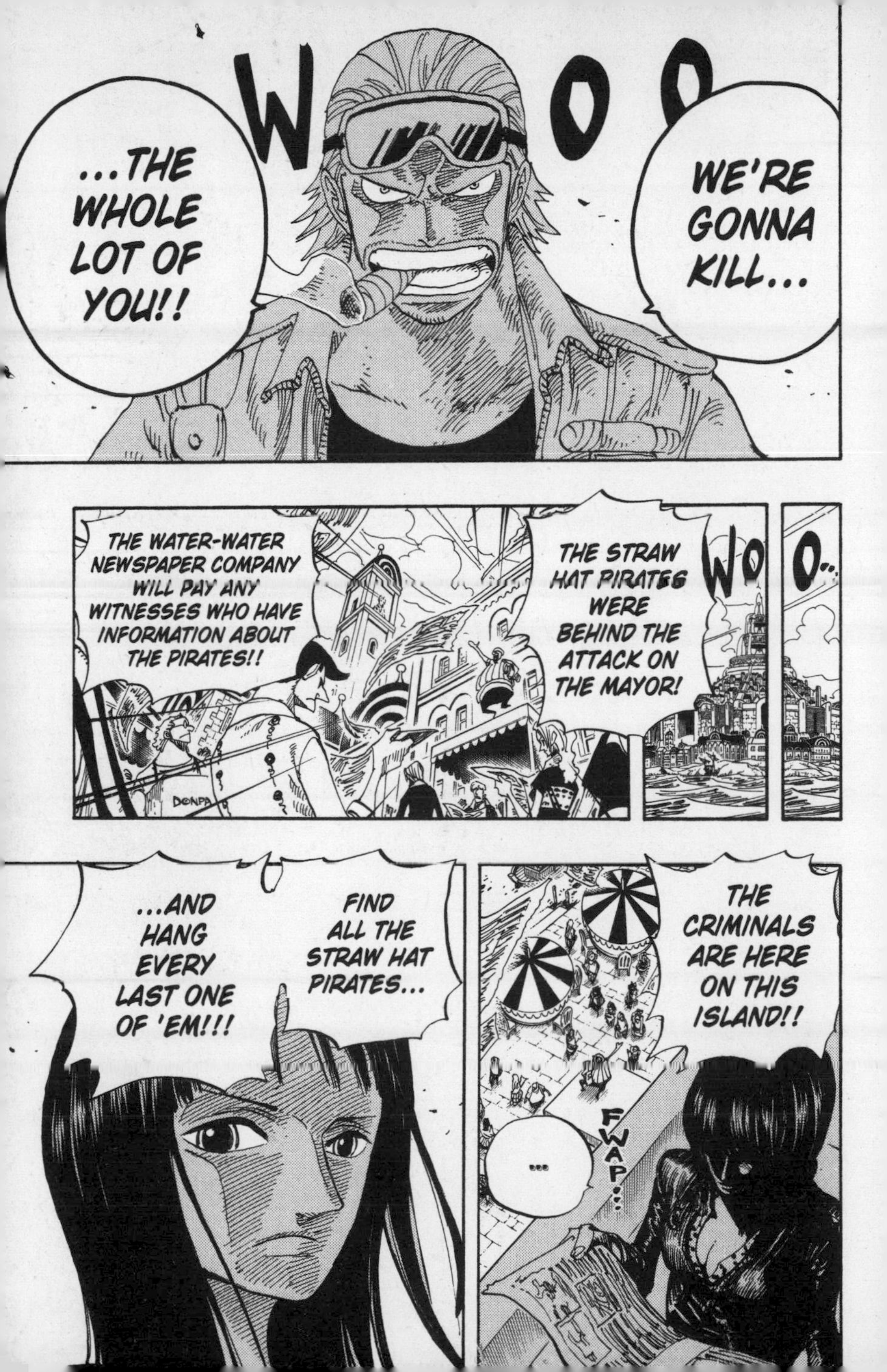
WOO
WE'RE GONNA KILL...
...THE WHOLE LOT OF YOU!!
WO O..
THE STRAW HAT PIRATES WERE BEHIND THE ATTACK ON THE MAYOR!
THE WATER-WATER NEWSPAPER COMPANY WILL PAY ANY WITNESSES WHO HAVE INFORMATION ABOUT THE PIRATES!!
DONPA
THE CRIMINALS ARE HERE ON THIS ISLAND!!
FWAP...
...
FIND ALL THE STRAW HAT PIRATES...
...AND HANG EVERY LAST ONE OF 'EM!!!

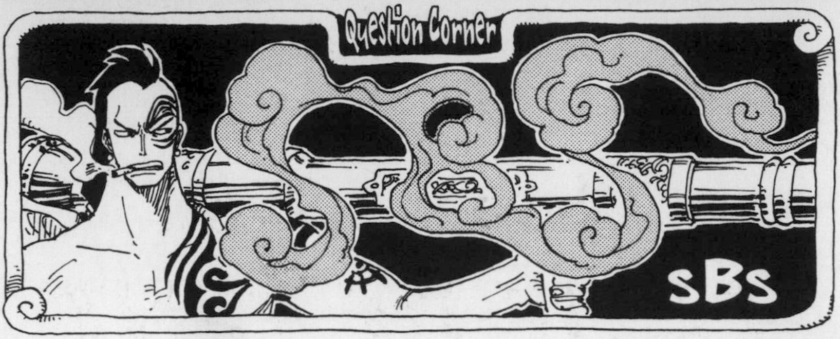
Question Corner
SBS

Reader: Hello, Oda Sensei! I am a very low-ranking guard in the mayor's Personal Guard, which is based in and active out of Water Seven. Let's have the captain of the guard begin the Question Corner this time! Sir, if you would!

Paulie: Hmm? Did you call me? Gwah! You there, Eiichiro Oda! Just what do you think you're wearing, sitting there drawing manga?! You're shameless! As if I could leave something like this to a shameless fellow like you! I'll start this off instead!

Let's begin the Question Corner!

--Jun

Oda: Oh, man, they've started it again... (SOB) Hello, everybody. This is a stark-naked Eiichiro Oda. ...Hold it! Who are you calling shameless?! And anyway, **don't tell anyone** I'm drawing manga in such a shameless state!

Q: Is saying "I'm sorry" a habit of Pagaya's? And why does he say "I'm sorry"?

A: I don't know. I'm sorry.

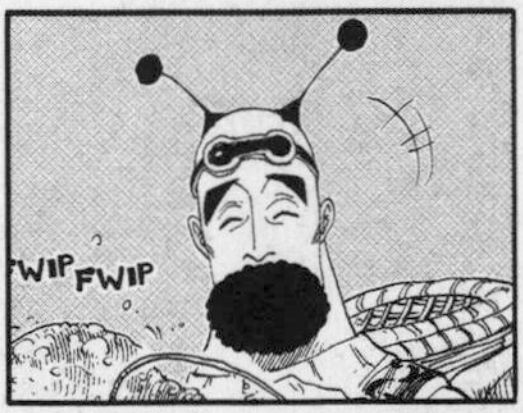
FWIP FWIP

Q: Oda Sensei, when you're low on power, do you borrow the power of the afro as well?

--Shii-kun ♡

A: But of course. No one could possibly manage to draw a weekly serial without afro power. I hope someday to become a champion.

Chapter 338:
COUP DE VENT

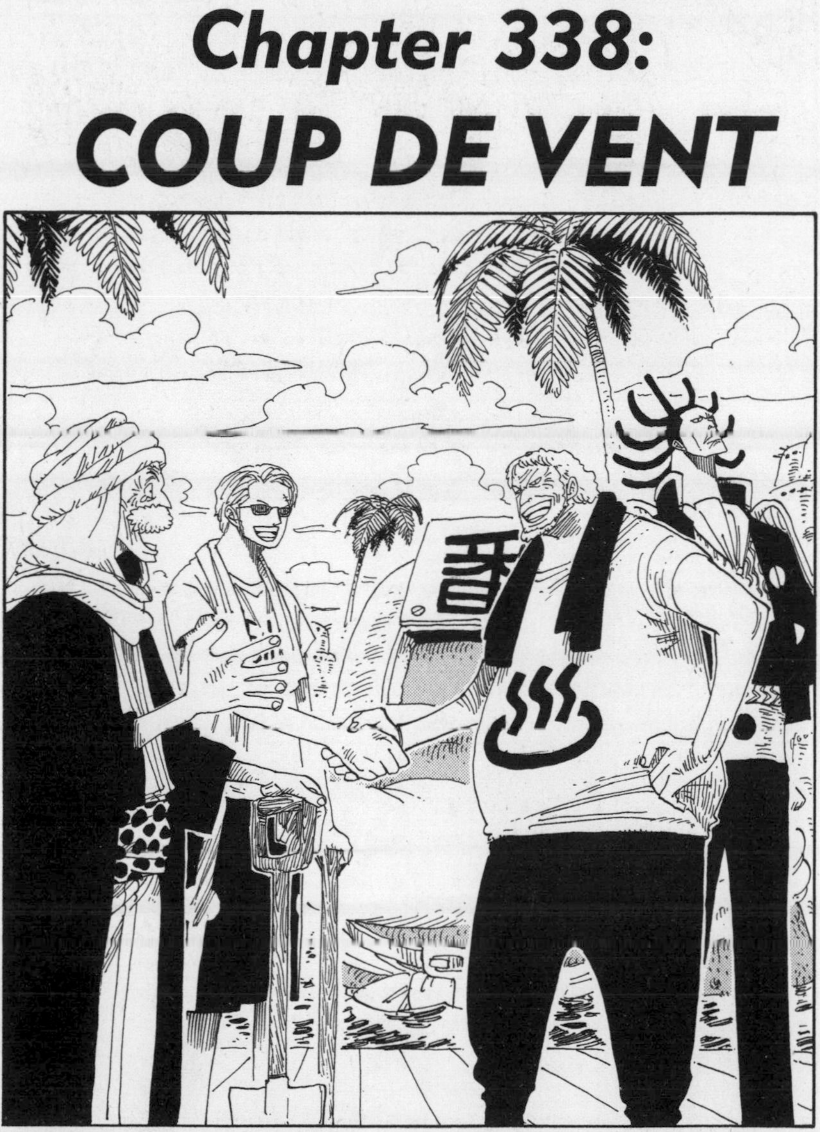

GEDATSU'S UNEXPECTED LIFE ON THE BLUE SEA, VOL. 22:
"GORO, KOZA'S UNCLE AND TOH-TOH'S LITTLE BROTHER, RETURNS HOME BY CHANCE"

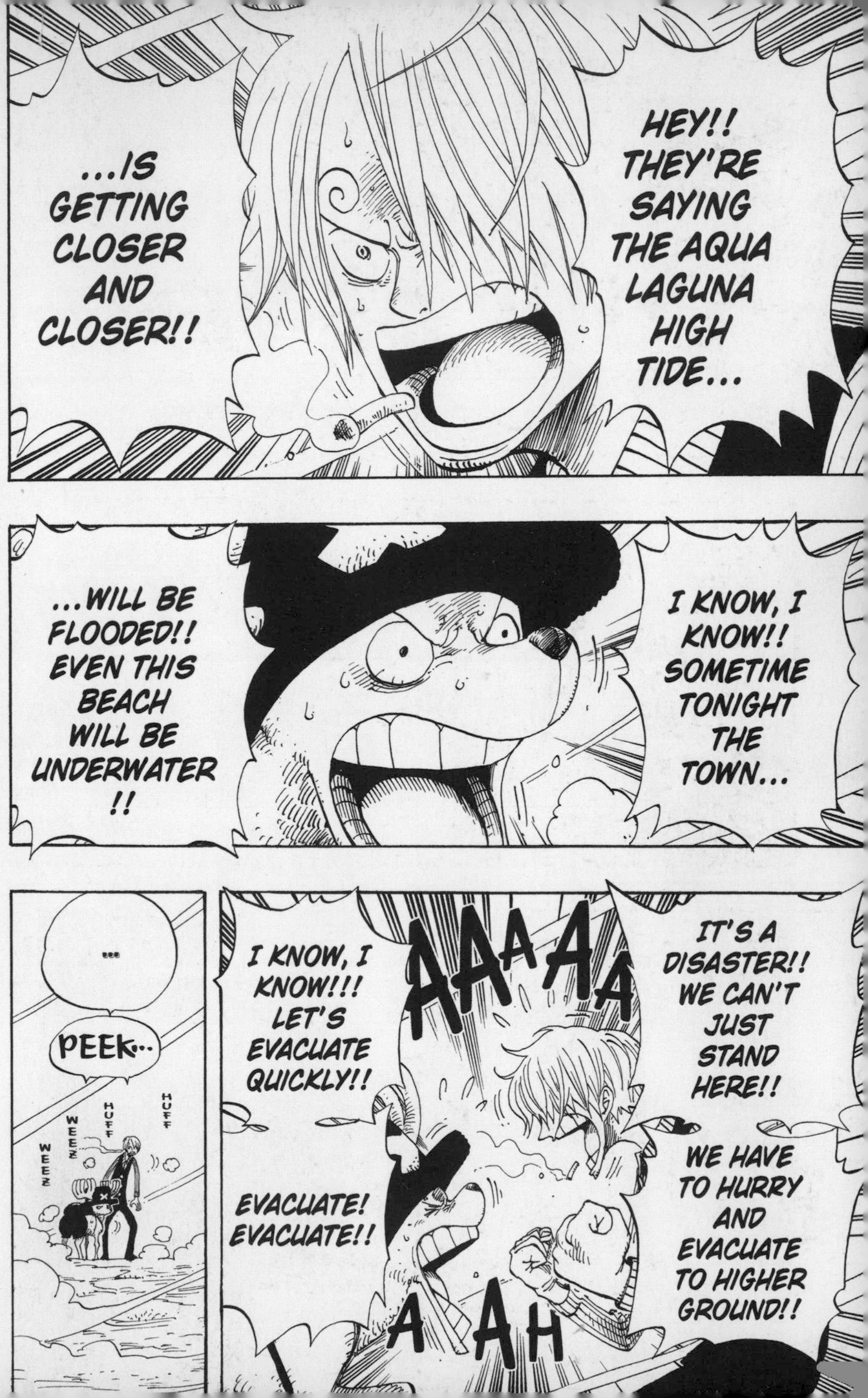
HEY!! THEY'RE SAYING THE AQUA LAGUNA HIGH TIDE...
...IS GETTING CLOSER AND CLOSER!!
I KNOW, I KNOW!! SOMETIME TONIGHT THE TOWN...
...WILL BE FLOODED!! EVEN THIS BEACH WILL BE UNDERWATER!!
IT'S A DISASTER!! WE CAN'T JUST STAND HERE!!
AAAAA
I KNOW, I KNOW!!! LET'S EVACUATE QUICKLY!!
WE HAVE TO HURRY AND EVACUATE TO HIGHER GROUND!!
EVACUATE! EVACUATE!!
AAH
...
PEEK...
HUFF HUFF
WEEZ WEEZ

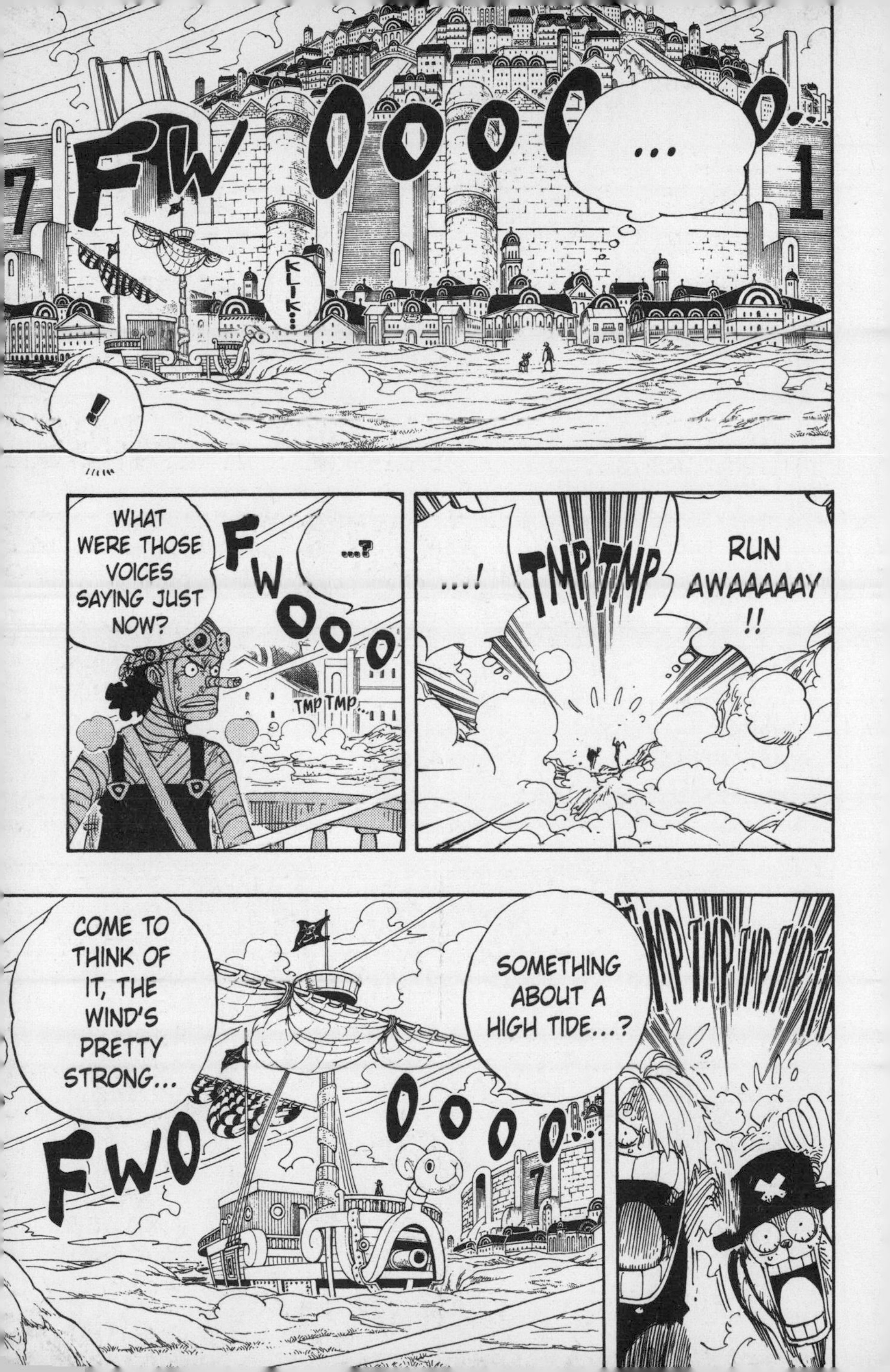

FWOOOOO...
...
7
1
KLIK...
!
RUN AWAAAAAY!!
TMP TMP
...!
...?
FWOOO
WHAT WERE THOSE VOICES SAYING JUST NOW?
TMP TMP...
TMP TMP TMP TMP
SOMETHING ABOUT A HIGH TIDE...?
COME TO THINK OF IT, THE WIND'S PRETTY STRONG...
FWOOOOO...

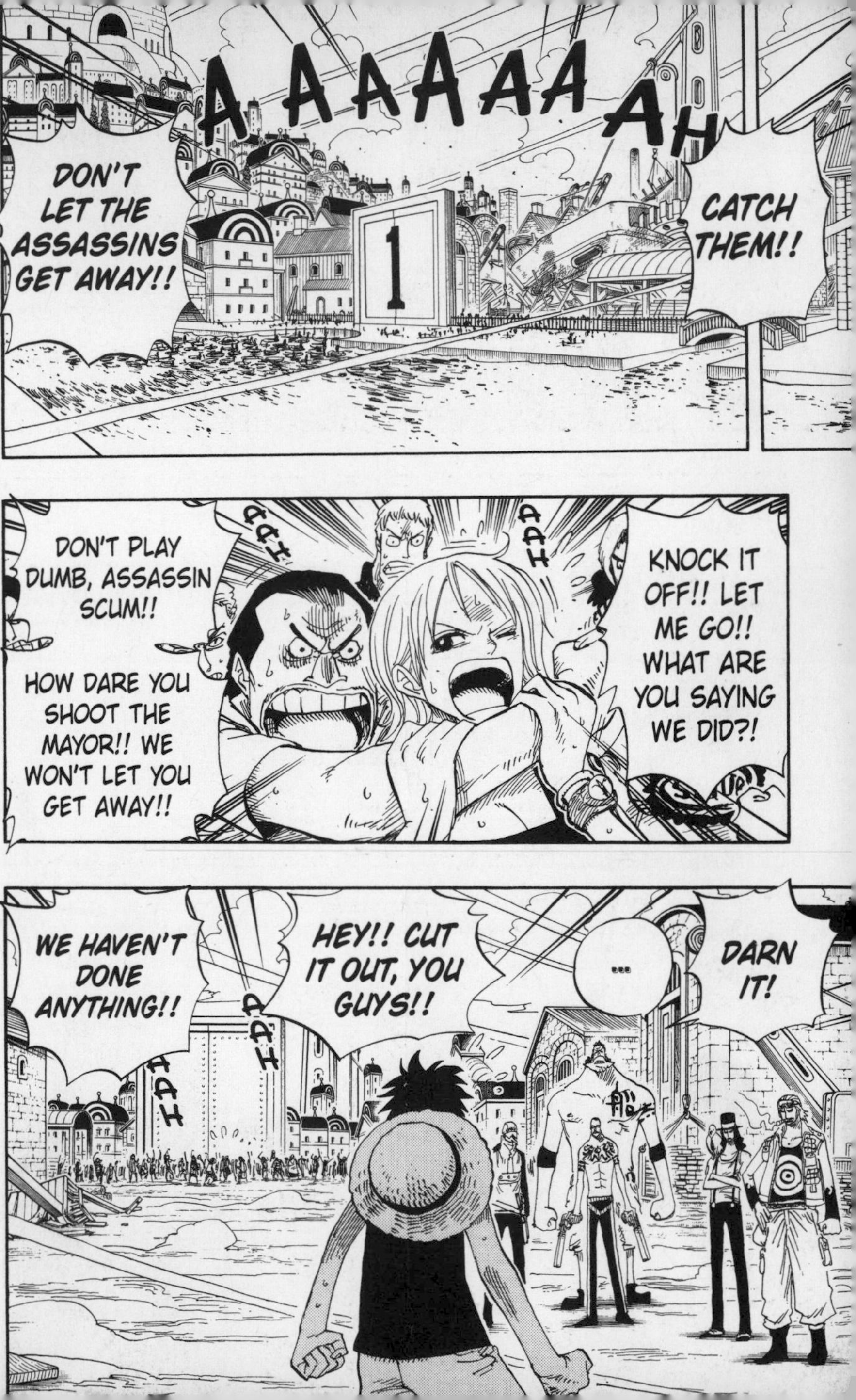

AAAAAAAH
CATCH THEM!!
DON'T LET THE ASSASSINS GET AWAY!!
AAAH
AAAH
KNOCK IT OFF!! LET ME GO!! WHAT ARE YOU SAYING WE DID?!
DON'T PLAY DUMB, ASSASSIN SCUM!!
HOW DARE YOU SHOOT THE MAYOR!! WE WON'T LET YOU GET AWAY!!
DARN IT!
...
HEY!! CUT IT OUT, YOU GUYS!!
AAAH
WE HAVEN'T DONE ANYTHING!!
AAAH

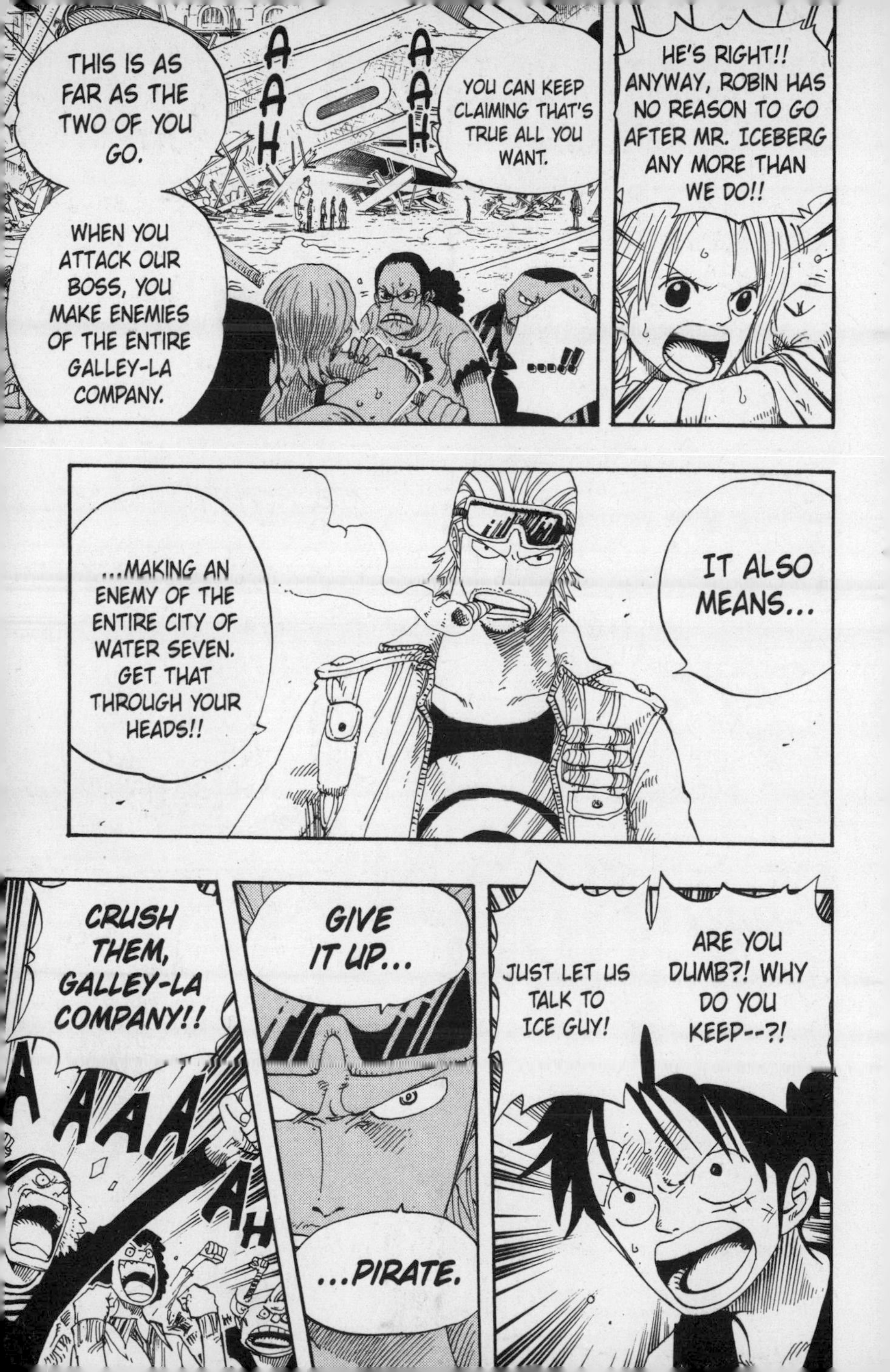
HE'S RIGHT!! ANYWAY, ROBIN HAS NO REASON TO GO AFTER MR. ICEBERG ANY MORE THAN WE DO!!
YOU CAN KEEP CLAIMING THAT'S TRUE ALL YOU WANT.
AAAH
AAAH
THIS IS AS FAR AS THE TWO OF YOU GO.
WHEN YOU ATTACK OUR BOSS, YOU MAKE ENEMIES OF THE ENTIRE GALLEY-LA COMPANY.
...!!
IT ALSO MEANS...
...MAKING AN ENEMY OF THE ENTIRE CITY OF WATER SEVEN. GET THAT THROUGH YOUR HEADS!!
ARE YOU DUMB?! WHY DO YOU KEEP--?!
JUST LET US TALK TO ICE GUY!
GIVE IT UP...
...PIRATE.
CRUSH THEM, GALLEY-LA COMPANY!!
AAAAH

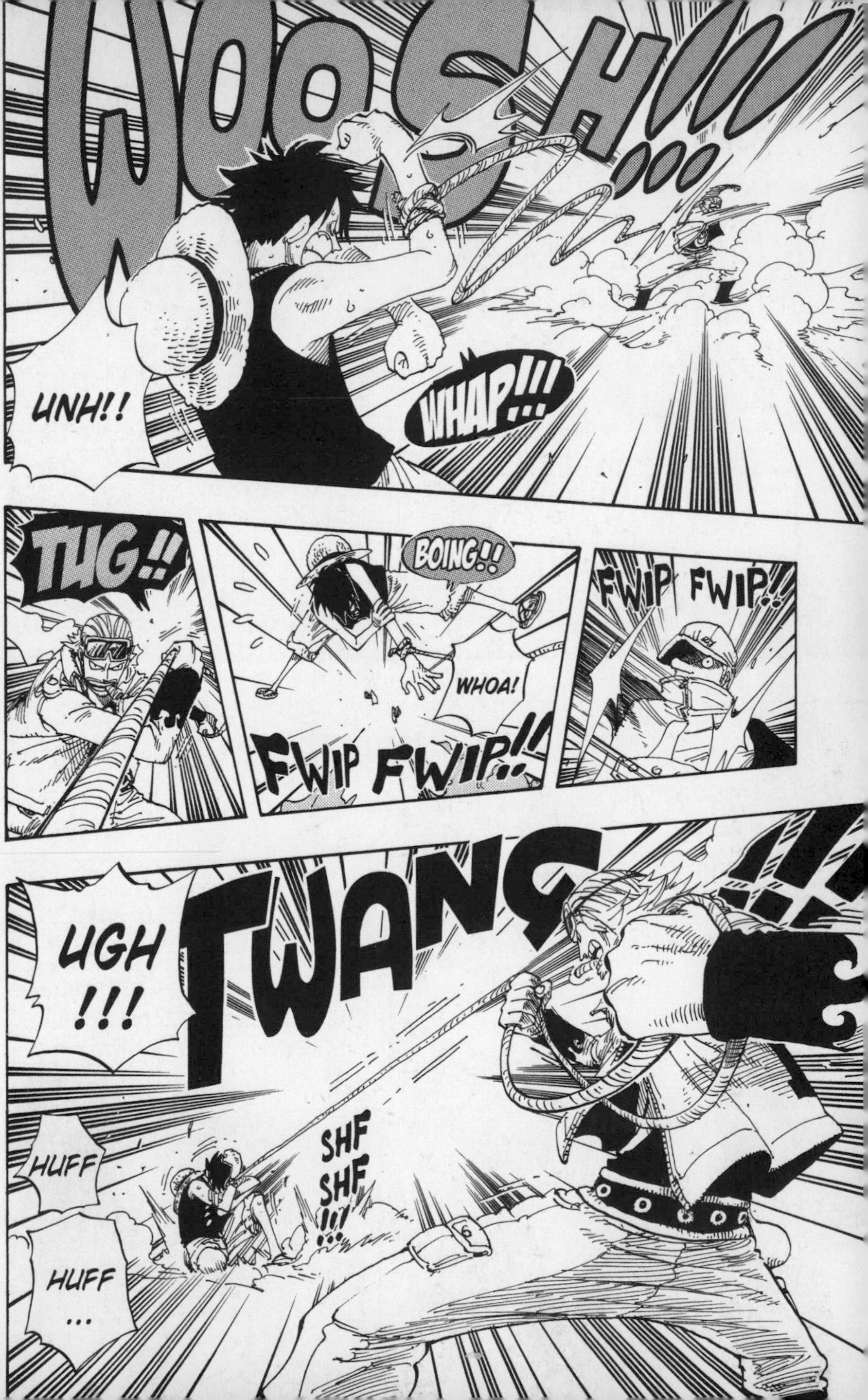
WOOSH!!!...
WHAP!!!
UNH!!
FWIP FWIP!!
BOING!!
WHOA!
FWIP FWIP!!
TUG!!
TWANG!!!
UGH !!!
SHF SHF !!!
HUFF
HUFF ...

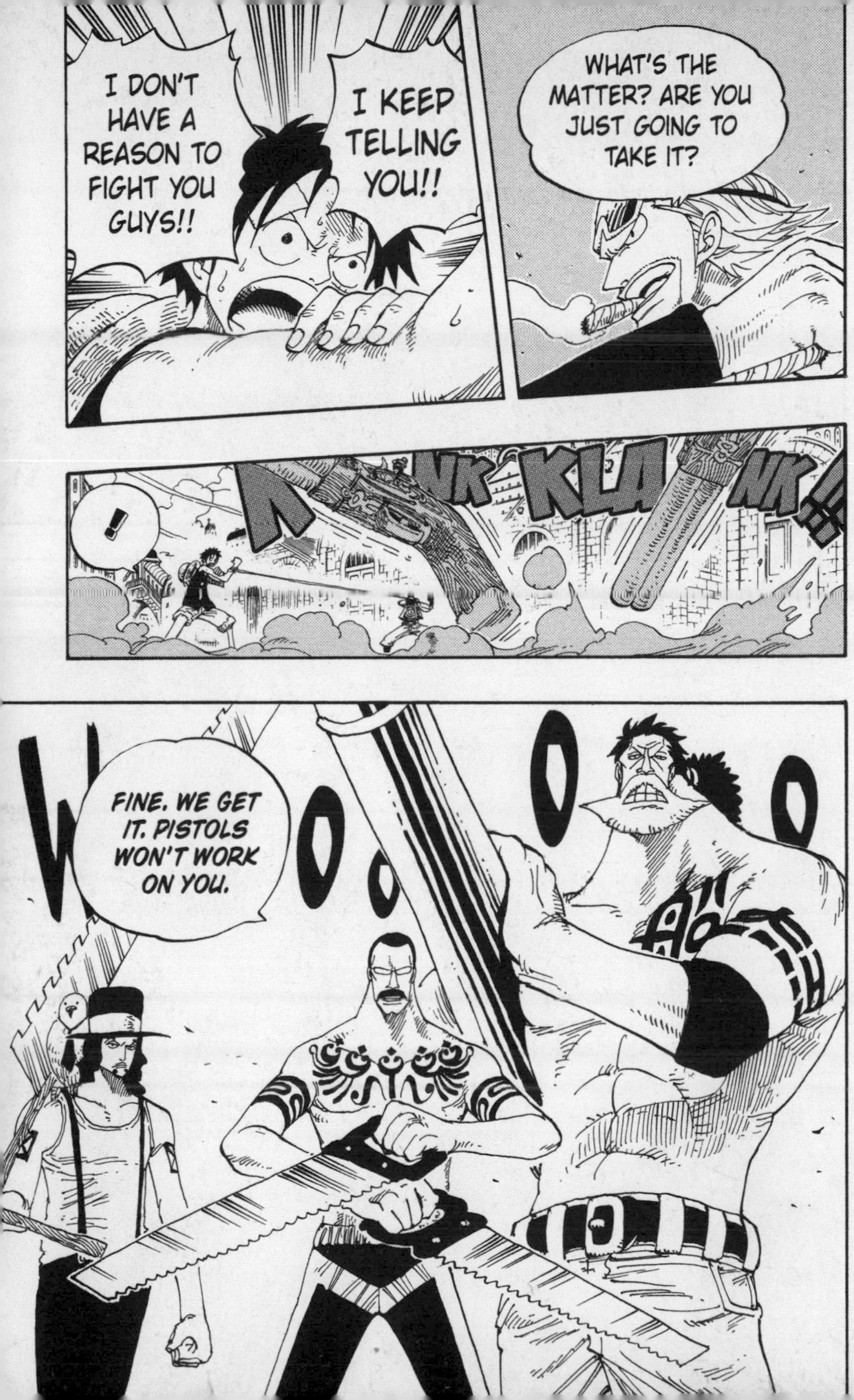
WHAT'S THE MATTER? ARE YOU JUST GOING TO TAKE IT?
I KEEP TELLING YOU!!
I DON'T HAVE A REASON TO FIGHT YOU GUYS!!
NK KLA NK!!
!
FINE. WE GET IT. PISTOLS WON'T WORK ON YOU.

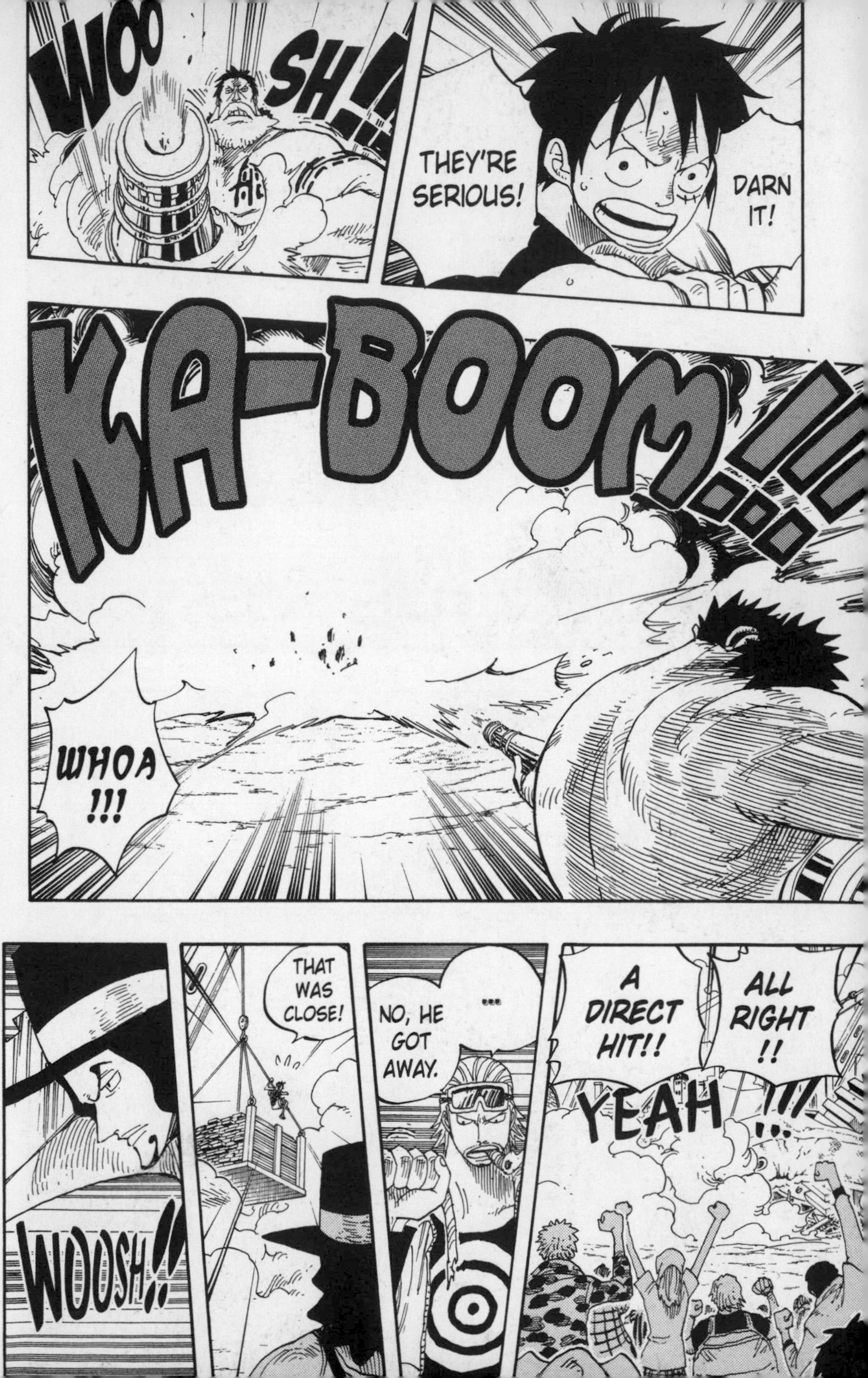
DARN IT!
THEY'RE SERIOUS!
WOOSH!!!
KA-BOOM!!!
WHOA!!!
ALL RIGHT!!
A DIRECT HIT!!
YEAH!!!
...
NO, HE GOT AWAY.
THAT WAS CLOSE!
WOOSH!!

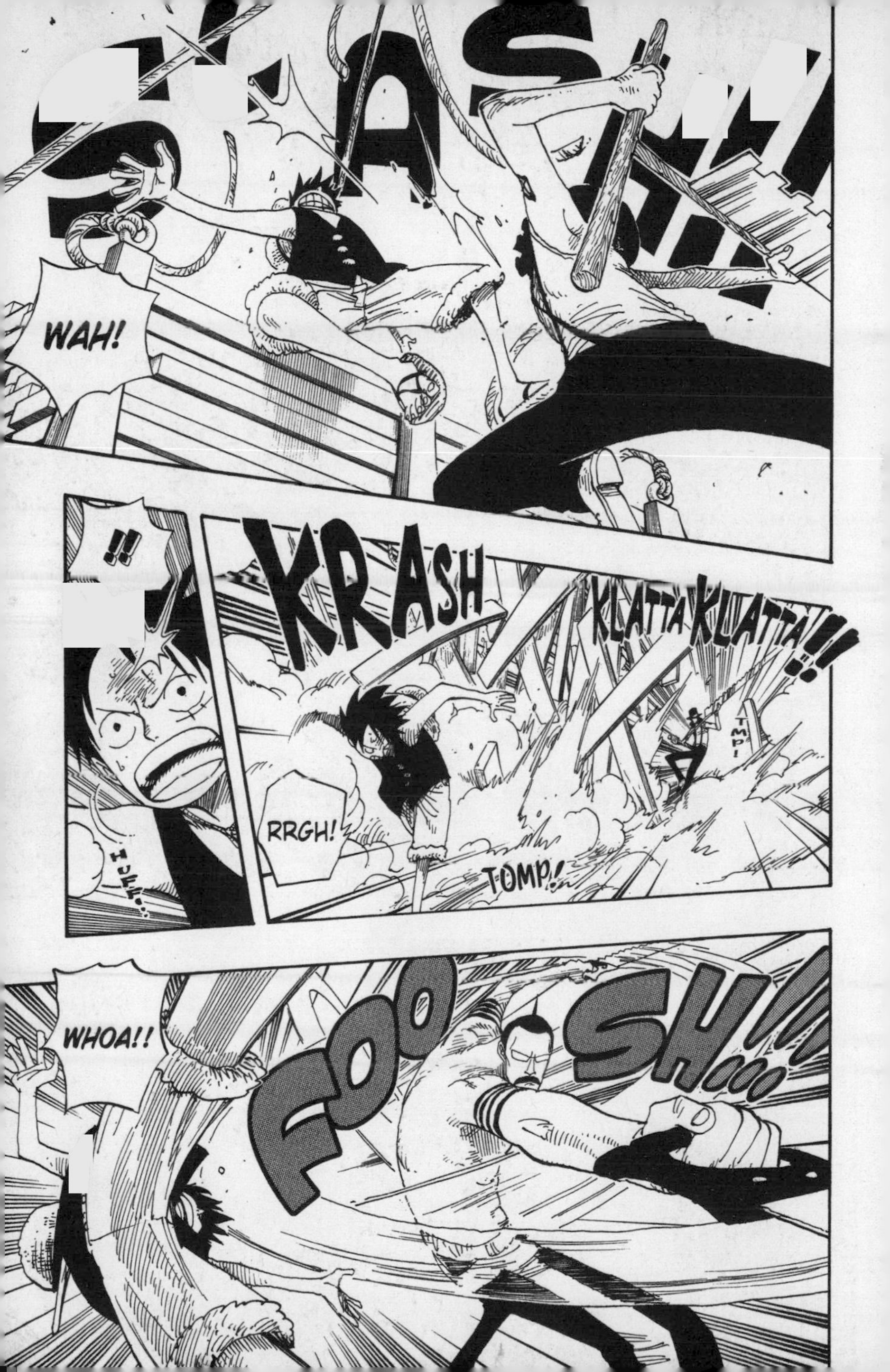
WAH!
KRASH
KLATTA KLATTA!!
TMP!
RRGH!
TOMP!
!!
HUFF...
FOOSH...!!
WHOA!!

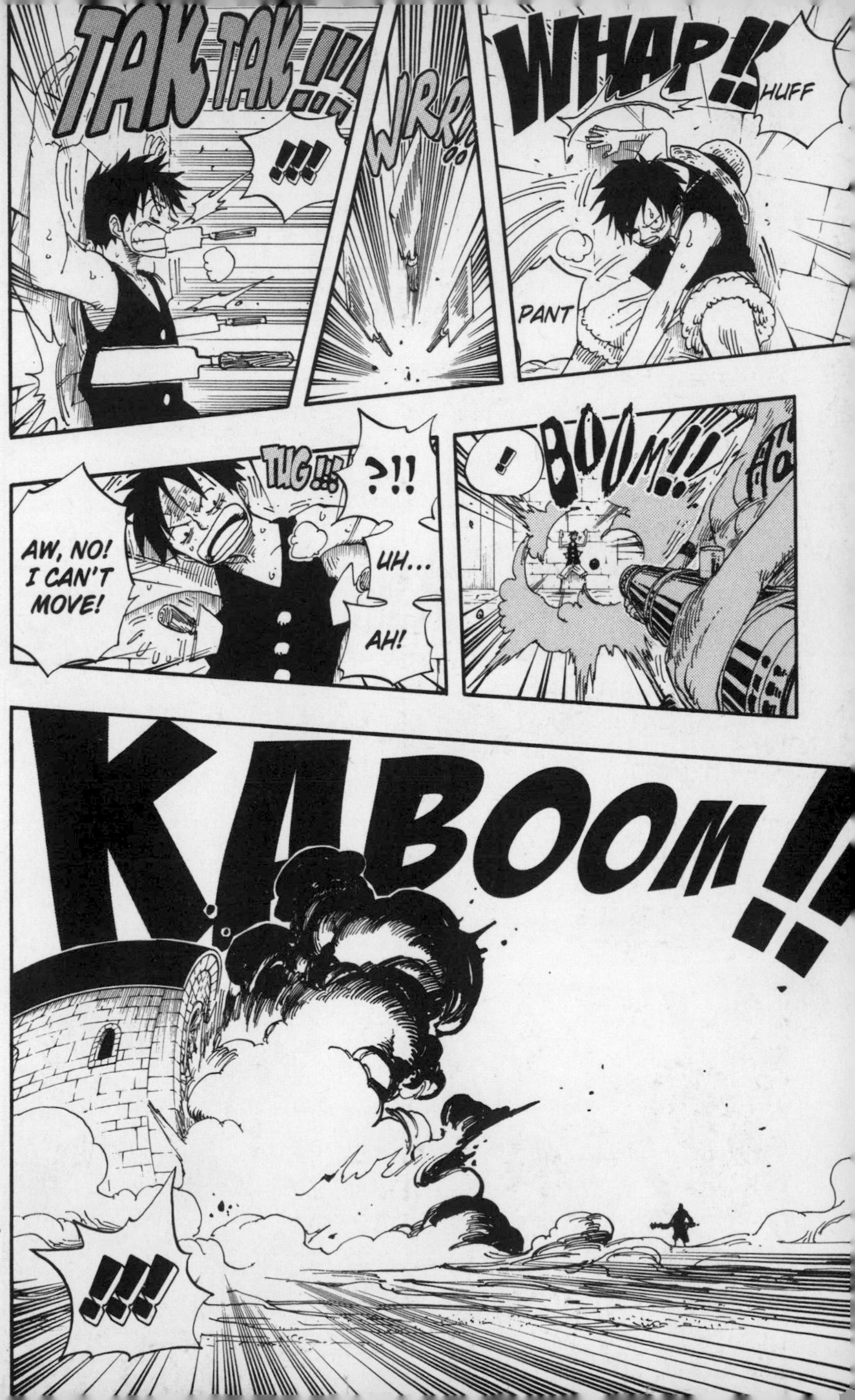
WHAP!!
HUFF
PANT
WIRR...
TAK TAK!!!
!!!
!
BOOM!!
?!!
TUG!!!
UH...
AH!
AW, NO! I CAN'T MOVE!
KABOOM!!
!!!

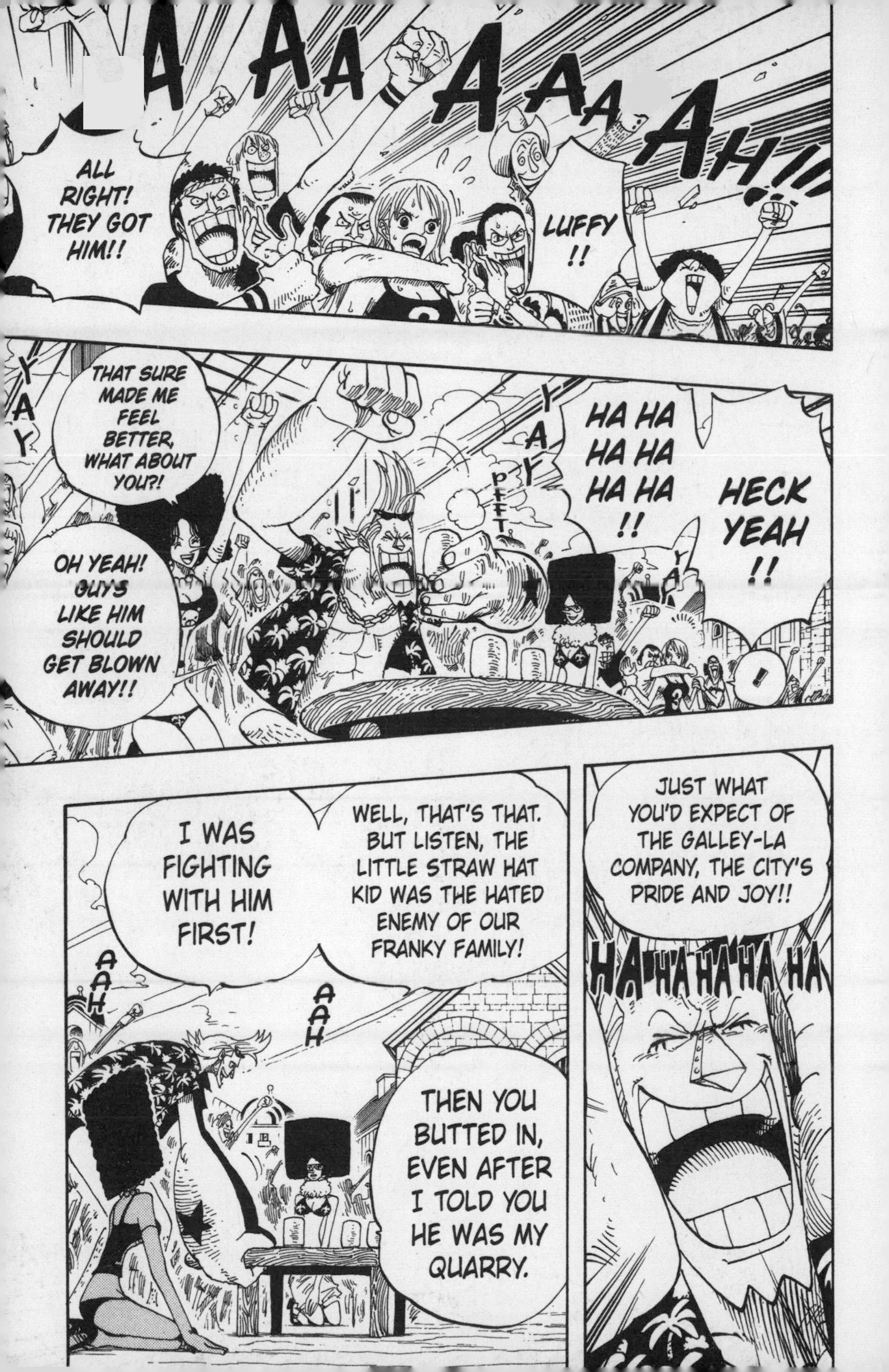
AAAAAAAAH!!!!
LUFFY!!
ALL RIGHT! THEY GOT HIM!!
HECK YEAH!!
HA HA HA HA HA HA!!
YAY
PFFT
YAY
THAT SURE MADE ME FEEL BETTER, WHAT ABOUT YOU?!
OH YEAH! GUYS LIKE HIM SHOULD GET BLOWN AWAY!!
YAY
!
JUST WHAT YOU'D EXPECT OF THE GALLEY-LA COMPANY, THE CITY'S PRIDE AND JOY!!
HA HA HA HA HA HA
WELL, THAT'S THAT. BUT LISTEN, THE LITTLE STRAW HAT KID WAS THE HATED ENEMY OF OUR FRANKY FAMILY!
I WAS FIGHTING WITH HIM FIRST!
AAAH
AAH
THEN YOU BUTTED IN, EVEN AFTER I TOLD YOU HE WAS MY QUARRY.

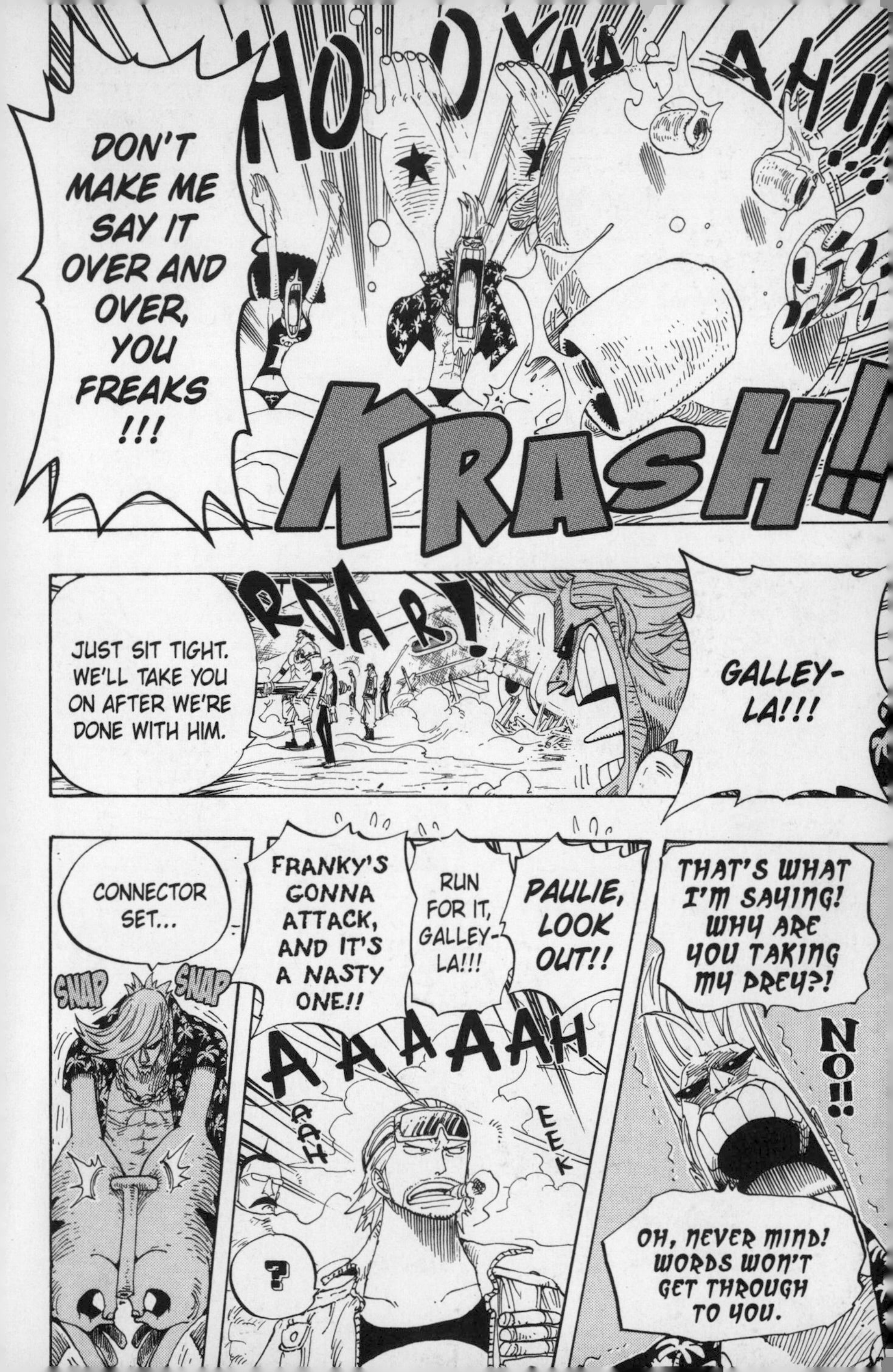

HOOYAAAAH!!!
DON'T MAKE ME SAY IT OVER AND OVER, YOU FREAKS!!!
KRASH!!
GALLEY-LA!!!
ROAR!
JUST SIT TIGHT. WE'LL TAKE YOU ON AFTER WE'RE DONE WITH HIM.
THAT'S WHAT I'M SAYING! WHY ARE YOU TAKING MY PREY?!
NO!!
OH, NEVER MIND! WORDS WON'T GET THROUGH TO YOU.
PAULIE, LOOK OUT!!
RUN FOR IT, GALLEY-LA!!!
FRANKY'S GONNA ATTACK, AND IT'S A NASTY ONE!!
AAAAAH
EEEK
AAH
?
CONNECTOR SET...
SNAP
SNAP

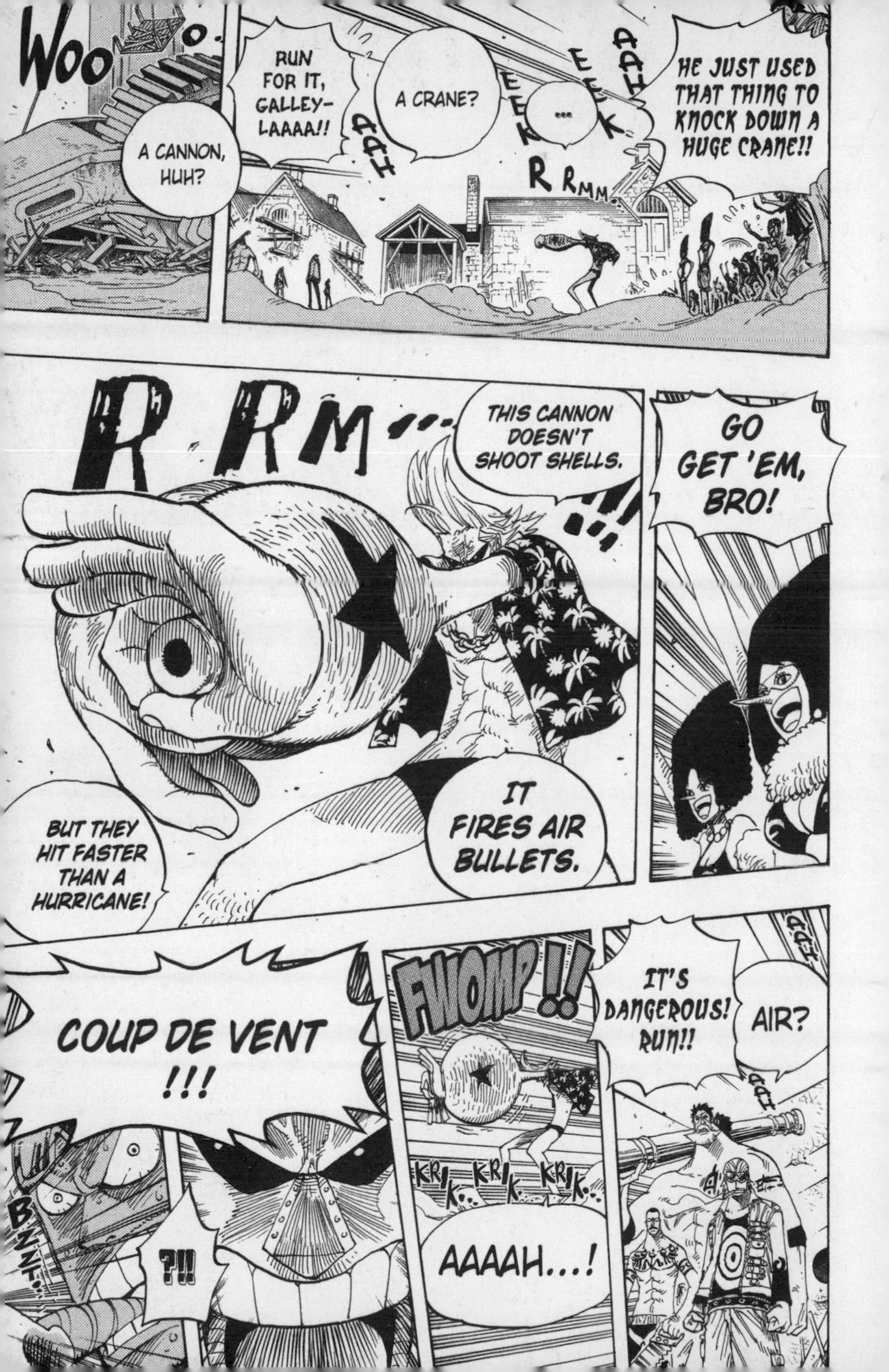
HE JUST USED THAT THING TO KNOCK DOWN A HUGE CRANE!!
AAAH
EEEK
...
A CRANE?
AAAH
RUN FOR IT, GALLEY-LAAAA!!
RRMM
WOO...
A CANNON, HUH?
GO GET 'EM, BRO!
THIS CANNON DOESN'T SHOOT SHELLS.
RRM...
IT FIRES AIR BULLETS.
BUT THEY HIT FASTER THAN A HURRICANE!
AIR?
IT'S DANGEROUS! RUN!!
FWOMP!!
KRIK KRIK KRIK
AAAAH...!
COUP DE VENT !!!
?!!
BZZT...

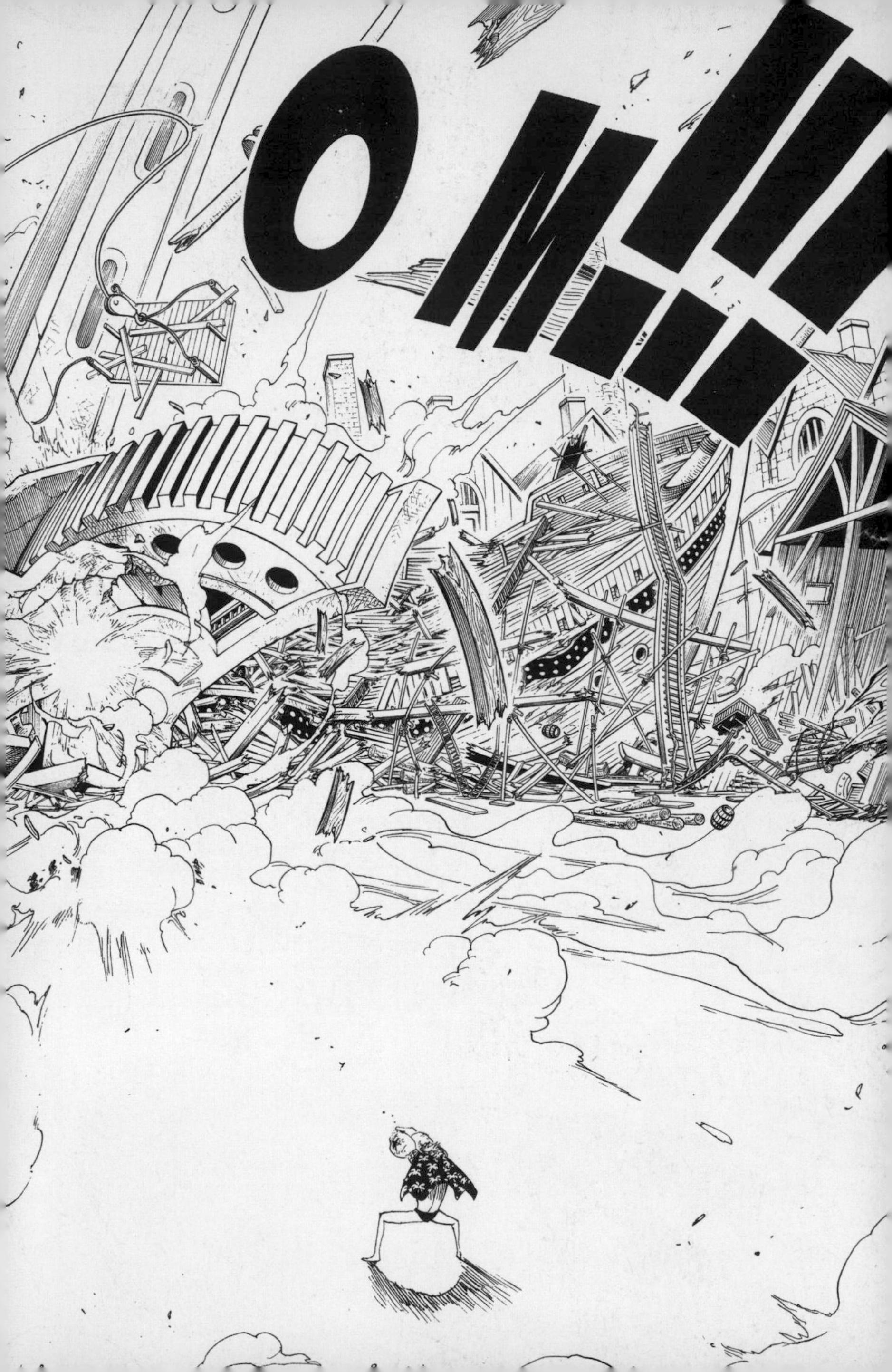
ON!!

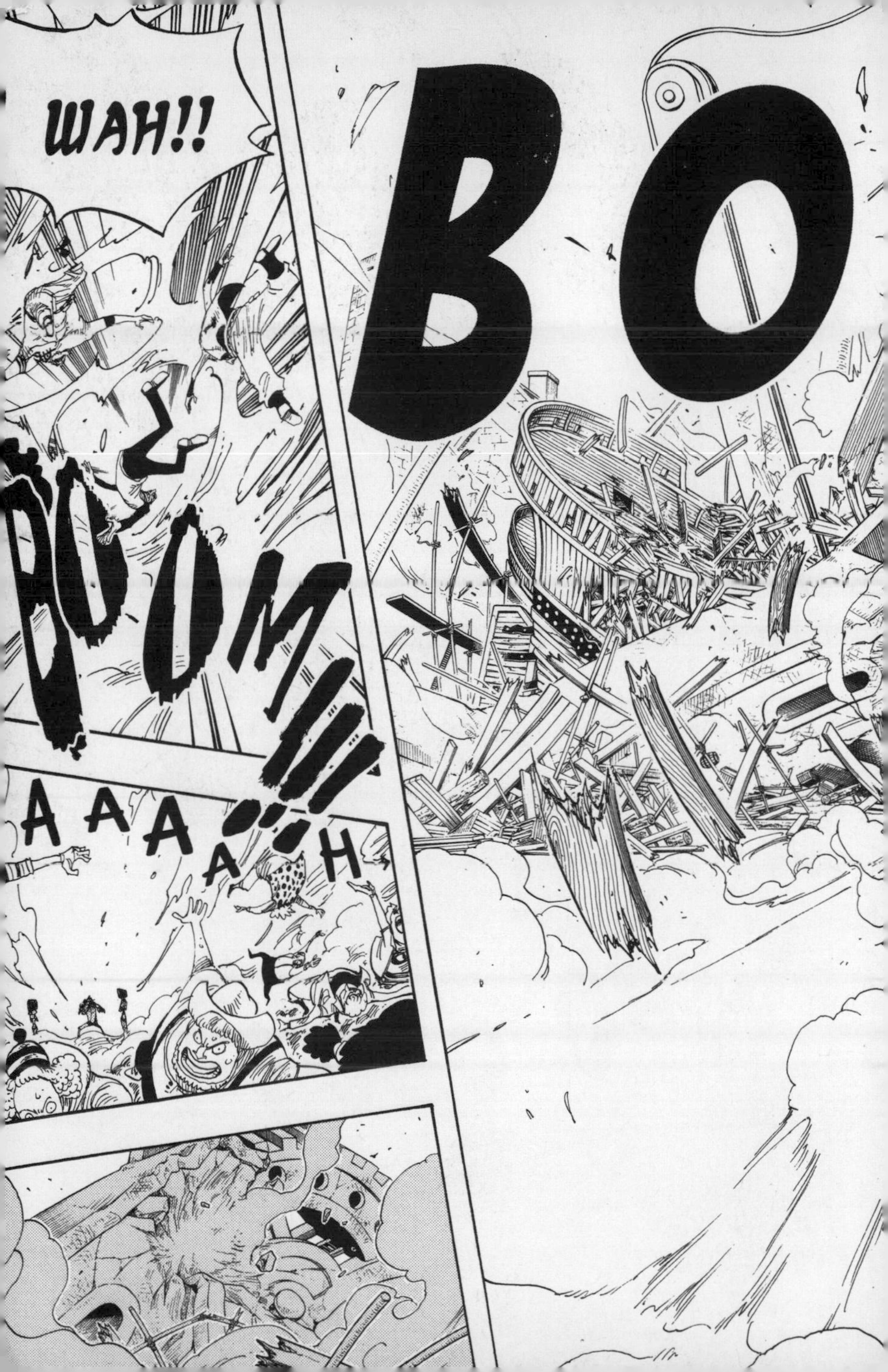
BOOM!!
WAH!!
BOOM!!!
AAAAAH

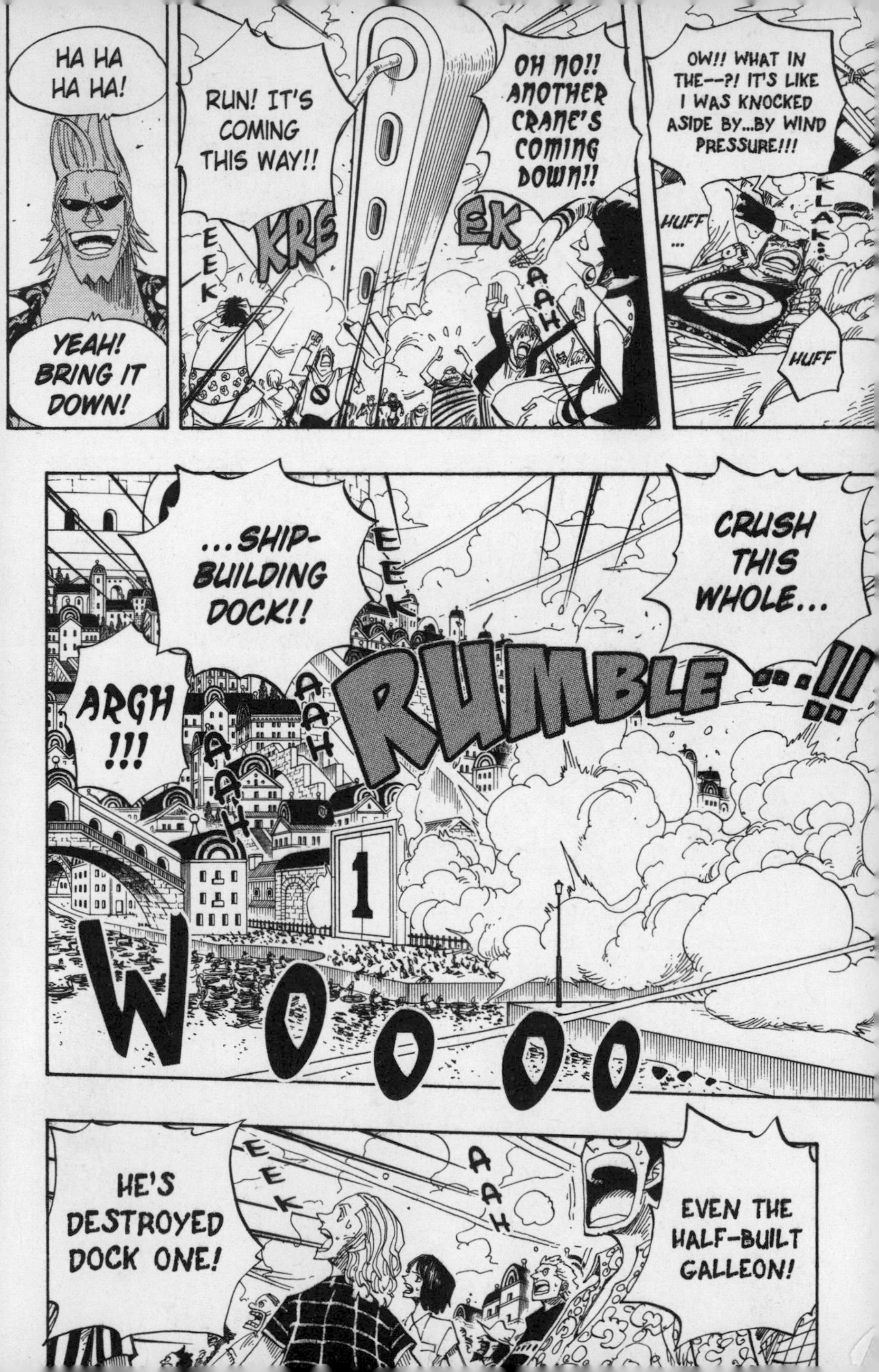

OW!! WHAT IN THE--?! IT'S LIKE I WAS KNOCKED ASIDE BY...BY WIND PRESSURE!!!
KLAK...
HUFF ...
HUFF
OH NO!! ANOTHER CRANE'S COMING DOWN!!
RUN! IT'S COMING THIS WAY!!
KRE EK
AAAH
EEEK
HA HA HA HA!
YEAH! BRING IT DOWN!
CRUSH THIS WHOLE...
...SHIP-BUILDING DOCK!!
EEEK
RUMBLE...!!
AAAH
AAAH
ARGH !!!
WOOOO
1
EVEN THE HALF-BUILT GALLEON!
AAAH
EEEK
HE'S DESTROYED DOCK ONE!

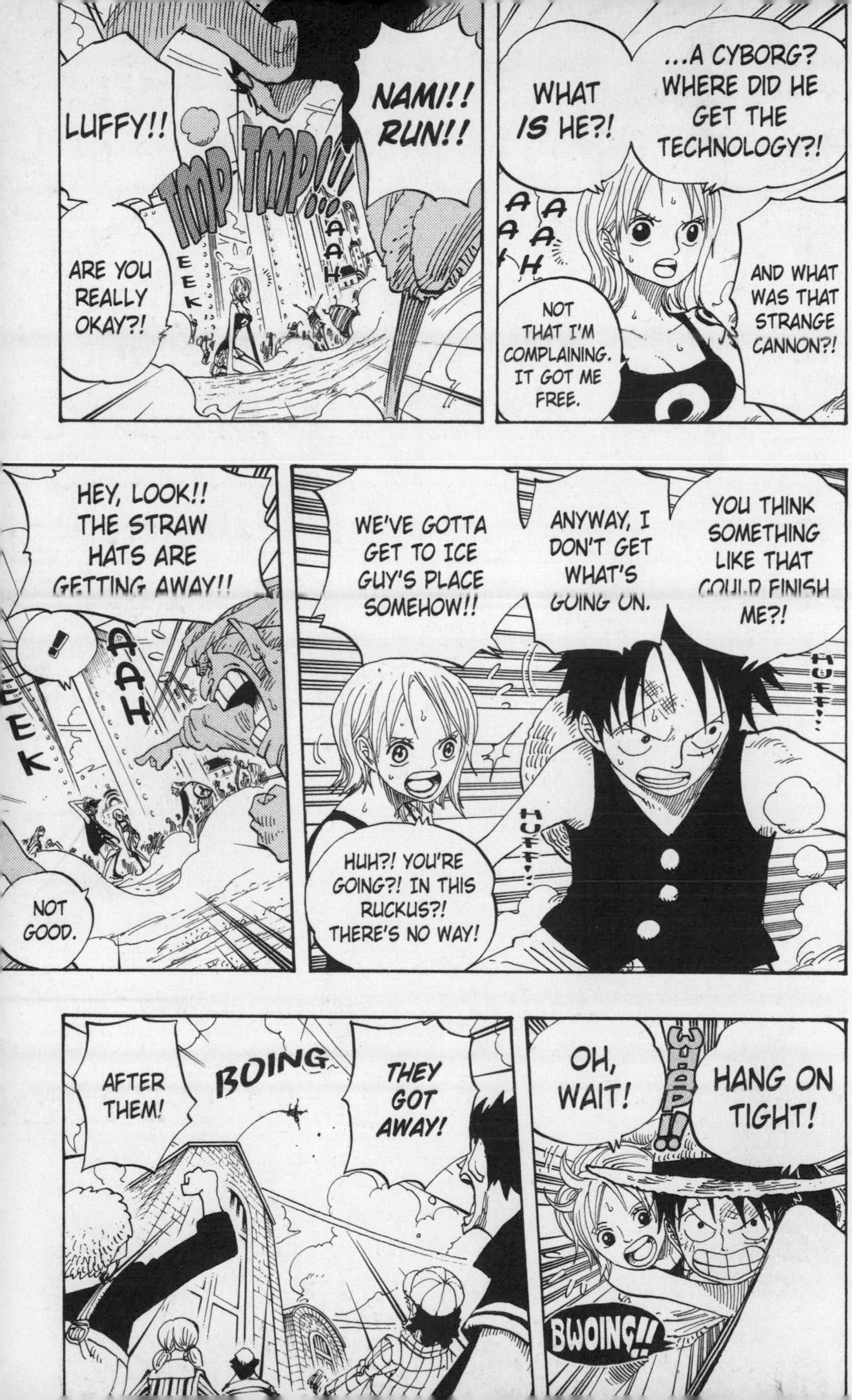
...A CYBORG? WHERE DID HE GET THE TECHNOLOGY?!
WHAT IS HE?!
AAAAH
AND WHAT WAS THAT STRANGE CANNON?!
NOT THAT I'M COMPLAINING. IT GOT ME FREE.
NAMI!! RUN!!
LUFFY!!
TMP TMP!!
AAAH
EEEK
ARE YOU REALLY OKAY?!
YOU THINK SOMETHING LIKE THAT COULD FINISH ME?!
HUFF
ANYWAY, I DON'T GET WHAT'S GOING ON.
WE'VE GOTTA GET TO ICE GUY'S PLACE SOMEHOW!!
HUFF
HUH?! YOU'RE GOING?! IN THIS RUCKUS?! THERE'S NO WAY!
HEY, LOOK!! THE STRAW HATS ARE GETTING AWAY!!
!
AAAH
EEEK
NOT GOOD.
HANG ON TIGHT!
WHAP!!
OH, WAIT!
BWOING!!
THEY GOT AWAY!
BOING
AFTER THEM!

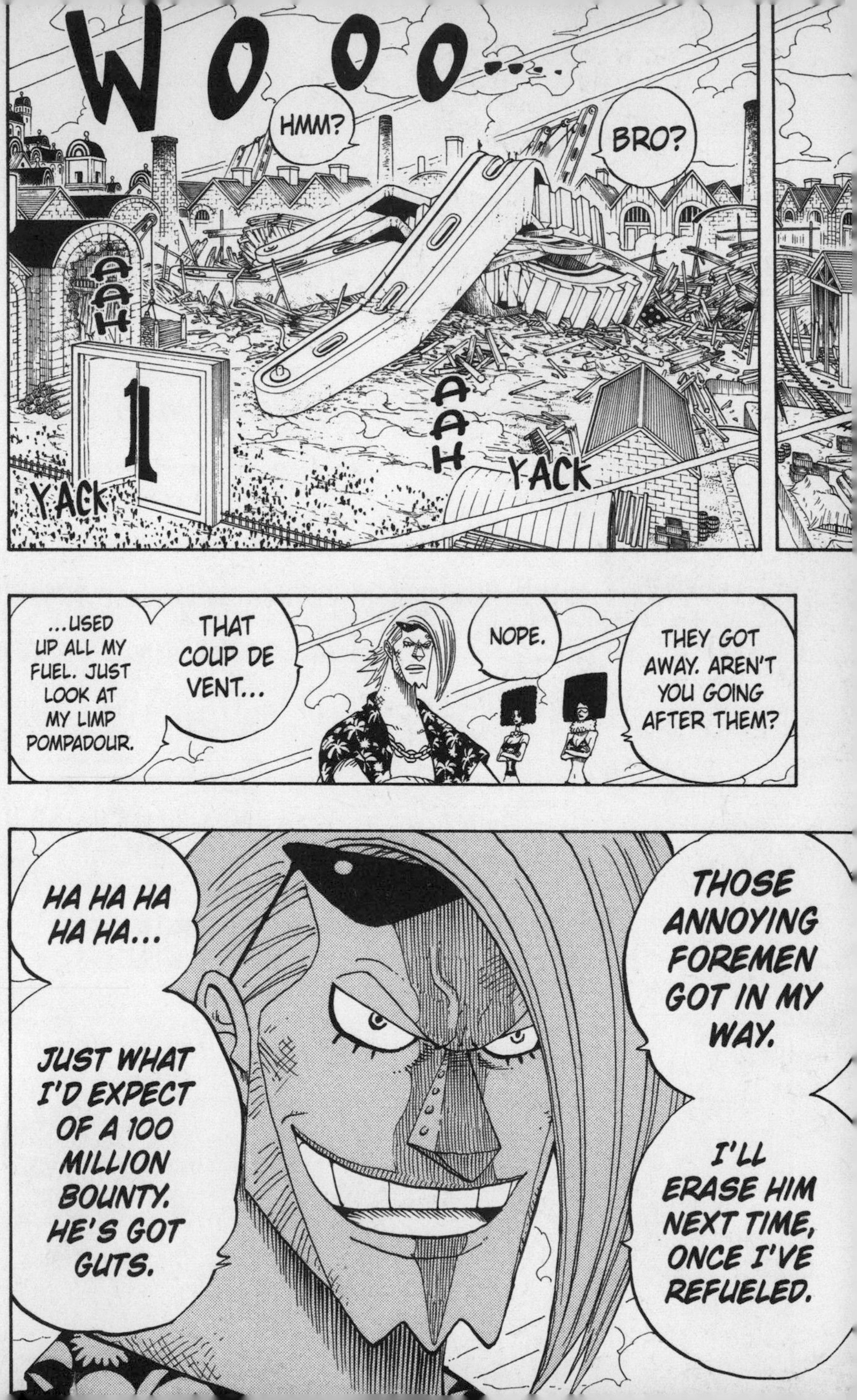
BRO?
HMM?
WOOO...
AAH
YACK
AAH
YACK
1
THEY GOT AWAY. AREN'T YOU GOING AFTER THEM?
NOPE.
THAT COUP DE VENT...
...USED UP ALL MY FUEL. JUST LOOK AT MY LIMP POMPADOUR.
THOSE ANNOYING FOREMEN GOT IN MY WAY.
I'LL ERASE HIM NEXT TIME, ONCE I'VE REFUELED.
HA HA HA HA HA...
JUST WHAT I'D EXPECT OF A 100 MILLION BOUNTY. HE'S GOT GUTS.

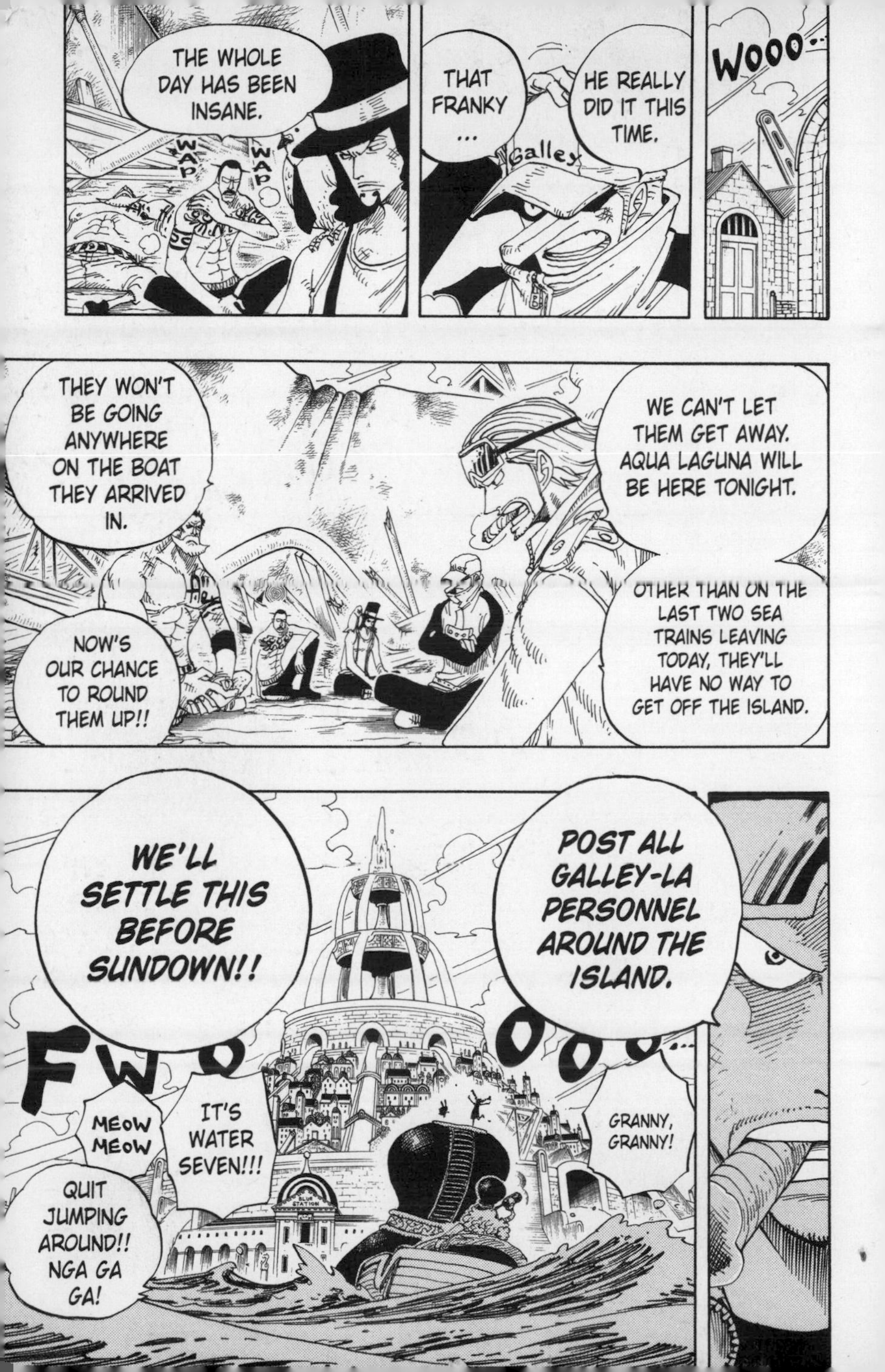
WOOO...
HE REALLY DID IT THIS TIME.
THAT FRANKY...
THE WHOLE DAY HAS BEEN INSANE.
WAP
WAP
WE CAN'T LET THEM GET AWAY. AQUA LAGUNA WILL BE HERE TONIGHT.
OTHER THAN ON THE LAST TWO SEA TRAINS LEAVING TODAY, THEY'LL HAVE NO WAY TO GET OFF THE ISLAND.
THEY WON'T BE GOING ANYWHERE ON THE BOAT THEY ARRIVED IN.
NOW'S OUR CHANCE TO ROUND THEM UP!!
POST ALL GALLEY-LA PERSONNEL AROUND THE ISLAND.
WE'LL SETTLE THIS BEFORE SUNDOWN!!
FWOOOO...
GRANNY, GRANNY!
IT'S WATER SEVEN!!!
MEOW MEOW
QUIT JUMPING AROUND!! NGA GA GA!

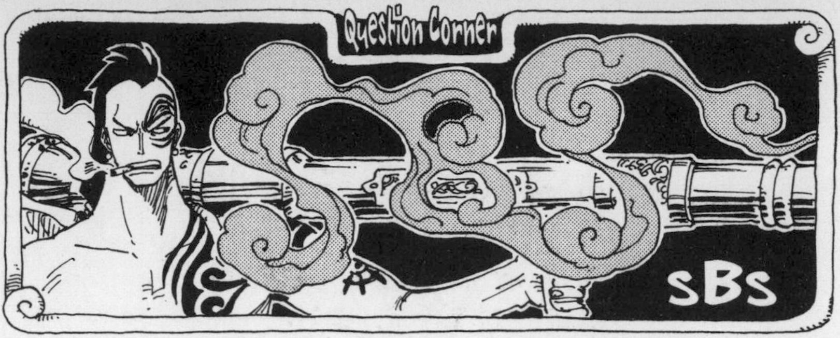
Question Corner
SBS

Q: Oda Sensei, I have a question. What's a cutlass? Is it a sword? Or a gun? Please tell me.

--Chopper Love

A: Yes, um, it's a sword like this. ⬇ They say it started out as a knife for cutting the meat off of animals, and was later shortened for sailors (including the navy). In One Piece, they're drawn like the figure on the right.

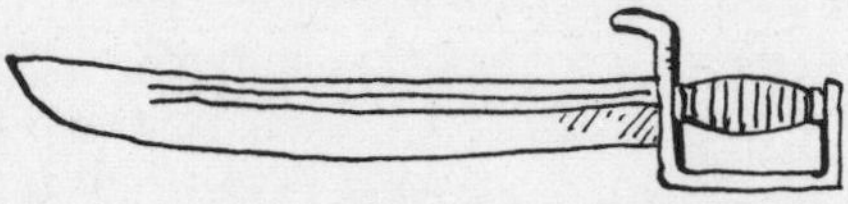

Cutlass (short and broad)

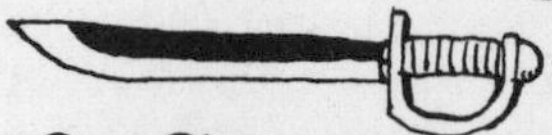

One Piece version

Q: Mr. Oda! Recently, those dream bugs of boys the world over--the Hercules and Atlas beetles--can be found in ordinary pet stores. What do you think about this? Grown-ups today couldn't have dreamed of such a thing when they were children, could they? Is it okay for every boy's dream to be fulfilled so easily? Please say something to today's children!

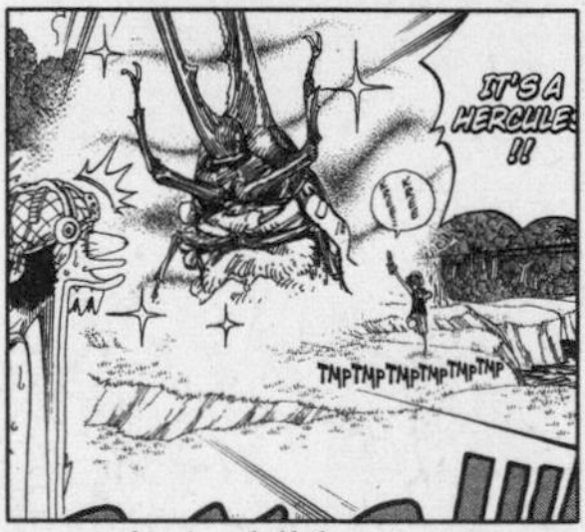
IT'S A HERCULES!!
TMPTMPTMPTMPTMPTMP

--Miyama-Stag-Beetles-Are-My-Life

A: I got a postcard from a very passionate adult. The reader is right. Way back when, you couldn't see real-life foreign bugs. When we were kids, we looked at guidebooks and fell head over heels for the biggest beetle in the world, the Hercules beetle. Nowadays in Japan you can just go and see one. It's amazing. When you think about it, it's the adults of today--the ones who spent their childhoods like we did--who fulfilled the dreams of boys today by showing them the bugs of the world. I think it's pretty terrific when you look at it that way.

Chapter 339: RUMORS

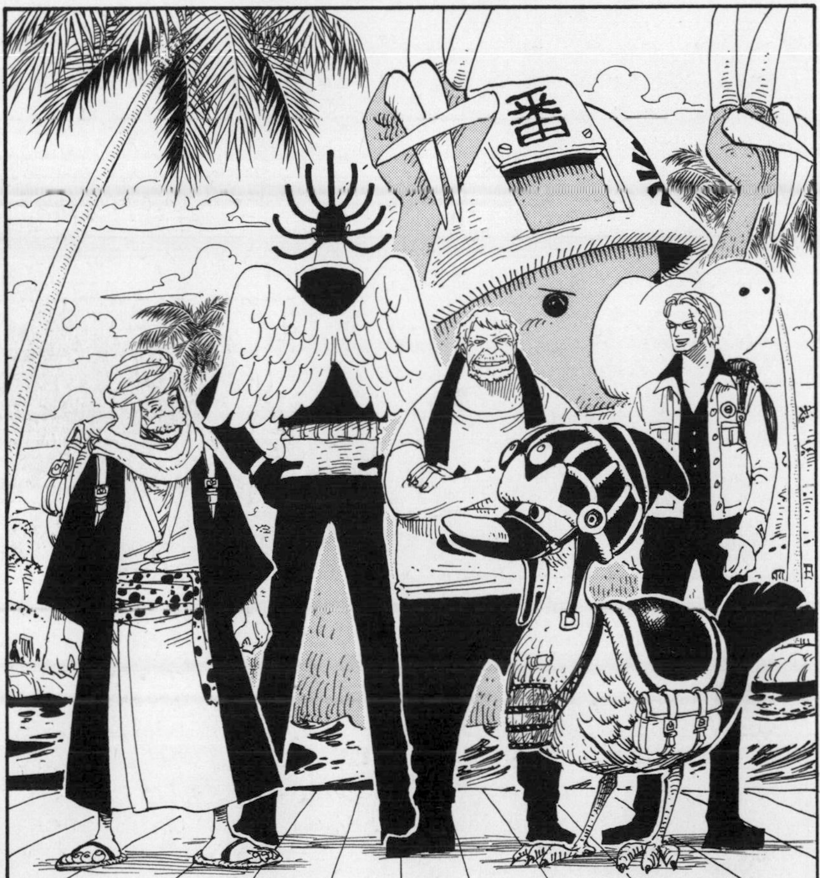
番

GEDATSU'S UNEXPECTED LIFE ON THE BLUE SEA, VOL. 23: "THE HOT SPRINGS INSPECTION SQUAD"

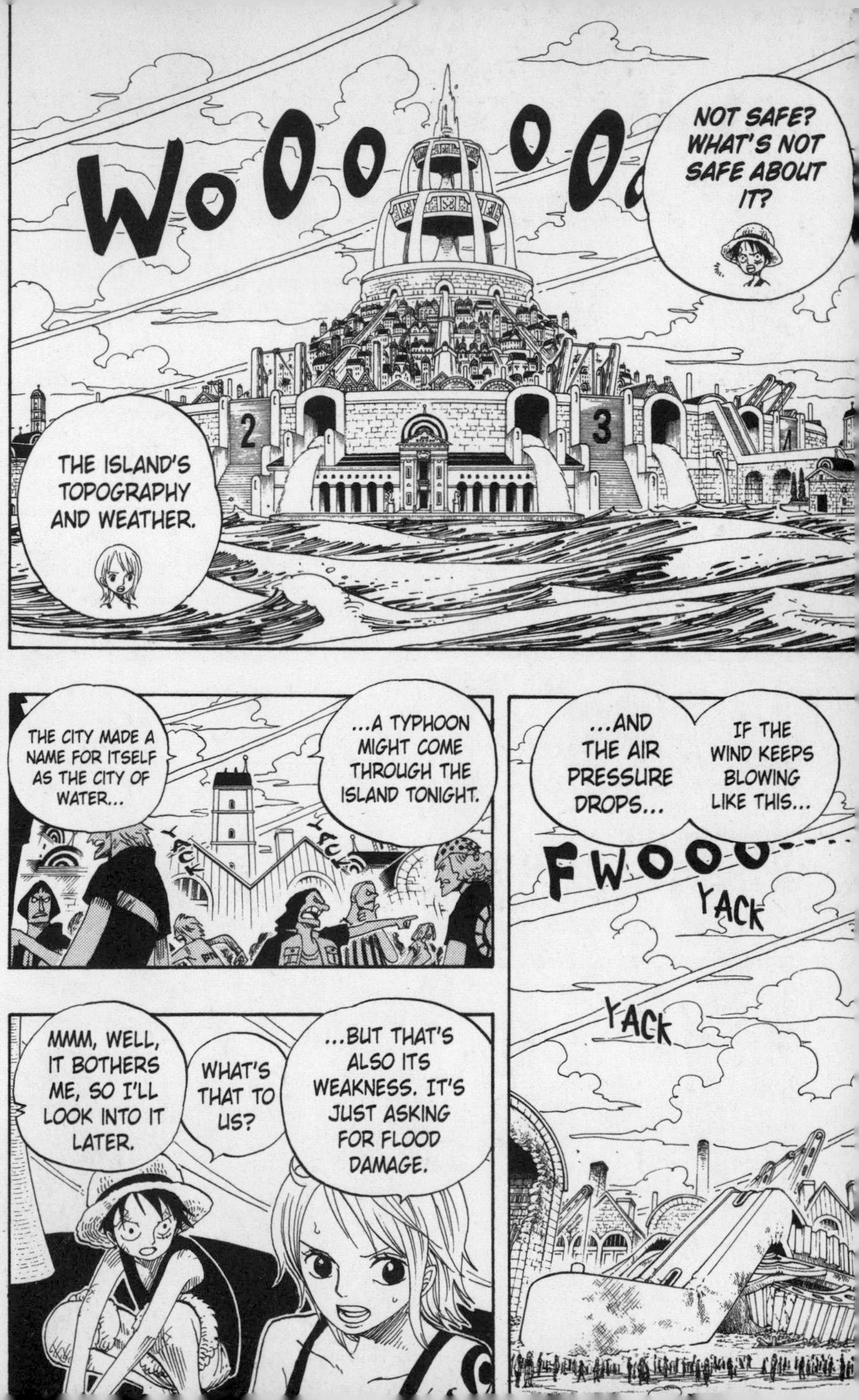
NOT SAFE? WHAT'S NOT SAFE ABOUT IT?
WoOO OOo
THE ISLAND'S TOPOGRAPHY AND WEATHER.
IF THE WIND KEEPS BLOWING LIKE THIS...
...AND THE AIR PRESSURE DROPS...
FWOOO
YACK
YACK
...A TYPHOON MIGHT COME THROUGH THE ISLAND TONIGHT.
THE CITY MADE A NAME FOR ITSELF AS THE CITY OF WATER...
YACK
YACK
...BUT THAT'S ALSO ITS WEAKNESS. IT'S JUST ASKING FOR FLOOD DAMAGE.
WHAT'S THAT TO US?
MMM, WELL, IT BOTHERS ME, SO I'LL LOOK INTO IT LATER.

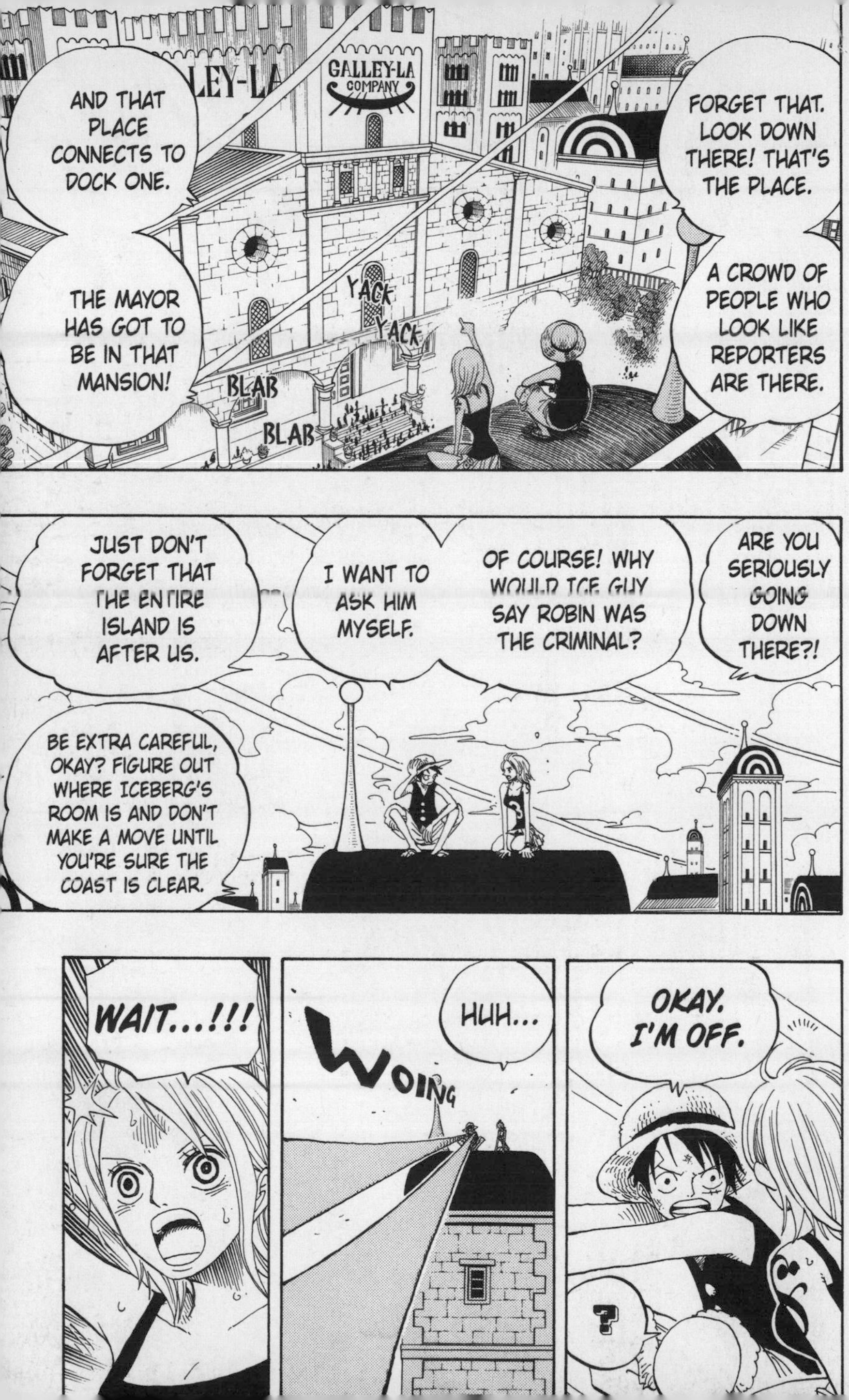
GALLEY-LA COMPANY
FORGET THAT. LOOK DOWN THERE! THAT'S THE PLACE.
A CROWD OF PEOPLE WHO LOOK LIKE REPORTERS ARE THERE.
AND THAT PLACE CONNECTS TO DOCK ONE.
THE MAYOR HAS GOT TO BE IN THAT MANSION!
YACK YACK
BLAB BLAB
ARE YOU SERIOUSLY GOING DOWN THERE?!
OF COURSE! WHY WOULD ICE GUY SAY ROBIN WAS THE CRIMINAL?
I WANT TO ASK HIM MYSELF.
JUST DON'T FORGET THAT THE ENTIRE ISLAND IS AFTER US.
BE EXTRA CAREFUL, OKAY? FIGURE OUT WHERE ICEBERG'S ROOM IS AND DON'T MAKE A MOVE UNTIL YOU'RE SURE THE COAST IS CLEAR.
OKAY. I'M OFF.
?
HUH...
WOING
WAIT...!!!

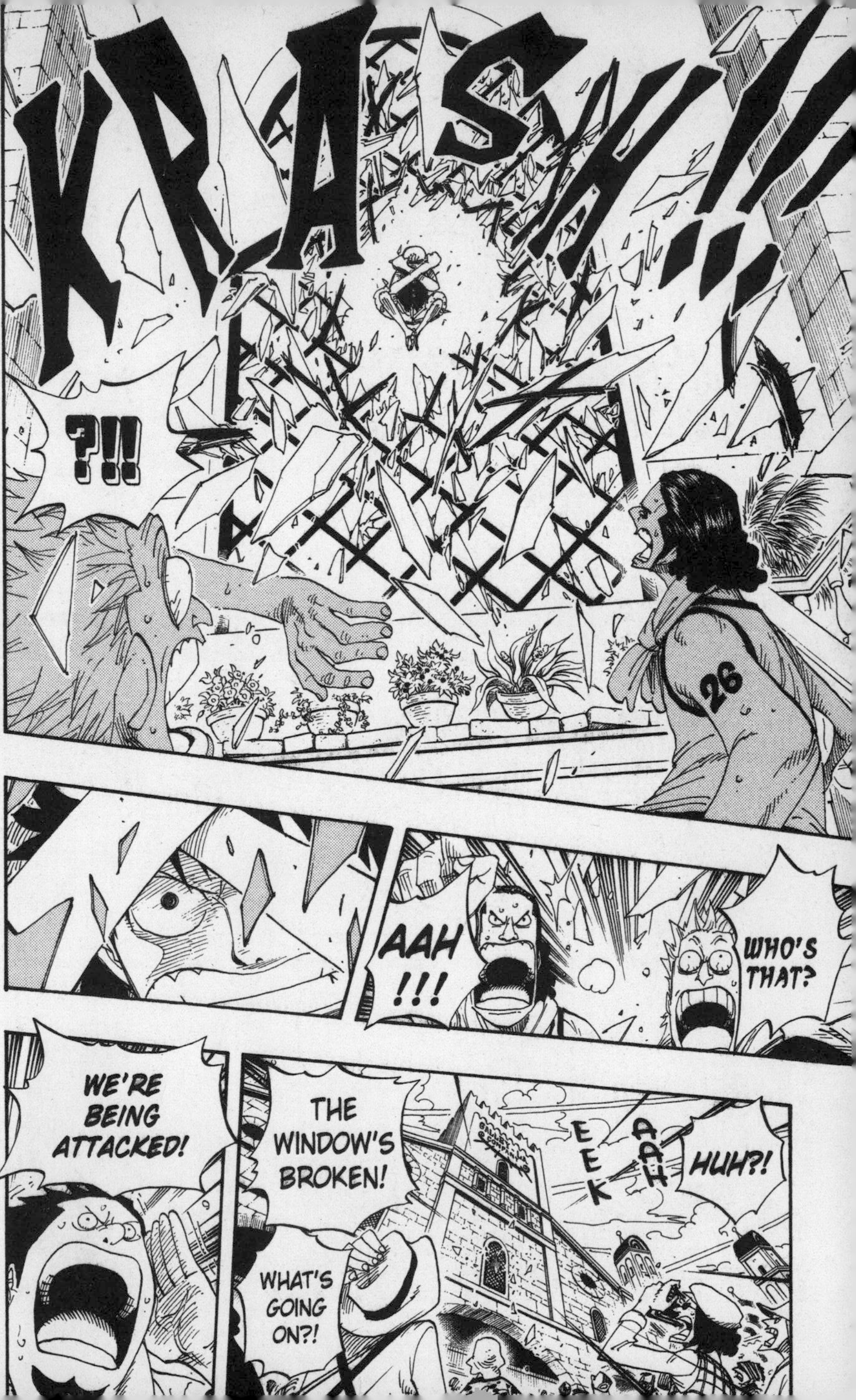
KRASH!!!
?!!
WHO'S THAT?
AAH !!!
HUH?!
AAH
EEK
THE WINDOW'S BROKEN!
WHAT'S GOING ON?!
WE'RE BEING ATTACKED!

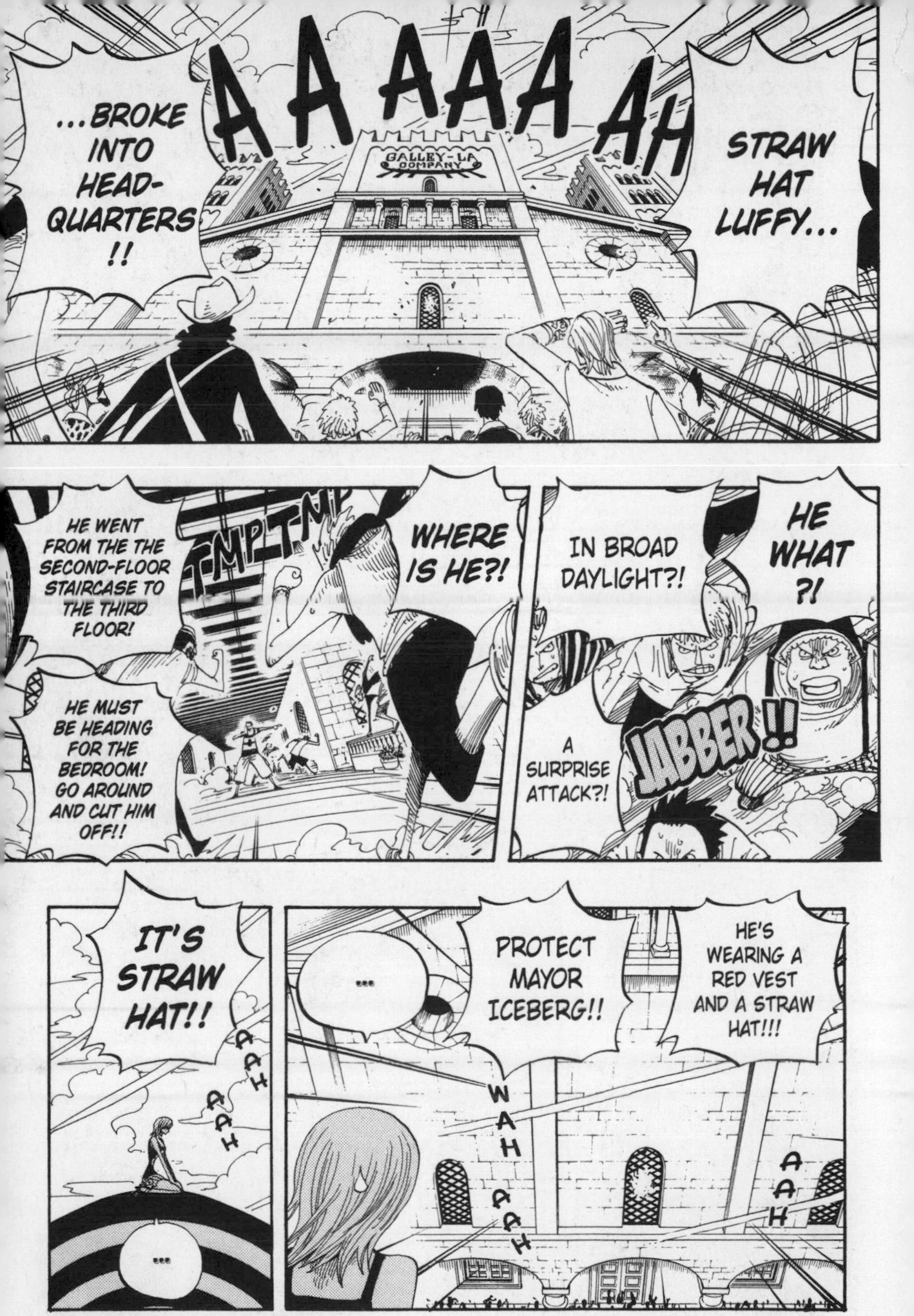
STRAW HAT LUFFY...
AAAAAAH
...BROKE INTO HEAD-QUARTERS !!
GALLEY-LA COMPANY
HE WHAT ?!
IN BROAD DAYLIGHT?!
JABBER!!
A SURPRISE ATTACK?!
WHERE IS HE?!
TMP TMP
HE WENT FROM THE THE SECOND-FLOOR STAIRCASE TO THE THIRD FLOOR!
HE MUST BE HEADING FOR THE BEDROOM! GO AROUND AND CUT HIM OFF!!
HE'S WEARING A RED VEST AND A STRAW HAT!!!
PROTECT MAYOR ICEBERG!!
...
AAAH
WAHAAAH
IT'S STRAW HAT!!
AAAH
AAAH
...

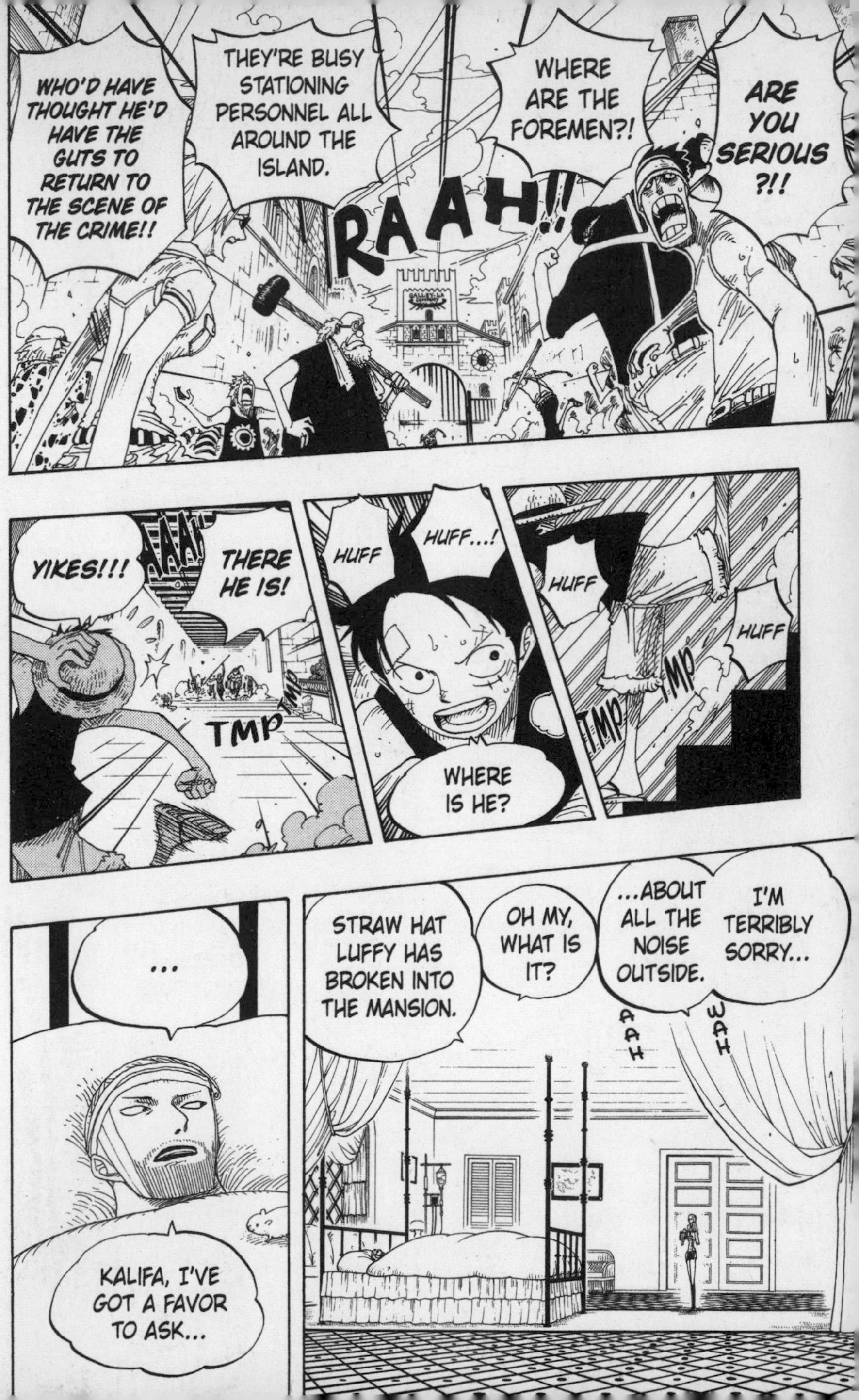
ARE YOU SERIOUS?!!
WHERE ARE THE FOREMEN?!
RAAH!!
THEY'RE BUSY STATIONING PERSONNEL ALL AROUND THE ISLAND.
WHO'D HAVE THOUGHT HE'D HAVE THE GUTS TO RETURN TO THE SCENE OF THE CRIME!!
HUFF
HUFF
TMP
TMP
HUFF...!
HUFF
WHERE IS HE?
THERE HE IS!
YIKES!!!
TMP TMP
TMP
I'M TERRIBLY SORRY...
...ABOUT ALL THE NOISE OUTSIDE.
WAH
AAH
OH MY, WHAT IS IT?
STRAW HAT LUFFY HAS BROKEN INTO THE MANSION.
...
KALIFA, I'VE GOT A FAVOR TO ASK...

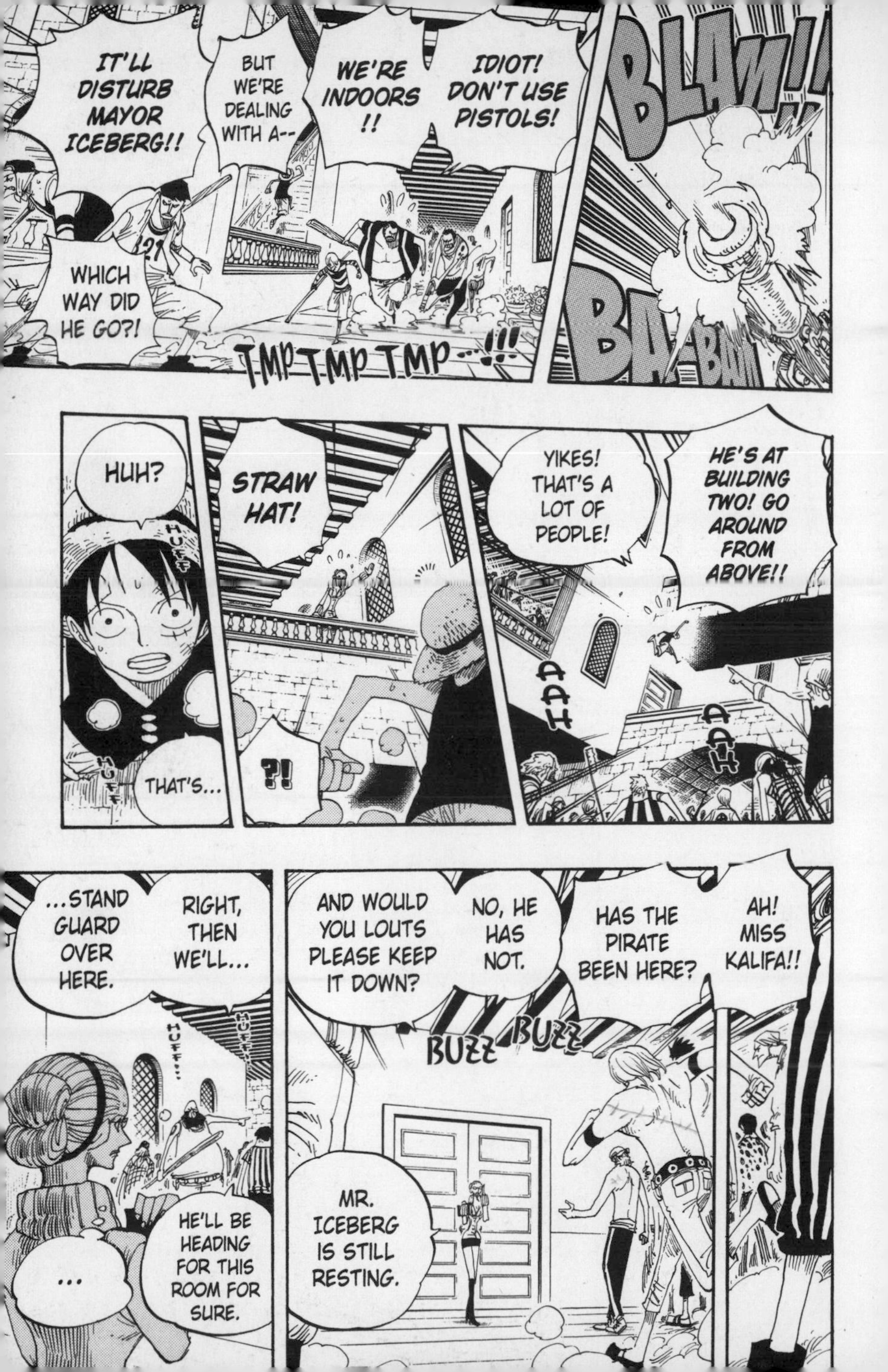
BLAM!!
BA-BAM
IDIOT! DON'T USE PISTOLS!
WE'RE INDOORS!!
BUT WE'RE DEALING WITH A--
IT'LL DISTURB MAYOR ICEBERG!!
WHICH WAY DID HE GO?!
TMP TMP TMP...!!
HE'S AT BUILDING TWO! GO AROUND FROM ABOVE!!
YIKES! THAT'S A LOT OF PEOPLE!
AAH
AAH
STRAW HAT!
?!
HUH?
HUFF
HUFF
THAT'S...
AH! MISS KALIFA!!
HAS THE PIRATE BEEN HERE?
NO, HE HAS NOT.
AND WOULD YOU LOUTS PLEASE KEEP IT DOWN?
BUZZ BUZZ
MR. ICEBERG IS STILL RESTING.
RIGHT, THEN WE'LL...
...STAND GUARD OVER HERE.
HUFF...
HUFF...
HE'LL BE HEADING FOR THIS ROOM FOR SURE.
...

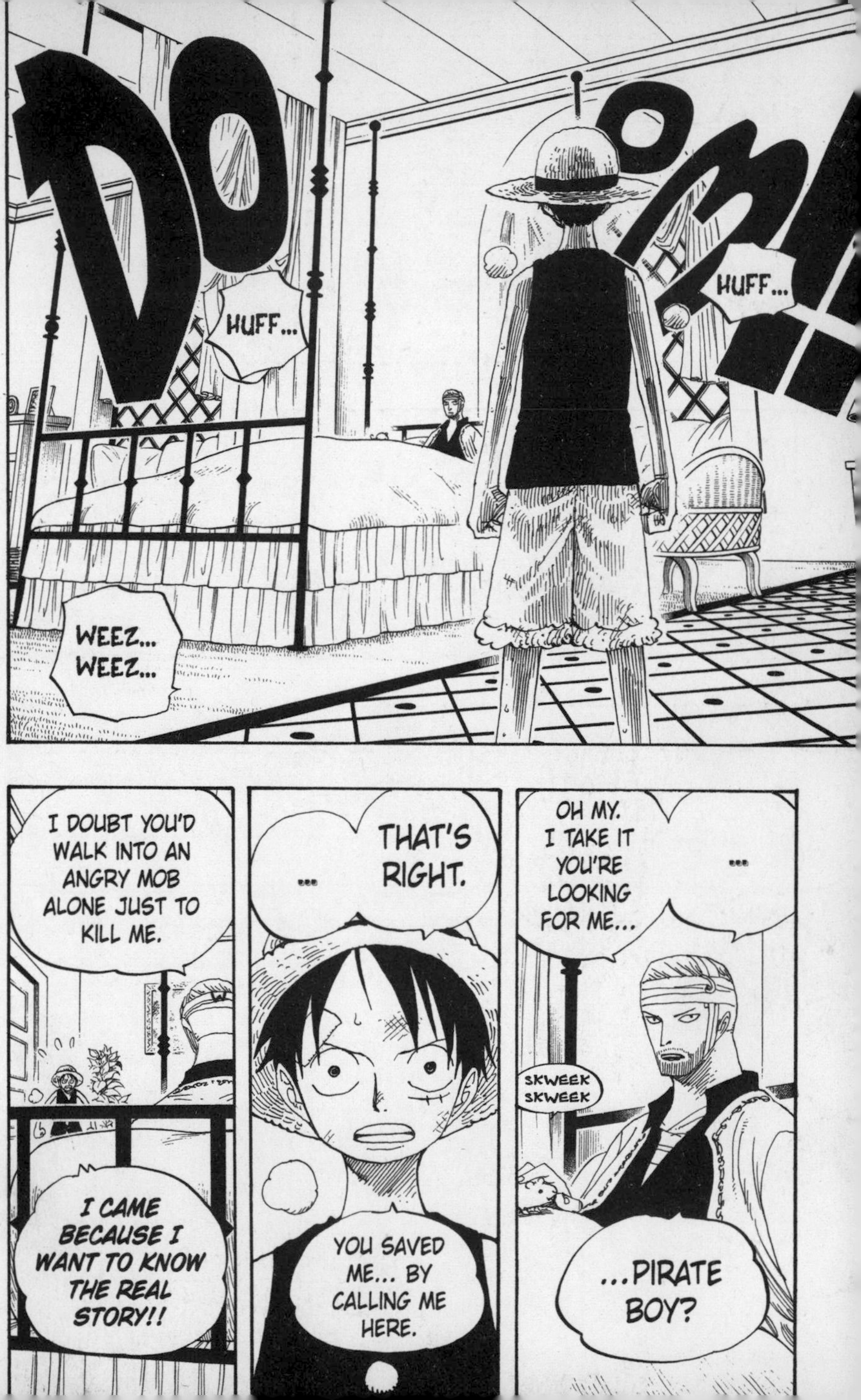
DOOM!!
HUFF...
HUFF...
WEEZ... WEEZ...
...
OH MY. I TAKE IT YOU'RE LOOKING FOR ME...
SKWEEK SKWEEK
...PIRATE BOY?
THAT'S RIGHT.
...
YOU SAVED ME... BY CALLING ME HERE.
I DOUBT YOU'D WALK INTO AN ANGRY MOB ALONE JUST TO KILL ME.
I CAME BECAUSE I WANT TO KNOW THE REAL STORY!!

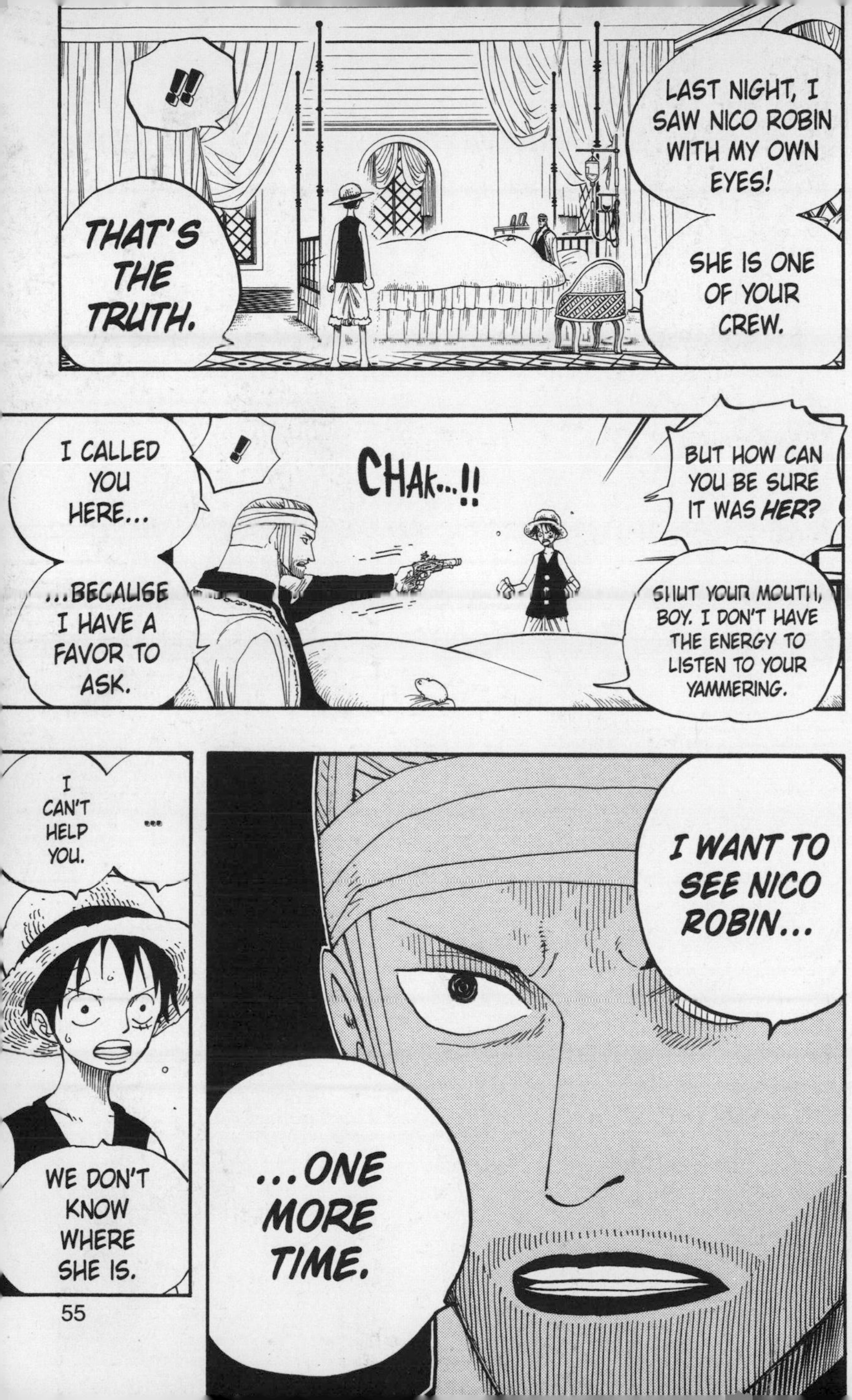
LAST NIGHT, I SAW NICO ROBIN WITH MY OWN EYES!
SHE IS ONE OF YOUR CREW.
!!
THAT'S THE TRUTH.
BUT HOW CAN YOU BE SURE IT WAS *HER*?
CHAK...!!
SHUT YOUR MOUTH, BOY. I DON'T HAVE THE ENERGY TO LISTEN TO YOUR YAMMERING.
!
I CALLED YOU HERE...
...BECAUSE I HAVE A FAVOR TO ASK.
I WANT TO SEE NICO ROBIN...
...ONE MORE TIME.
...
I CAN'T HELP YOU.
WE DON'T KNOW WHERE SHE IS.

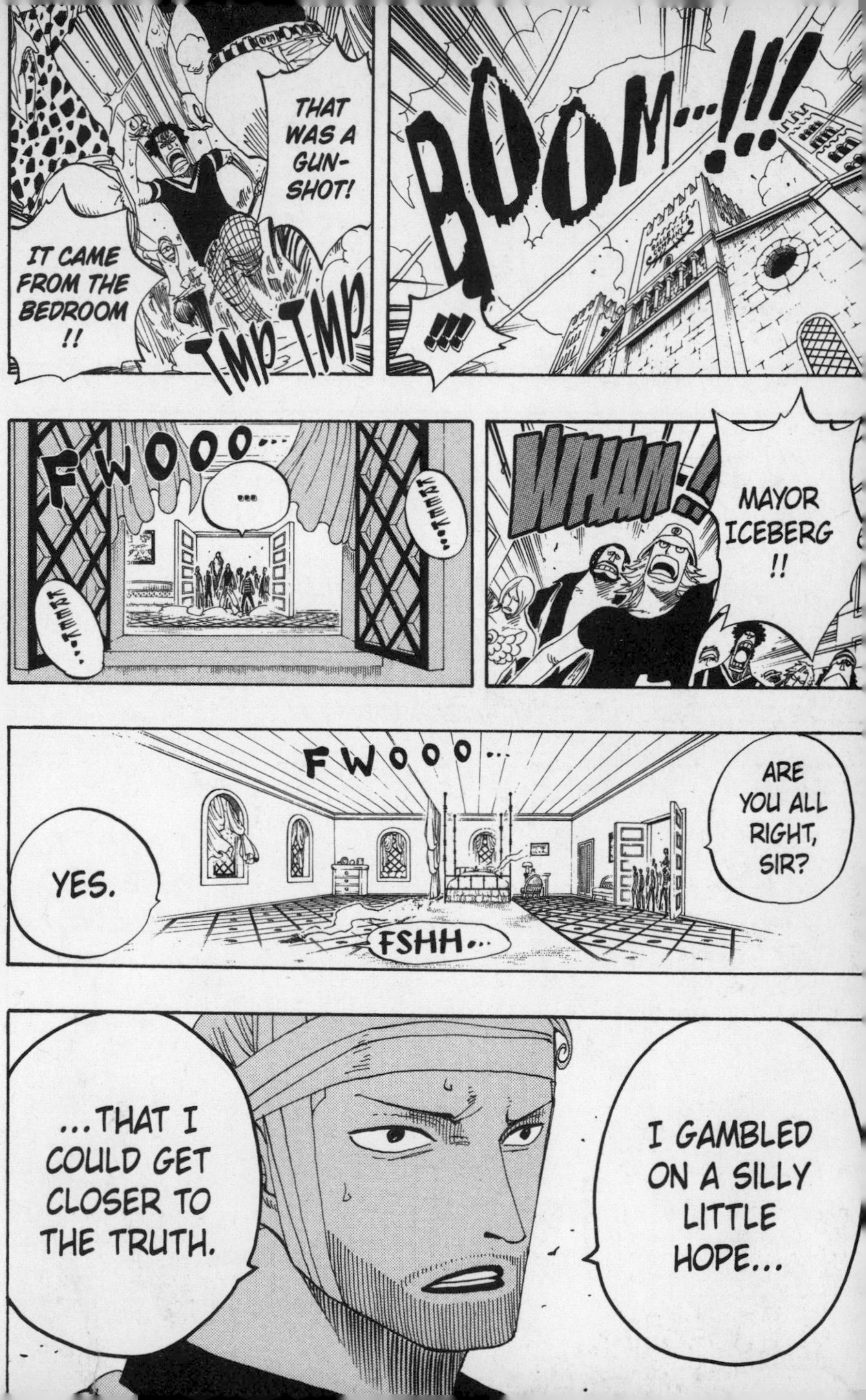
BOOM...!!!
!!!
THAT WAS A GUN-SHOT!
IT CAME FROM THE BEDROOM !!
TMP TMP
WHAM!!
MAYOR ICEBERG !!
KREEK...
...
FWOOO...
KREEK...
ARE YOU ALL RIGHT, SIR?
FWOOO...
YES.
FSHH...
I GAMBLED ON A SILLY LITTLE HOPE...
...THAT I COULD GET CLOSER TO THE TRUTH.

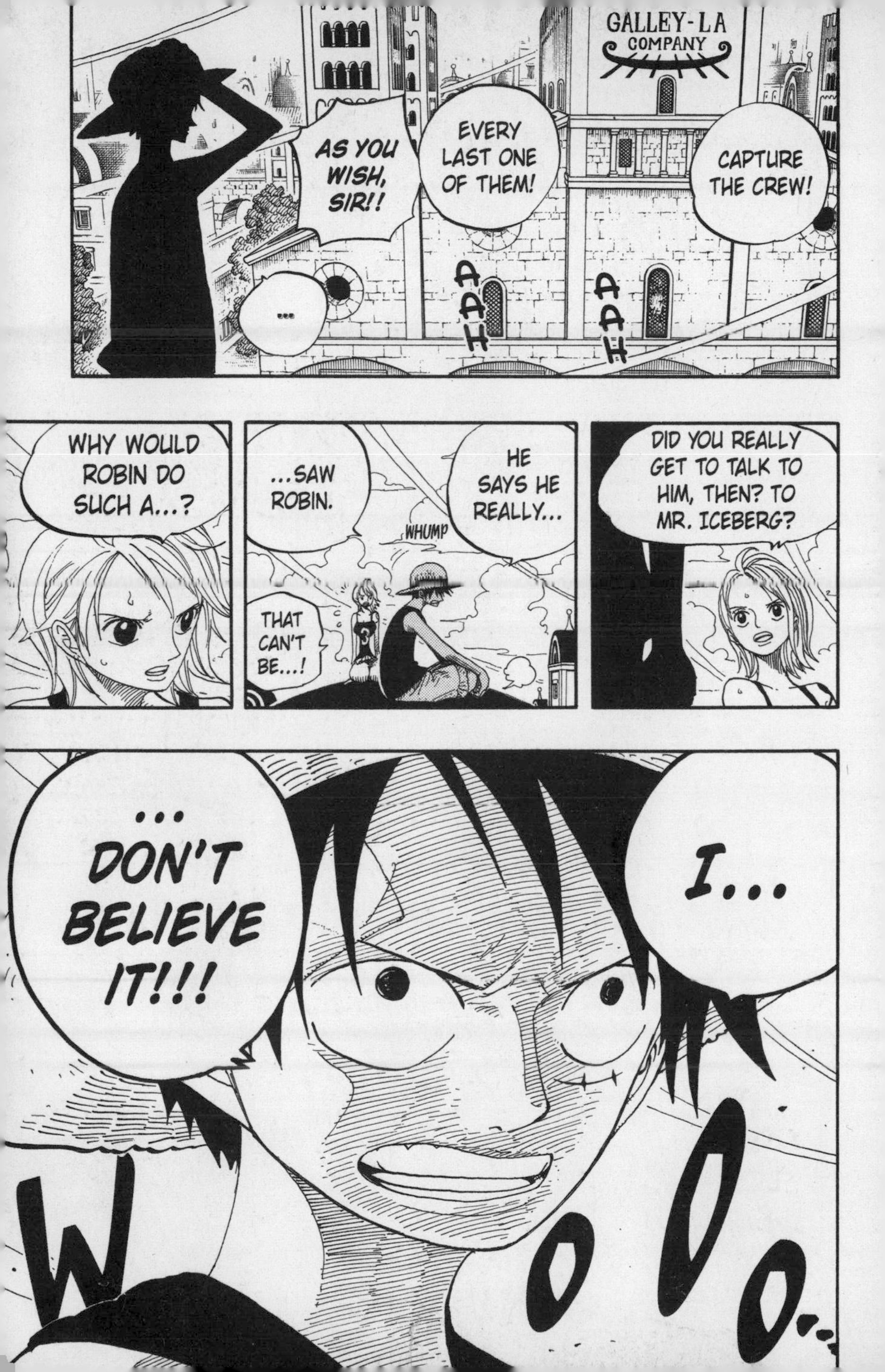
GALLEY-LA COMPANY
CAPTURE THE CREW!
EVERY LAST ONE OF THEM!
AS YOU WISH, SIR!!
AAH
AAH
...
DID YOU REALLY GET TO TALK TO HIM, THEN? TO MR. ICEBERG?
HE SAYS HE REALLY...
...SAW ROBIN.
WHUMP
THAT CAN'T BE...!
WHY WOULD ROBIN DO SUCH A...?
I...
...DON'T BELIEVE IT!!!
WOOOO...

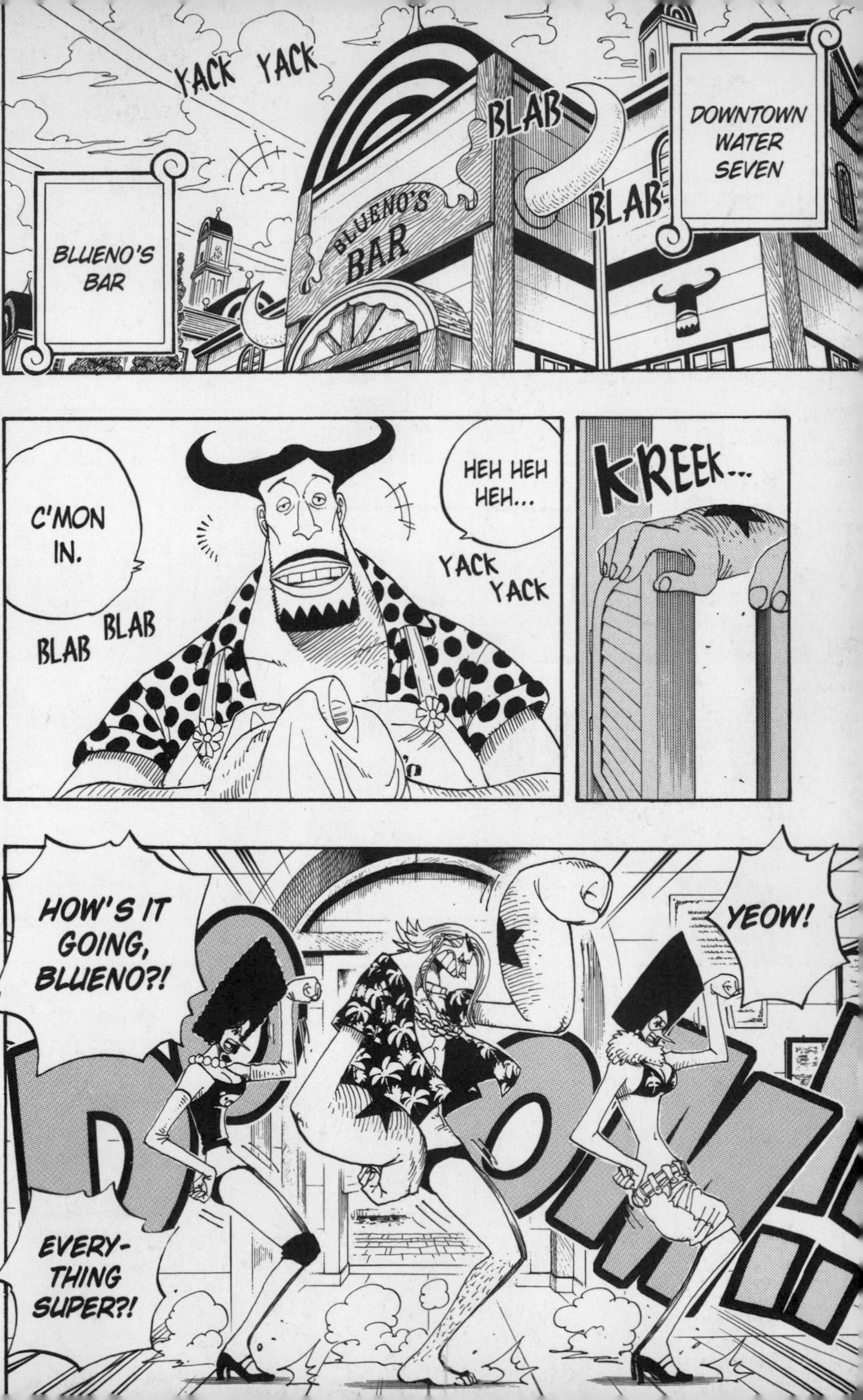
DOWNTOWN WATER SEVEN
BLAB
BLAB
BLUENO'S BAR
YACK YACK
BLUENO'S BAR
KREEK...
HEH HEH HEH...
YACK YACK
C'MON IN.
BLAB BLAB
YEOW!
HOW'S IT GOING, BLUENO?!
EVERY-THING SUPER?!

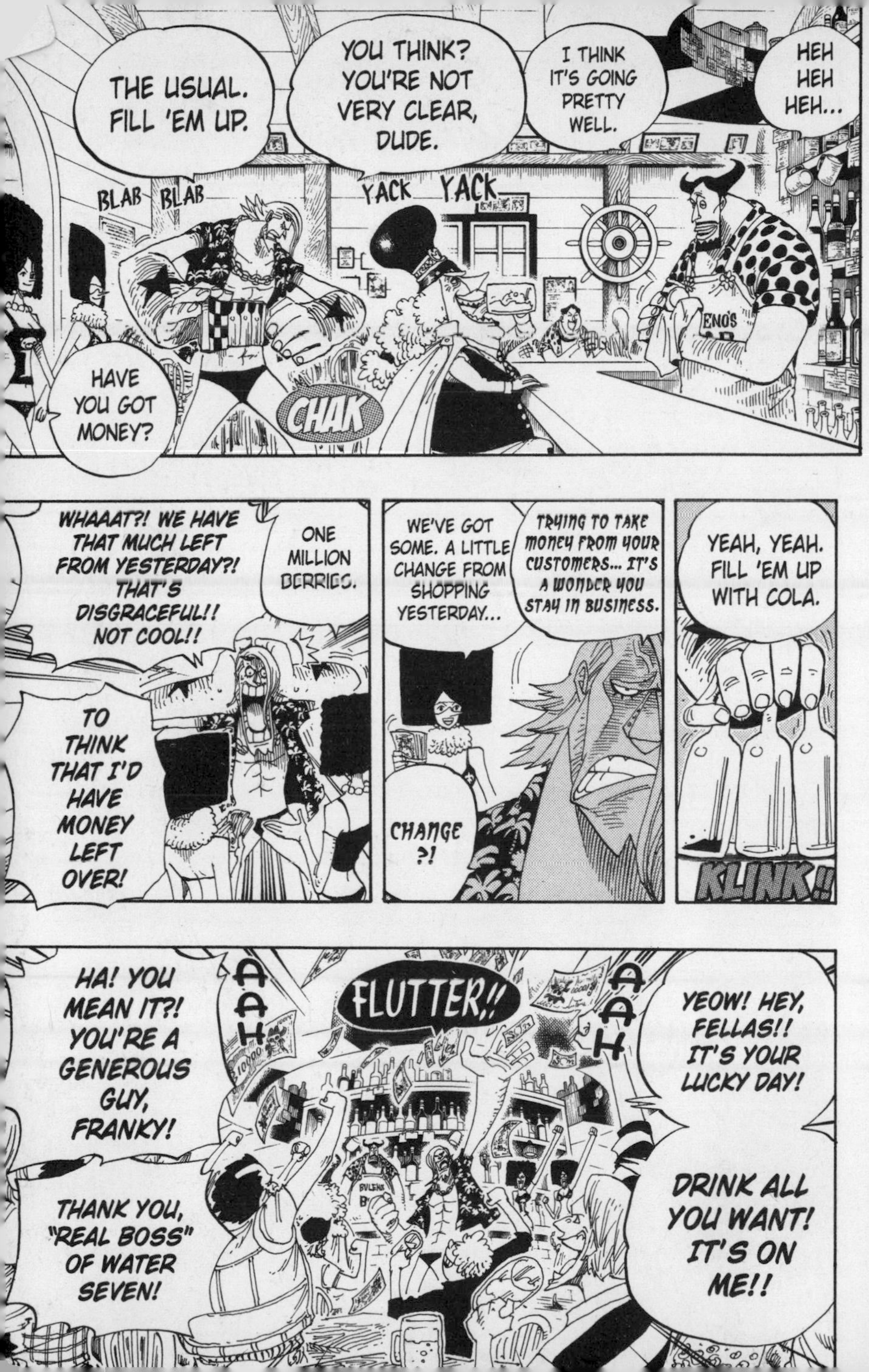
HEH HEH HEH...
I THINK IT'S GOING PRETTY WELL.
YOU THINK? YOU'RE NOT VERY CLEAR, DUDE.
YACK YACK
THE USUAL. FILL 'EM UP.
BLAB BLAB
CHAK
HAVE YOU GOT MONEY?
YEAH, YEAH. FILL 'EM UP WITH COLA.
KLINK!!
TRYING TO TAKE MONEY FROM YOUR CUSTOMERS... IT'S A WONDER YOU STAY IN BUSINESS.
WE'VE GOT SOME. A LITTLE CHANGE FROM SHOPPING YESTERDAY...
CHANGE ?!
ONE MILLION BERRIES.
WHAAAT?! WE HAVE THAT MUCH LEFT FROM YESTERDAY?! THAT'S DISGRACEFUL!! NOT COOL!!
TO THINK THAT I'D HAVE MONEY LEFT OVER!
YEOW! HEY, FELLAS!! IT'S YOUR LUCKY DAY!
DRINK ALL YOU WANT! IT'S ON ME!!
AAH
FLUTTER!!
AAH
HA! YOU MEAN IT?! YOU'RE A GENEROUS GUY, FRANKY!
THANK YOU, "REAL BOSS" OF WATER SEVEN!

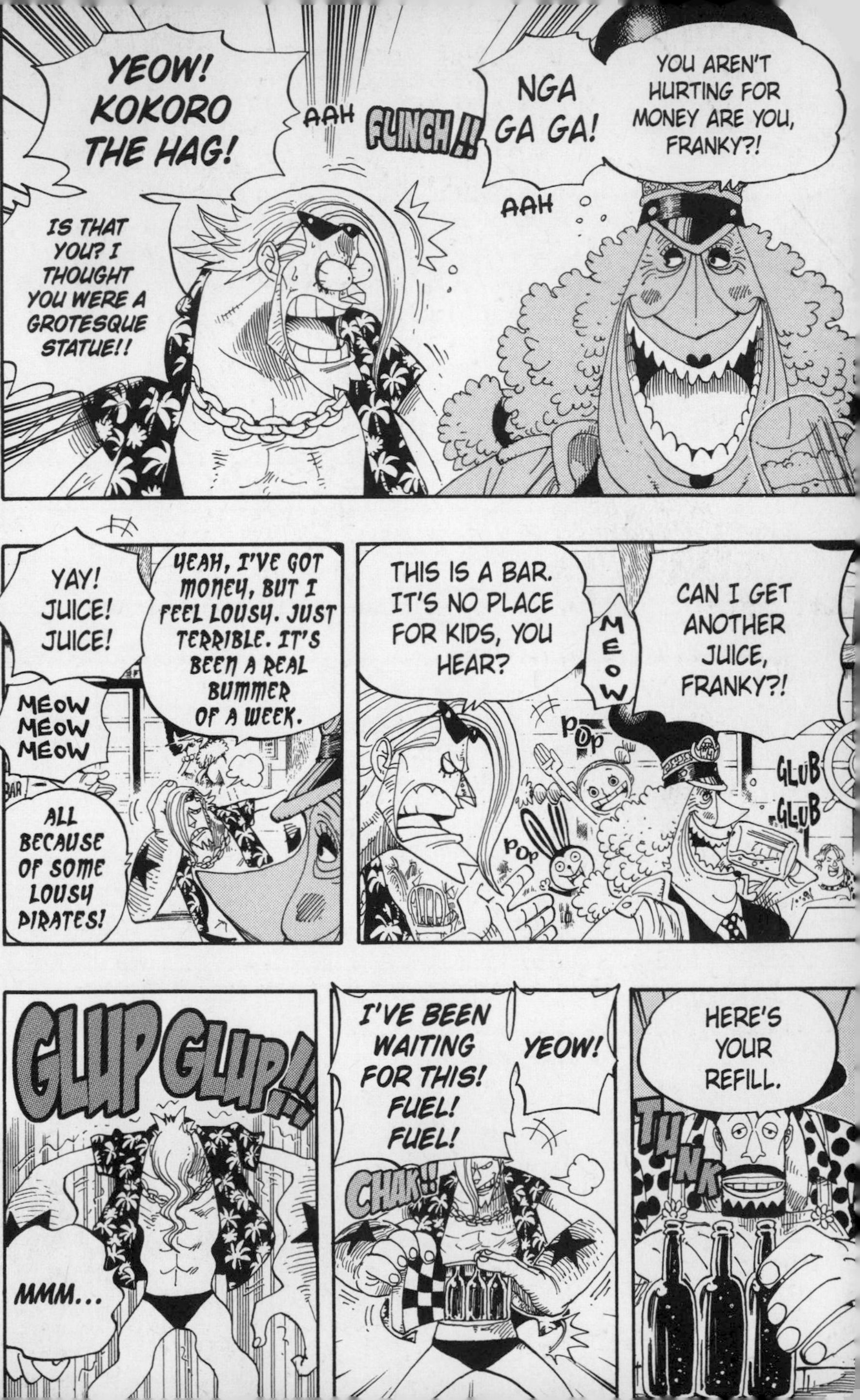
YOU AREN'T HURTING FOR MONEY ARE YOU, FRANKY?!
NGA GA GA!
AAH
FLINCH!!
AAH
YEOW! KOKORO THE HAG!
IS THAT YOU? I THOUGHT YOU WERE A GROTESQUE STATUE!!
CAN I GET ANOTHER JUICE, FRANKY?!
MEOW
THIS IS A BAR. IT'S NO PLACE FOR KIDS, YOU HEAR?
POP
GLUB GLUB
POP
YEAH, I'VE GOT MONEY, BUT I FEEL LOUSY. JUST TERRIBLE. IT'S BEEN A REAL BUMMER OF A WEEK.
YAY! JUICE! JUICE!
MEOW MEOW MEOW
ALL BECAUSE OF SOME LOUSY PIRATES!
HERE'S YOUR REFILL.
TUNK
YEOW!
I'VE BEEN WAITING FOR THIS! FUEL! FUEL!
CHAK!!
GLUP GLUP!!
MMM...

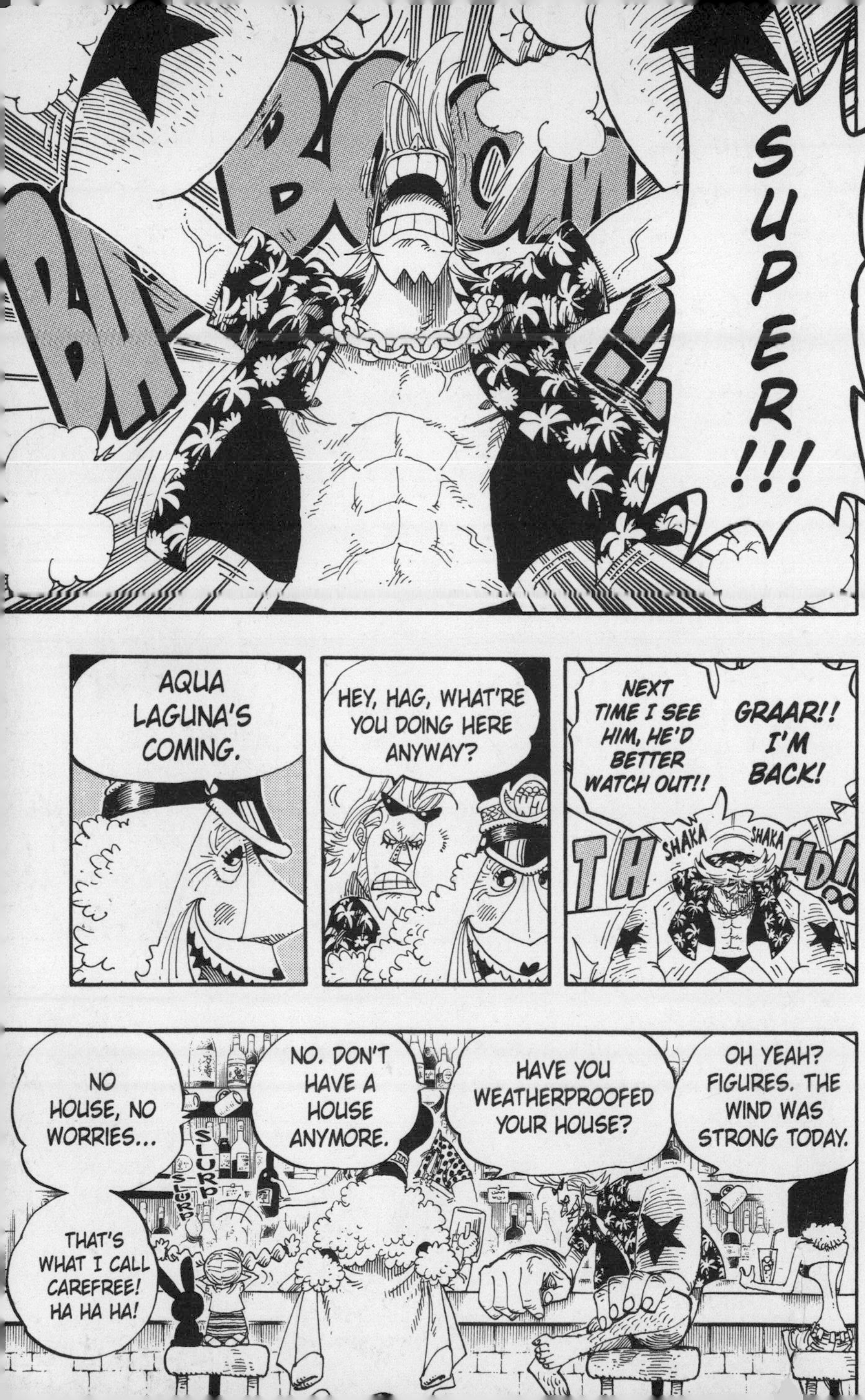
SUPER!!!
GRAAR!! I'M BACK!
NEXT TIME I SEE HIM, HE'D BETTER WATCH OUT!!
SHAKA
SHAKA
HEY, HAG, WHAT'RE YOU DOING HERE ANYWAY?
AQUA LAGUNA'S COMING.
OH YEAH? FIGURES. THE WIND WAS STRONG TODAY.
HAVE YOU WEATHERPROOFED YOUR HOUSE?
NO. DON'T HAVE A HOUSE ANYMORE.
NO HOUSE, NO WORRIES...
SLURP
SLURP
THAT'S WHAT I CALL CAREFREE! HA HA HA!

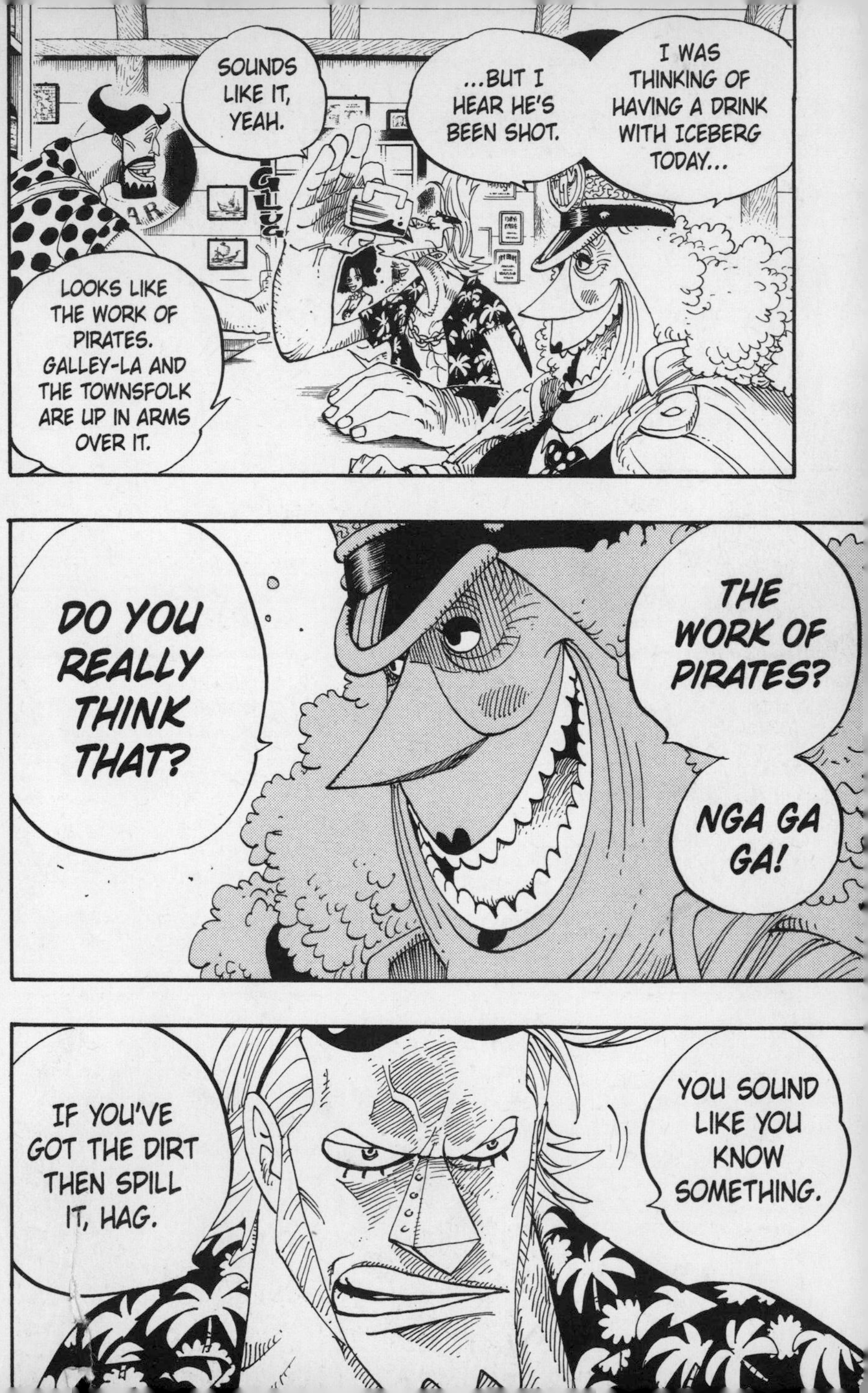
I WAS THINKING OF HAVING A DRINK WITH ICEBERG TODAY...
...BUT I HEAR HE'S BEEN SHOT.
SOUNDS LIKE IT, YEAH.
GLUG
LOOKS LIKE THE WORK OF PIRATES. GALLEY-LA AND THE TOWNSFOLK ARE UP IN ARMS OVER IT.
THE WORK OF PIRATES?
NGA GA GA!
DO YOU REALLY THINK THAT?
YOU SOUND LIKE YOU KNOW SOMETHING.
IF YOU'VE GOT THE DIRT THEN SPILL IT, HAG.

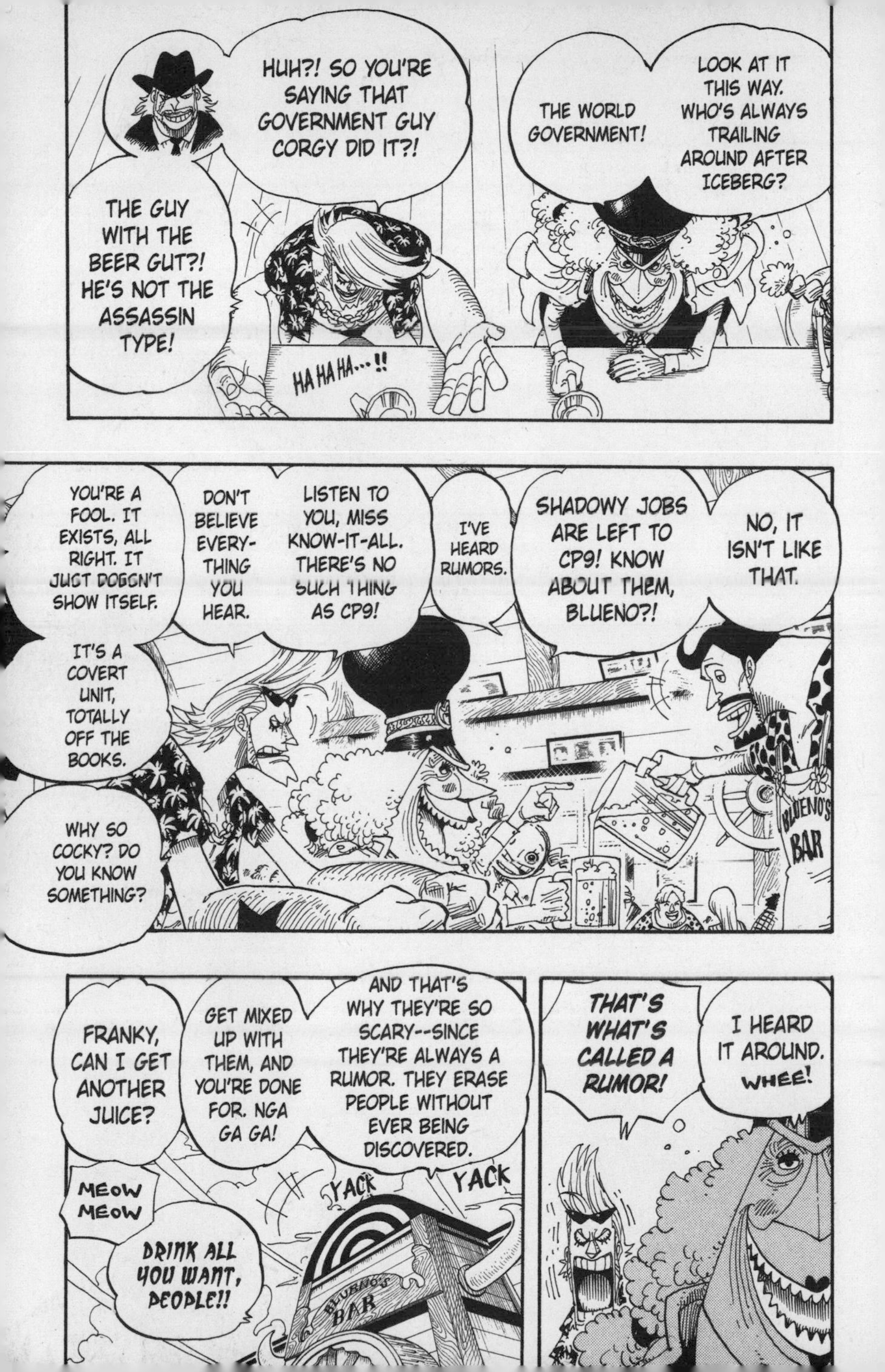
LOOK AT IT THIS WAY. WHO'S ALWAYS TRAILING AROUND AFTER ICEBERG?
THE WORLD GOVERNMENT!
HUH?! SO YOU'RE SAYING THAT GOVERNMENT GUY CORGY DID IT?!
THE GUY WITH THE BEER GUT?! HE'S NOT THE ASSASSIN TYPE!
HA HA HA...!!
NO, IT ISN'T LIKE THAT.
SHADOWY JOBS ARE LEFT TO CP9! KNOW ABOUT THEM, BLUENO?!
I'VE HEARD RUMORS.
LISTEN TO YOU, MISS KNOW-IT-ALL. THERE'S NO SUCH THING AS CP9!
DON'T BELIEVE EVERY-THING YOU HEAR.
YOU'RE A FOOL. IT EXISTS, ALL RIGHT. IT JUST DOESN'T SHOW ITSELF.
IT'S A COVERT UNIT, TOTALLY OFF THE BOOKS.
BLUENO'S BAR
WHY SO COCKY? DO YOU KNOW SOMETHING?
I HEARD IT AROUND. WHEE!
THAT'S WHAT'S CALLED A RUMOR!
AND THAT'S WHY THEY'RE SO SCARY--SINCE THEY'RE ALWAYS A RUMOR. THEY ERASE PEOPLE WITHOUT EVER BEING DISCOVERED.
GET MIXED UP WITH THEM, AND YOU'RE DONE FOR. NGA GA GA!
FRANKY, CAN I GET ANOTHER JUICE?
YACK
YACK
MEOW MEOW
DRINK ALL YOU WANT, PEOPLE!!
BLUENO'S BAR

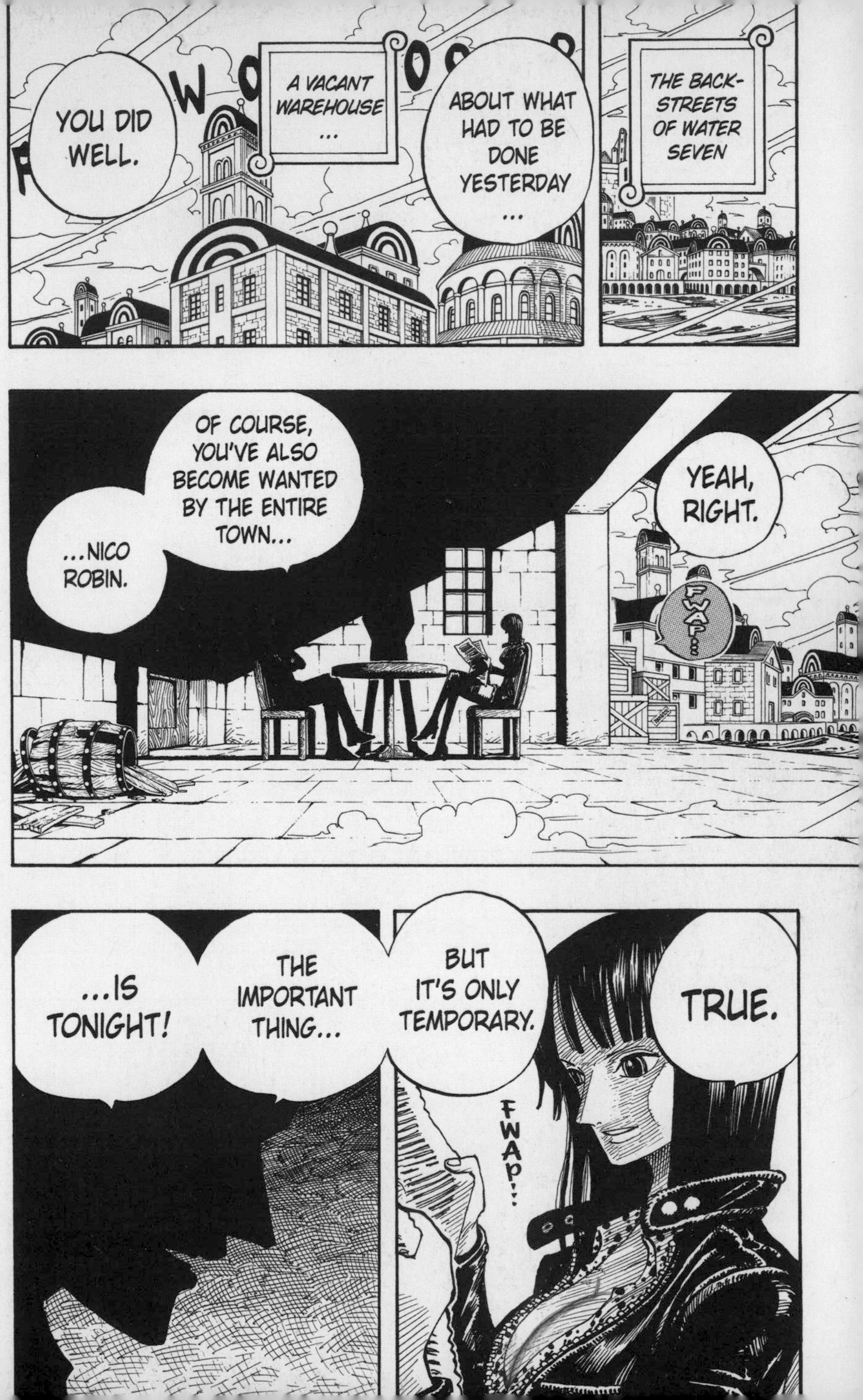
THE BACK-STREETS OF WATER SEVEN
ABOUT WHAT HAD TO BE DONE YESTERDAY ...
A VACANT WAREHOUSE ...
YOU DID WELL.
YEAH, RIGHT.
OF COURSE, YOU'VE ALSO BECOME WANTED BY THE ENTIRE TOWN...
...NICO ROBIN.
FWAP..
TRUE.
FWAP!!
BUT IT'S ONLY TEMPORARY.
THE IMPORTANT THING...
...IS TONIGHT!

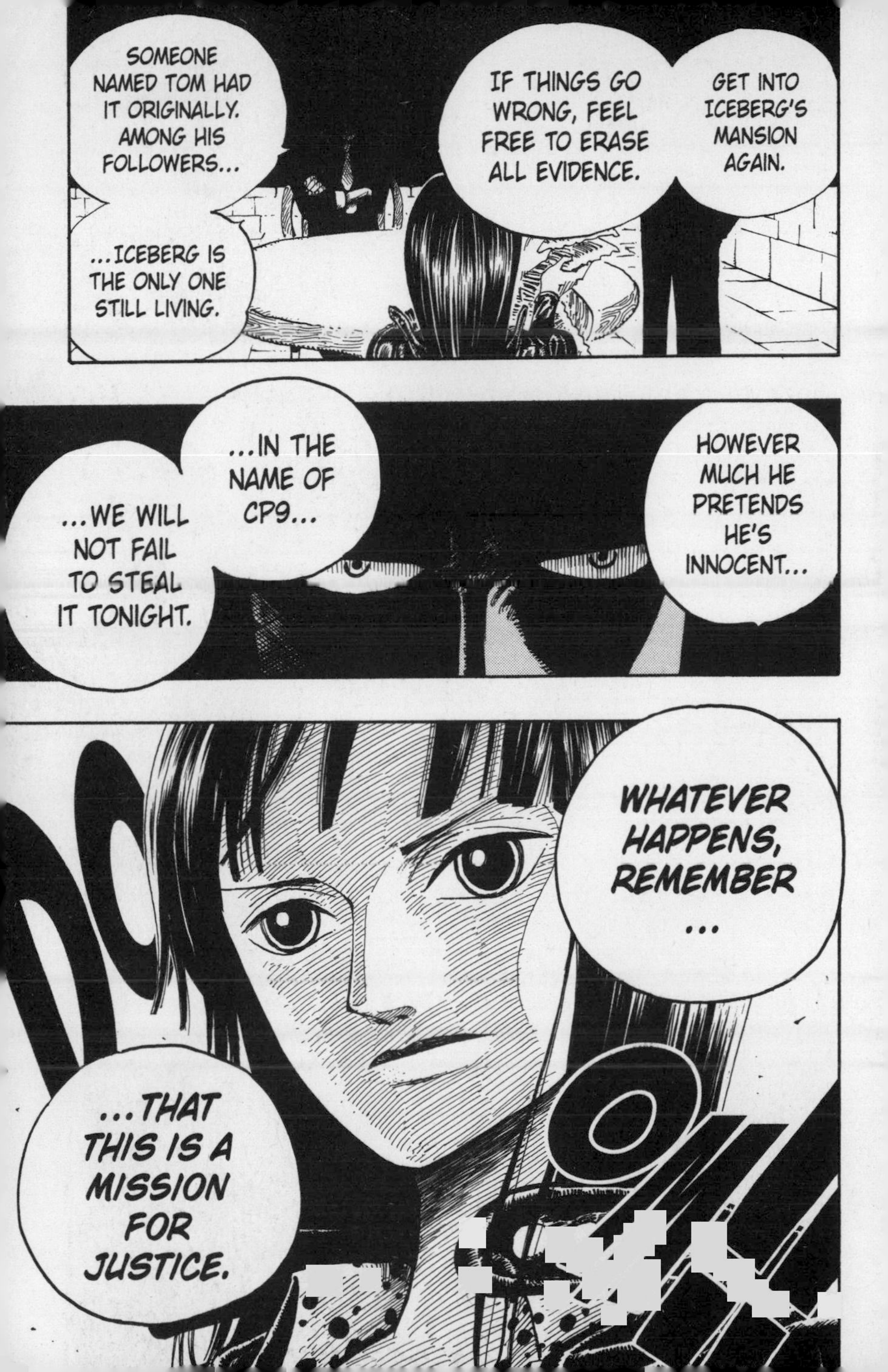
GET INTO ICEBERG'S MANSION AGAIN.
IF THINGS GO WRONG, FEEL FREE TO ERASE ALL EVIDENCE.
SOMEONE NAMED TOM HAD IT ORIGINALLY. AMONG HIS FOLLOWERS...
...ICEBERG IS THE ONLY ONE STILL LIVING.
HOWEVER MUCH HE PRETENDS HE'S INNOCENT...
...IN THE NAME OF CP9...
...WE WILL NOT FAIL TO STEAL IT TONIGHT.
WHATEVER HAPPENS, REMEMBER ...
...THAT THIS IS A MISSION FOR JUSTICE.

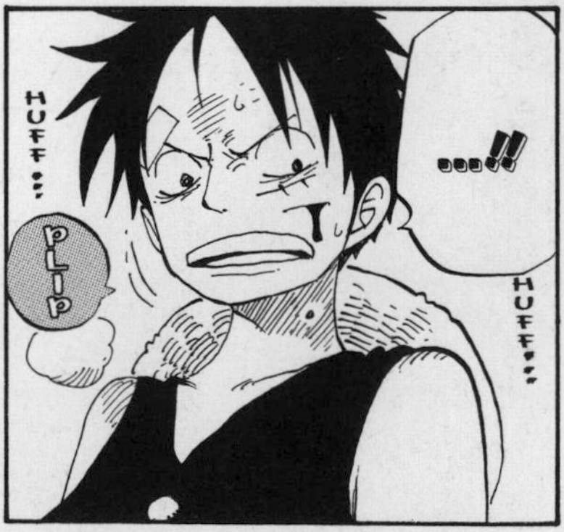
...!!
HUFF...
HUFF...
PLIP

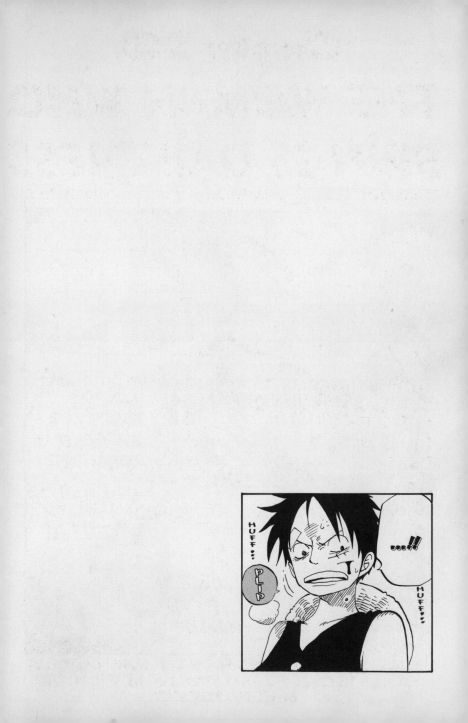

Chapter 340:

THE WOMAN WHO BRINGS DARKNESS

TEXT ABOVE MAIN ENTRANCE SAYS "BATHS"; ABOVE DOORS, "MEN" AND "WOMEN"; ON FLAG, "UNEXPECTED BATHS"--ED.

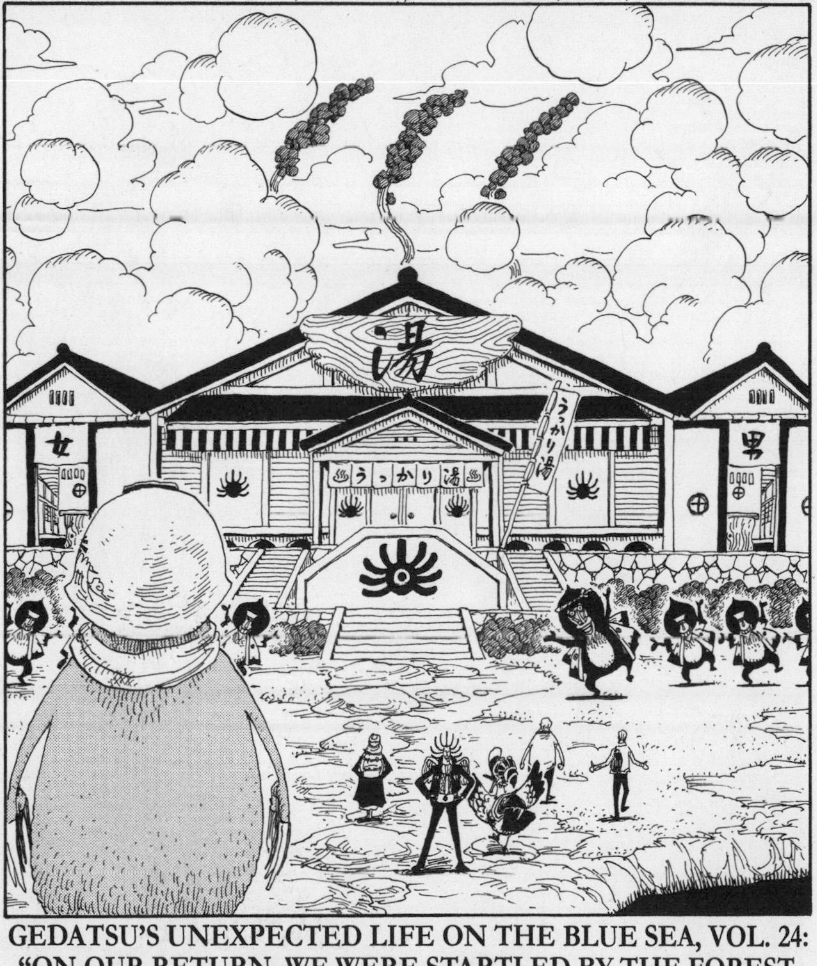
湯
男
うっかり湯
うっかり湯
女

GEDATSU'S UNEXPECTED LIFE ON THE BLUE SEA, VOL. 24: "ON OUR RETURN, WE WERE STARTLED BY THE FOREST BOSS'S BIG PROJECT"

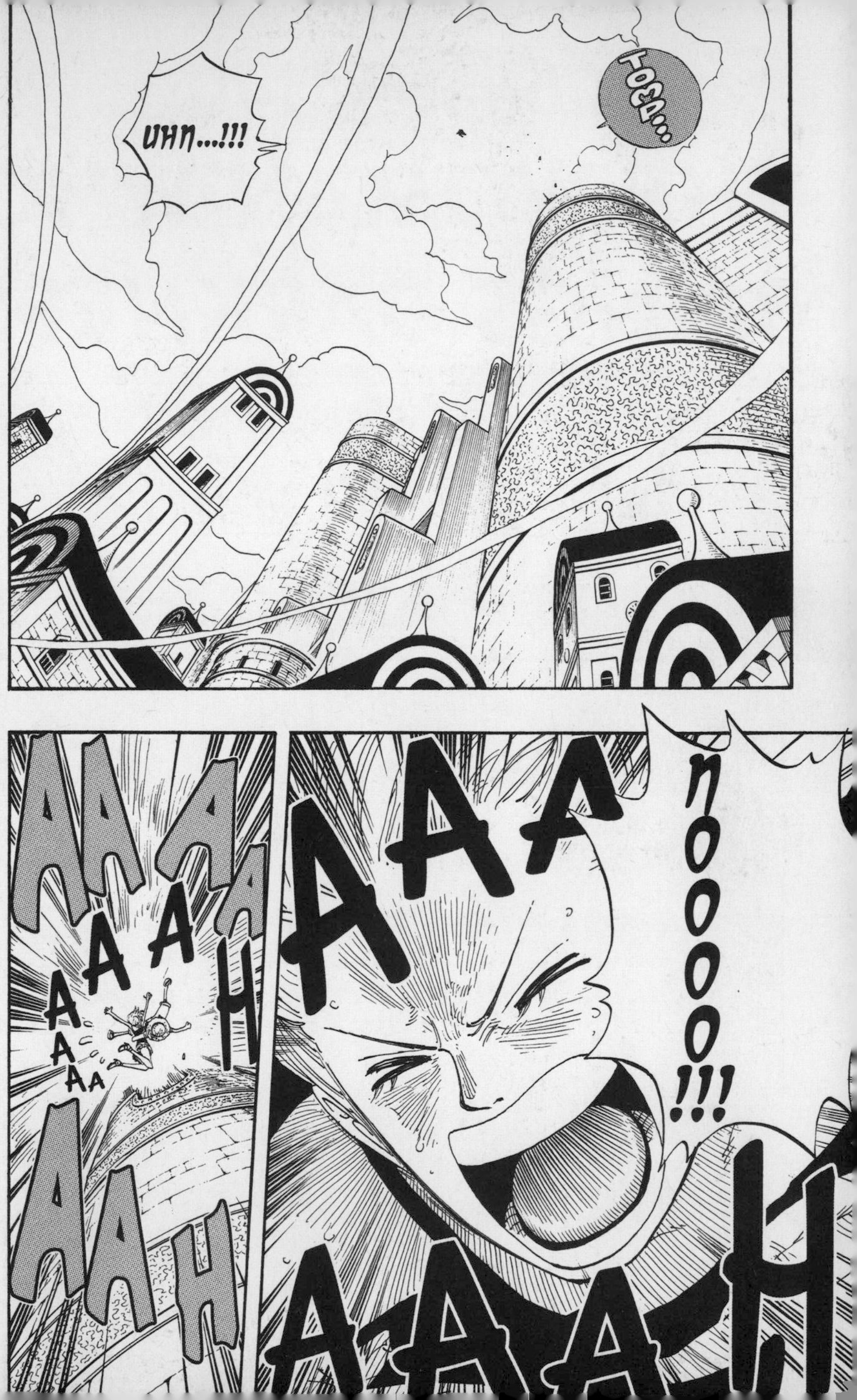
TOMP...
UHN...!!!
NOOOOO!!!
AAAAAH
AAAAAAAAAH
AAAAAAH

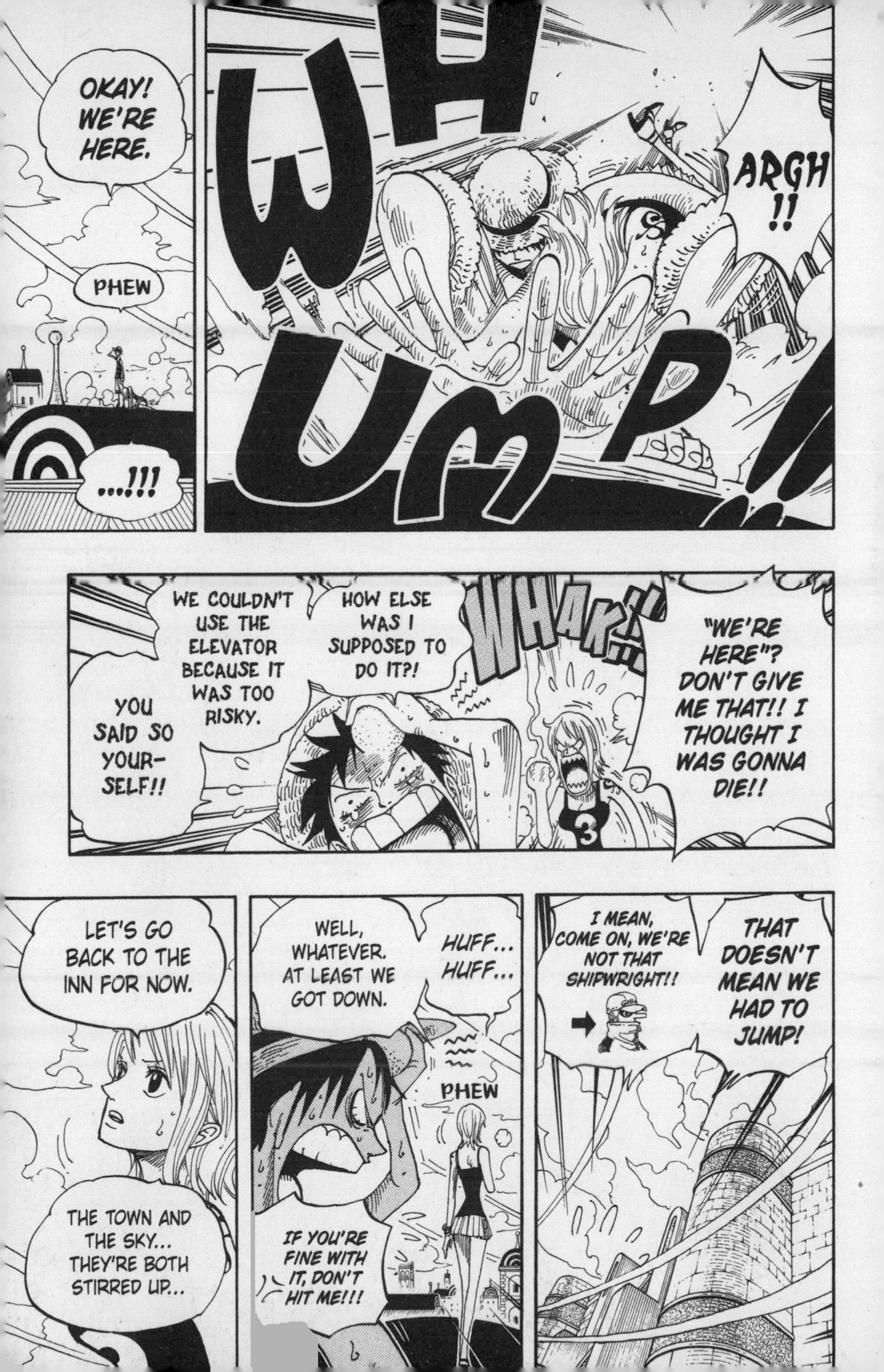
WHUMP!!
ARGH !!
OKAY! WE'RE HERE.
PHEW
...!!!
WHAK!!
"WE'RE HERE"? DON'T GIVE ME THAT!! I THOUGHT I WAS GONNA DIE!!
HOW ELSE WAS I SUPPOSED TO DO IT?!
WE COULDN'T USE THE ELEVATOR BECAUSE IT WAS TOO RISKY.
YOU SAID SO YOUR-SELF!!
THAT DOESN'T MEAN WE HAD TO JUMP!
I MEAN, COME ON, WE'RE NOT THAT SHIPWRIGHT!!
HUFF... HUFF...
WELL, WHATEVER. AT LEAST WE GOT DOWN.
PHEW
IF YOU'RE FINE WITH IT, DON'T HIT ME!!!
LET'S GO BACK TO THE INN FOR NOW.
THE TOWN AND THE SKY... THEY'RE BOTH STIRRED UP...

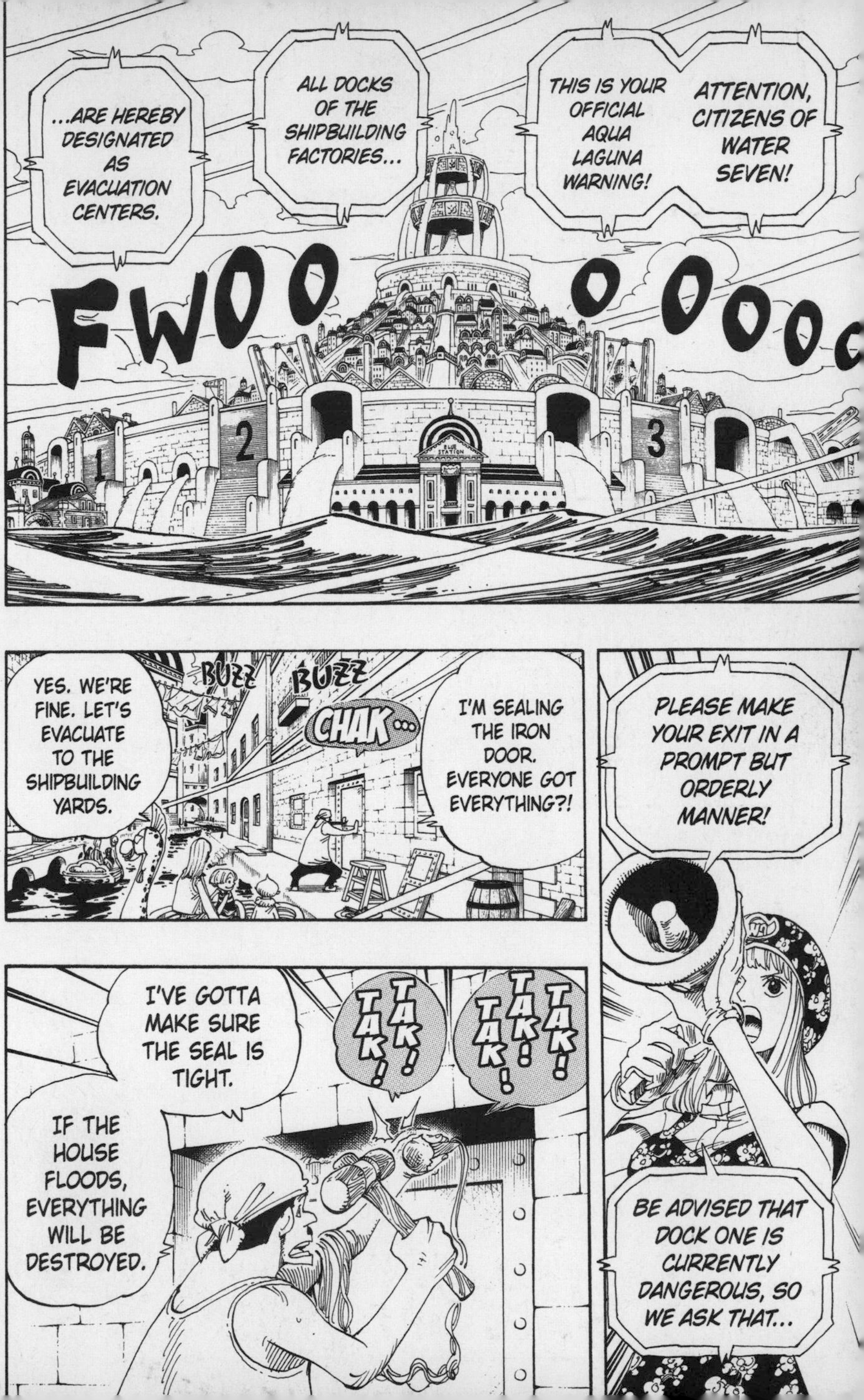

ATTENTION, CITIZENS OF WATER SEVEN!
THIS IS YOUR OFFICIAL AQUA LAGUNA WARNING!
ALL DOCKS OF THE SHIPBUILDING FACTORIES...
...ARE HEREBY DESIGNATED AS EVACUATION CENTERS.
FWOOOOOO
PLEASE MAKE YOUR EXIT IN A PROMPT BUT ORDERLY MANNER!
BE ADVISED THAT DOCK ONE IS CURRENTLY DANGEROUS, SO WE ASK THAT...
BUZZ BUZZ
CHAK...
I'M SEALING THE IRON DOOR. EVERYONE GOT EVERYTHING?!
YES. WE'RE FINE. LET'S EVACUATE TO THE SHIPBUILDING YARDS.
TAK! TAK! TAK! TAK! TAK!
I'VE GOTTA MAKE SURE THE SEAL IS TIGHT.
IF THE HOUSE FLOODS, EVERYTHING WILL BE DESTROYED.

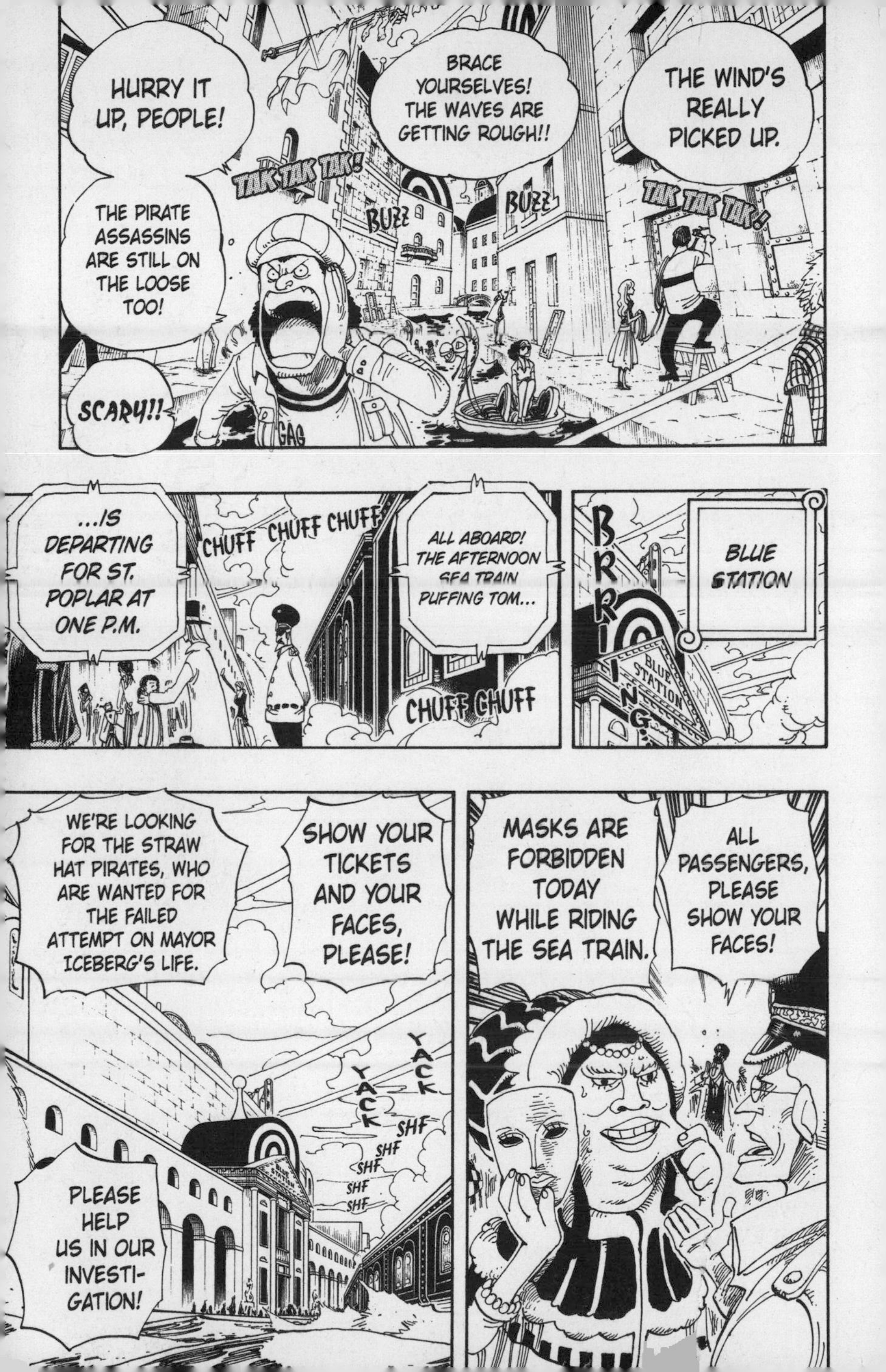
THE WIND'S REALLY PICKED UP.
BRACE YOURSELVES! THE WAVES ARE GETTING ROUGH!!
HURRY IT UP, PEOPLE!
TAK TAK TAK!
BUZZ
BUZZ
TAK TAK TAK!
THE PIRATE ASSASSINS ARE STILL ON THE LOOSE TOO!
SCARY!!
GAG
BLUE STATION
BRRRING...
BLUE STATION
ALL ABOARD! THE AFTERNOON SEA TRAIN PUFFING TOM...
CHUFF CHUFF CHUFF
...IS DEPARTING FOR ST. POPLAR AT ONE P.M.
CHUFF CHUFF
ALL PASSENGERS, PLEASE SHOW YOUR FACES!
MASKS ARE FORBIDDEN TODAY WHILE RIDING THE SEA TRAIN.
SHOW YOUR TICKETS AND YOUR FACES, PLEASE!
WE'RE LOOKING FOR THE STRAW HAT PIRATES, WHO ARE WANTED FOR THE FAILED ATTEMPT ON MAYOR ICEBERG'S LIFE.
YACK
YACK
SHF
SHF
SHF
SHF
SHF
PLEASE HELP US IN OUR INVESTIGATION!

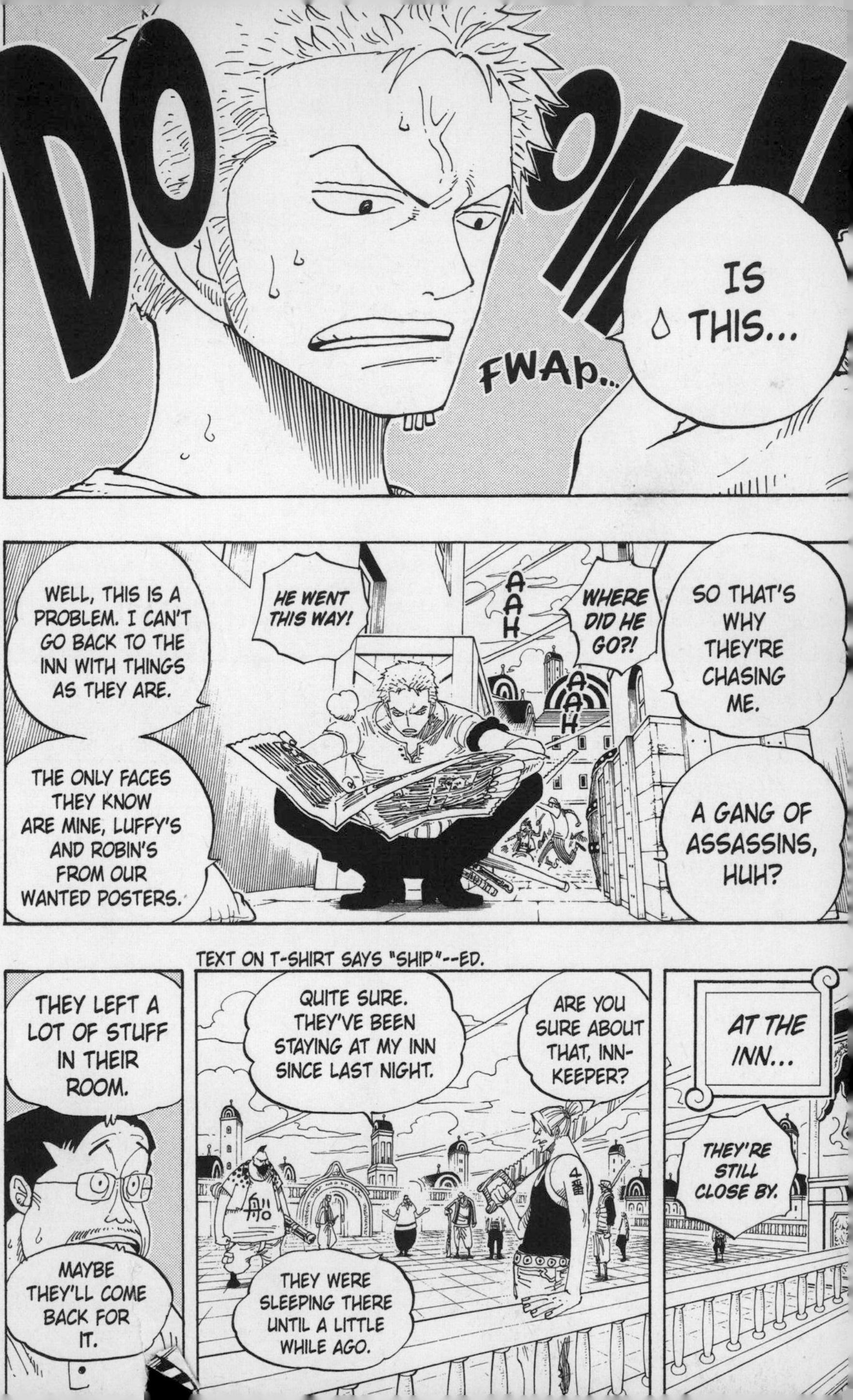
DOOON
IS THIS...
FWAp...
SO THAT'S WHY THEY'RE CHASING ME.
A GANG OF ASSASSINS, HUH?
WHERE DID HE GO?!
AAAH
AAAH
HE WENT THIS WAY!
WELL, THIS IS A PROBLEM. I CAN'T GO BACK TO THE INN WITH THINGS AS THEY ARE.
THE ONLY FACES THEY KNOW ARE MINE, LUFFY'S AND ROBIN'S FROM OUR WANTED POSTERS.
TEXT ON T-SHIRT SAYS "SHIP"--ED.
AT THE INN...
THEY'RE STILL CLOSE BY.
ARE YOU SURE ABOUT THAT, INN-KEEPER?
QUITE SURE. THEY'VE BEEN STAYING AT MY INN SINCE LAST NIGHT.
THEY WERE SLEEPING THERE UNTIL A LITTLE WHILE AGO.
THEY LEFT A LOT OF STUFF IN THEIR ROOM.
MAYBE THEY'LL COME BACK FOR IT.

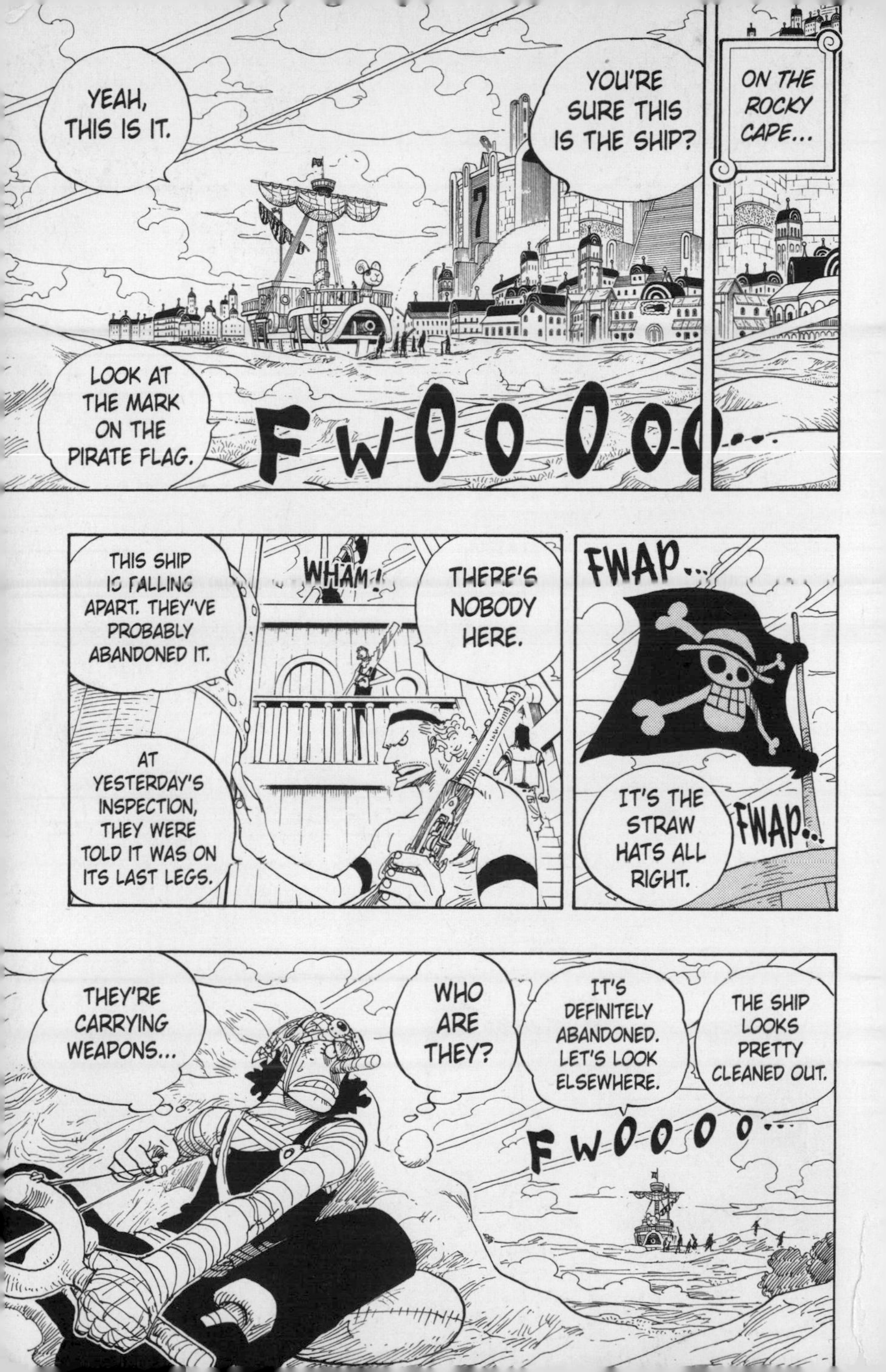
ON THE ROCKY CAPE...
YOU'RE SURE THIS IS THE SHIP?
YEAH, THIS IS IT.
FWOOOO...
LOOK AT THE MARK ON THE PIRATE FLAG.
FWAP...
IT'S THE STRAW HATS ALL RIGHT.
FWAP...
THERE'S NOBODY HERE.
WHAM!
THIS SHIP IS FALLING APART. THEY'VE PROBABLY ABANDONED IT.
AT YESTERDAY'S INSPECTION, THEY WERE TOLD IT WAS ON ITS LAST LEGS.
THE SHIP LOOKS PRETTY CLEANED OUT.
IT'S DEFINITELY ABANDONED. LET'S LOOK ELSEWHERE.
WHO ARE THEY?
THEY'RE CARRYING WEAPONS...
FWOOOO...

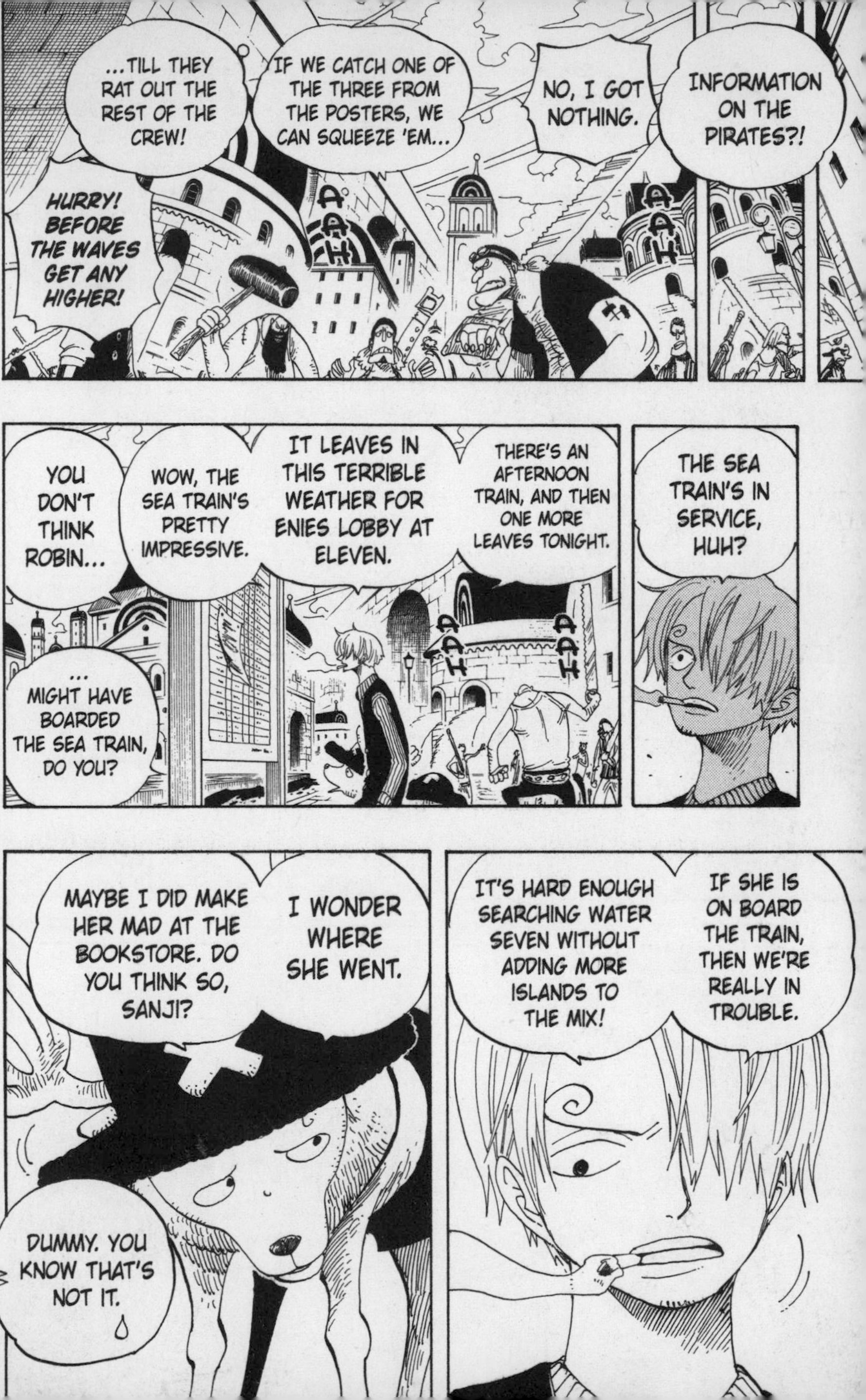
INFORMATION ON THE PIRATES?!
NO, I GOT NOTHING.
IF WE CATCH ONE OF THE THREE FROM THE POSTERS, WE CAN SQUEEZE 'EM...
...TILL THEY RAT OUT THE REST OF THE CREW!
HURRY! BEFORE THE WAVES GET ANY HIGHER!
AAH
THE SEA TRAIN'S IN SERVICE, HUH?
THERE'S AN AFTERNOON TRAIN, AND THEN ONE MORE LEAVES TONIGHT.
IT LEAVES IN THIS TERRIBLE WEATHER FOR ENIES LOBBY AT ELEVEN.
WOW, THE SEA TRAIN'S PRETTY IMPRESSIVE.
YOU DON'T THINK ROBIN...
...MIGHT HAVE BOARDED THE SEA TRAIN, DO YOU?
IF SHE IS ON BOARD THE TRAIN, THEN WE'RE REALLY IN TROUBLE.
IT'S HARD ENOUGH SEARCHING WATER SEVEN WITHOUT ADDING MORE ISLANDS TO THE MIX!
I WONDER WHERE SHE WENT.
MAYBE I DID MAKE HER MAD AT THE BOOKSTORE. DO YOU THINK SO, SANJI?
DUMMY. YOU KNOW THAT'S NOT IT.

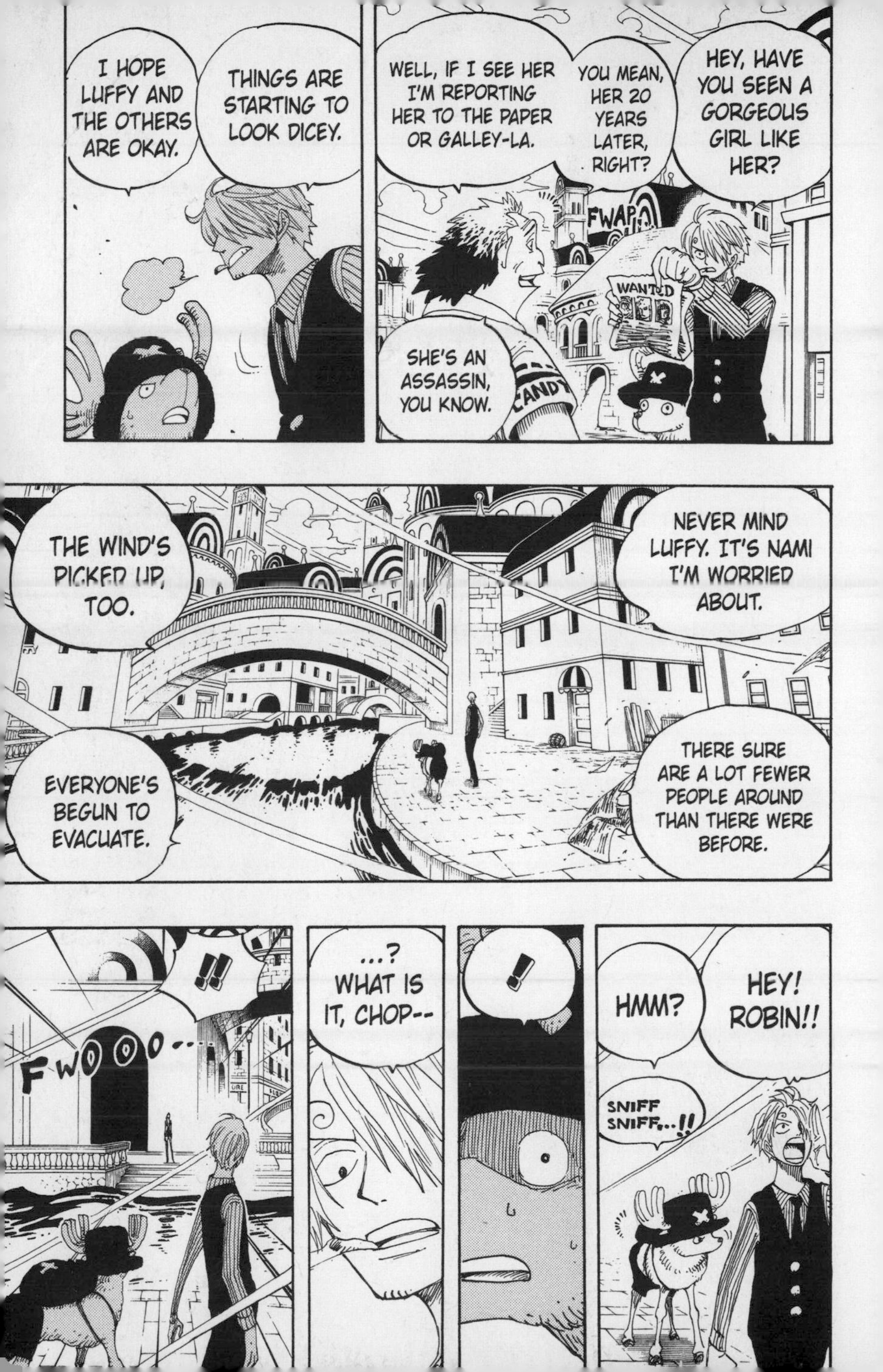

HEY, HAVE YOU SEEN A GORGEOUS GIRL LIKE HER?
WANTED
YOU MEAN, HER 20 YEARS LATER, RIGHT?
FWAP
WELL, IF I SEE HER I'M REPORTING HER TO THE PAPER OR GALLEY-LA.
SHE'S AN ASSASSIN, YOU KNOW.
CANDY
THINGS ARE STARTING TO LOOK DICEY.
I HOPE LUFFY AND THE OTHERS ARE OKAY.
NEVER MIND LUFFY. IT'S NAMI I'M WORRIED ABOUT.
THE WIND'S PICKED UP, TOO.
THERE SURE ARE A LOT FEWER PEOPLE AROUND THAN THERE WERE BEFORE.
EVERYONE'S BEGUN TO EVACUATE.
HEY! ROBIN!!
HMM?
SNIFF SNIFF...!!
!
...? WHAT IS IT, CHOP--
!!
FWOOO...

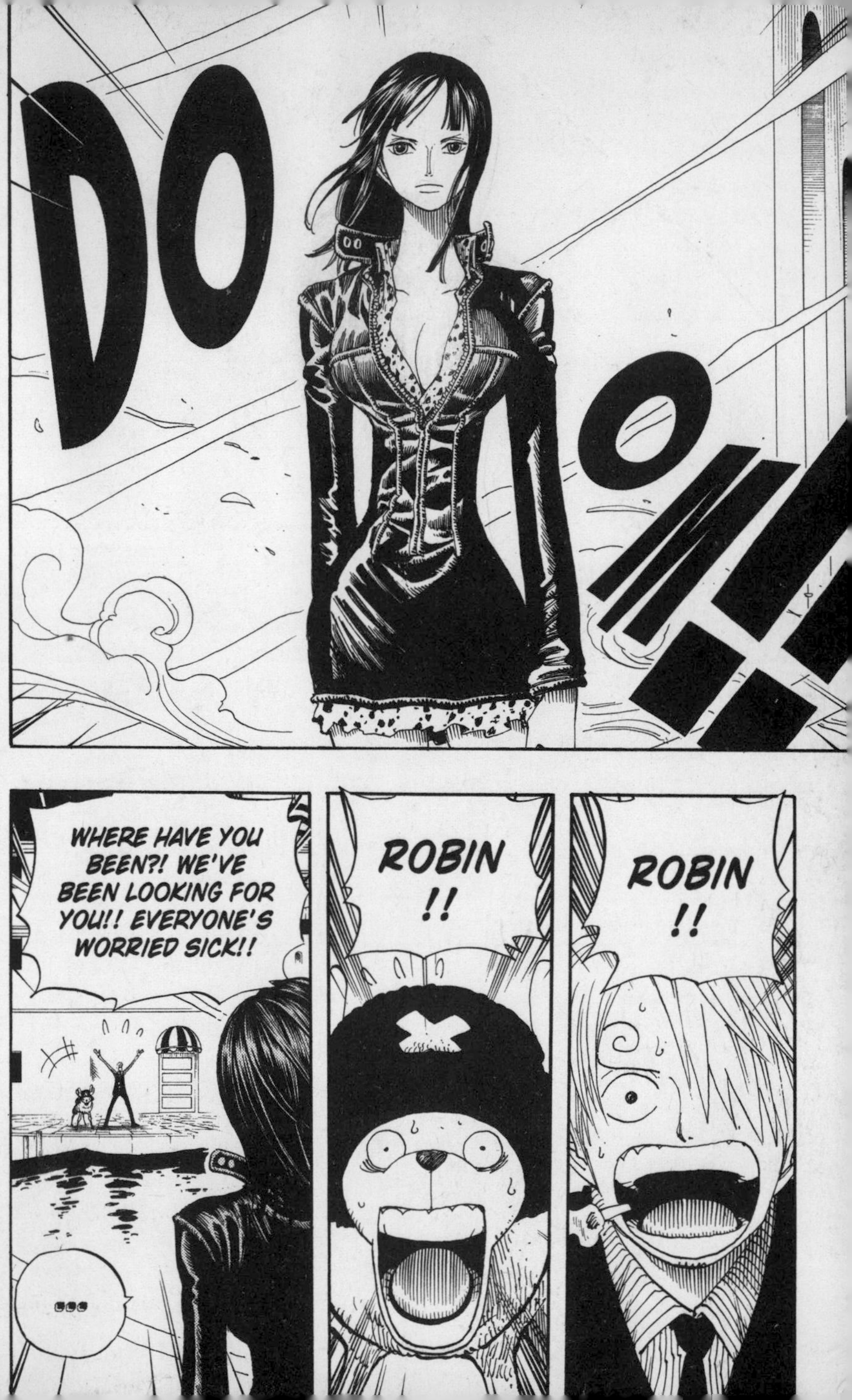
DOON
ROBIN !!
ROBIN !!
WHERE HAVE YOU BEEN?! WE'VE BEEN LOOKING FOR YOU!! EVERYONE'S WORRIED SICK!!
...

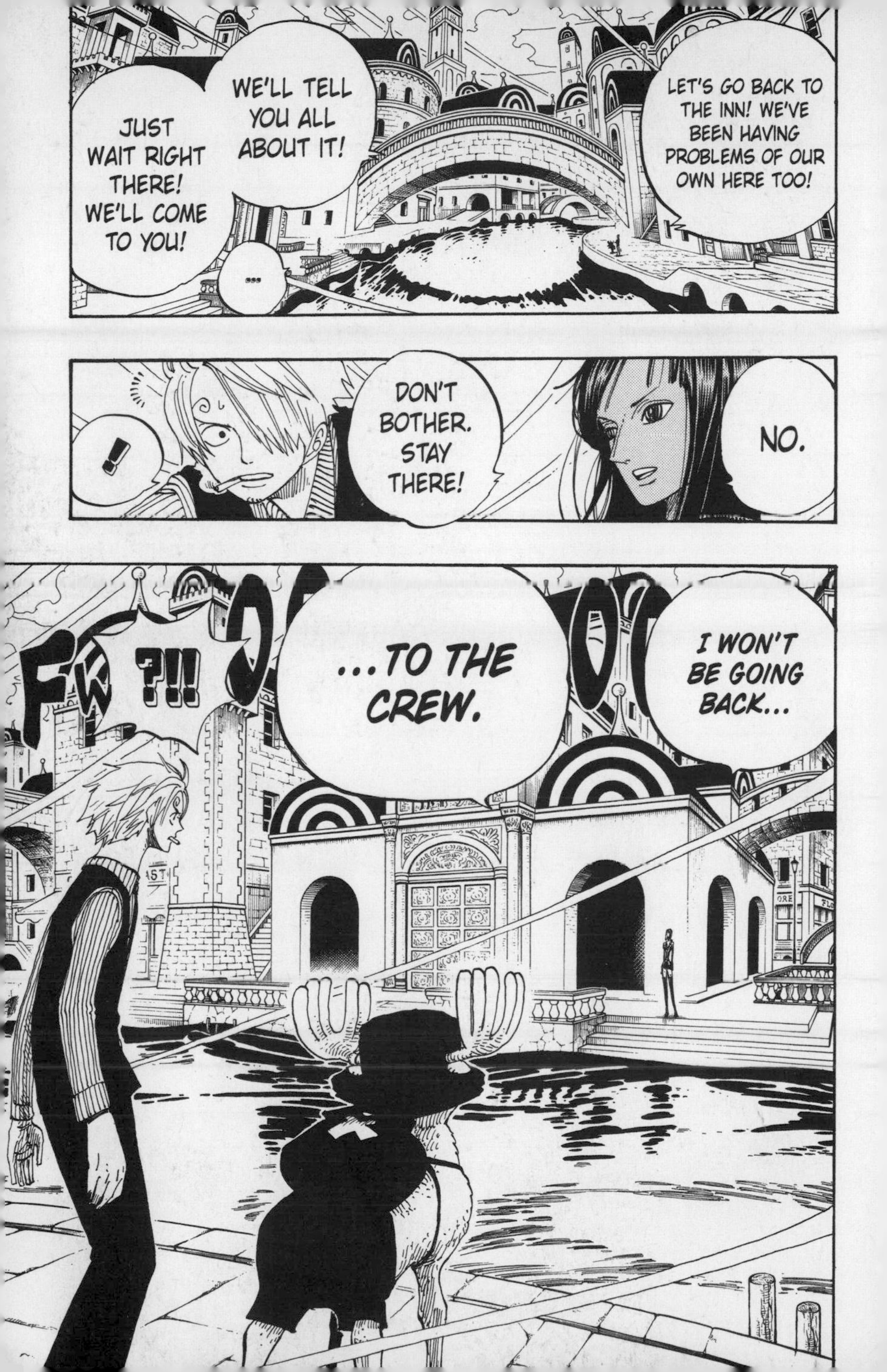
LET'S GO BACK TO THE INN! WE'VE BEEN HAVING PROBLEMS OF OUR OWN HERE TOO!
WE'LL TELL YOU ALL ABOUT IT!
JUST WAIT RIGHT THERE! WE'LL COME TO YOU!
...
NO.
DON'T BOTHER. STAY THERE!
!
I WON'T BE GOING BACK...
...TO THE CREW.
?!!

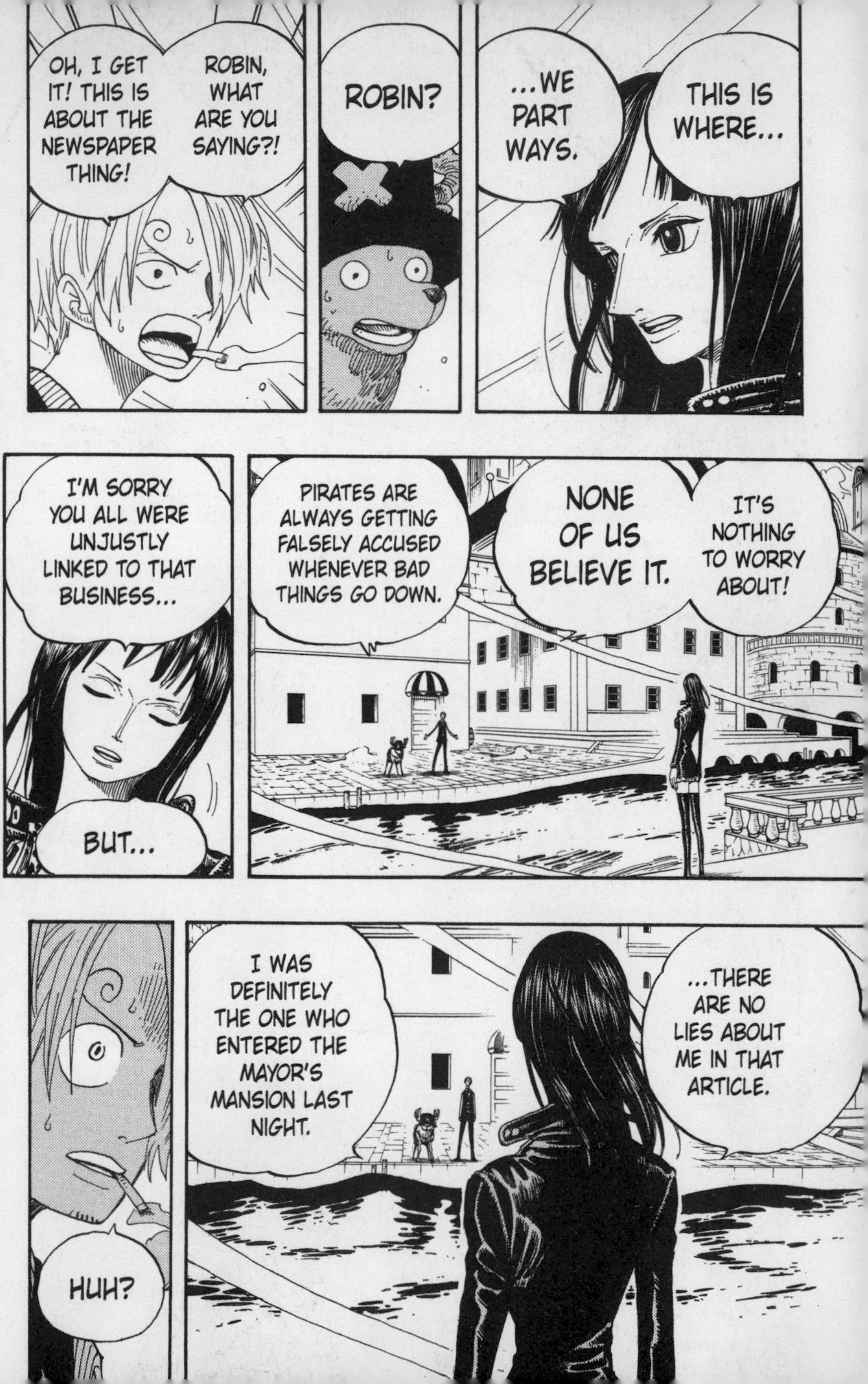
THIS IS WHERE...
...WE PART WAYS.
ROBIN?
ROBIN, WHAT ARE YOU SAYING?!
OH, I GET IT! THIS IS ABOUT THE NEWSPAPER THING!
IT'S NOTHING TO WORRY ABOUT!
NONE OF US BELIEVE IT.
PIRATES ARE ALWAYS GETTING FALSELY ACCUSED WHENEVER BAD THINGS GO DOWN.
I'M SORRY YOU ALL WERE UNJUSTLY LINKED TO THAT BUSINESS...
BUT...
...THERE ARE NO LIES ABOUT ME IN THAT ARTICLE.
I WAS DEFINITELY THE ONE WHO ENTERED THE MAYOR'S MANSION LAST NIGHT.
HUH?

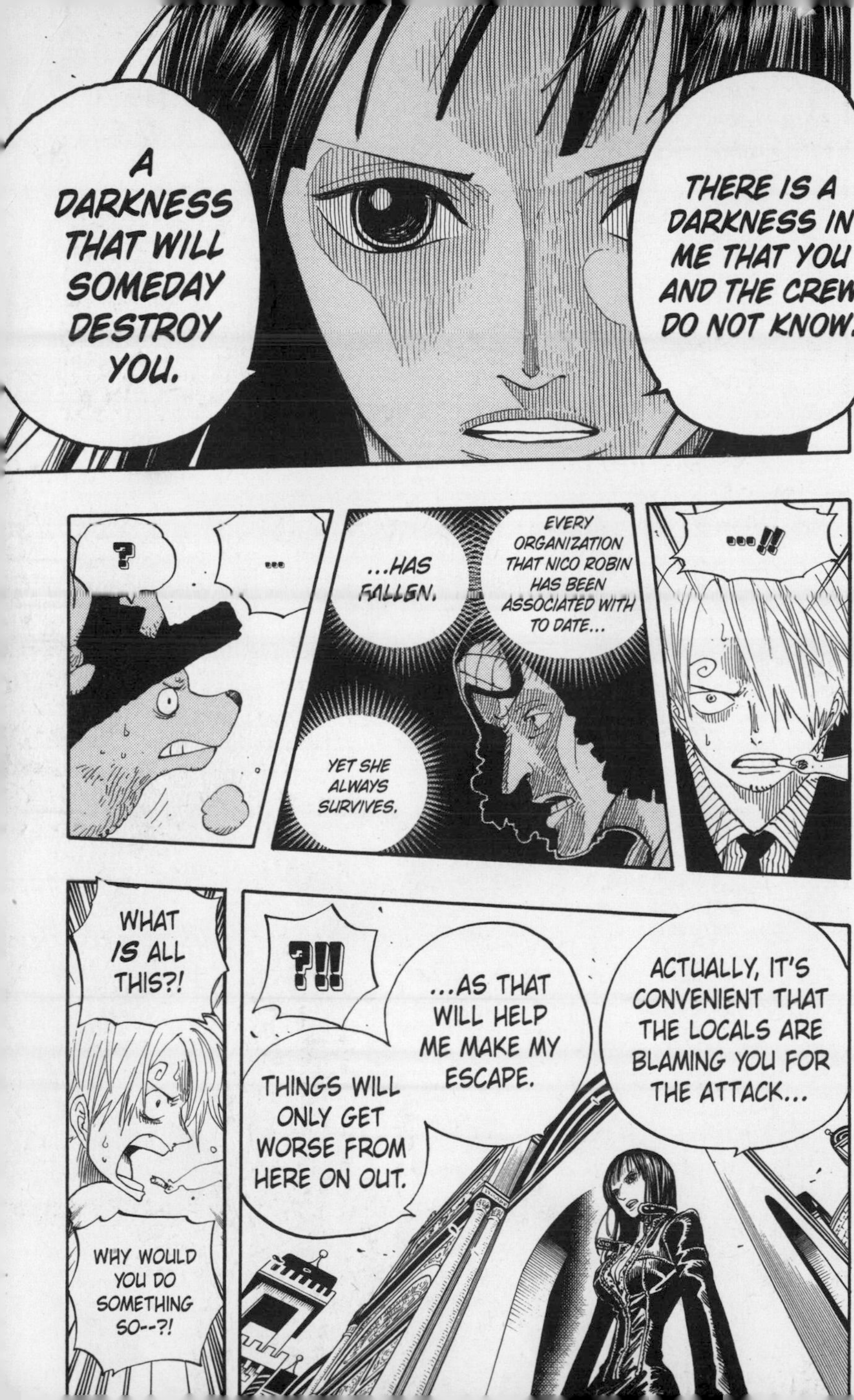
THERE IS A DARKNESS IN ME THAT YOU AND THE CREW DO NOT KNOW.
A DARKNESS THAT WILL SOMEDAY DESTROY YOU.
...!!
EVERY ORGANIZATION THAT NICO ROBIN HAS BEEN ASSOCIATED WITH TO DATE...
...HAS FALLEN.
YET SHE ALWAYS SURVIVES.
...
?
ACTUALLY, IT'S CONVENIENT THAT THE LOCALS ARE BLAMING YOU FOR THE ATTACK...
...AS THAT WILL HELP ME MAKE MY ESCAPE.
?!!
THINGS WILL ONLY GET WORSE FROM HERE ON OUT.
WHAT IS ALL THIS?!
WHY WOULD YOU DO SOMETHING SO--?!

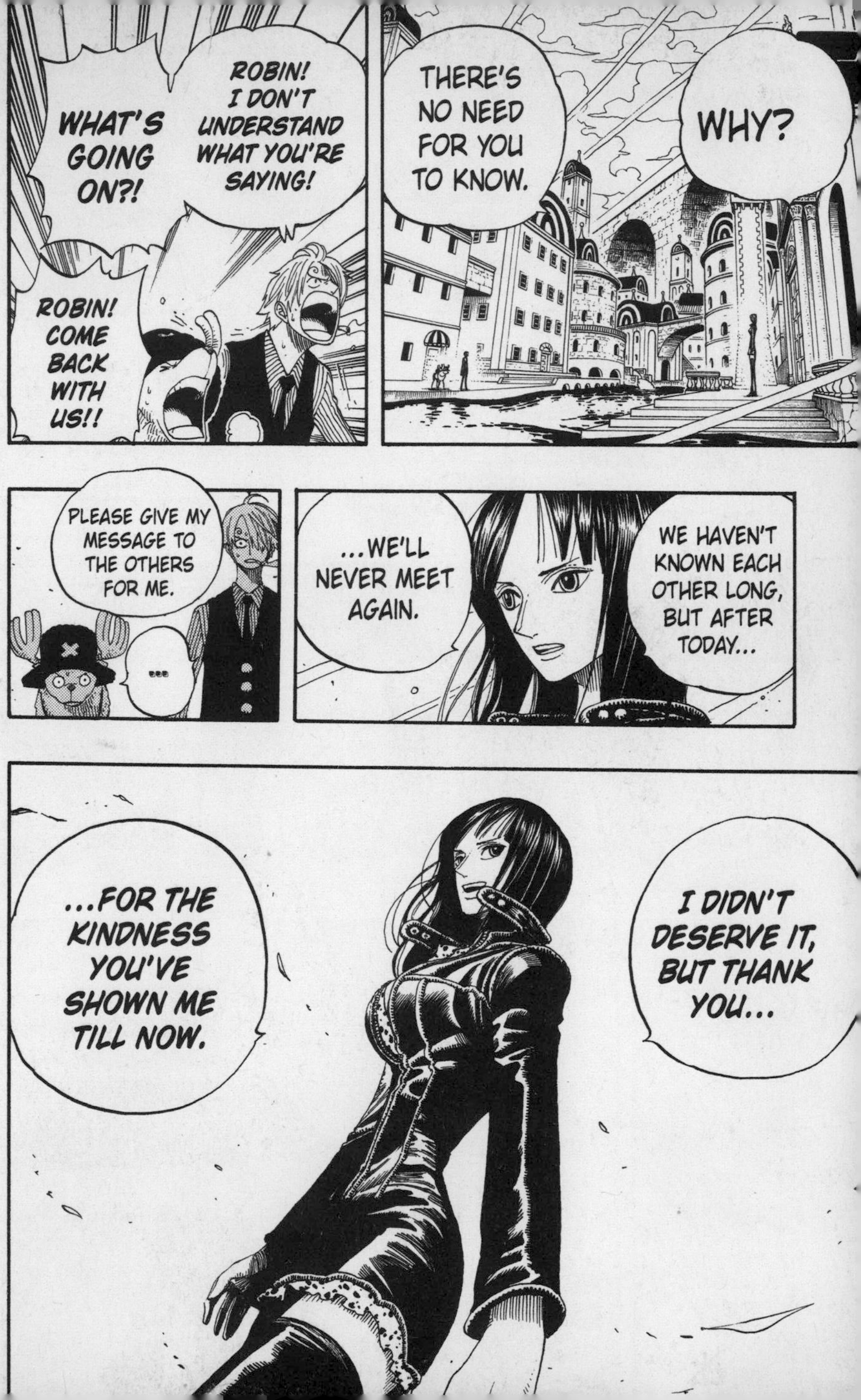
WHY?
THERE'S NO NEED FOR YOU TO KNOW.
ROBIN! I DON'T UNDERSTAND WHAT YOU'RE SAYING!
WHAT'S GOING ON?!
ROBIN! COME BACK WITH US!!
WE HAVEN'T KNOWN EACH OTHER LONG, BUT AFTER TODAY...
...WE'LL NEVER MEET AGAIN.
PLEASE GIVE MY MESSAGE TO THE OTHERS FOR ME.
...
I DIDN'T DESERVE IT, BUT THANK YOU...
...FOR THE KINDNESS YOU'VE SHOWN ME TILL NOW.

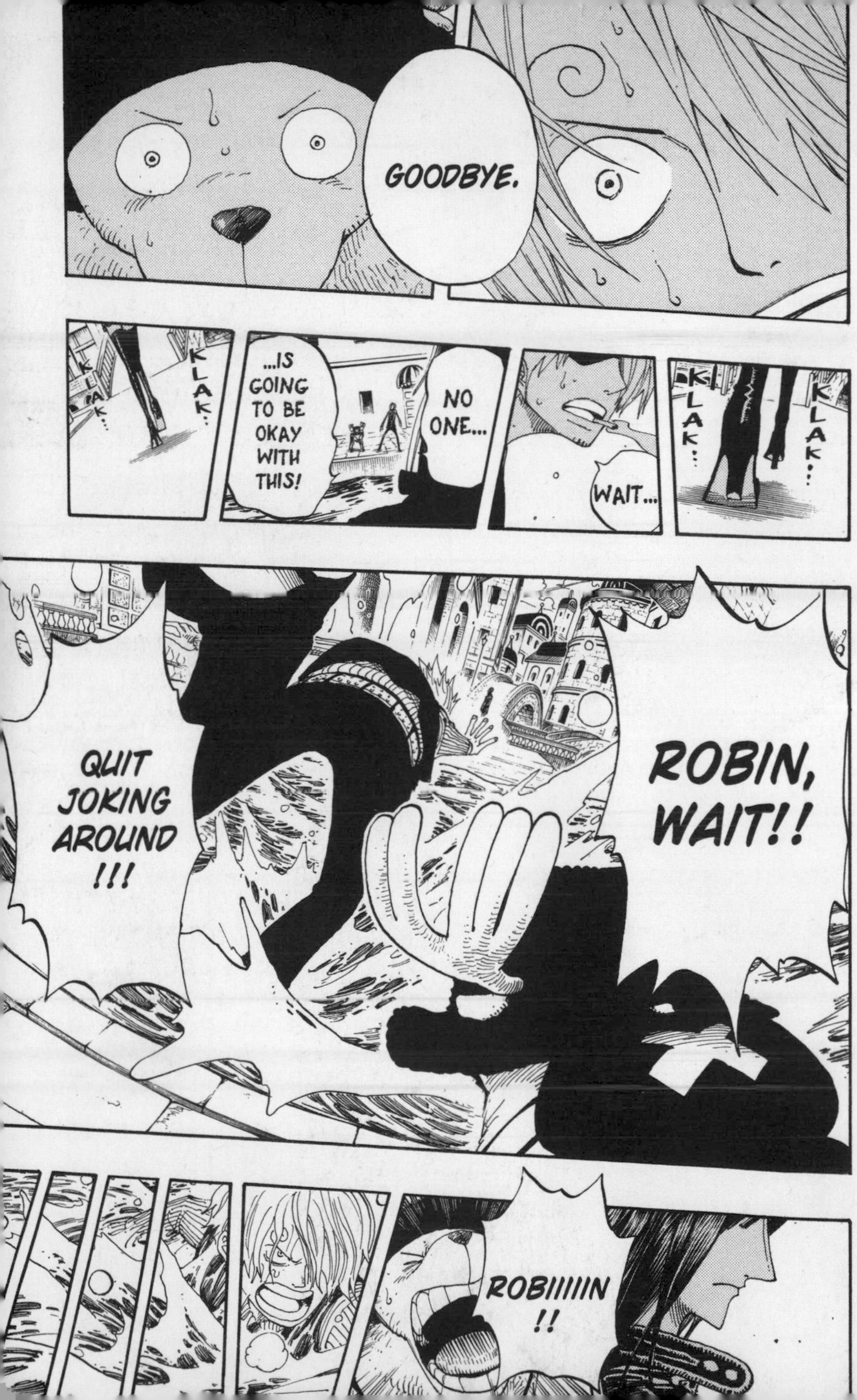
GOODBYE.
KLAK KLAK...
KLAK...
WAIT...
NO ONE...
...IS GOING TO BE OKAY WITH THIS!
KLAK
KLAK...
ROBIN, WAIT!!
QUIT JOKING AROUND!!!
ROBIIIIIN!!

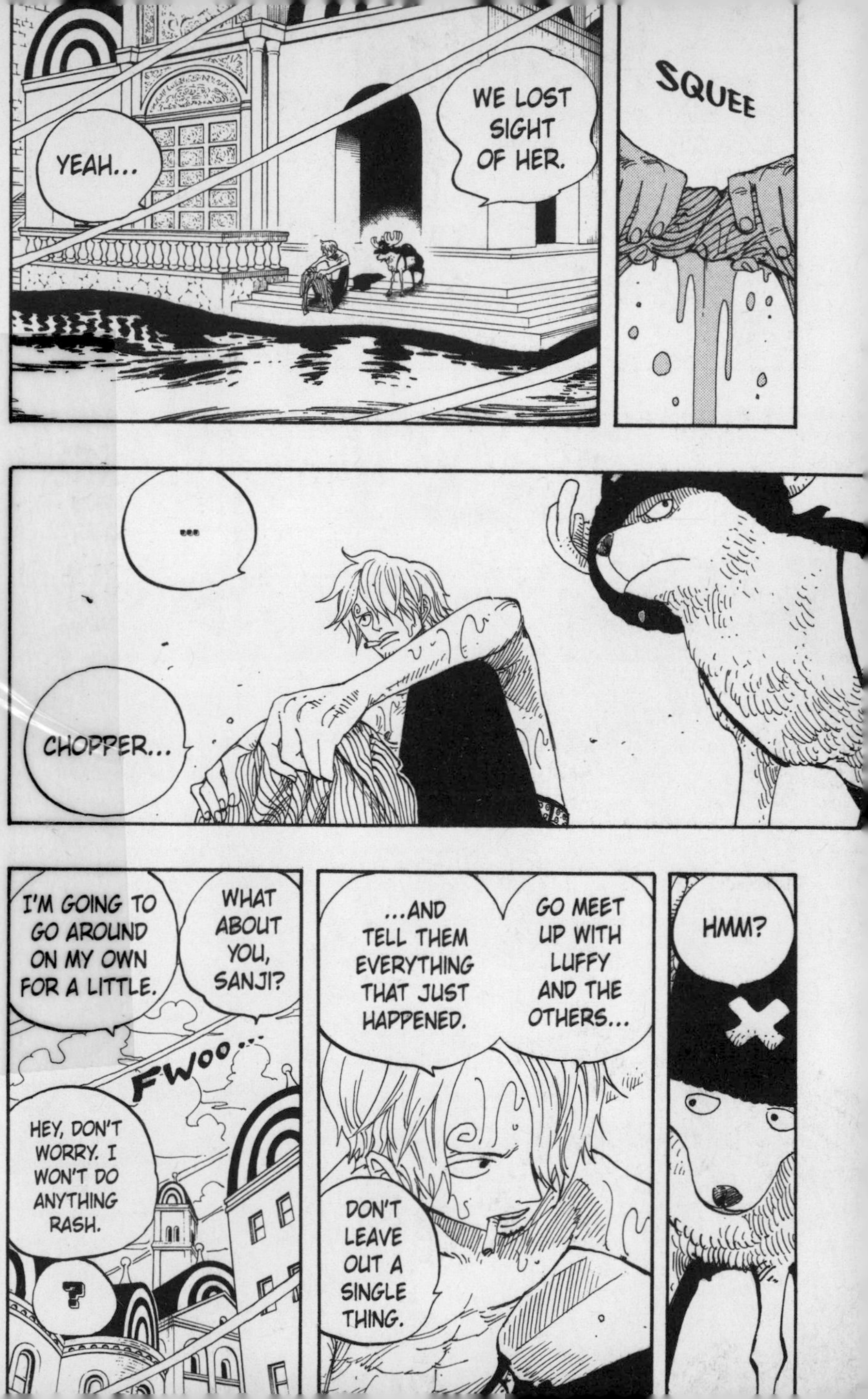
SQUEE
WE LOST SIGHT OF HER.
YEAH...
...
CHOPPER...
HMM?
GO MEET UP WITH LUFFY AND THE OTHERS...
...AND TELL THEM EVERYTHING THAT JUST HAPPENED.
DON'T LEAVE OUT A SINGLE THING.
WHAT ABOUT YOU, SANJI?
I'M GOING TO GO AROUND ON MY OWN FOR A LITTLE.
FWOO...
HEY, DON'T WORRY. I WON'T DO ANYTHING RASH.
?

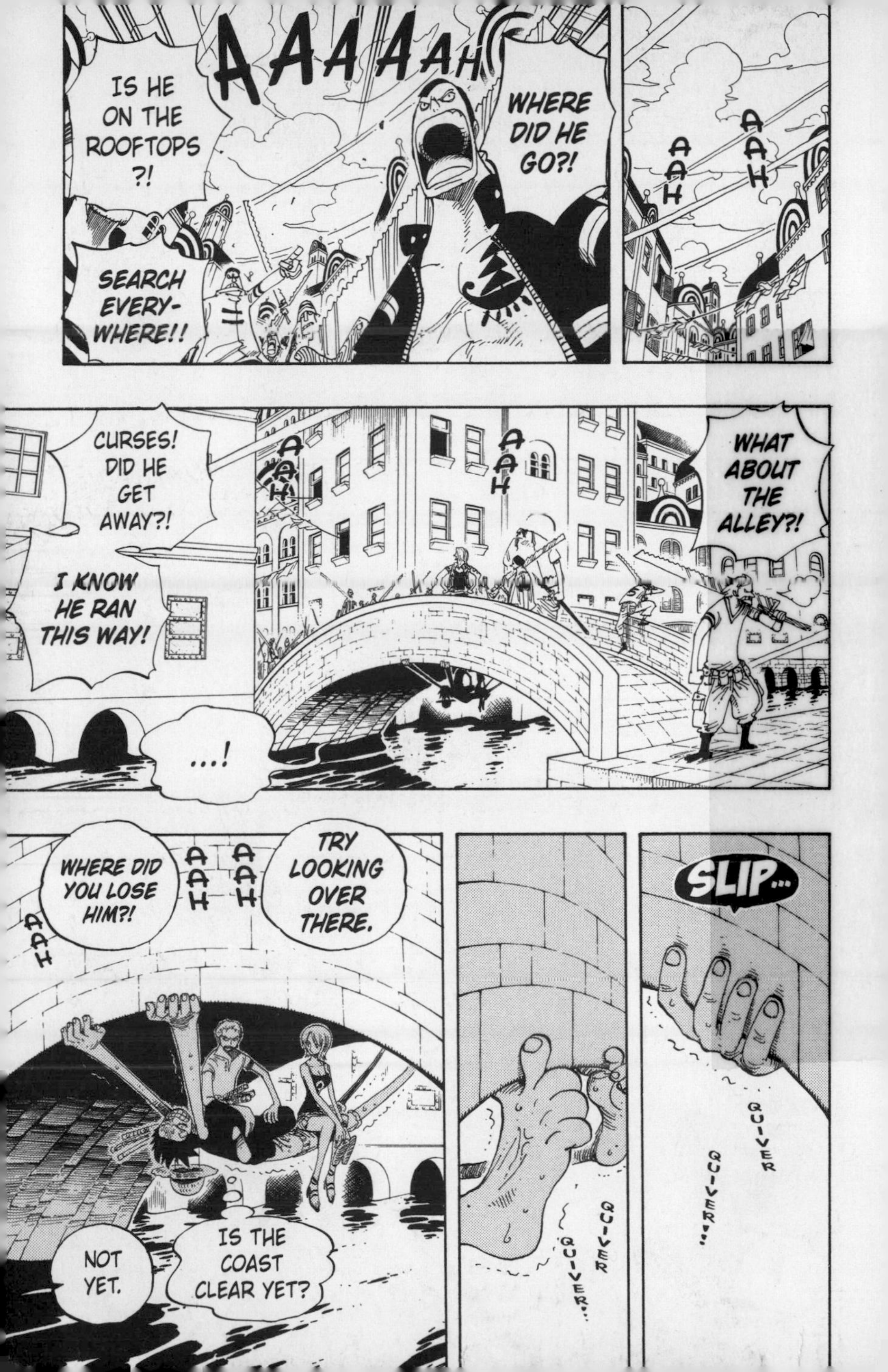
AAH
AAH
AAAAAAH
WHERE DID HE GO?!
IS HE ON THE ROOFTOPS ?!
SEARCH EVERY-WHERE!!
WHAT ABOUT THE ALLEY?!
AAH
AAH
CURSES! DID HE GET AWAY?!
I KNOW HE RAN THIS WAY!
...!
SLIP...
QUIVER
QUIVER...
QUIVER
QUIVER...
TRY LOOKING OVER THERE.
AAH
AAH
WHERE DID YOU LOSE HIM?!
AAH
IS THE COAST CLEAR YET?
NOT YET.

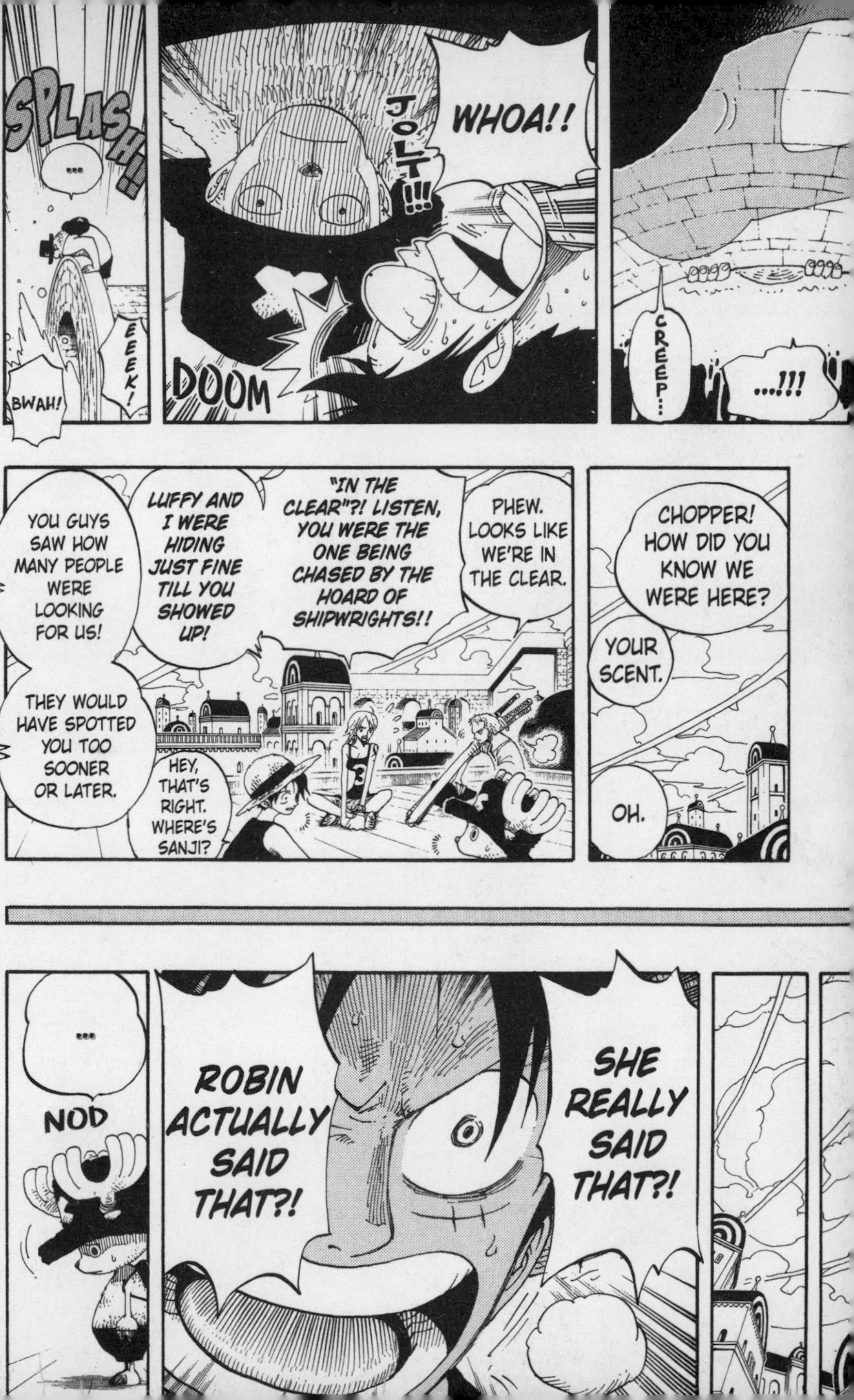
CREEP...
...!!!
WHOA!!
JOLT!!!
DOOM
SPLASH!!
...
EEEEK!
BWAH!
CHOPPER! HOW DID YOU KNOW WE WERE HERE?
YOUR SCENT.
OH.
PHEW. LOOKS LIKE WE'RE IN THE CLEAR.
"IN THE CLEAR"?! LISTEN, YOU WERE THE ONE BEING CHASED BY THE HOARD OF SHIPWRIGHTS!!
LUFFY AND I WERE HIDING JUST FINE TILL YOU SHOWED UP!
YOU GUYS SAW HOW MANY PEOPLE WERE LOOKING FOR US!
THEY WOULD HAVE SPOTTED YOU TOO SOONER OR LATER.
HEY, THAT'S RIGHT. WHERE'S SANJI?
SHE REALLY SAID THAT?!
ROBIN ACTUALLY SAID THAT?!
...
NOD

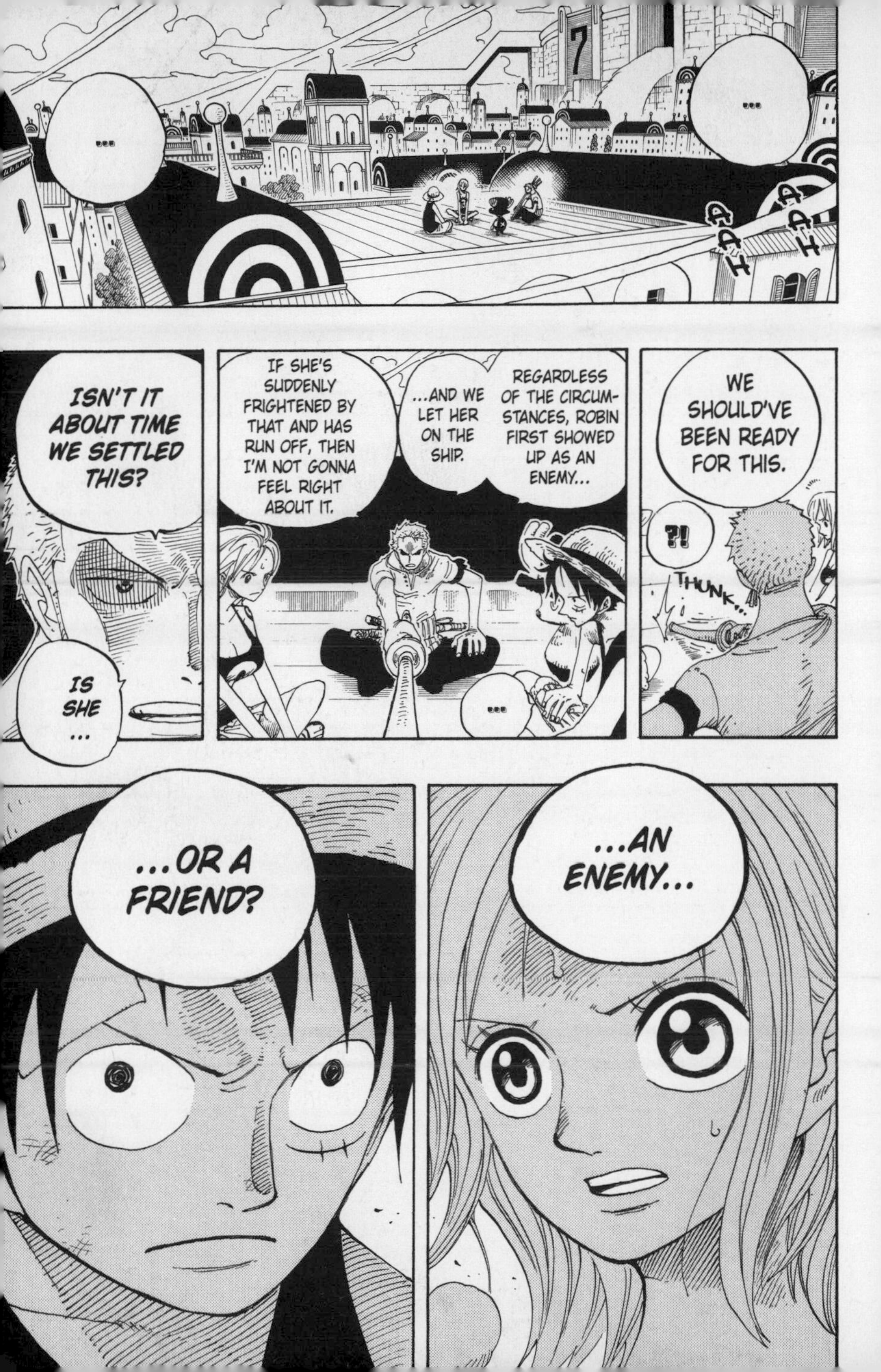
...
AAAH
AAAH
...
WE SHOULD'VE BEEN READY FOR THIS.
?!
THUNK...
REGARDLESS OF THE CIRCUM-STANCES, ROBIN FIRST SHOWED UP AS AN ENEMY...
...AND WE LET HER ON THE SHIP.
IF SHE'S SUDDENLY FRIGHTENED BY THAT AND HAS RUN OFF, THEN I'M NOT GONNA FEEL RIGHT ABOUT IT.
...
ISN'T IT ABOUT TIME WE SETTLED THIS?
IS SHE ...
...AN ENEMY...
...OR A FRIEND?

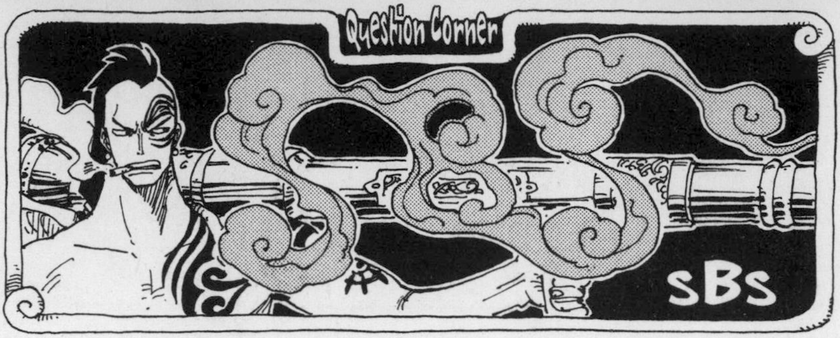
Question Corner
SBS

Q: What sort of guy was the then-Mr. 7, the one who tried to scout Zolo for Baroque Works?

--Dollar Piece

A:

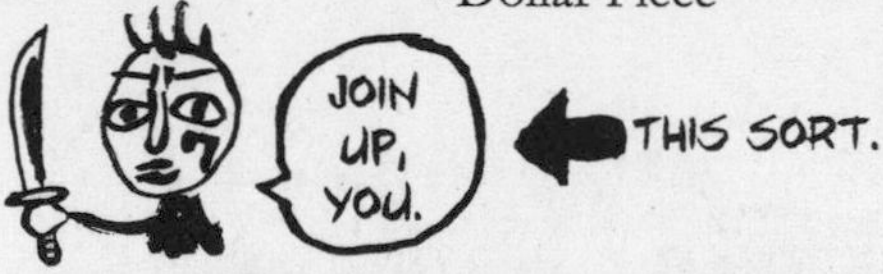
JOIN UP, YOU.
THIS SORT.

Q: In chapter 322 ("Puffing Tom") Zolo called Sanji "Dart Boy"? Why "Dart Boy"?

--Lovely Eyelashes

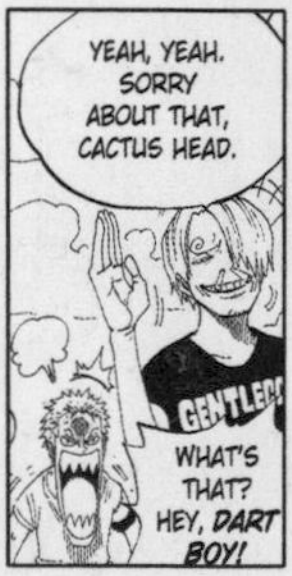
YEAH, YEAH. SORRY ABOUT THAT, CACTUS HEAD.
WHAT'S THAT? HEY, DART BOY!

A: That was a bit hard to get, wasn't it? I got several questions about that. I think he meant the dartboard, instead of darts, seeing as it's like a spiral. Seriously, why does he say weird things like that?! That Zolo!

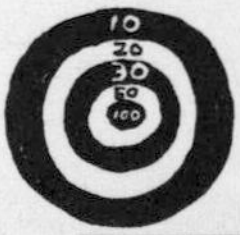
10
20
30
50
100

Q: What percentages of a deer, a racoon, a reindeer and a human would you have to combine to get Chopper?

--Chopper Love ♡

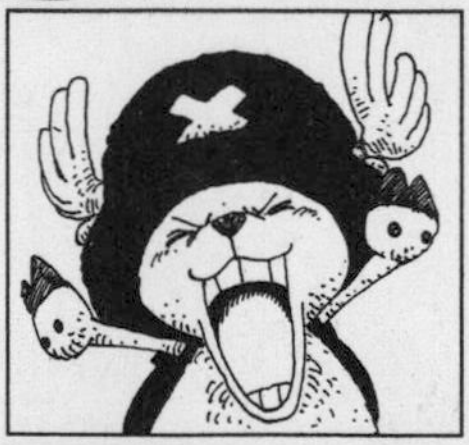

A: Ten percent deer, 10 percent racoon, 10 percent reindeer and 10 percent human, if you please.

Q: Does Kami Eneru like apples?

--Raiden

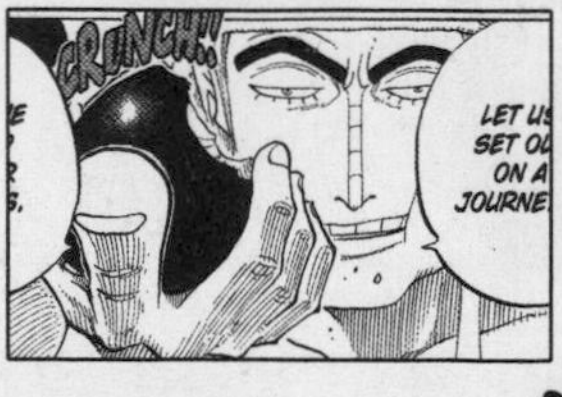
CRUNCH!!

A: Yes. He does. I like 'em too. Oh, you didn't ask about me? I like pears too! Oh, you didn't ask about me?

Chapter 341:
DEMON

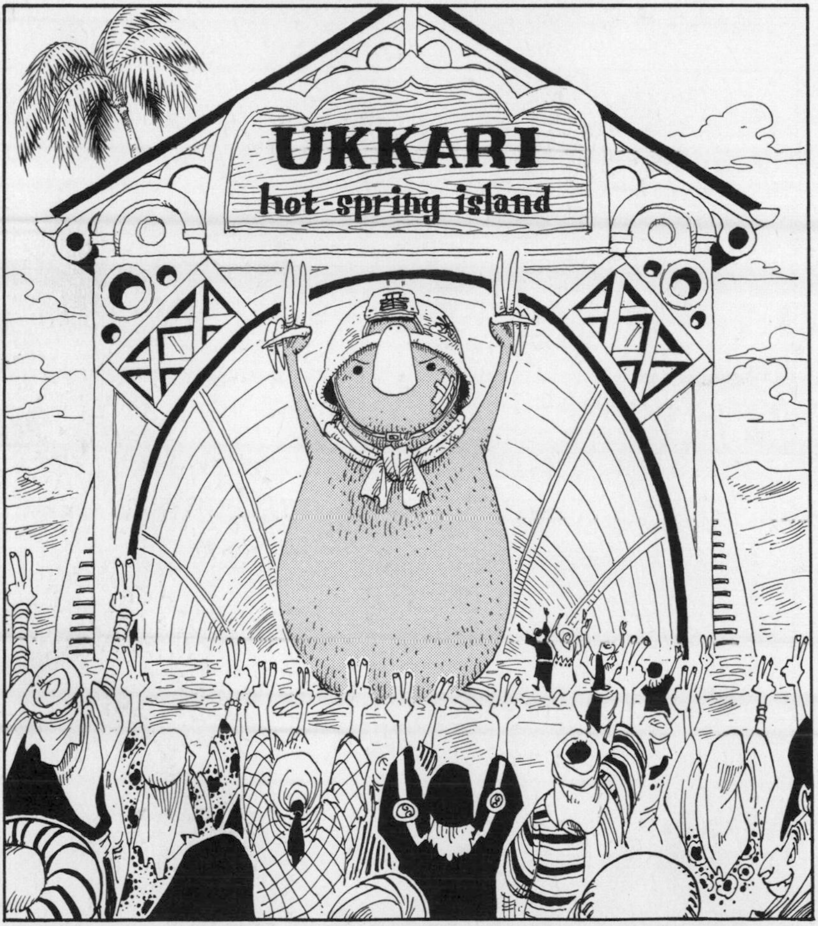
UKKARI
hot-spring island

GEDATSU'S UNEXPECTED LIFE ON THE BLUE SEA, VOL. 25:
"A TUNNEL TO THE UNEXPECTED HOT SPRING ISLAND OPENS IN THE COUNTRY OF SAND"

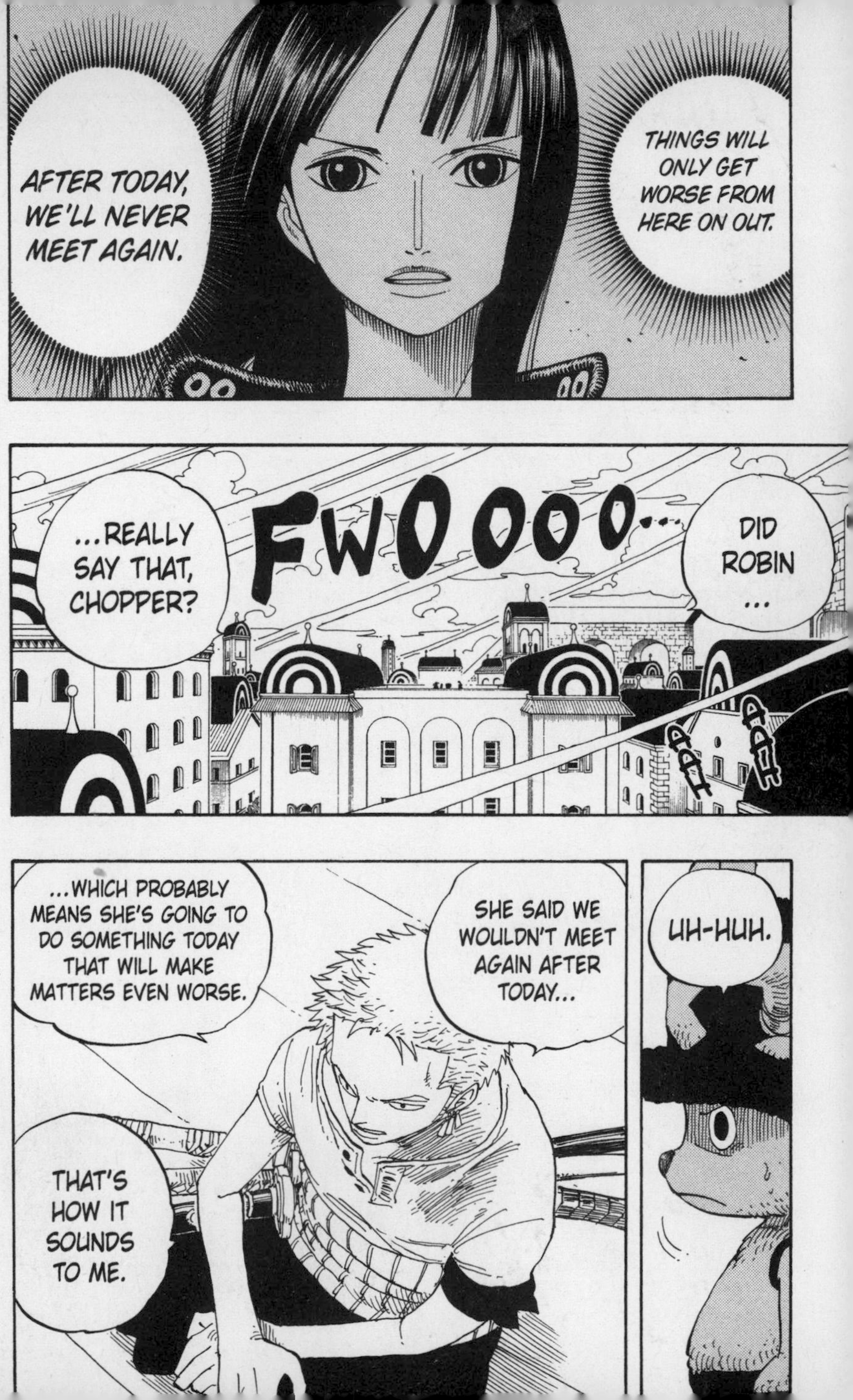
THINGS WILL ONLY GET WORSE FROM HERE ON OUT.
AFTER TODAY, WE'LL NEVER MEET AGAIN.
DID ROBIN ...
FWOOOO...
...REALLY SAY THAT, CHOPPER?
UH-HUH.
SHE SAID WE WOULDN'T MEET AGAIN AFTER TODAY...
...WHICH PROBABLY MEANS SHE'S GOING TO DO SOMETHING TODAY THAT WILL MAKE MATTERS EVEN WORSE.
THAT'S HOW IT SOUNDS TO ME.

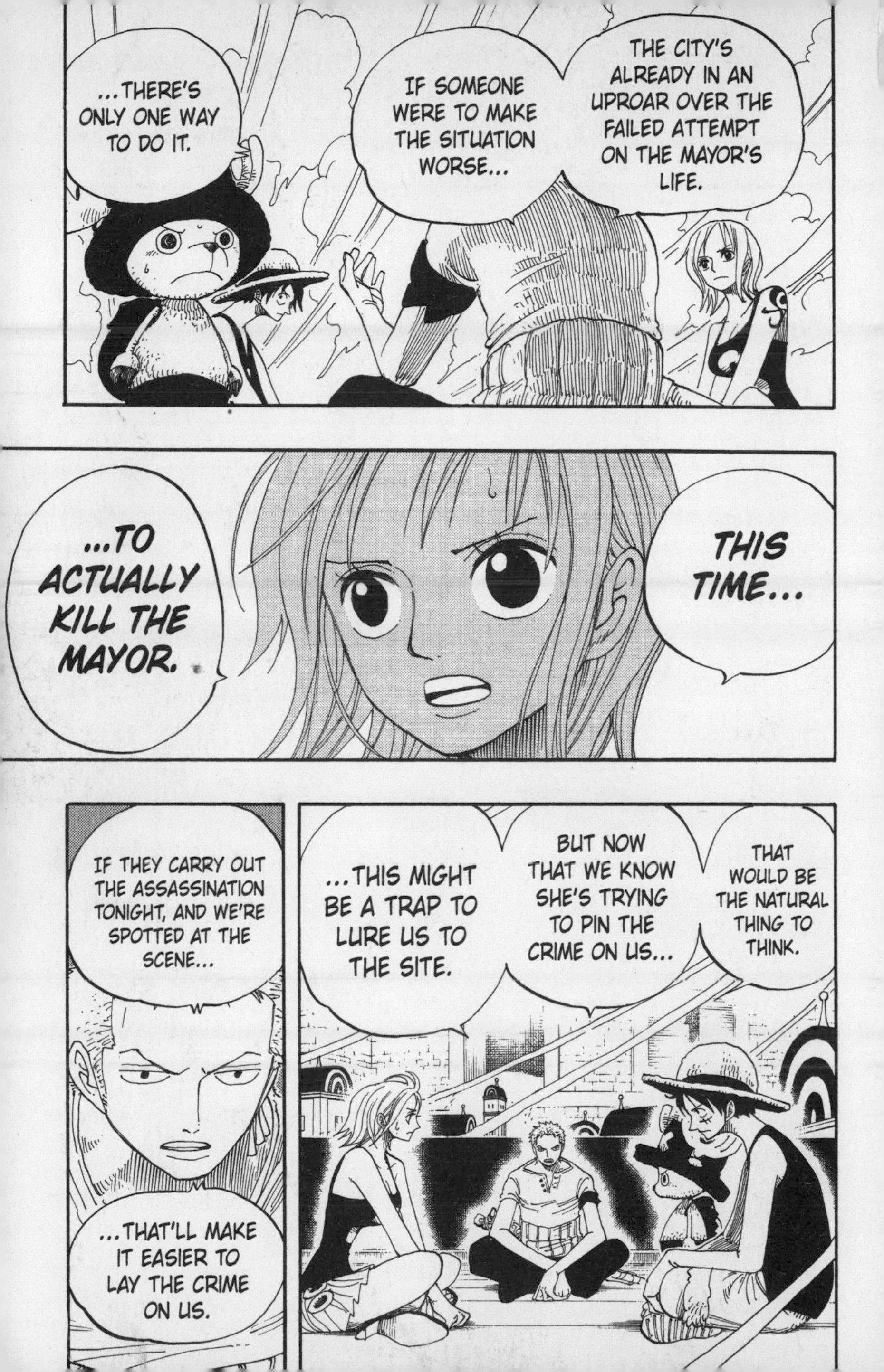
THE CITY'S ALREADY IN AN UPROAR OVER THE FAILED ATTEMPT ON THE MAYOR'S LIFE.
IF SOMEONE WERE TO MAKE THE SITUATION WORSE...
...THERE'S ONLY ONE WAY TO DO IT.
THIS TIME...
...TO ACTUALLY KILL THE MAYOR.
THAT WOULD BE THE NATURAL THING TO THINK.
BUT NOW THAT WE KNOW SHE'S TRYING TO PIN THE CRIME ON US...
...THIS MIGHT BE A TRAP TO LURE US TO THE SITE.
IF THEY CARRY OUT THE ASSASSINATION TONIGHT, AND WE'RE SPOTTED AT THE SCENE...
...THAT'LL MAKE IT EASIER TO LAY THE CRIME ON US.

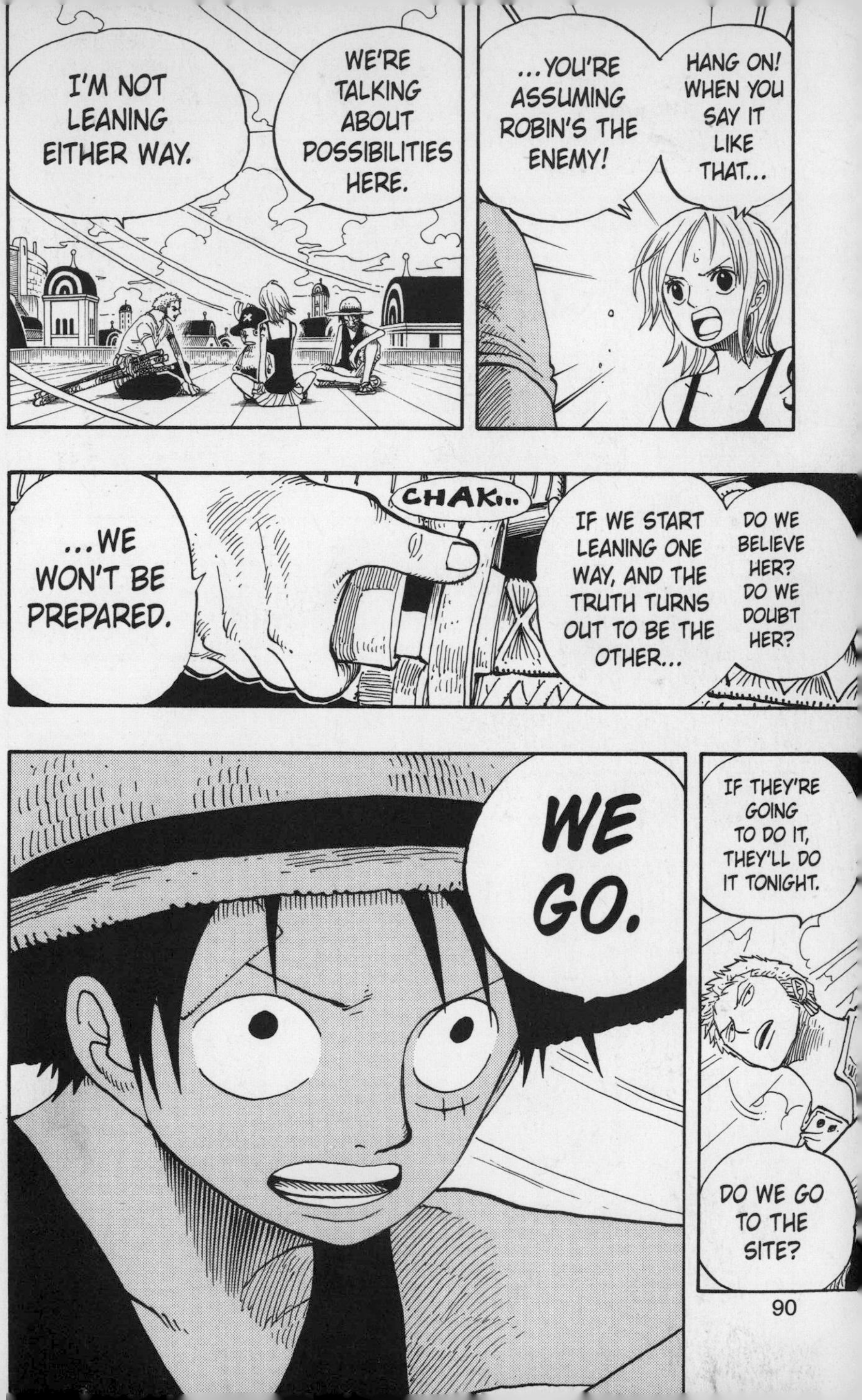
HANG ON! WHEN YOU SAY IT LIKE THAT...
...YOU'RE ASSUMING ROBIN'S THE ENEMY!
WE'RE TALKING ABOUT POSSIBILITIES HERE.
I'M NOT LEANING EITHER WAY.
DO WE BELIEVE HER? DO WE DOUBT HER?
IF WE START LEANING ONE WAY, AND THE TRUTH TURNS OUT TO BE THE OTHER...
CHAK...
...WE WON'T BE PREPARED.
IF THEY'RE GOING TO DO IT, THEY'LL DO IT TONIGHT.
DO WE GO TO THE SITE?
WE GO.

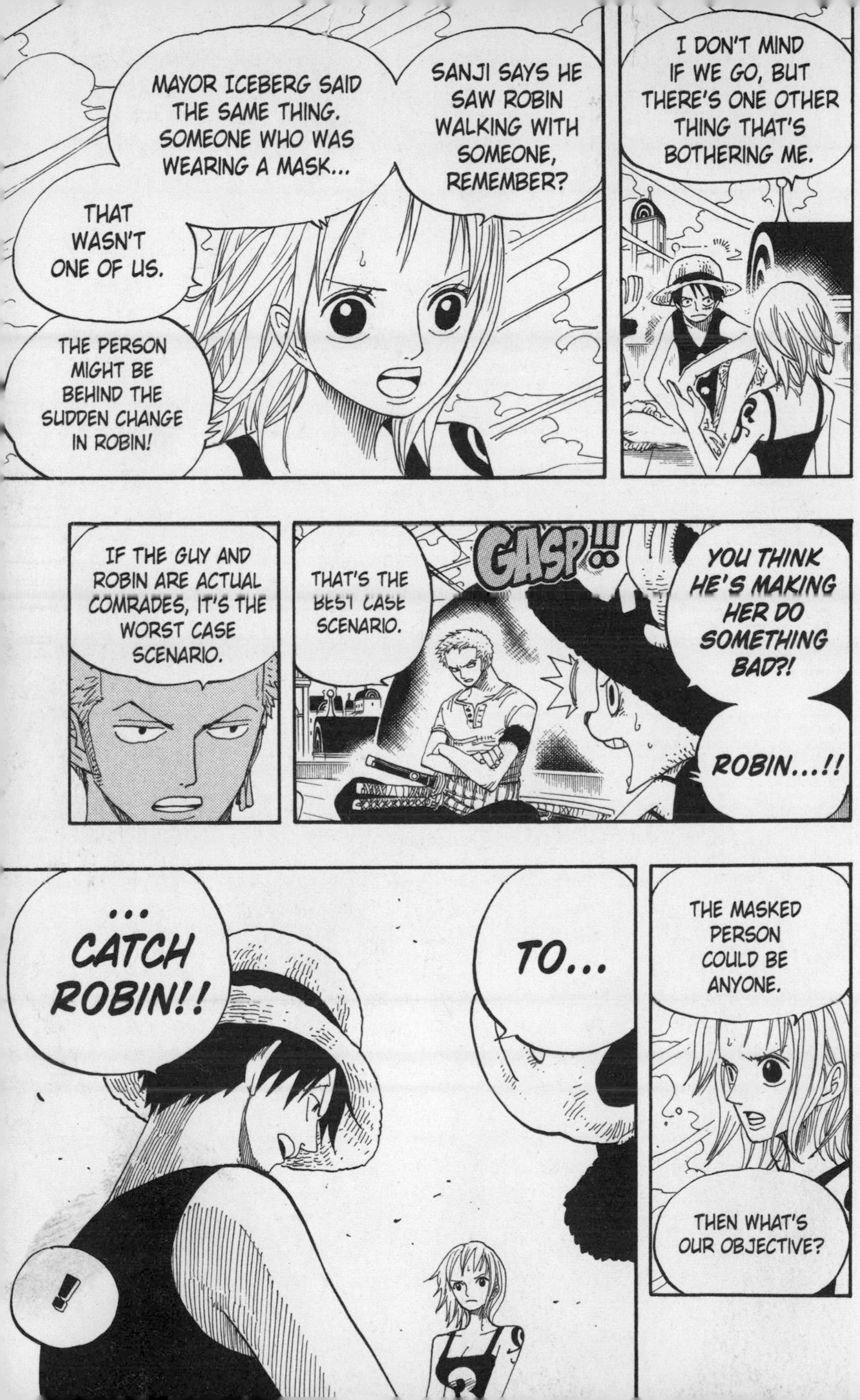
I DON'T MIND IF WE GO, BUT THERE'S ONE OTHER THING THAT'S BOTHERING ME.
SANJI SAYS HE SAW ROBIN WALKING WITH SOMEONE, REMEMBER?
MAYOR ICEBERG SAID THE SAME THING. SOMEONE WHO WAS WEARING A MASK...
THAT WASN'T ONE OF US.
THE PERSON MIGHT BE BEHIND THE SUDDEN CHANGE IN ROBIN!
GASP!!
YOU THINK HE'S MAKING HER DO SOMETHING BAD?!
ROBIN...!!
THAT'S THE BEST CASE SCENARIO.
IF THE GUY AND ROBIN ARE ACTUAL COMRADES, IT'S THE WORST CASE SCENARIO.
THE MASKED PERSON COULD BE ANYONE.
THEN WHAT'S OUR OBJECTIVE?
TO...
... CATCH ROBIN!!
!

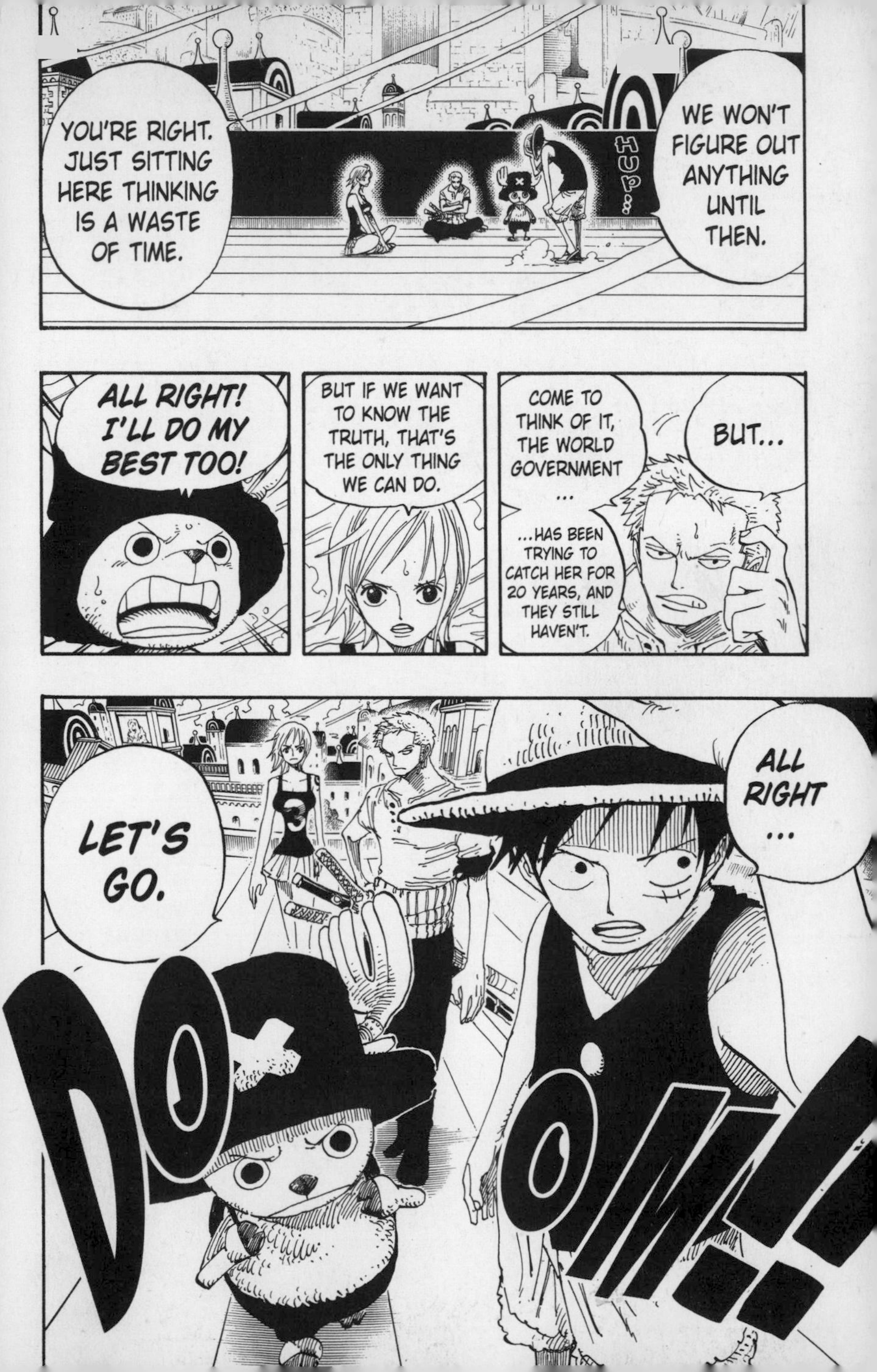

WE WON'T FIGURE OUT ANYTHING UNTIL THEN.
HUP..!
YOU'RE RIGHT. JUST SITTING HERE THINKING IS A WASTE OF TIME.
BUT...
COME TO THINK OF IT, THE WORLD GOVERNMENT ...
...HAS BEEN TRYING TO CATCH HER FOR 20 YEARS, AND THEY STILL HAVEN'T.
BUT IF WE WANT TO KNOW THE TRUTH, THAT'S THE ONLY THING WE CAN DO.
ALL RIGHT! I'LL DO MY BEST TOO!
ALL RIGHT ...
LET'S GO.
DOOM!!

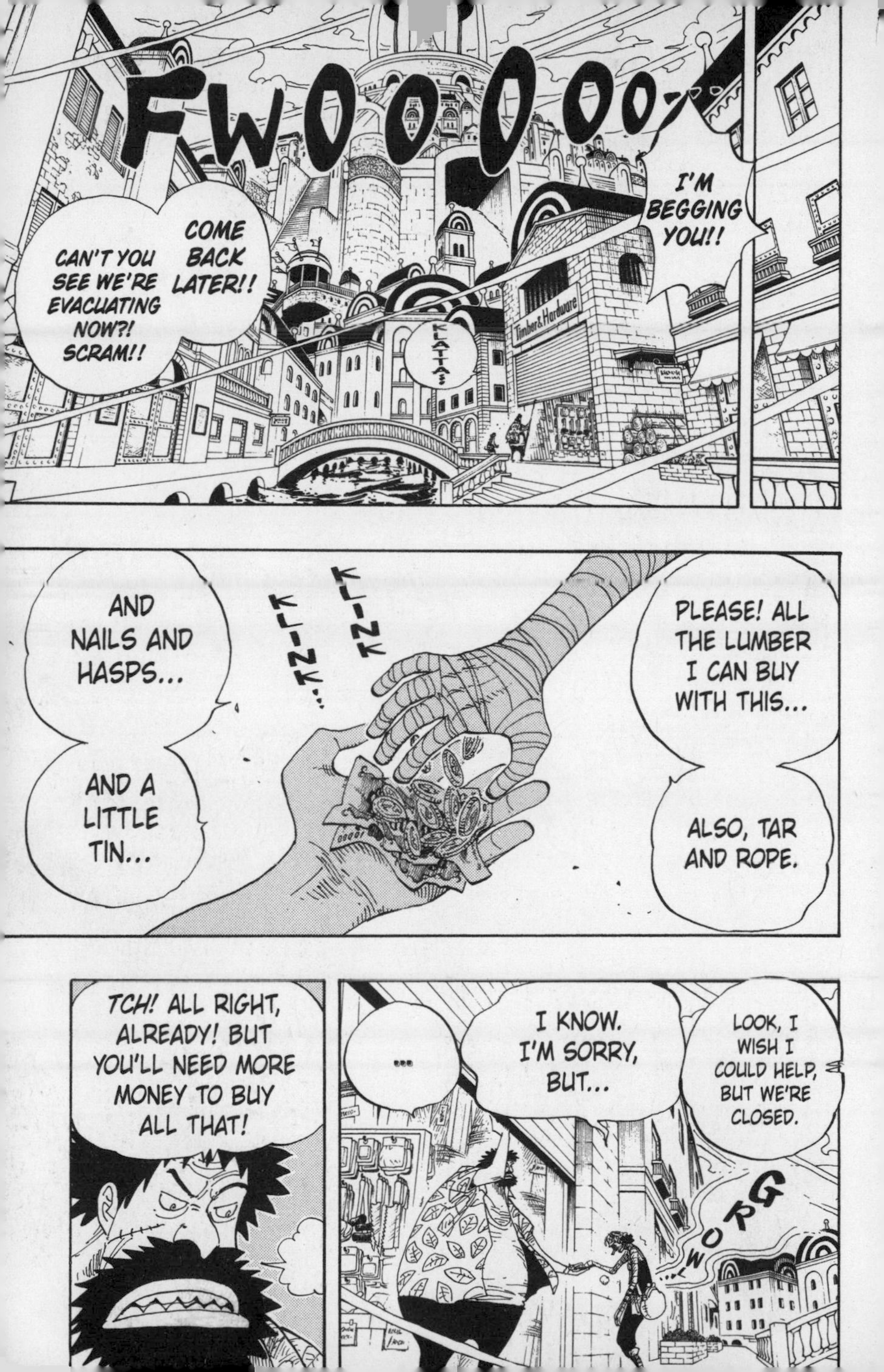
FWOOOOOO
I'M BEGGING YOU!!
COME BACK LATER!!
CAN'T YOU SEE WE'RE EVACUATING NOW?! SCRAM!!
KLATTA?
Timber & Hardware
PLEASE! ALL THE LUMBER I CAN BUY WITH THIS...
ALSO, TAR AND ROPE.
KLINK
KLINK...
AND NAILS AND HASPS...
AND A LITTLE TIN...
LOOK, I WISH I COULD HELP, BUT WE'RE CLOSED.
I KNOW. I'M SORRY, BUT...
...
WORG
TCH! ALL RIGHT, ALREADY! BUT YOU'LL NEED MORE MONEY TO BUY ALL THAT!

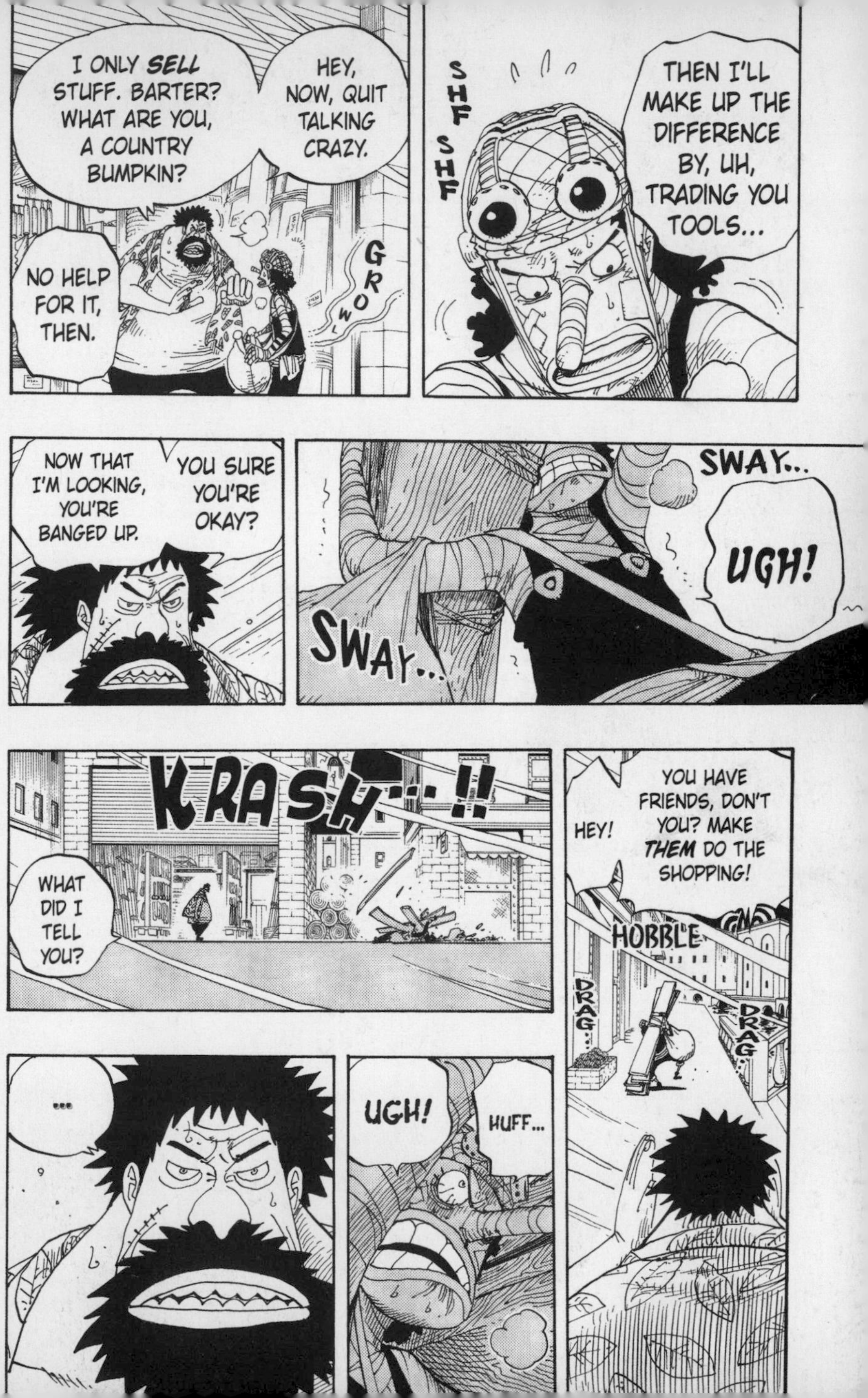

SHF SHF
THEN I'LL MAKE UP THE DIFFERENCE BY, UH, TRADING YOU TOOLS...
HEY, NOW, QUIT TALKING CRAZY.
I ONLY **SELL** STUFF. BARTER? WHAT ARE YOU, A COUNTRY BUMPKIN?
GROWL
NO HELP FOR IT, THEN.
SWAY...
UGH!
SWAY...
YOU SURE YOU'RE OKAY?
NOW THAT I'M LOOKING, YOU'RE BANGED UP.
YOU HAVE FRIENDS, DON'T YOU? MAKE ***THEM*** DO THE SHOPPING!
HEY!
HOBBLE
DRAG...
DRAG...
KRASH...!!
WHAT DID I TELL YOU?
HUFF...
UGH!
...

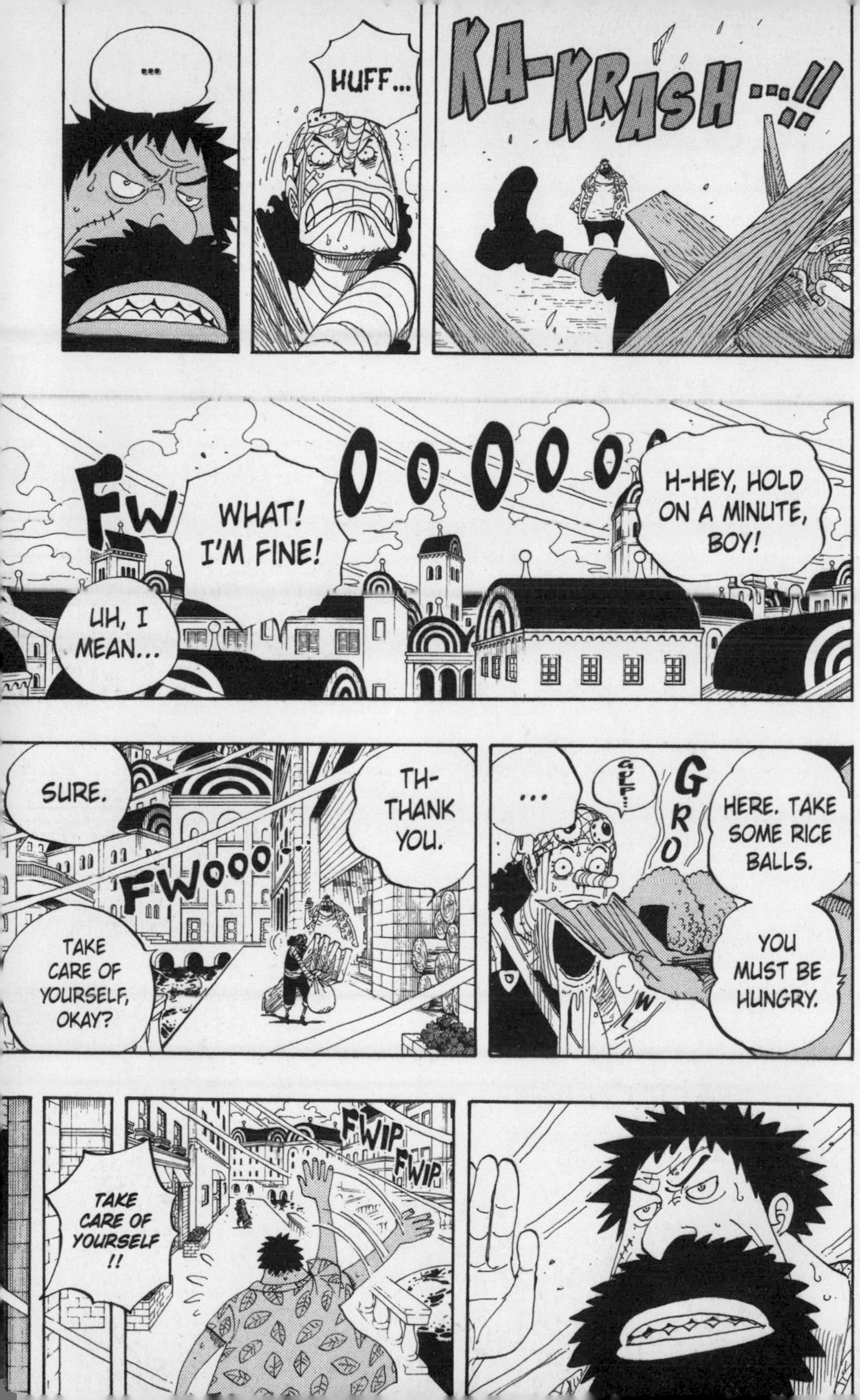
KA-KRASH...!!
HUFF...
...
H-HEY, HOLD ON A MINUTE, BOY!
OOOOO
WHAT! I'M FINE!
FW
UH, I MEAN...
HERE. TAKE SOME RICE BALLS.
YOU MUST BE HUNGRY.
GRO
GULP...
...
WL
TH-THANK YOU.
SURE.
FWOOO
TAKE CARE OF YOURSELF, OKAY?
FWIP FWIP
TAKE CARE OF YOURSELF !!

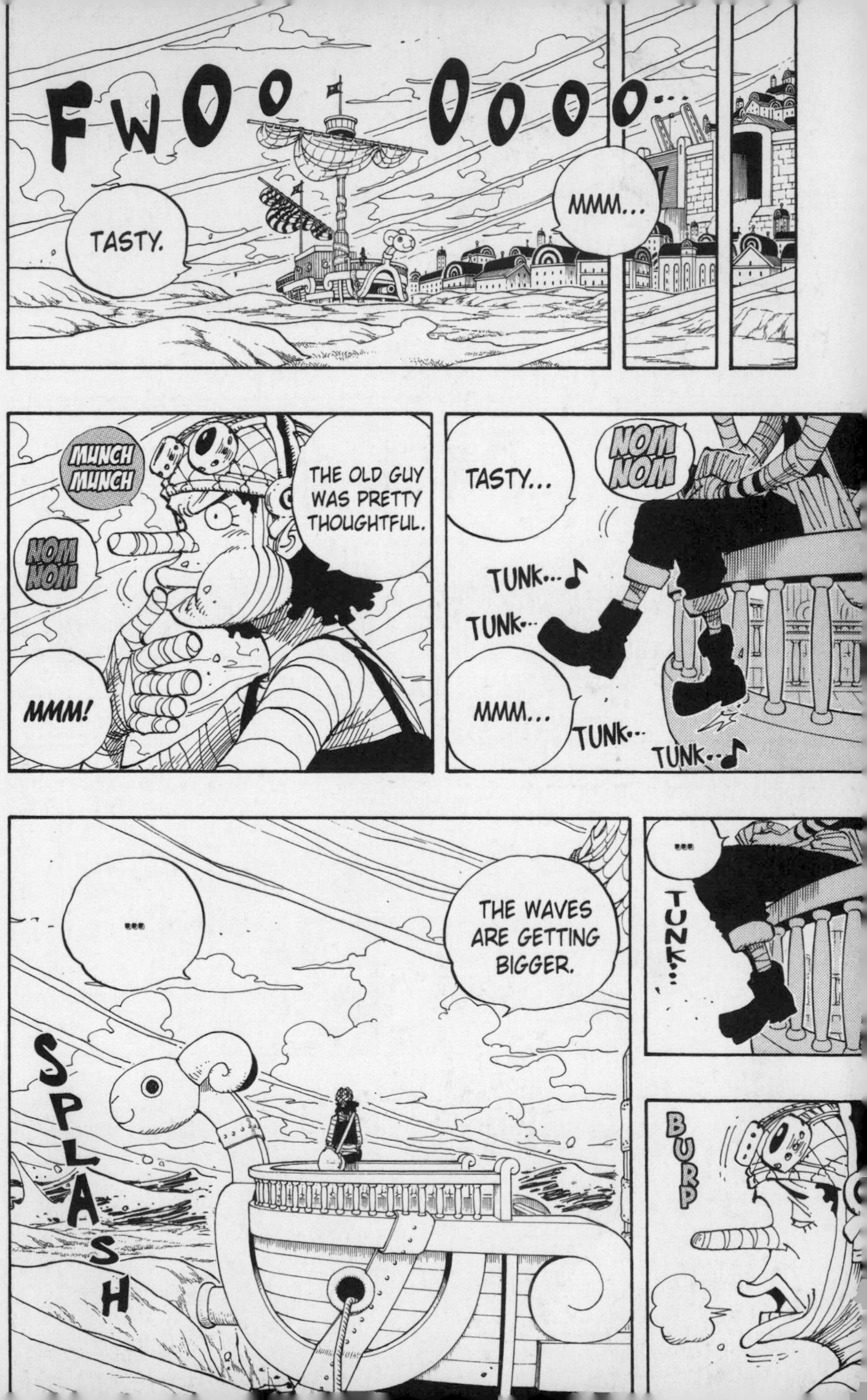
FWOOOOOO...
MMM...
TASTY.
NOM NOM
TASTY...
TUNK...♪
TUNK...
MMM...
TUNK...
TUNK...♪
THE OLD GUY WAS PRETTY THOUGHTFUL.
MUNCH MUNCH
NOM NOM
MMM!
...
TUNK...
BURP
THE WAVES ARE GETTING BIGGER.
...
SPLASH

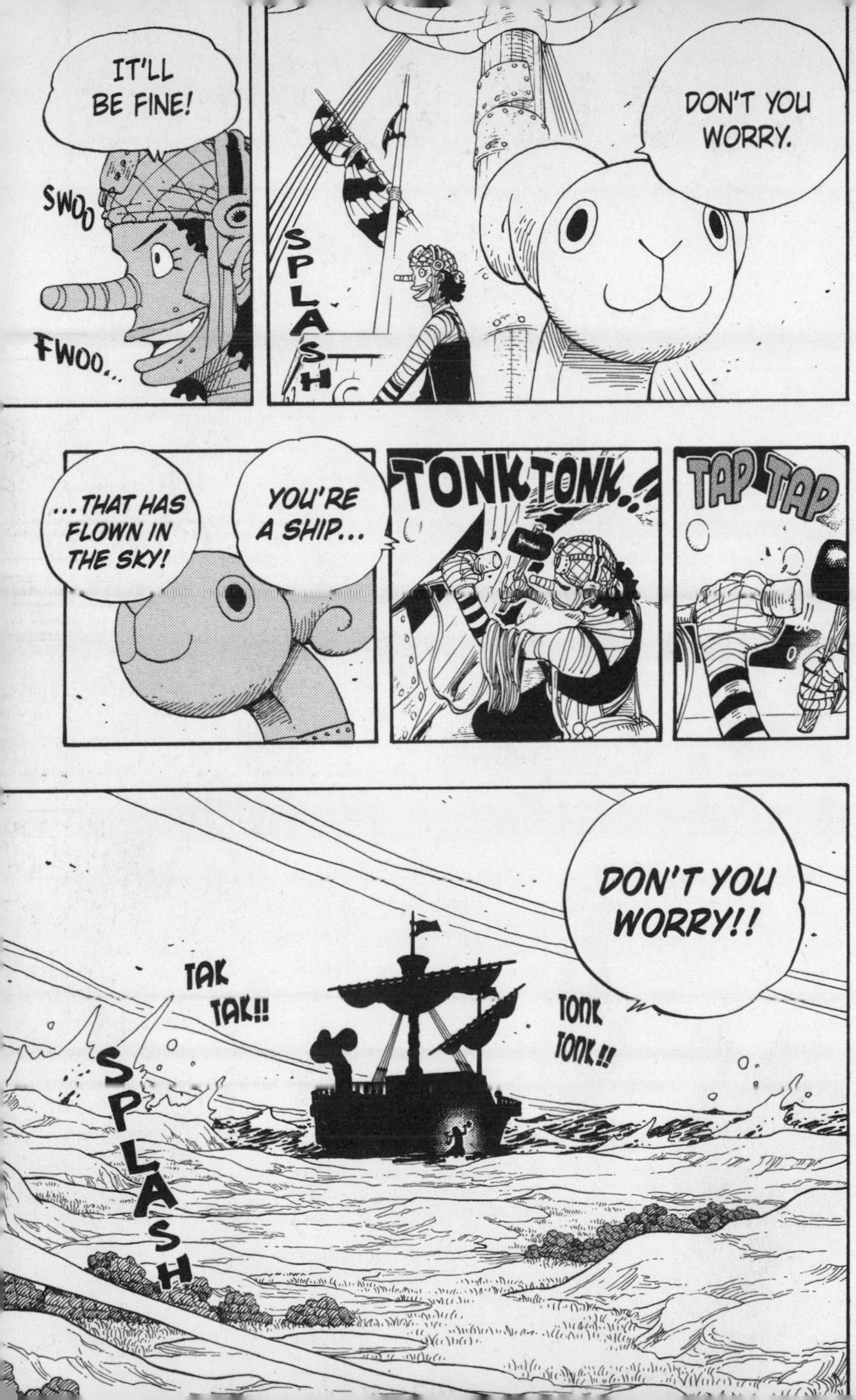
DON'T YOU WORRY.
SPLASH
IT'LL BE FINE!
SWOO
FWOO...
TAP TAP
TONK TONK..
YOU'RE A SHIP...
...THAT HAS FLOWN IN THE SKY!
DON'T YOU WORRY!!
TONK TONK!!
TAK TAK!!
SPLASH

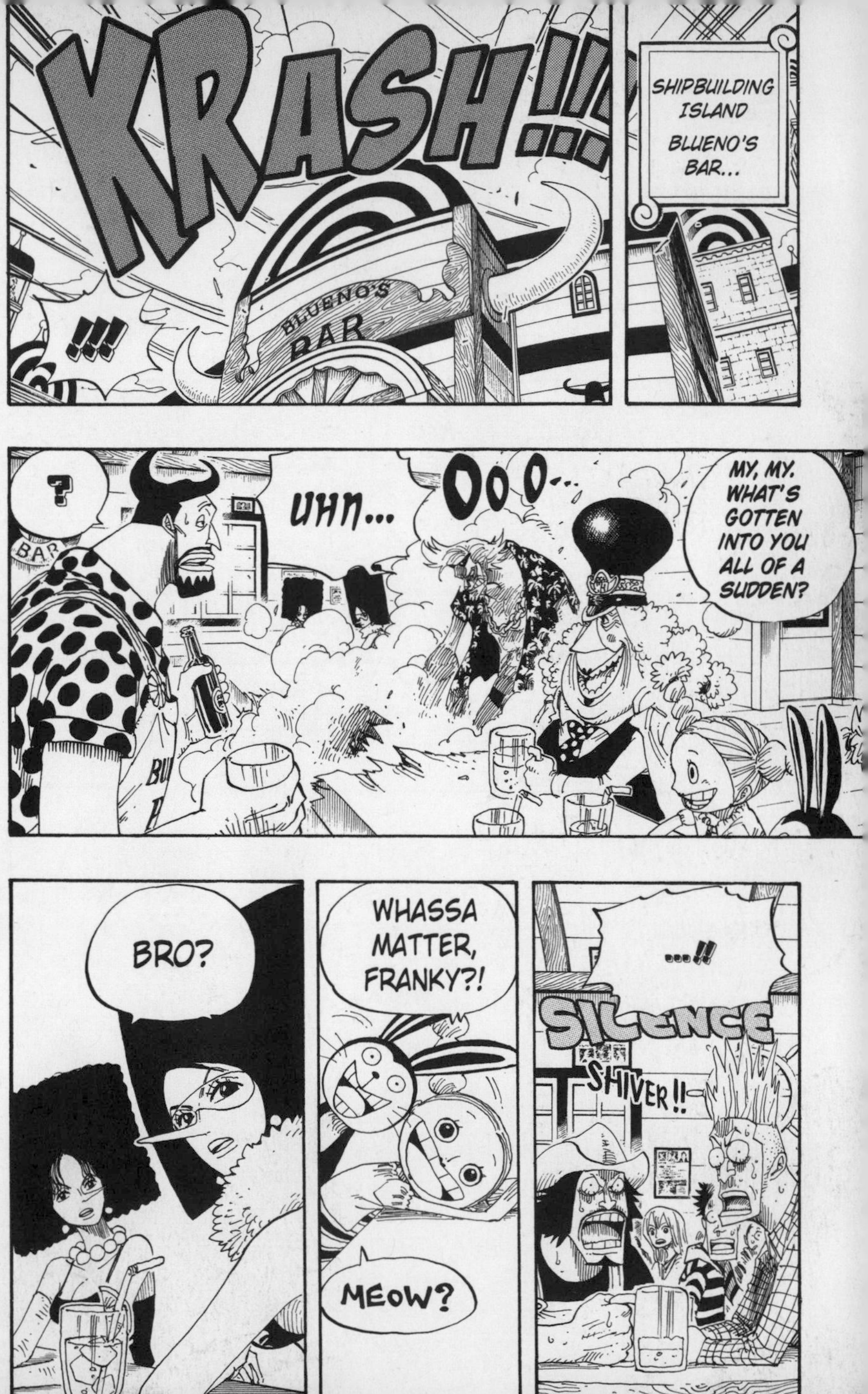
SHIPBUILDING ISLAND
BLUENO'S BAR...
KRASH!!!
BLUENO'S BAR
!!!
MY, MY. WHAT'S GOTTEN INTO YOU ALL OF A SUDDEN?
OOO...
UHN...
?
BAR
...!!
SILENCE
SHIVER!!
WHASSA MATTER, FRANKY?!
MEOW?
BRO?

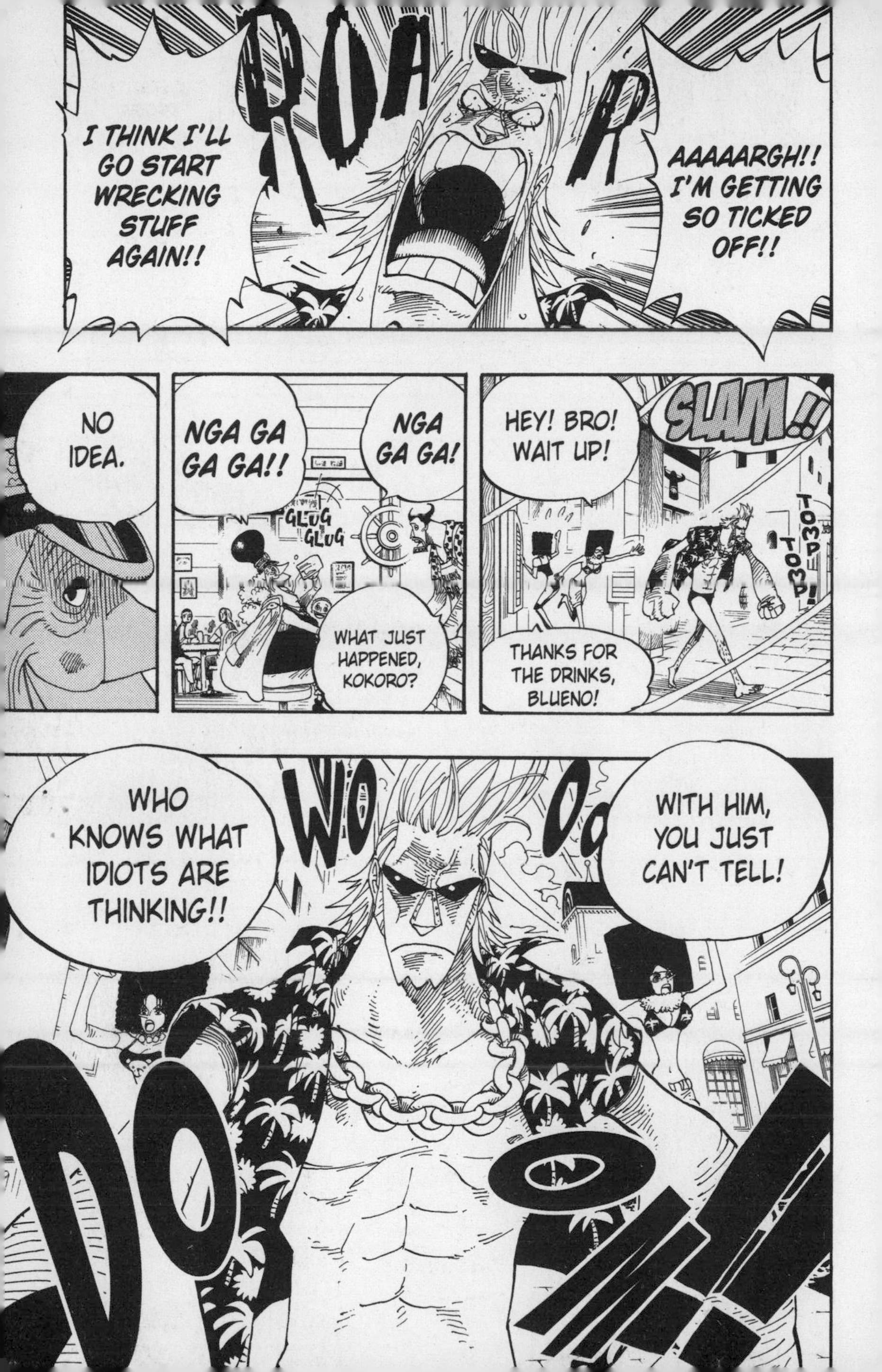
ROAR
AAAAARGH!! I'M GETTING SO TICKED OFF!!
I THINK I'LL GO START WRECKING STUFF AGAIN!!
SLAM!!
HEY! BRO! WAIT UP!
TOMP TOMP!
THANKS FOR THE DRINKS, BLUENO!
NGA GA GA!
NGA GA GA GA!!
GLUG GLUG
WHAT JUST HAPPENED, KOKORO?
NO IDEA.
WITH HIM, YOU JUST CAN'T TELL!
WHO KNOWS WHAT IDIOTS ARE THINKING!!

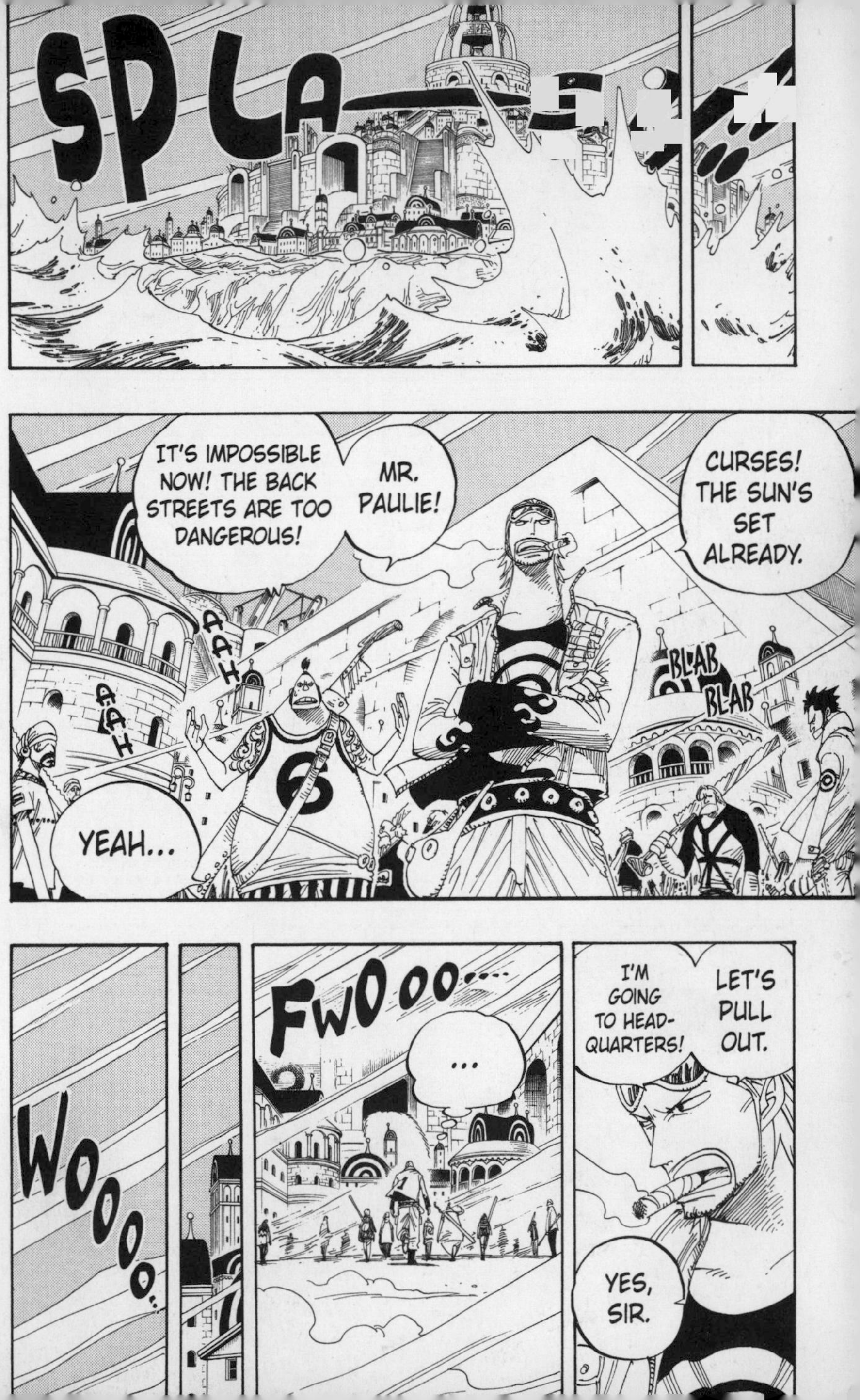
SPLA—
CURSES! THE SUN'S SET ALREADY.
MR. PAULIE!
IT'S IMPOSSIBLE NOW! THE BACK STREETS ARE TOO DANGEROUS!
BLAB BLAB
AAAH
AAAH
YEAH...
LET'S PULL OUT.
I'M GOING TO HEAD-QUARTERS!
YES, SIR.
FWOOO...
...
WOOOO

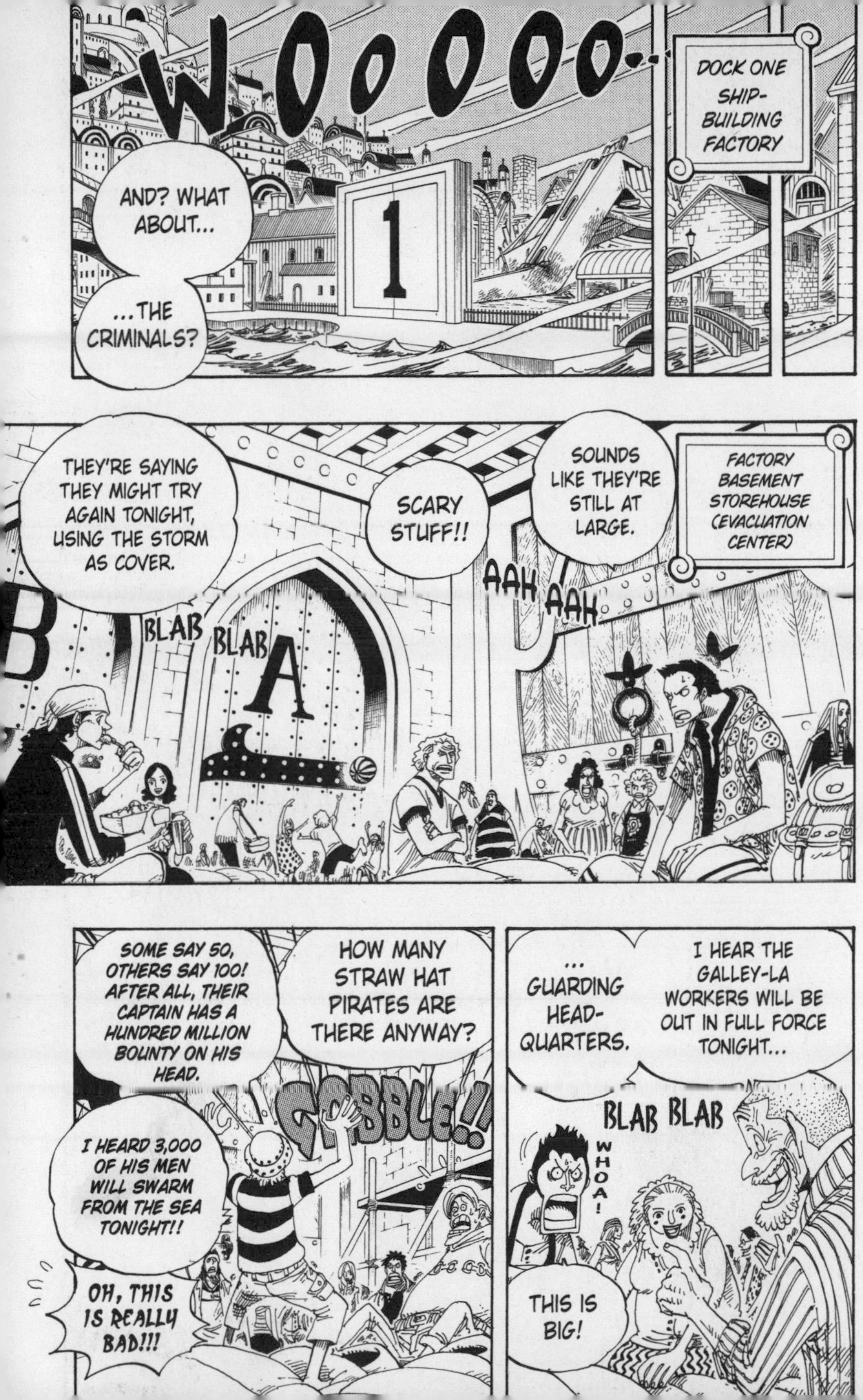
DOCK ONE SHIP-BUILDING FACTORY
WOOOOO...
AND? WHAT ABOUT...
...THE CRIMINALS?
FACTORY BASEMENT STOREHOUSE (EVACUATION CENTER)
SOUNDS LIKE THEY'RE STILL AT LARGE.
SCARY STUFF!!
THEY'RE SAYING THEY MIGHT TRY AGAIN TONIGHT, USING THE STORM AS COVER.
AAH AAH
BLAB BLAB
I HEAR THE GALLEY-LA WORKERS WILL BE OUT IN FULL FORCE TONIGHT...
...GUARDING HEAD-QUARTERS.
BLAB BLAB
WHOA!
THIS IS BIG!
HOW MANY STRAW HAT PIRATES ARE THERE ANYWAY?
SOME SAY 50, OTHERS SAY 100! AFTER ALL, THEIR CAPTAIN HAS A HUNDRED MILLION BOUNTY ON HIS HEAD.
GOBBLE!!
I HEARD 3,000 OF HIS MEN WILL SWARM FROM THE SEA TONIGHT!!
OH, THIS IS REALLY BAD!!!

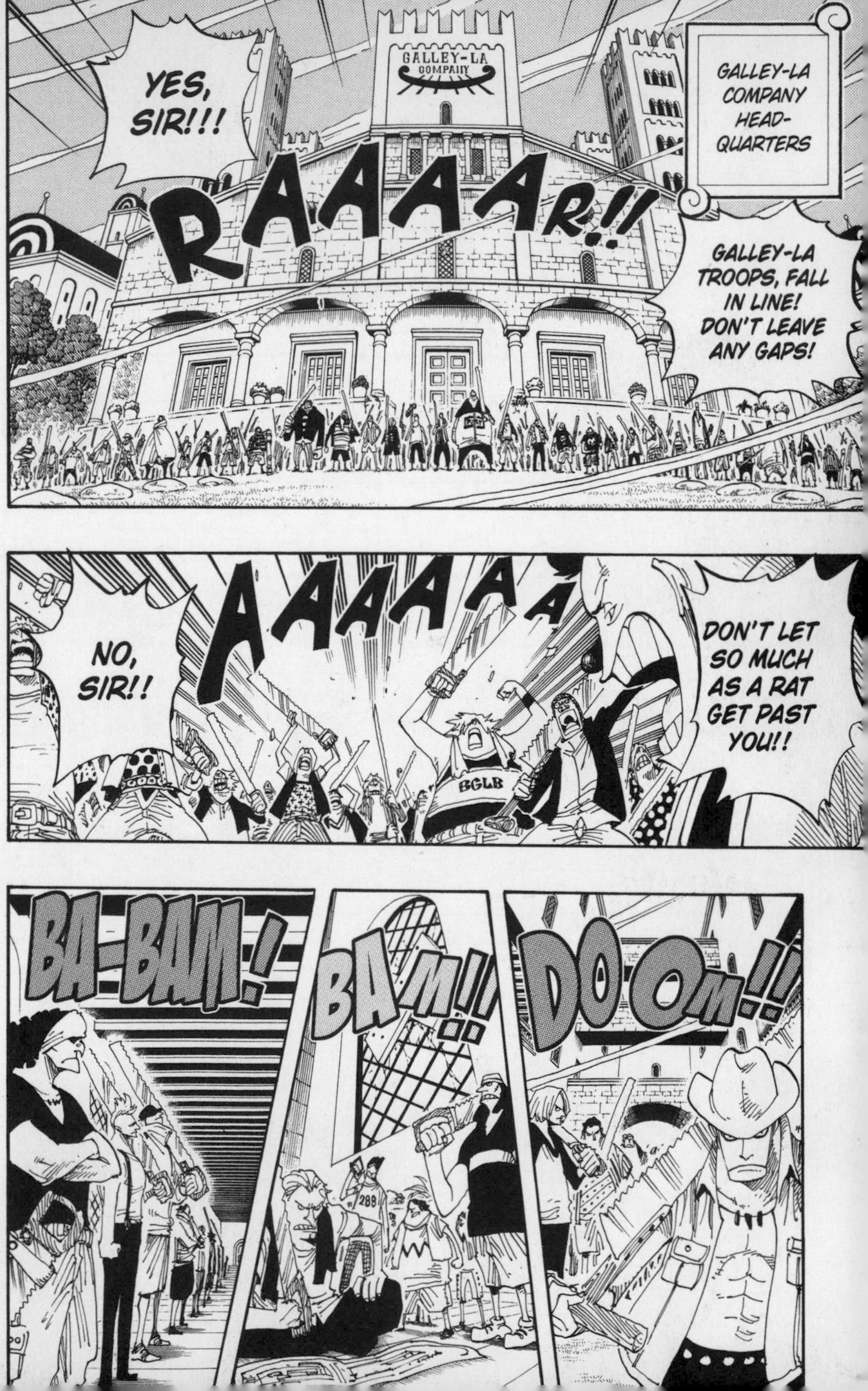
GALLEY-LA COMPANY HEAD-QUARTERS
GALLEY-LA TROOPS, FALL IN LINE! DON'T LEAVE ANY GAPS!
GALLEY-LA COMPANY
RAAAAAR!!
YES, SIR!!!
DON'T LET SO MUCH AS A RAT GET PAST YOU!!
AAAAAA
NO, SIR!!
BGLB
DOOM!!
BAM!!
BA-BAM!

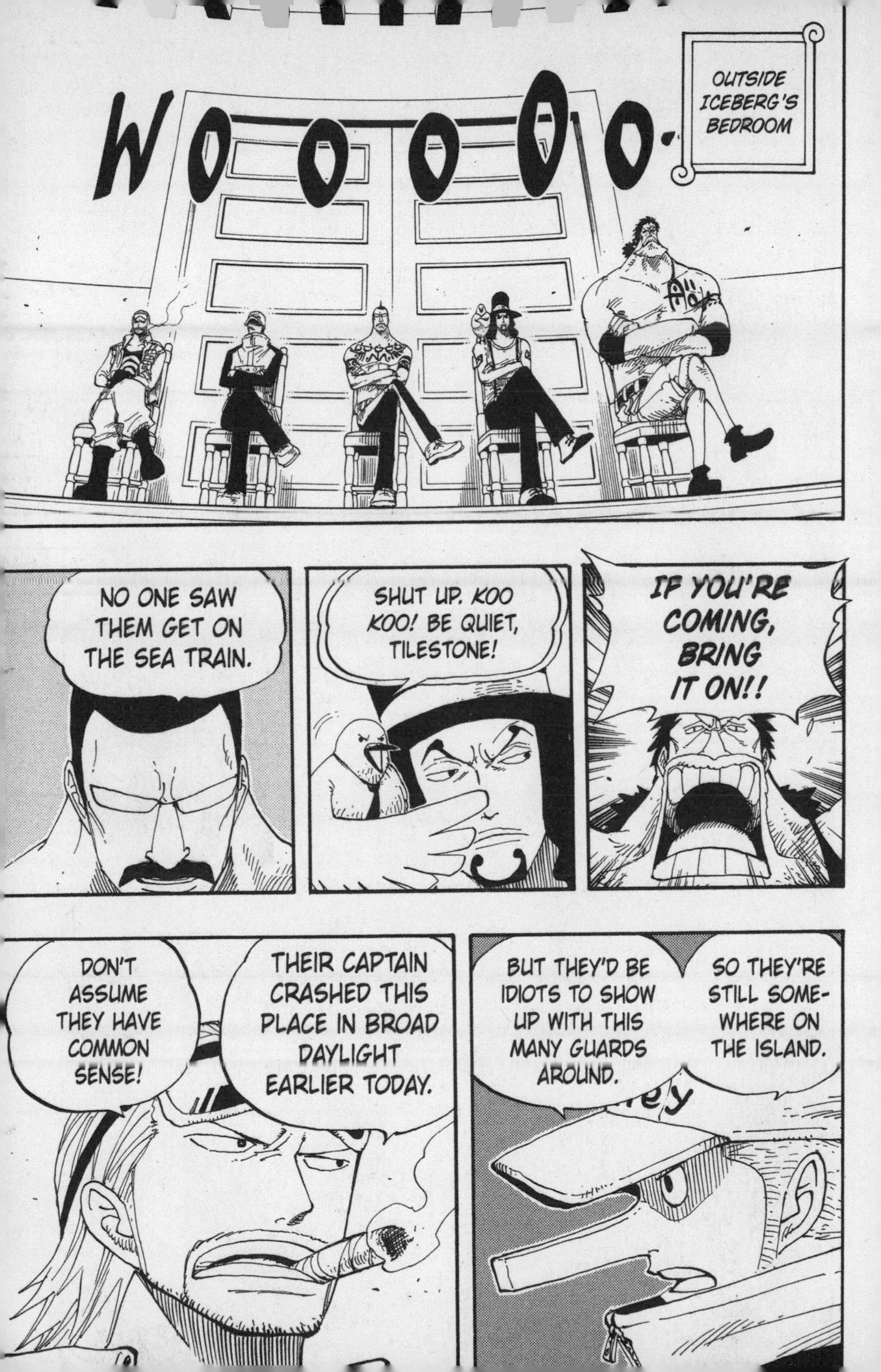
OUTSIDE ICEBERG'S BEDROOM
WOOOOO·
IF YOU'RE COMING, BRING IT ON!!
SHUT UP. KOO KOO! BE QUIET, TILESTONE!
NO ONE SAW THEM GET ON THE SEA TRAIN.
SO THEY'RE STILL SOME-WHERE ON THE ISLAND.
BUT THEY'D BE IDIOTS TO SHOW UP WITH THIS MANY GUARDS AROUND.
THEIR CAPTAIN CRASHED THIS PLACE IN BROAD DAYLIGHT EARLIER TODAY.
DON'T ASSUME THEY HAVE COMMON SENSE!

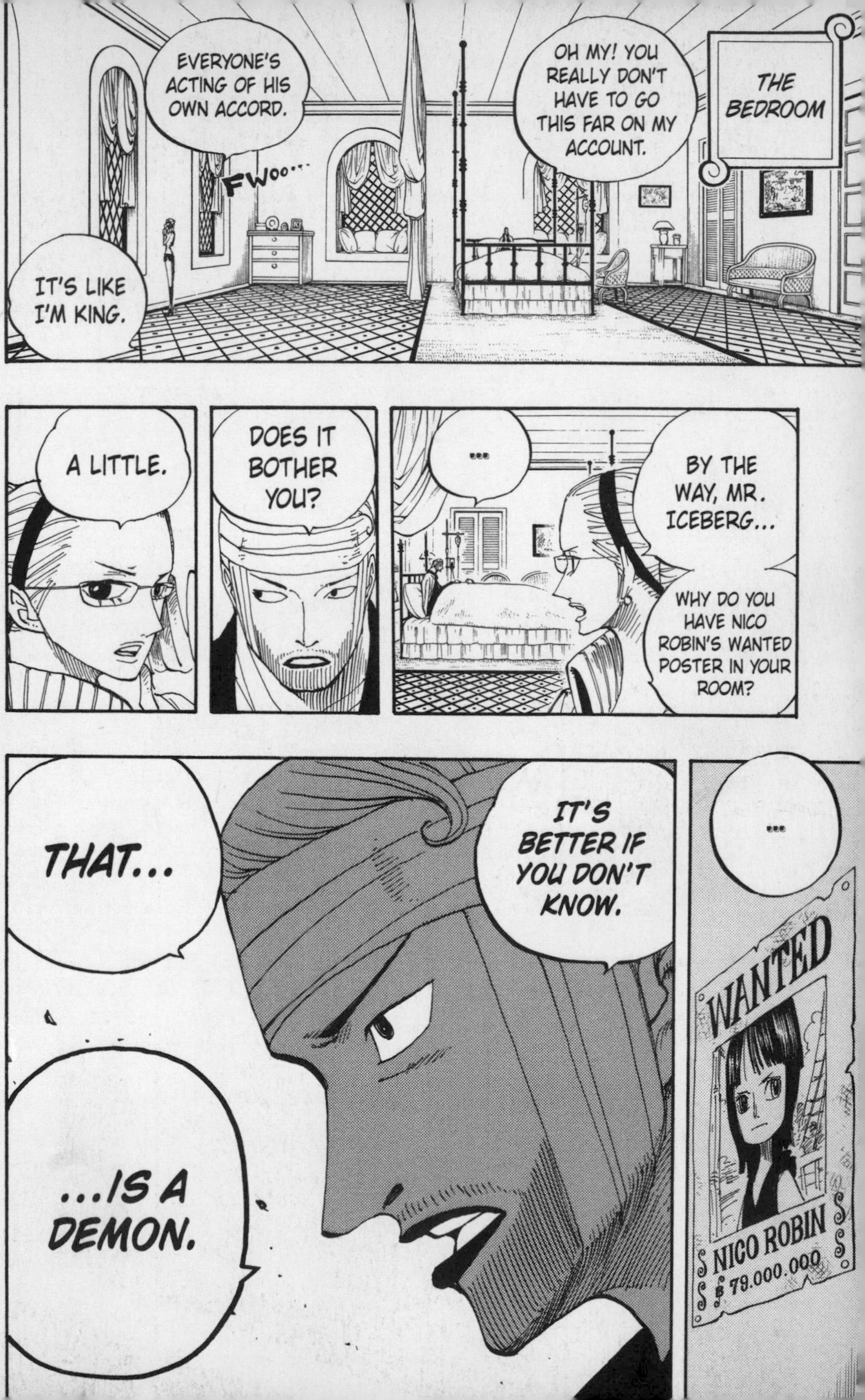
THE BEDROOM
OH MY! YOU REALLY DON'T HAVE TO GO THIS FAR ON MY ACCOUNT.
FWOO...
EVERYONE'S ACTING OF HIS OWN ACCORD.
IT'S LIKE I'M KING.
BY THE WAY, MR. ICEBERG...
WHY DO YOU HAVE NICO ROBIN'S WANTED POSTER IN YOUR ROOM?
...
DOES IT BOTHER YOU?
A LITTLE.
...
WANTED
NICO ROBIN
฿79.000.000
IT'S BETTER IF YOU DON'T KNOW.
THAT...
...IS A DEMON.

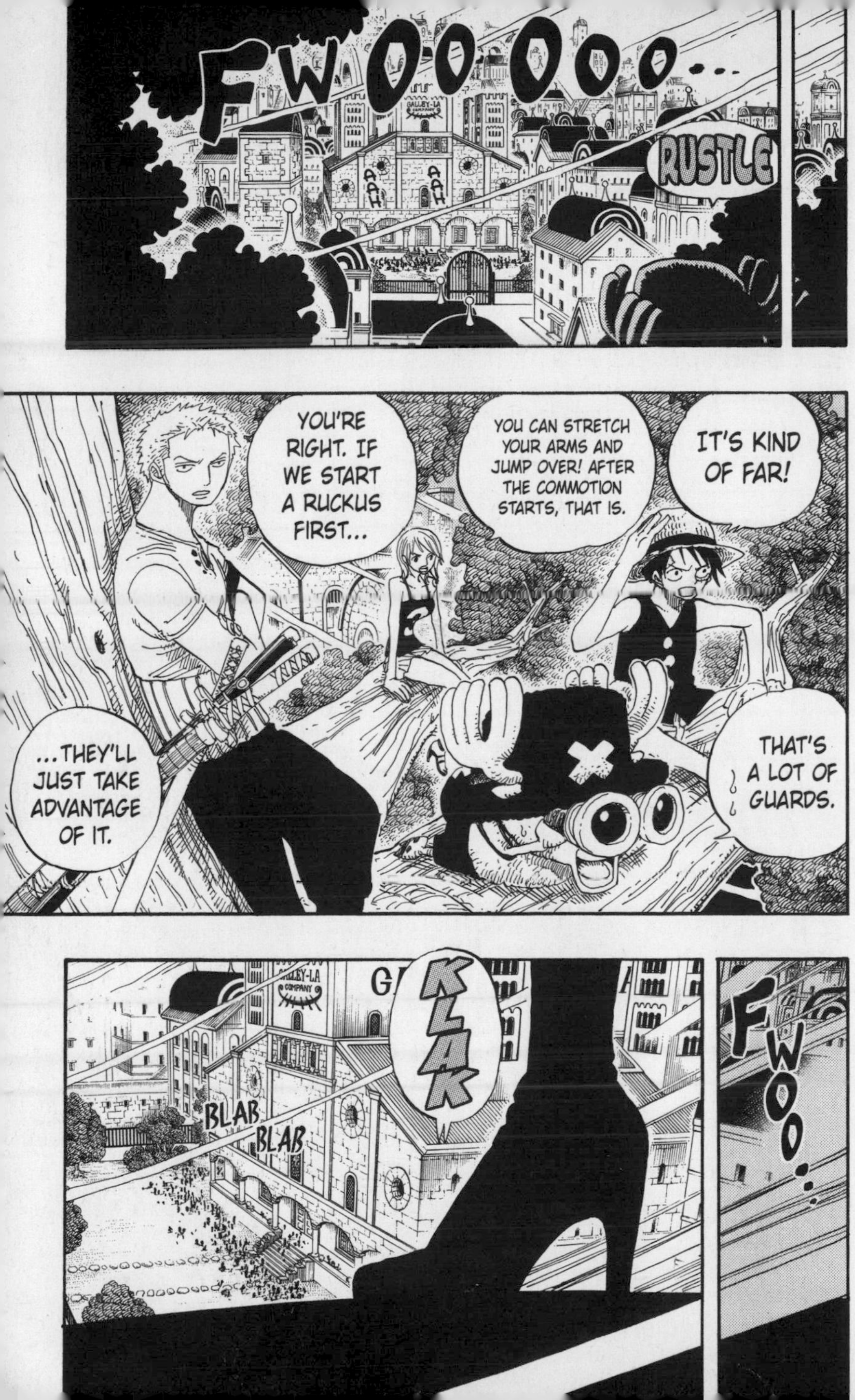
FWOOOOO...
GALLEY-LA COMPANY
AAAH
AAAH
RUSTLE
THAT'S A LOT OF GUARDS.
IT'S KIND OF FAR!
YOU CAN STRETCH YOUR ARMS AND JUMP OVER! AFTER THE COMMOTION STARTS, THAT IS.
YOU'RE RIGHT. IF WE START A RUCKUS FIRST...
...THEY'LL JUST TAKE ADVANTAGE OF IT.
FWOO...
KLAK
GALLEY-LA COMPANY
BLAB BLAB

ONE PIECE **STORYBOARD PREVIEW!!** #21

"I Don't Know Anybody Like This"

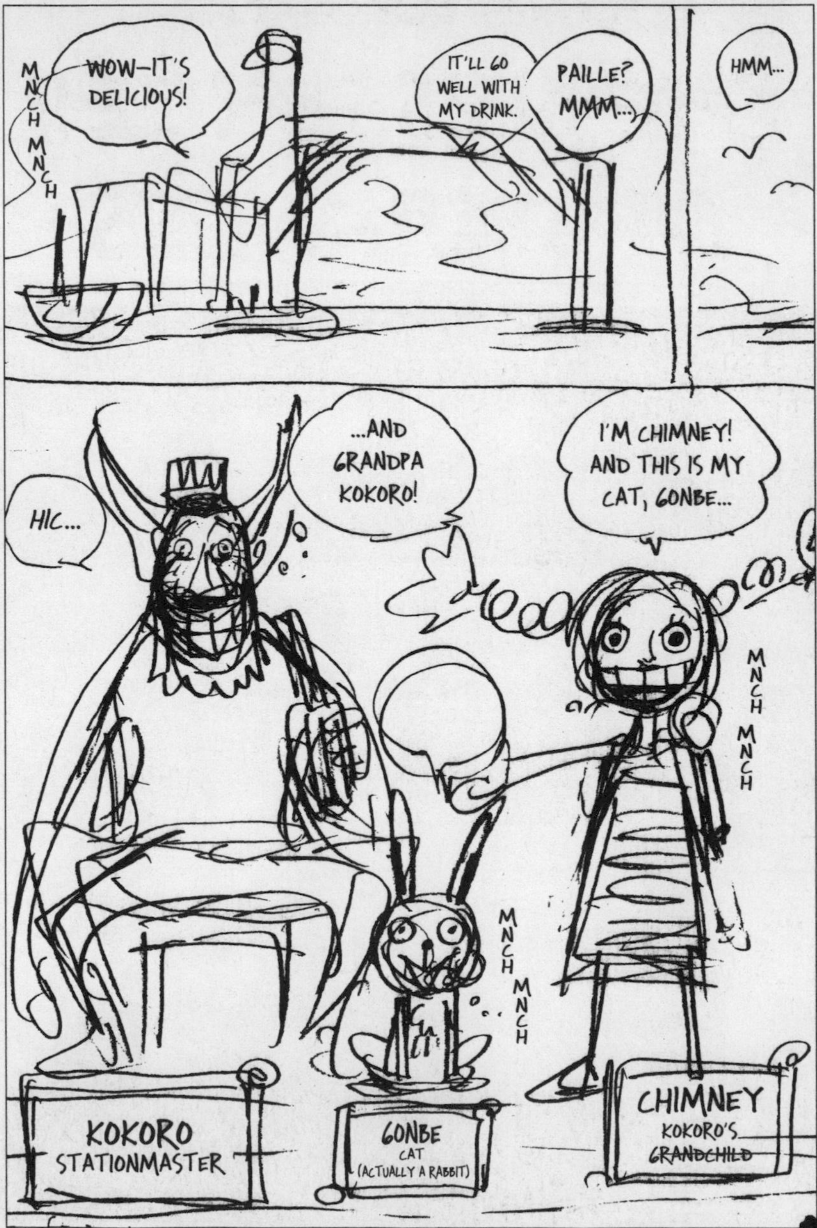
HMM...
PAILLE? MMM...
IT'LL GO WELL WITH MY DRINK.
WOW—IT'S DELICIOUS!
MNCH MNCH MNCH
I'M CHIMNEY! AND THIS IS MY CAT, GONBE...
...AND GRANDPA KOKORO!
HIC...
MNCH MNCH
MNCH MNCH
CHIMNEY
KOKORO'S GRANDCHILD
GONBE
CAT
(ACTUALLY A RABBIT)
KOKORO
STATIONMASTER

IN THIS VERSION, CHIMNEY INTRODUCES KOKORO AS "GRANDPA." SEE THE ORIGINAL VERSION IN VOLUME 34, P. 126--ED.

Chapter 342:

THE MESSENGER OF DARKNESS

TEXT ON FLAG SAYS "UNEXPECTED BATHS"--ED.

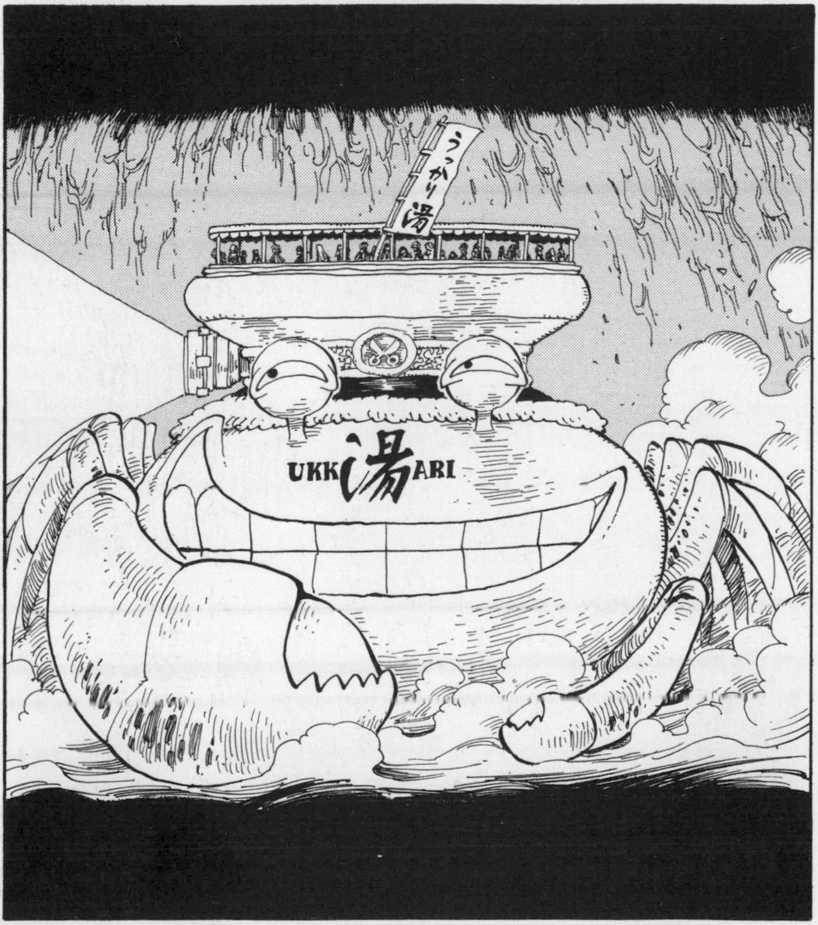
うっかり湯
UKK湯ARI

GEDATSU'S UNEXPECTED LIFE ON THE BLUE SEA, VOL. 26:
"PINCERS'S OCEAN FLOOR BUS SERVICE BEGINS"

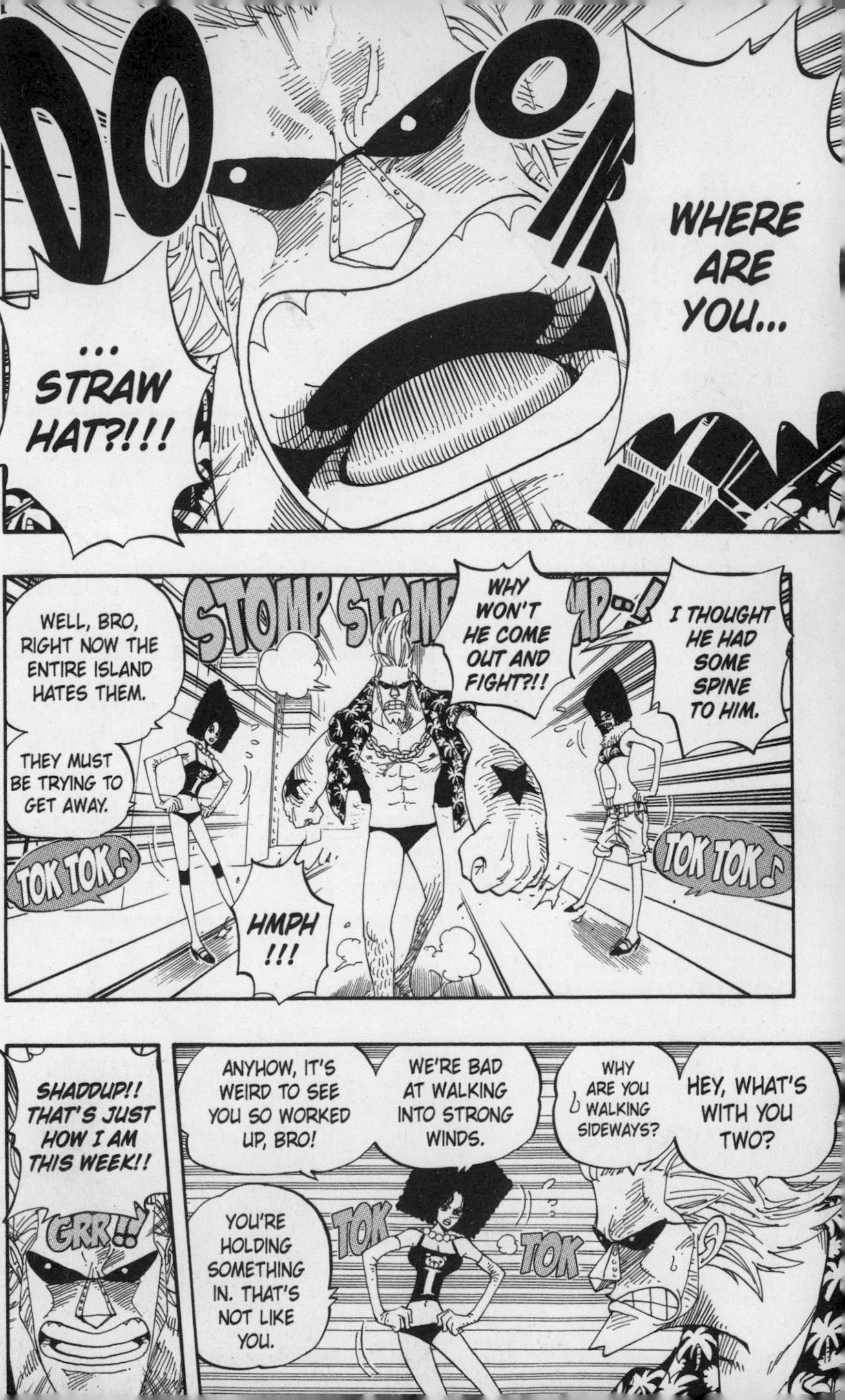
DOOM
WHERE ARE YOU...
...STRAW HAT?!!!
I THOUGHT HE HAD SOME SPINE TO HIM.
WHY WON'T HE COME OUT AND FIGHT?!!
STOMP STOM
TOK TOK ♪
WELL, BRO, RIGHT NOW THE ENTIRE ISLAND HATES THEM.
THEY MUST BE TRYING TO GET AWAY.
HMPH!!!
TOK TOK ♪
HEY, WHAT'S WITH YOU TWO?
WHY ARE YOU WALKING SIDEWAYS?
WE'RE BAD AT WALKING INTO STRONG WINDS.
ANYHOW, IT'S WEIRD TO SEE YOU SO WORKED UP, BRO!
TOK TOK
YOU'RE HOLDING SOMETHING IN. THAT'S NOT LIKE YOU.
SHADDUP!! THAT'S JUST HOW I AM THIS WEEK!!
GRR!!

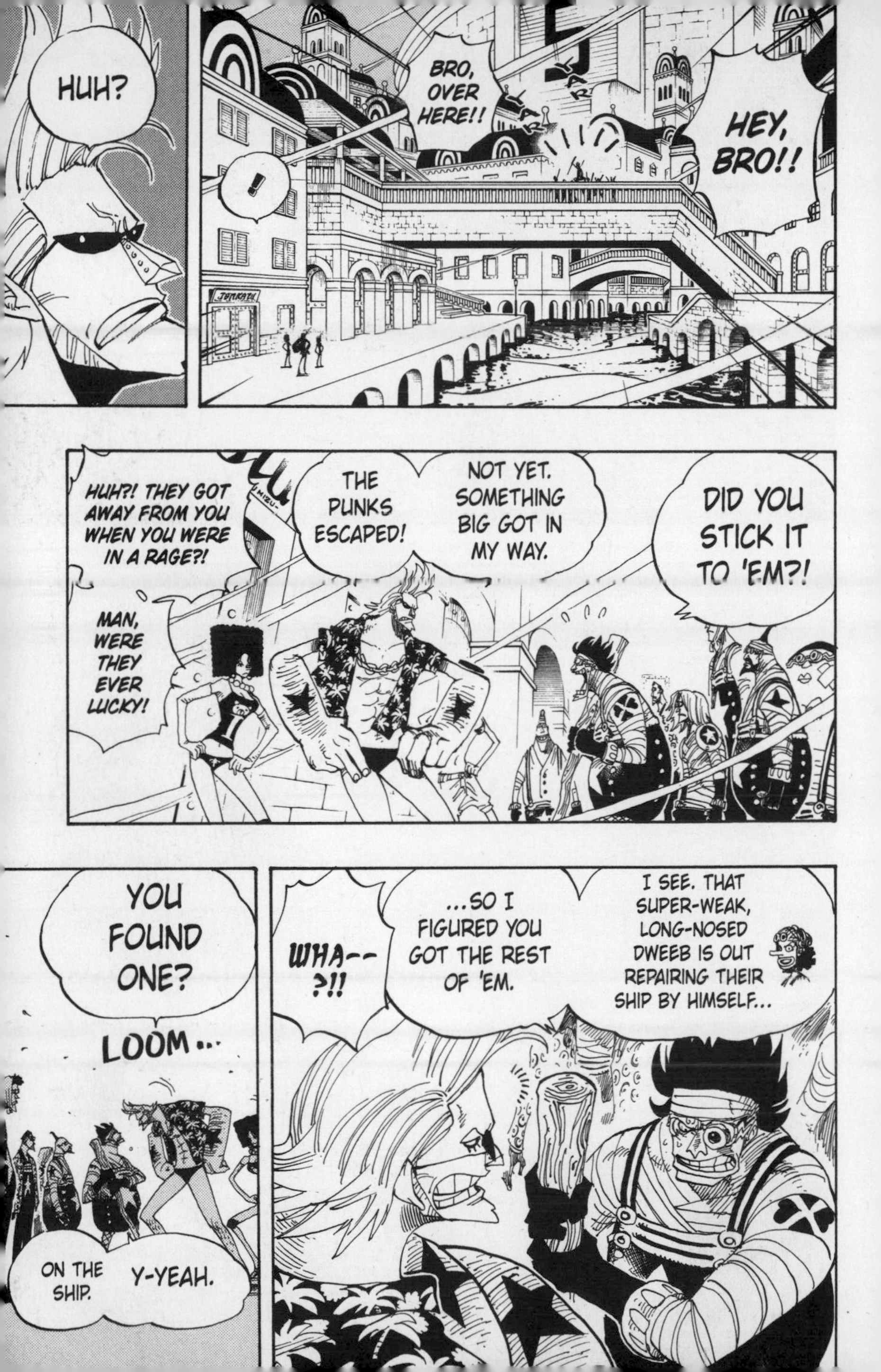
HEY, BRO!!
BRO, OVER HERE!!
!
HUH?
DID YOU STICK IT TO 'EM?!
NOT YET. SOMETHING BIG GOT IN MY WAY.
THE PUNKS ESCAPED!
HUH?! THEY GOT AWAY FROM YOU WHEN YOU WERE IN A RAGE?!
MAN, WERE THEY EVER LUCKY!
I SEE. THAT SUPER-WEAK, LONG-NOSED DWEEB IS OUT REPAIRING THEIR SHIP BY HIMSELF...
...SO I FIGURED YOU GOT THE REST OF 'EM.
WHA--?!!
YOU FOUND ONE?
LOOM...
Y-YEAH.
ON THE SHIP.

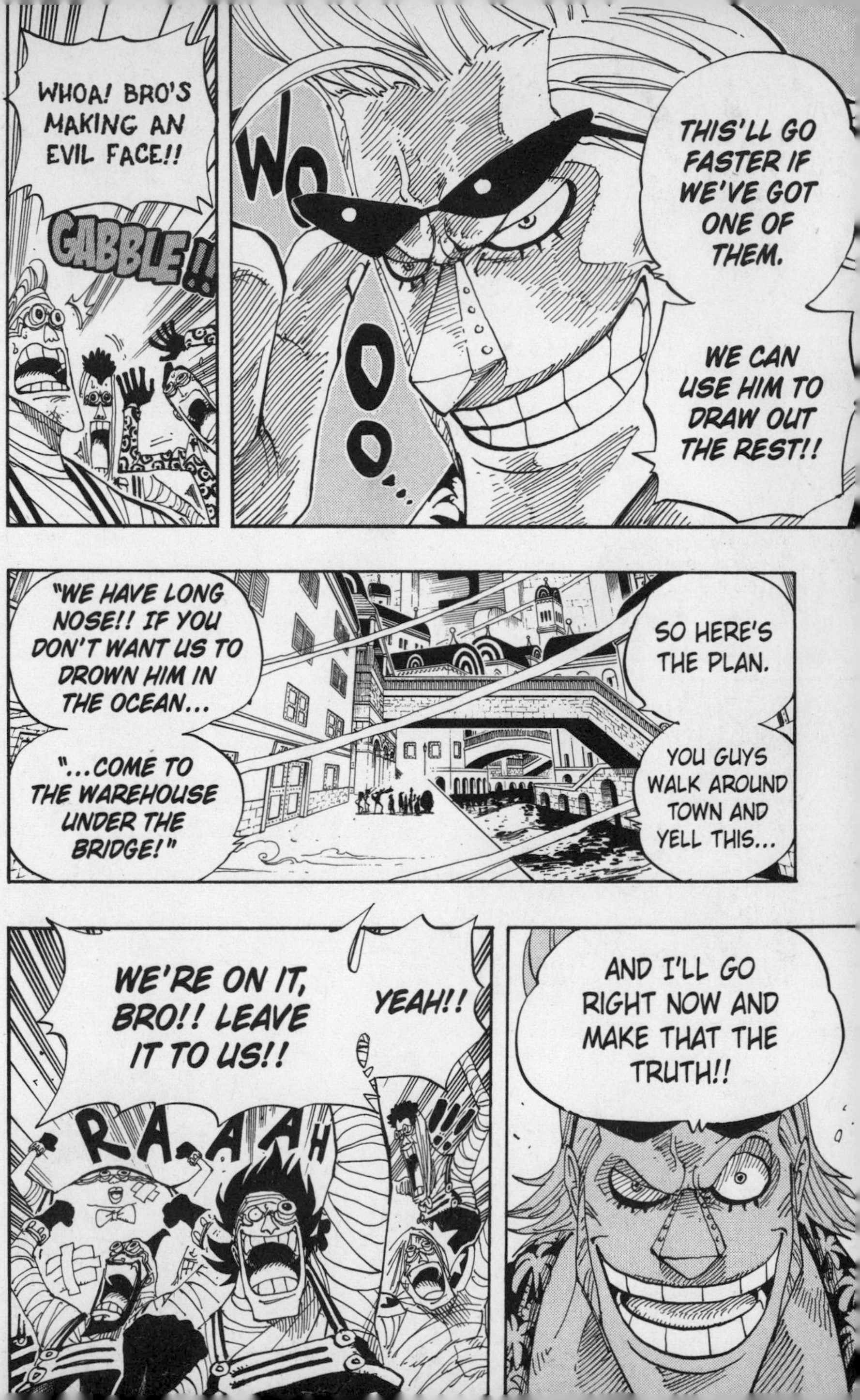
THIS'LL GO FASTER IF WE'VE GOT ONE OF THEM.
WE CAN USE HIM TO DRAW OUT THE REST!!
WOOOO...
WHOA! BRO'S MAKING AN EVIL FACE!!
GABBLE!!
SO HERE'S THE PLAN.
YOU GUYS WALK AROUND TOWN AND YELL THIS...
"WE HAVE LONG NOSE!! IF YOU DON'T WANT US TO DROWN HIM IN THE OCEAN...
"...COME TO THE WAREHOUSE UNDER THE BRIDGE!"
AND I'LL GO RIGHT NOW AND MAKE THAT THE TRUTH!!
YEAH!!
WE'RE ON IT, BRO!! LEAVE IT TO US!!
RAAAH
!!!

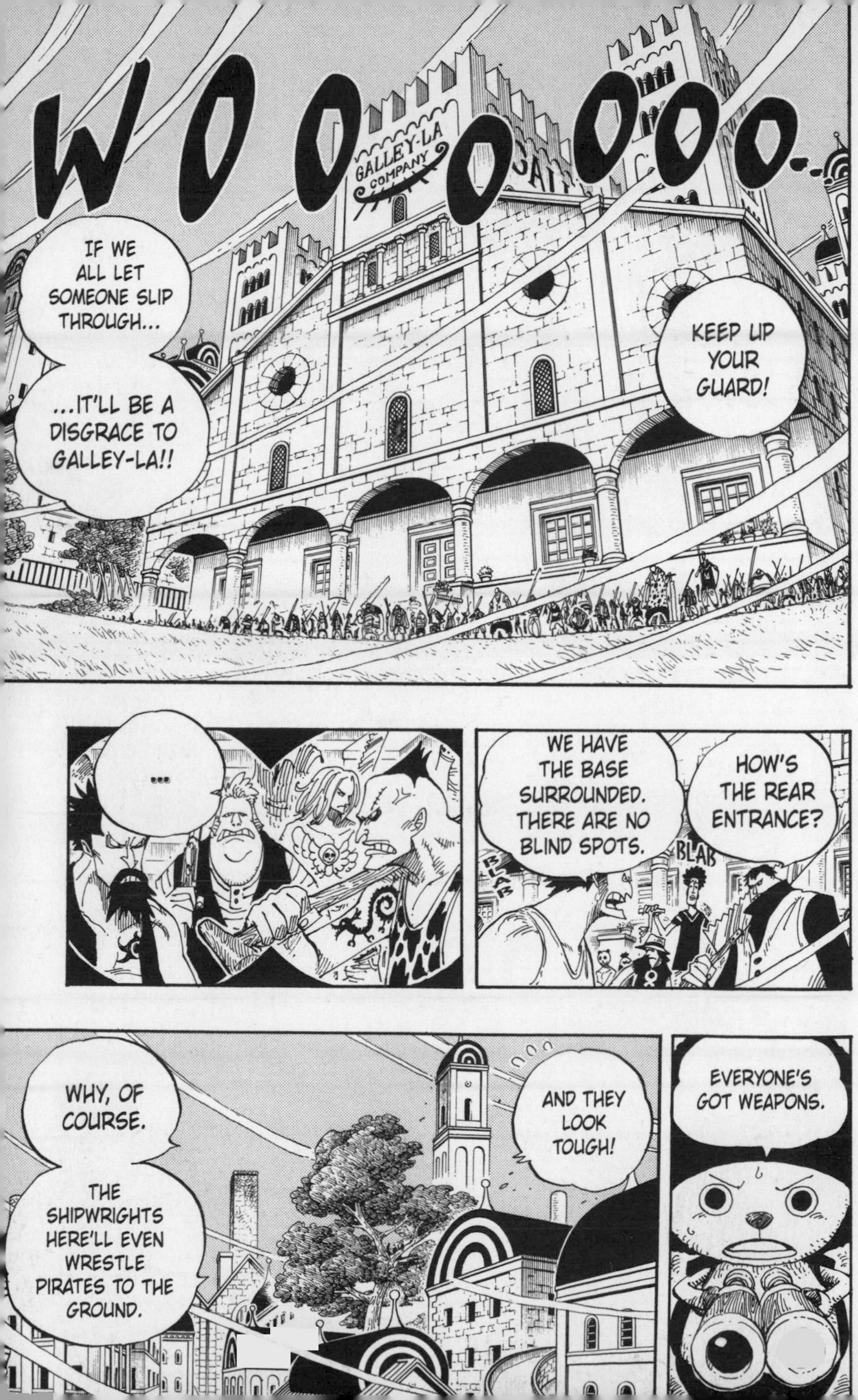
WOOOOOOO...
GALLEY-LA COMPANY
KEEP UP YOUR GUARD!
IF WE ALL LET SOMEONE SLIP THROUGH...
...IT'LL BE A DISGRACE TO GALLEY-LA!!
HOW'S THE REAR ENTRANCE?
WE HAVE THE BASE SURROUNDED. THERE ARE NO BLIND SPOTS.
BLAB
BLAB
...
EVERYONE'S GOT WEAPONS.
AND THEY LOOK TOUGH!
WHY, OF COURSE.
THE SHIPWRIGHTS HERE'LL EVEN WRESTLE PIRATES TO THE GROUND.

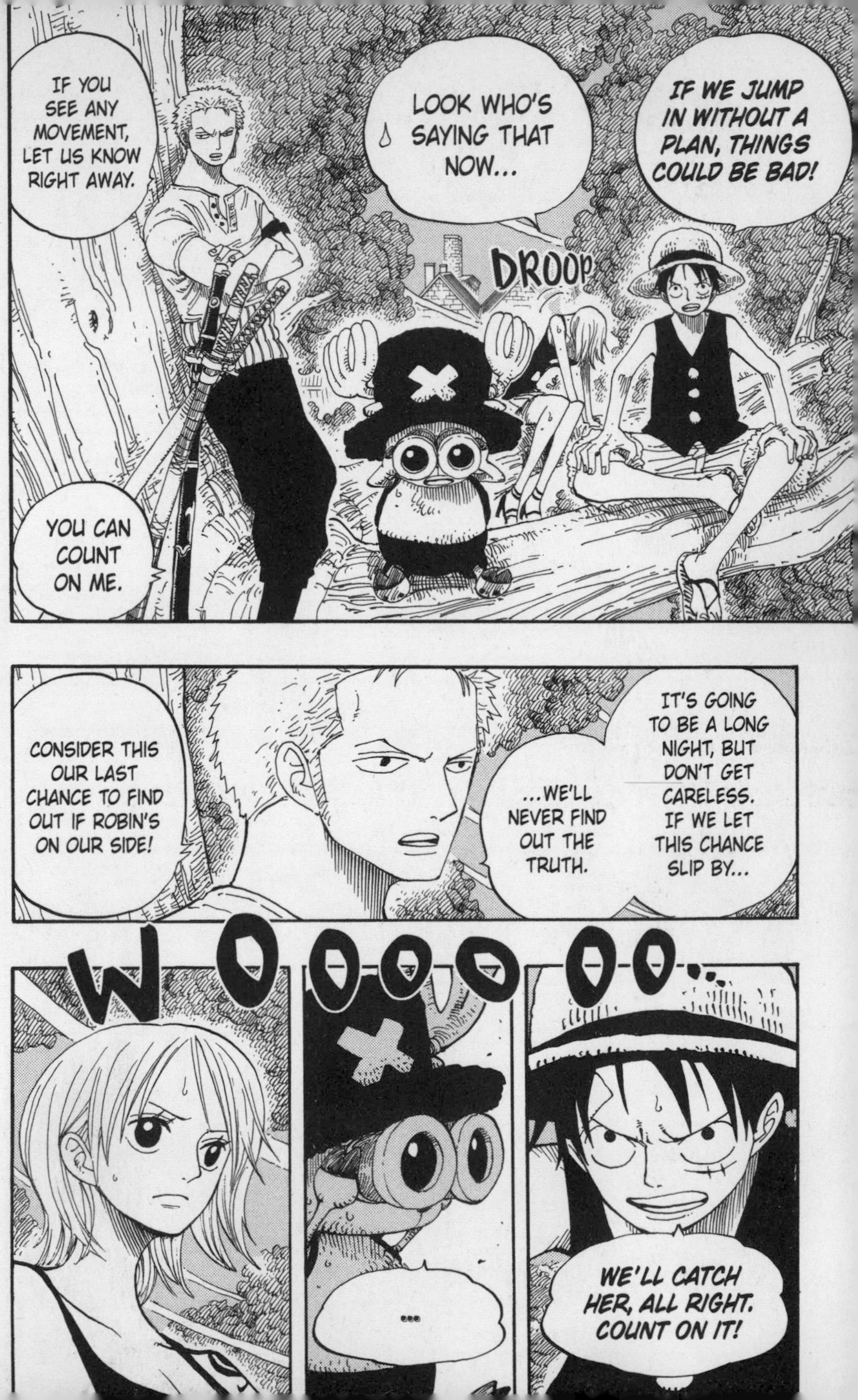
IF WE JUMP IN WITHOUT A PLAN, THINGS COULD BE BAD!
LOOK WHO'S SAYING THAT NOW...
DROOP
IF YOU SEE ANY MOVEMENT, LET US KNOW RIGHT AWAY.
YOU CAN COUNT ON ME.
IT'S GOING TO BE A LONG NIGHT, BUT DON'T GET CARELESS. IF WE LET THIS CHANCE SLIP BY...
...WE'LL NEVER FIND OUT THE TRUTH.
CONSIDER THIS OUR LAST CHANCE TO FIND OUT IF ROBIN'S ON OUR SIDE!
WOOOOOO...
WE'LL CATCH HER, ALL RIGHT. COUNT ON IT!
...

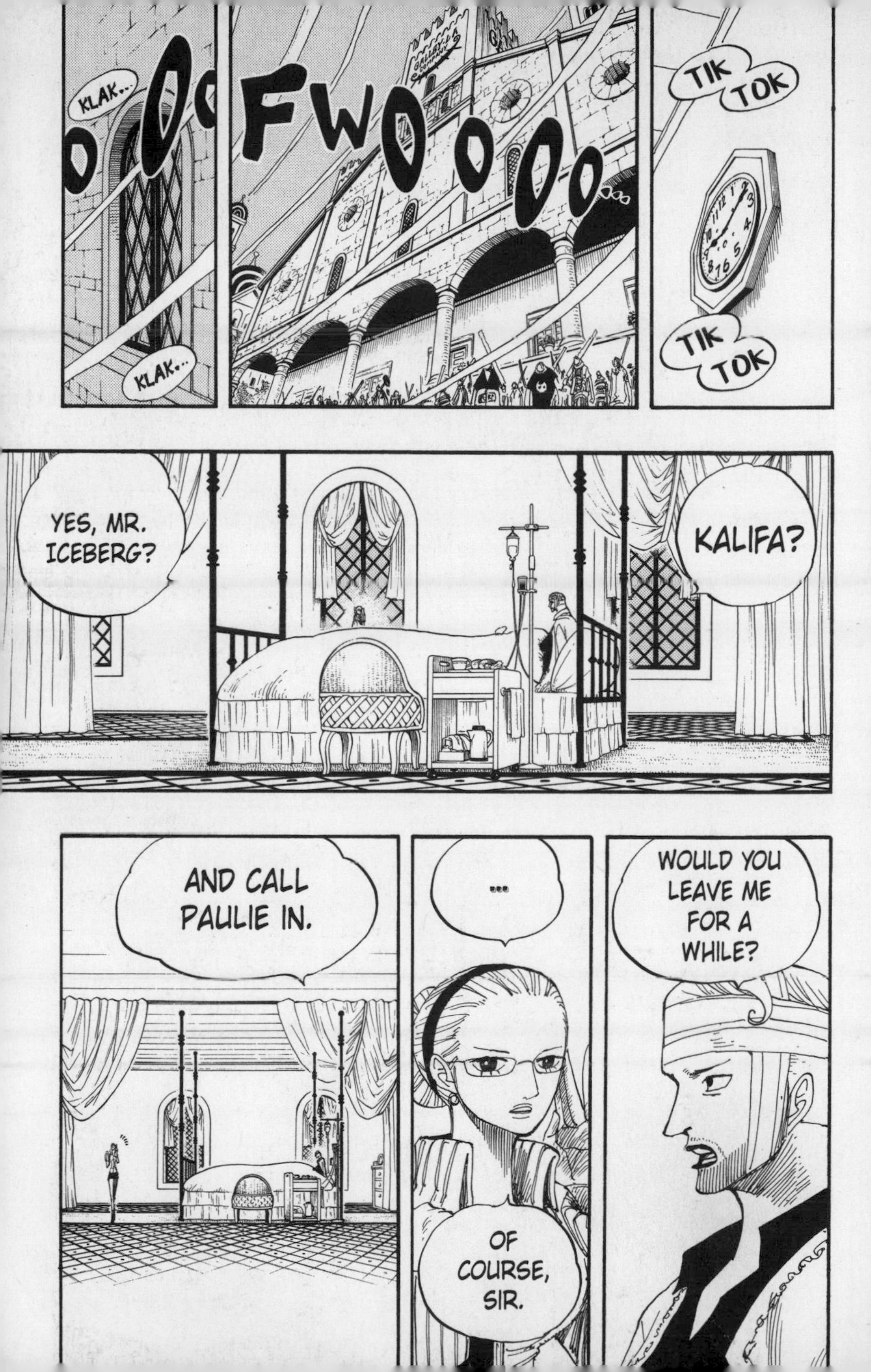
TIK TOK
TIK TOK
FWOOOOO
KLAK...
KLAK...
KALIFA?
YES, MR. ICEBERG?
WOULD YOU LEAVE ME FOR A WHILE?
...
OF COURSE, SIR.
AND CALL PAULIE IN.

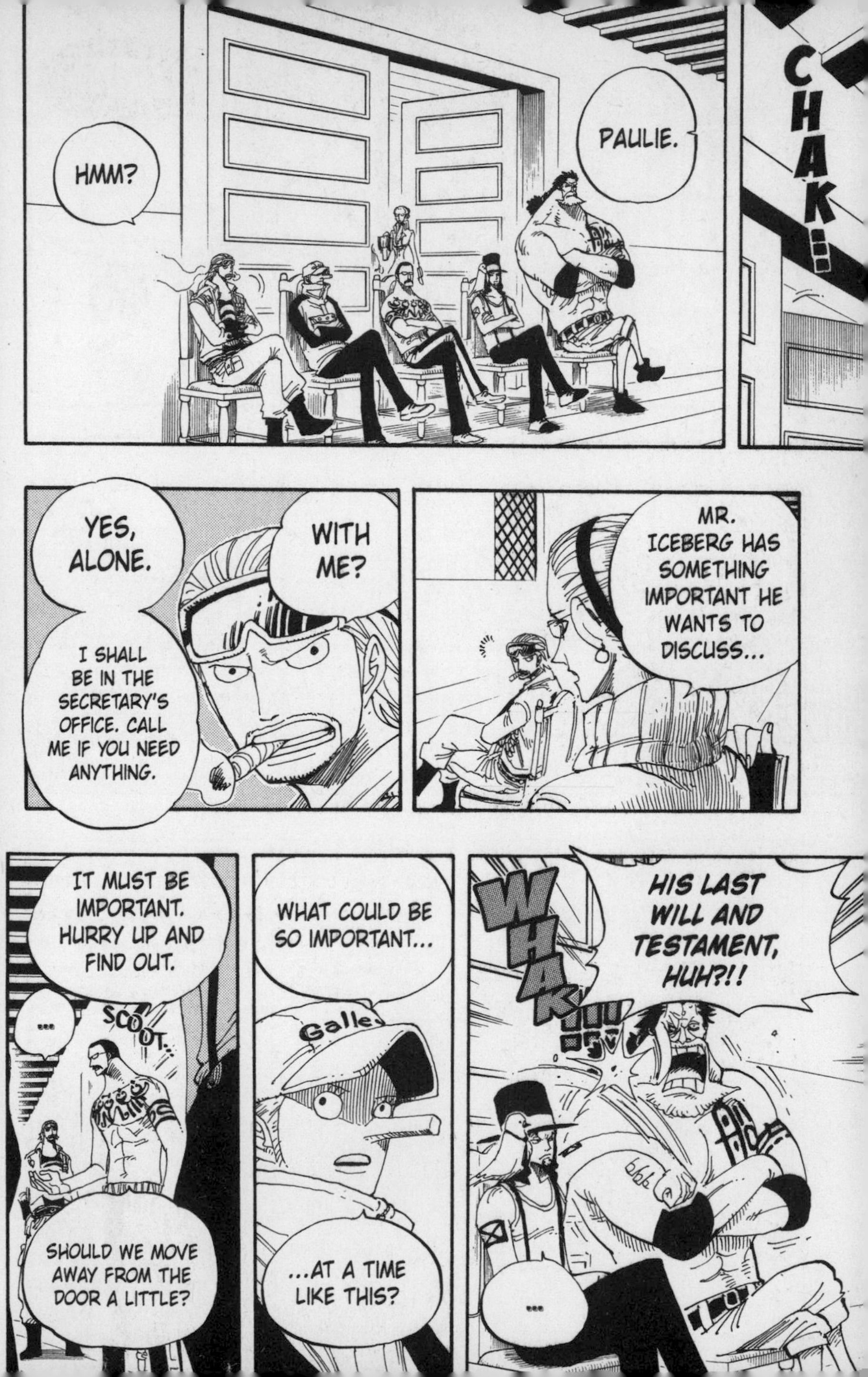
CHAK...
PAULIE.
HMM?
MR. ICEBERG HAS SOMETHING IMPORTANT HE WANTS TO DISCUSS...
WITH ME?
YES, ALONE.
I SHALL BE IN THE SECRETARY'S OFFICE. CALL ME IF YOU NEED ANYTHING.
HIS LAST WILL AND TESTAMENT, HUH?!!
WHAK
...
WHAT COULD BE SO IMPORTANT...
...AT A TIME LIKE THIS?
IT MUST BE IMPORTANT. HURRY UP AND FIND OUT.
...
SCOOT...
SHOULD WE MOVE AWAY FROM THE DOOR A LITTLE?

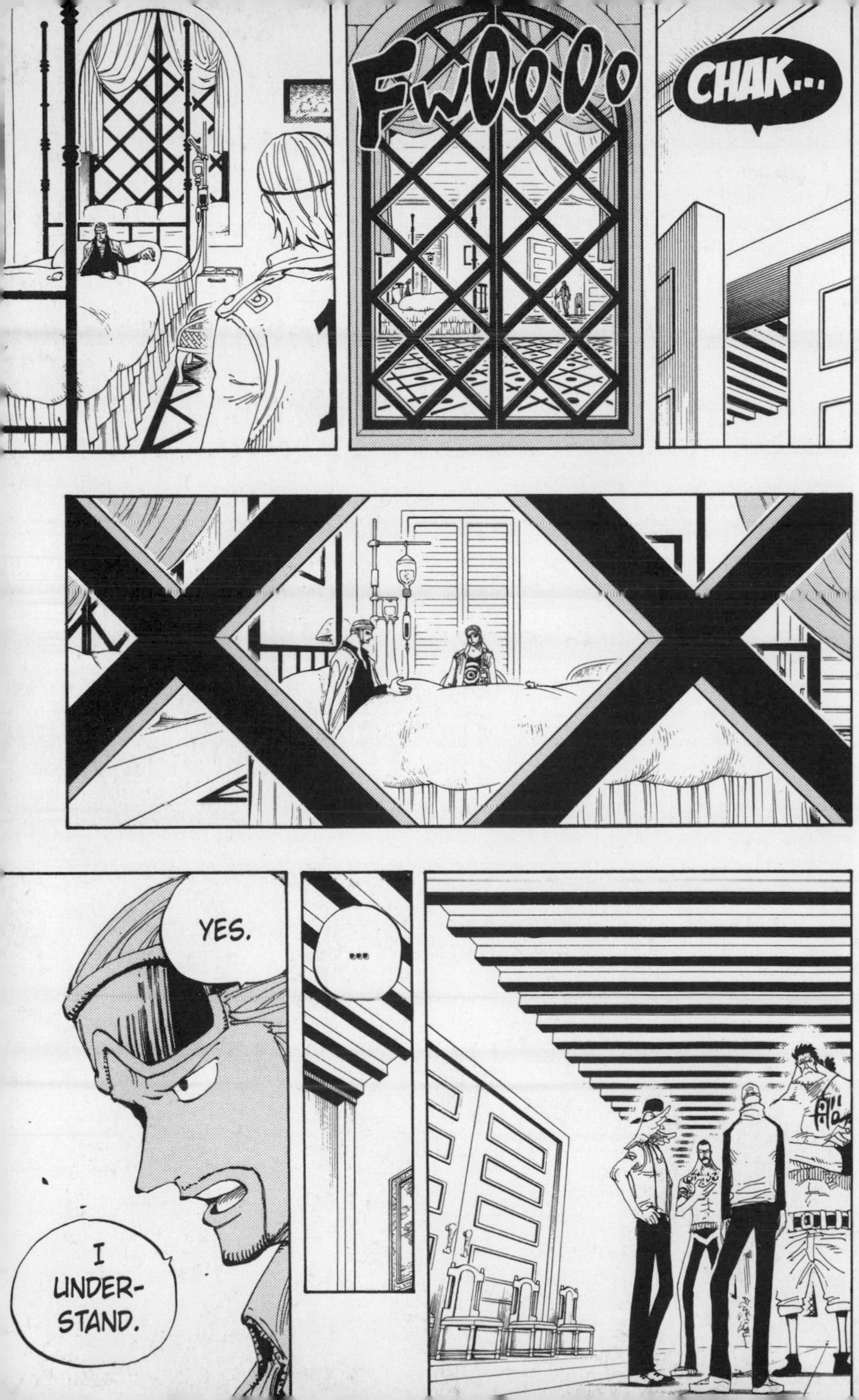
CHAK...
FWOOOO
...
YES.
I UNDER-STAND.

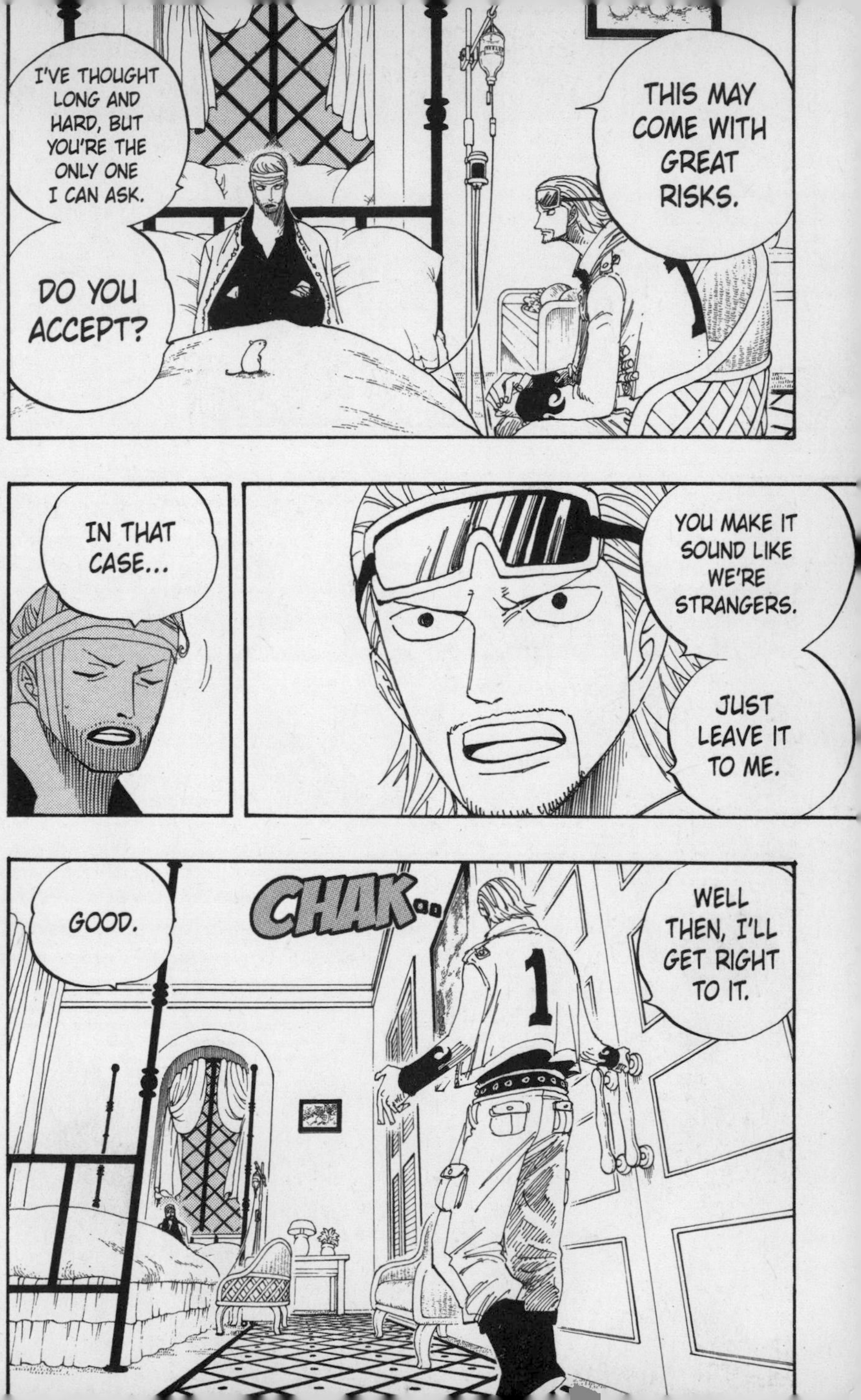
THIS MAY COME WITH GREAT RISKS.
I'VE THOUGHT LONG AND HARD, BUT YOU'RE THE ONLY ONE I CAN ASK.
DO YOU ACCEPT?
YOU MAKE IT SOUND LIKE WE'RE STRANGERS.
JUST LEAVE IT TO ME.
IN THAT CASE...
WELL THEN, I'LL GET RIGHT TO IT.
CHAK..
GOOD.

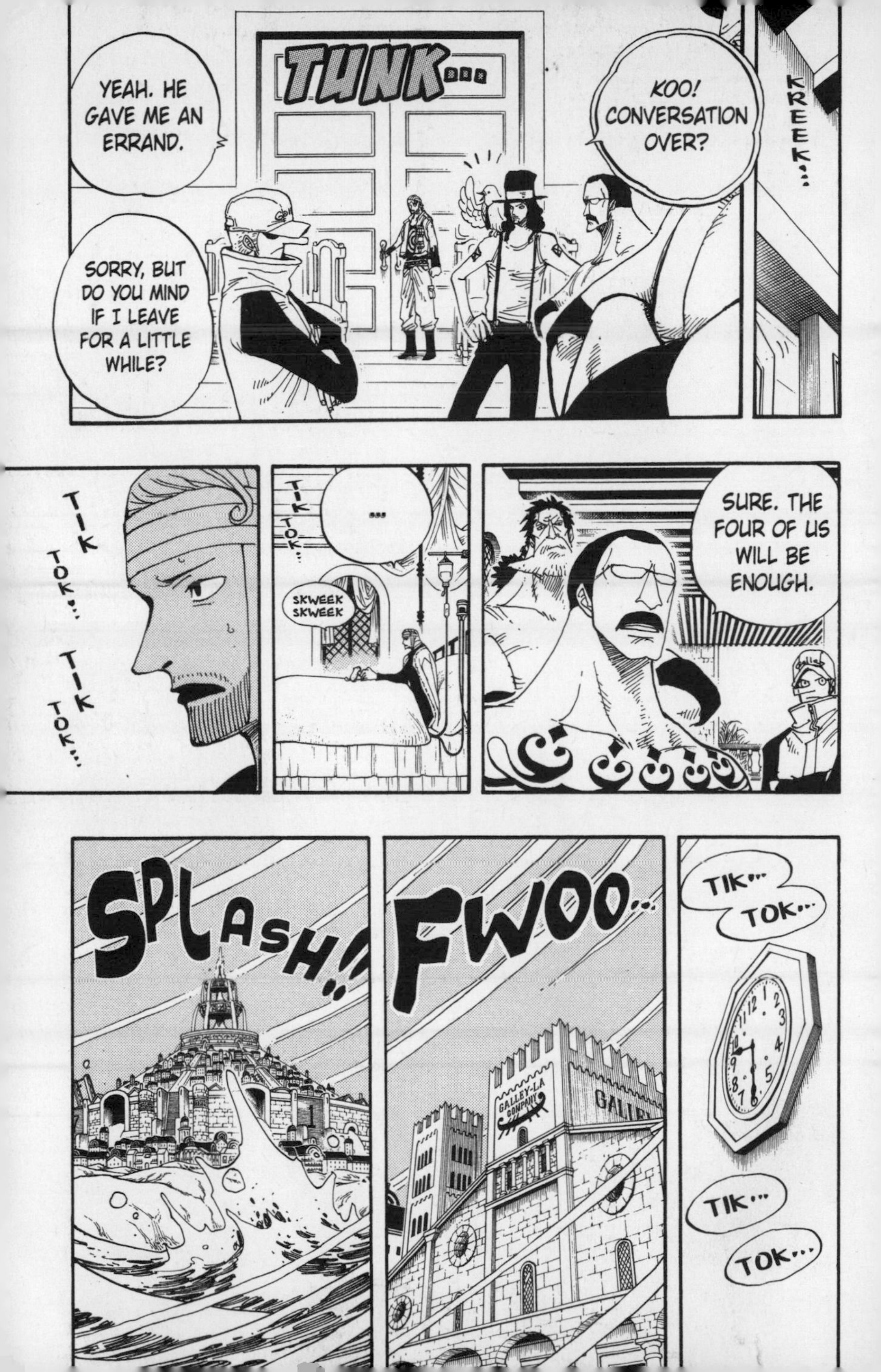
KREEK...
KOO! CONVERSATION OVER?
TUNK...
YEAH. HE GAVE ME AN ERRAND.
SORRY, BUT DO YOU MIND IF I LEAVE FOR A LITTLE WHILE?
SURE. THE FOUR OF US WILL BE ENOUGH.
TIK TOK...
...
SKWEEK SKWEEK
TIK TOK... TIK TOK...
TIK... TOK...
TIK... TOK...
FWOO...
SPLASH!!
GALLEY-LA COMPANY

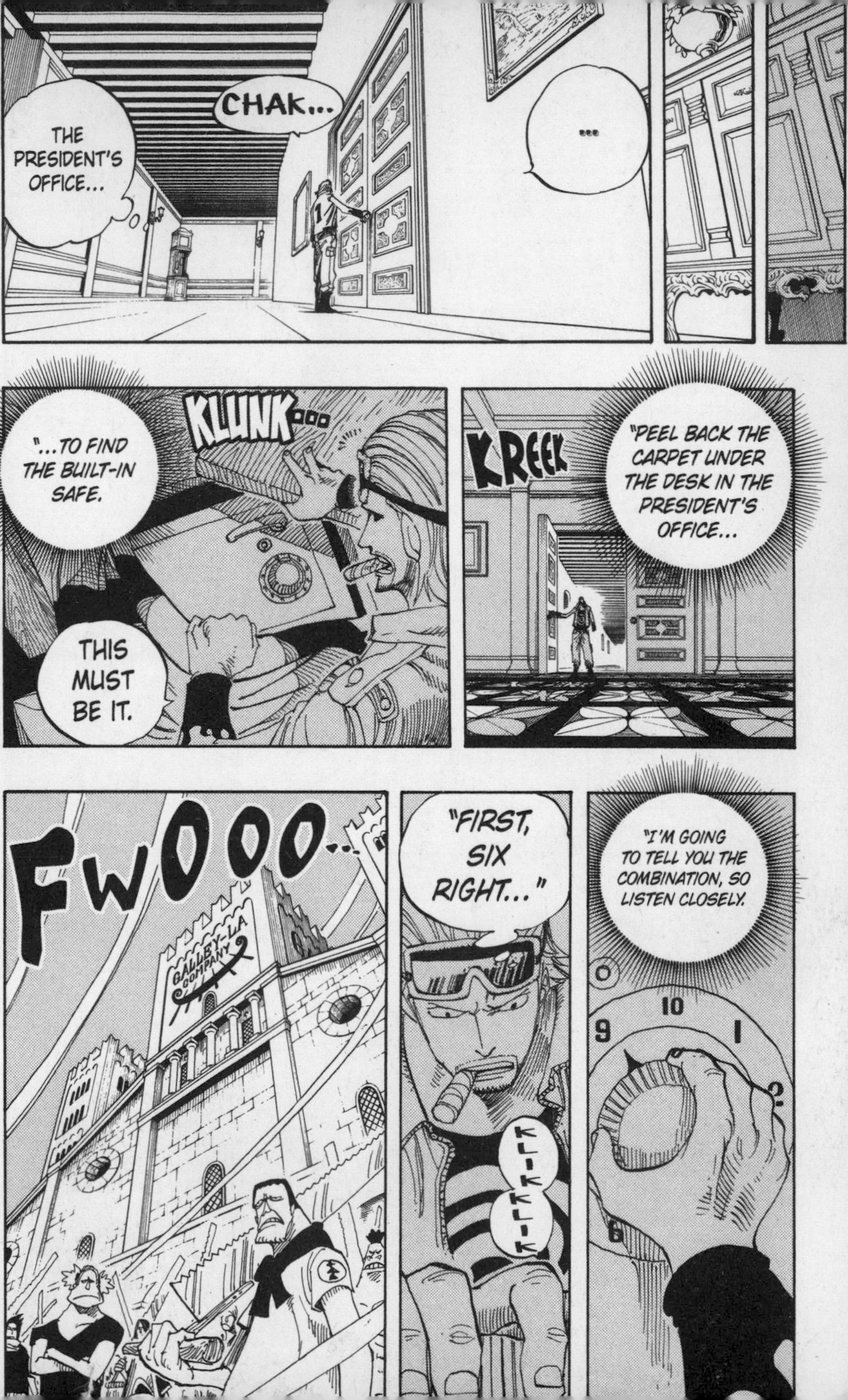
...
CHAK...
THE PRESIDENT'S OFFICE...
"PEEL BACK THE CARPET UNDER THE DESK IN THE PRESIDENT'S OFFICE...
KREEK
KLUNK...
"...TO FIND THE BUILT-IN SAFE.
THIS MUST BE IT.
"I'M GOING TO TELL YOU THE COMBINATION, SO LISTEN CLOSELY.
"FIRST, SIX RIGHT..."
KLIK KLIK KLIK
FWOOO...
GALLEY-LA COMPANY

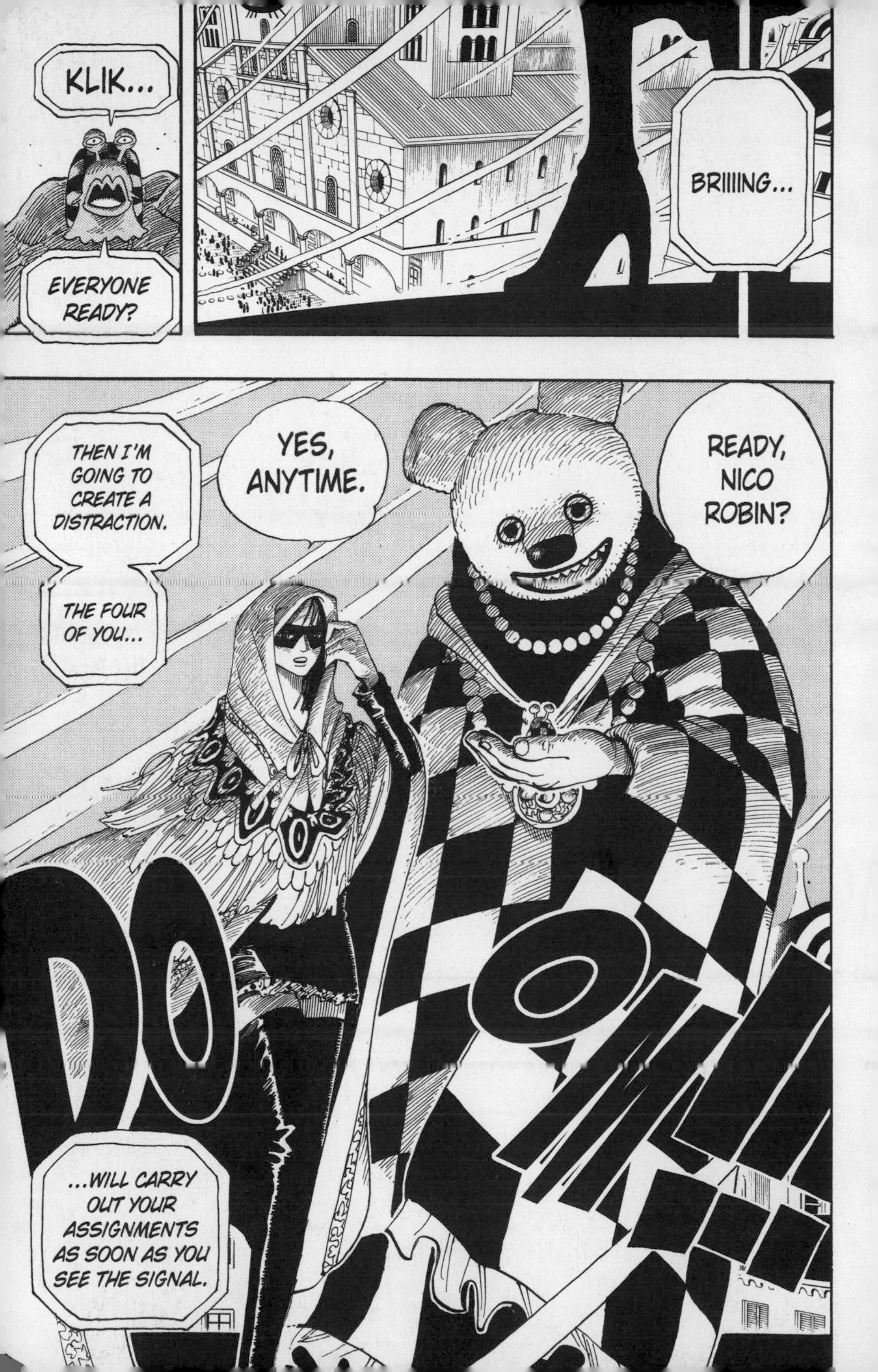
BRIIIING...
KLIK...
EVERYONE READY?
READY, NICO ROBIN?
YES, ANYTIME.
THEN I'M GOING TO CREATE A DISTRACTION.
THE FOUR OF YOU...
...WILL CARRY OUT YOUR ASSIGNMENTS AS SOON AS YOU SEE THE SIGNAL.
DOOM

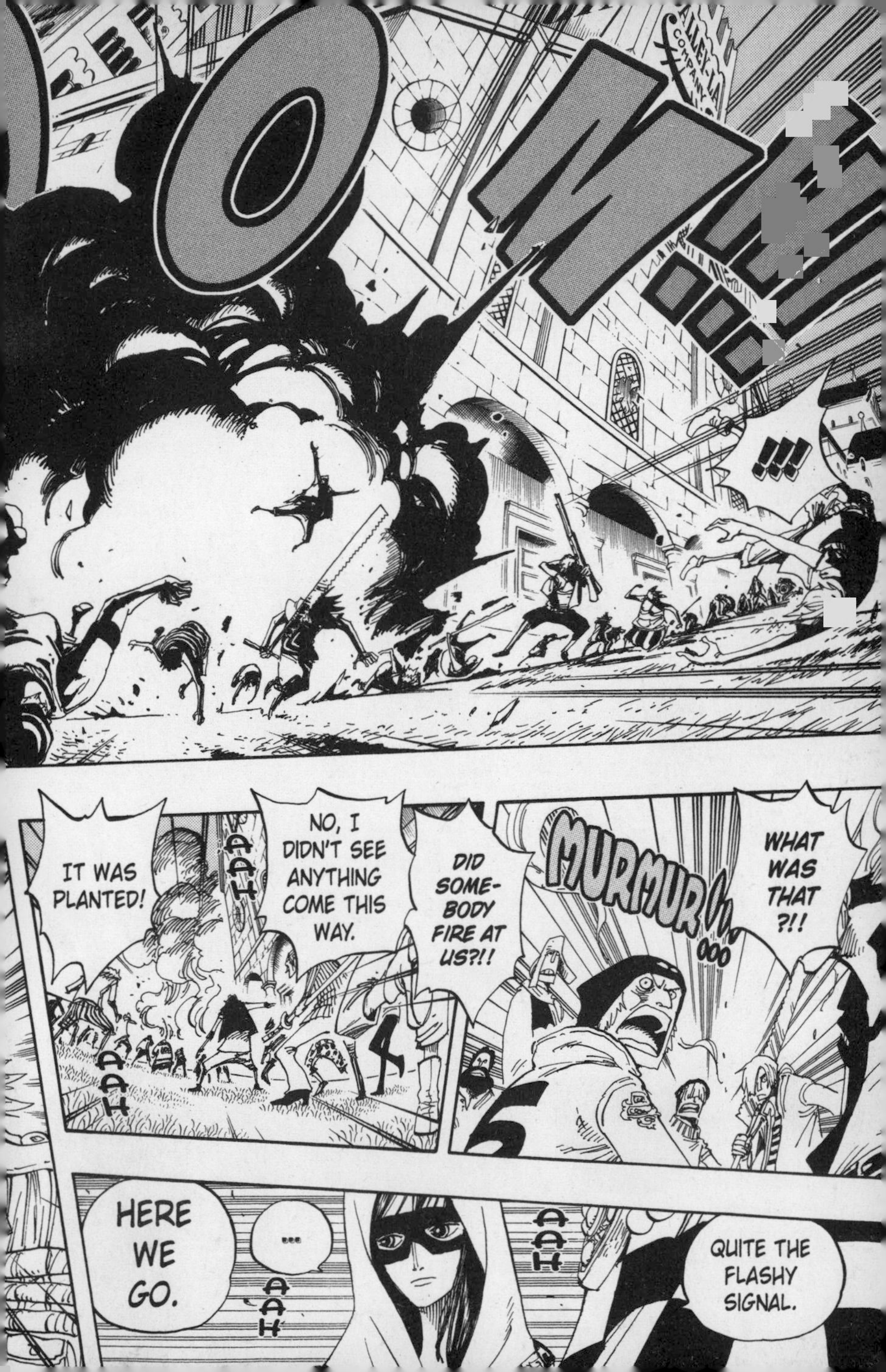
!!!
WHAT WAS THAT?!!
MURMUR
DID SOME-BODY FIRE AT US?!!
NO, I DIDN'T SEE ANYTHING COME THIS WAY.
AAAH
IT WAS PLANTED!
AAAH
QUITE THE FLASHY SIGNAL.
AAAH
AAAH
...
HERE WE GO.

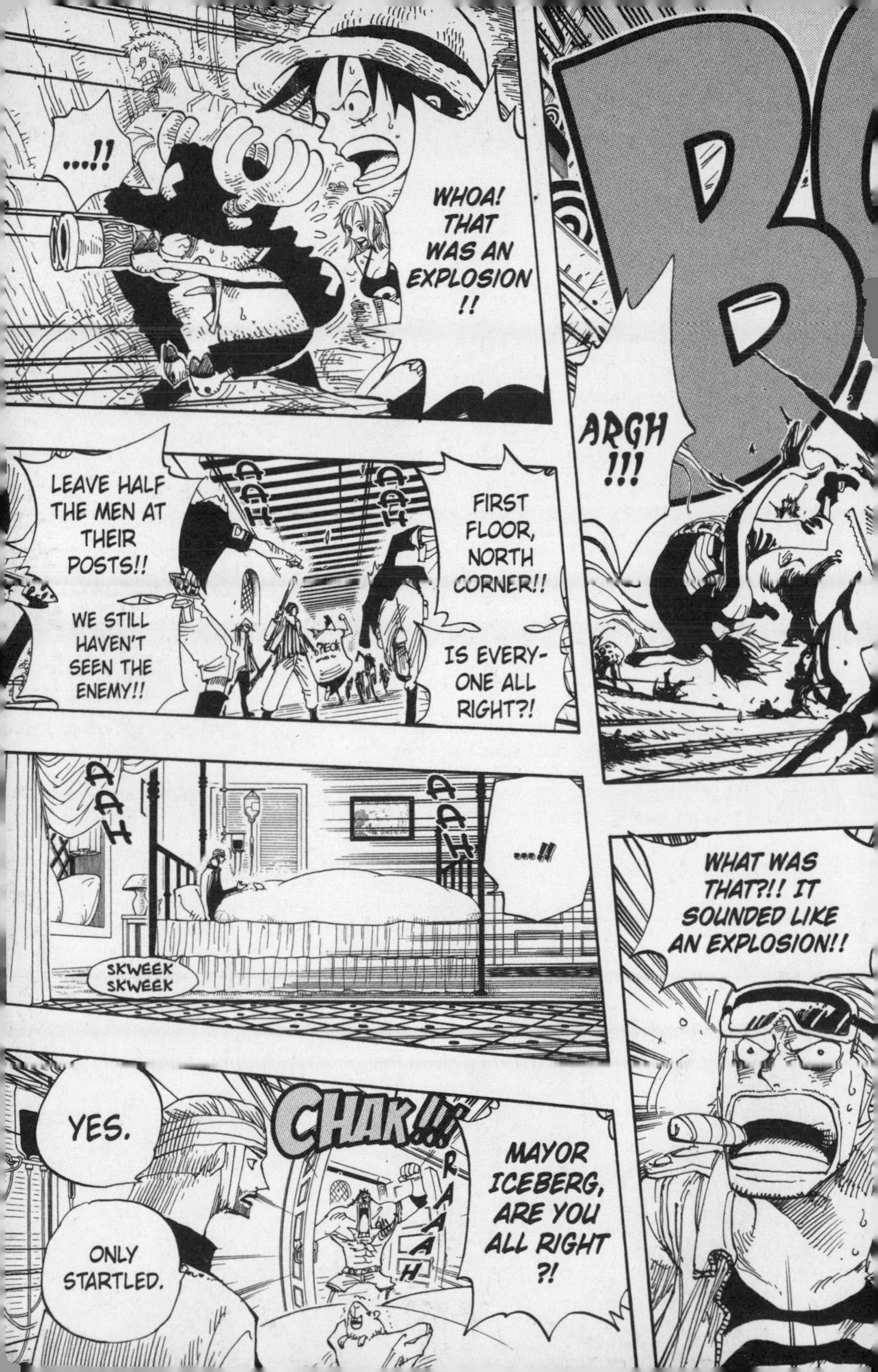
BO
ARGH!!!
WHOA! THAT WAS AN EXPLOSION!!
...!!
FIRST FLOOR, NORTH CORNER!!
AAH
AAH
IS EVERY-ONE ALL RIGHT?!
LEAVE HALF THE MEN AT THEIR POSTS!!
WE STILL HAVEN'T SEEN THE ENEMY!!
WHAT WAS THAT?!! IT SOUNDED LIKE AN EXPLOSION!!
...!!
AAH
AAH
SKWEEK SKWEEK
MAYOR ICEBERG, ARE YOU ALL RIGHT?!
CHAK!!!
RAAAAH
YES.
ONLY STARTLED.

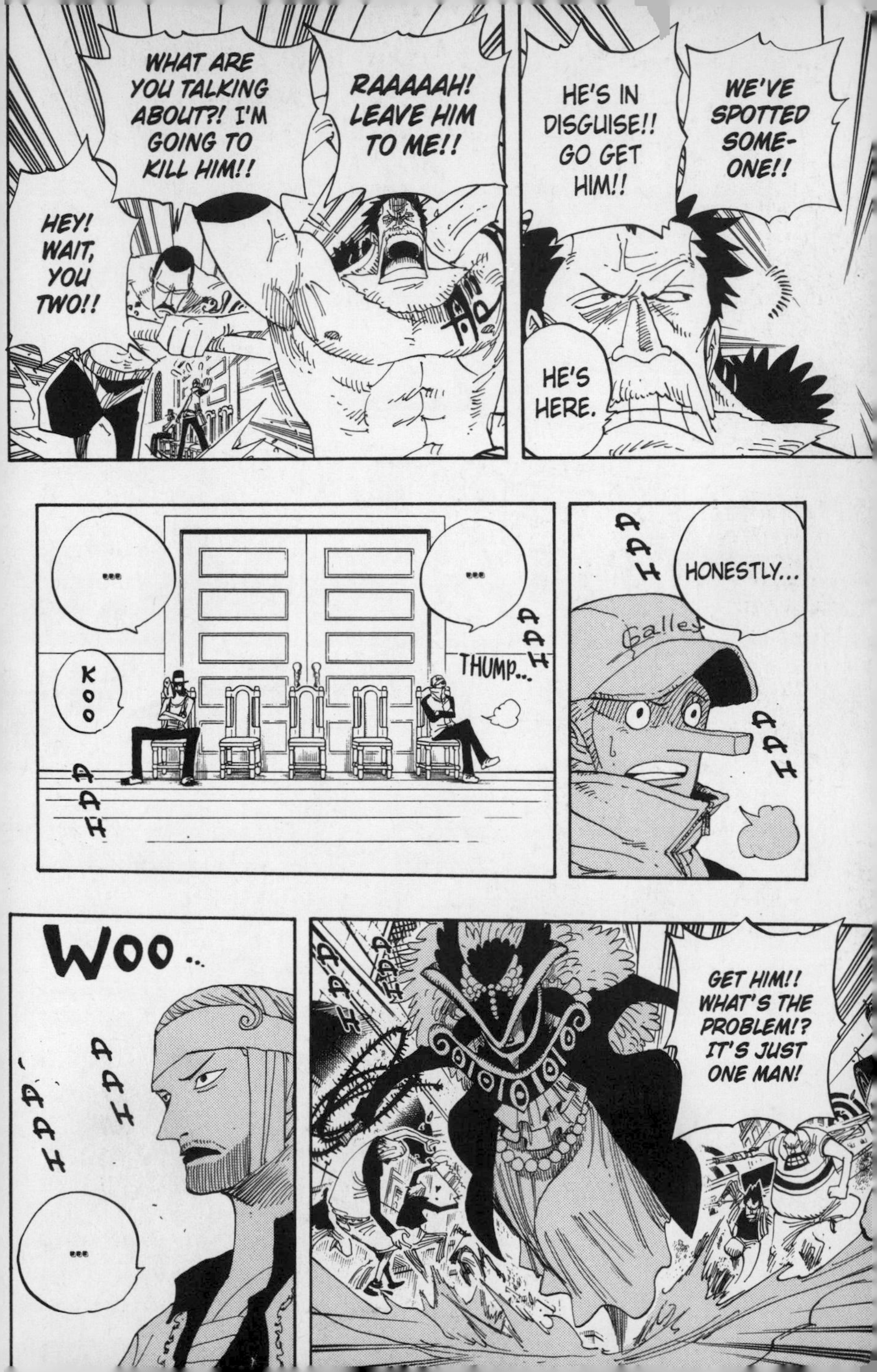
WE'VE SPOTTED SOME-ONE!!
HE'S IN DISGUISE!! GO GET HIM!!
HE'S HERE.
RAAAAAH! LEAVE HIM TO ME!!
WHAT ARE YOU TALKING ABOUT?! I'M GOING TO KILL HIM!!
HEY! WAIT, YOU TWO!!
AAH
HONESTLY...
AAH
...
AAH
THUMP...
...
KOO
AAH
GET HIM!! WHAT'S THE PROBLEM!? IT'S JUST ONE MAN!
WOO..
AAH
AAH
...

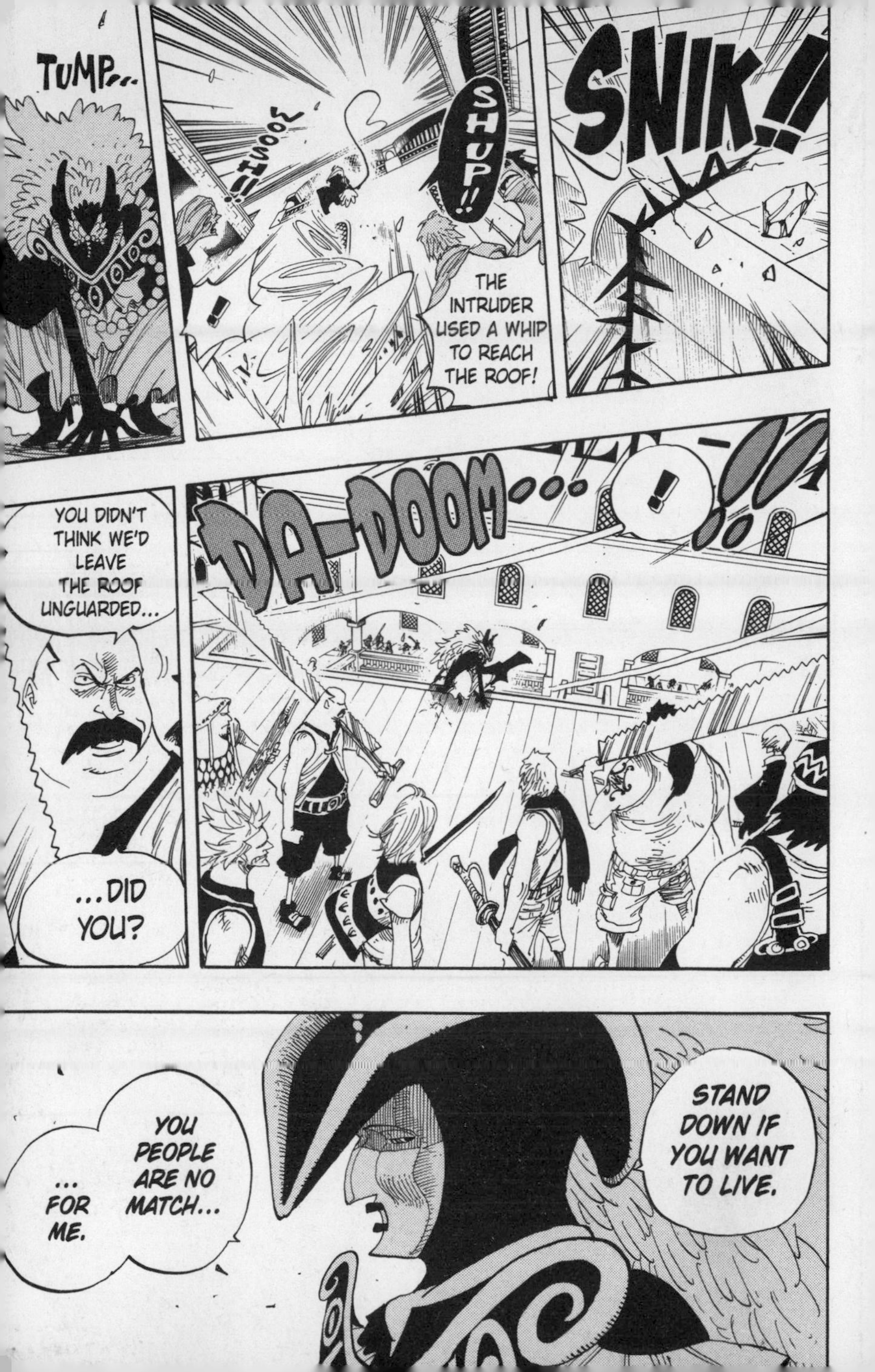
SNIK!!
SHUP!!
WOOSH!!
THE INTRUDER USED A WHIP TO REACH THE ROOF!
TUMP...
DA-DOOM...
!!
YOU DIDN'T THINK WE'D LEAVE THE ROOF UNGUARDED...
...DID YOU?
STAND DOWN IF YOU WANT TO LIVE.
YOU PEOPLE ARE NO MATCH...
... FOR ME.

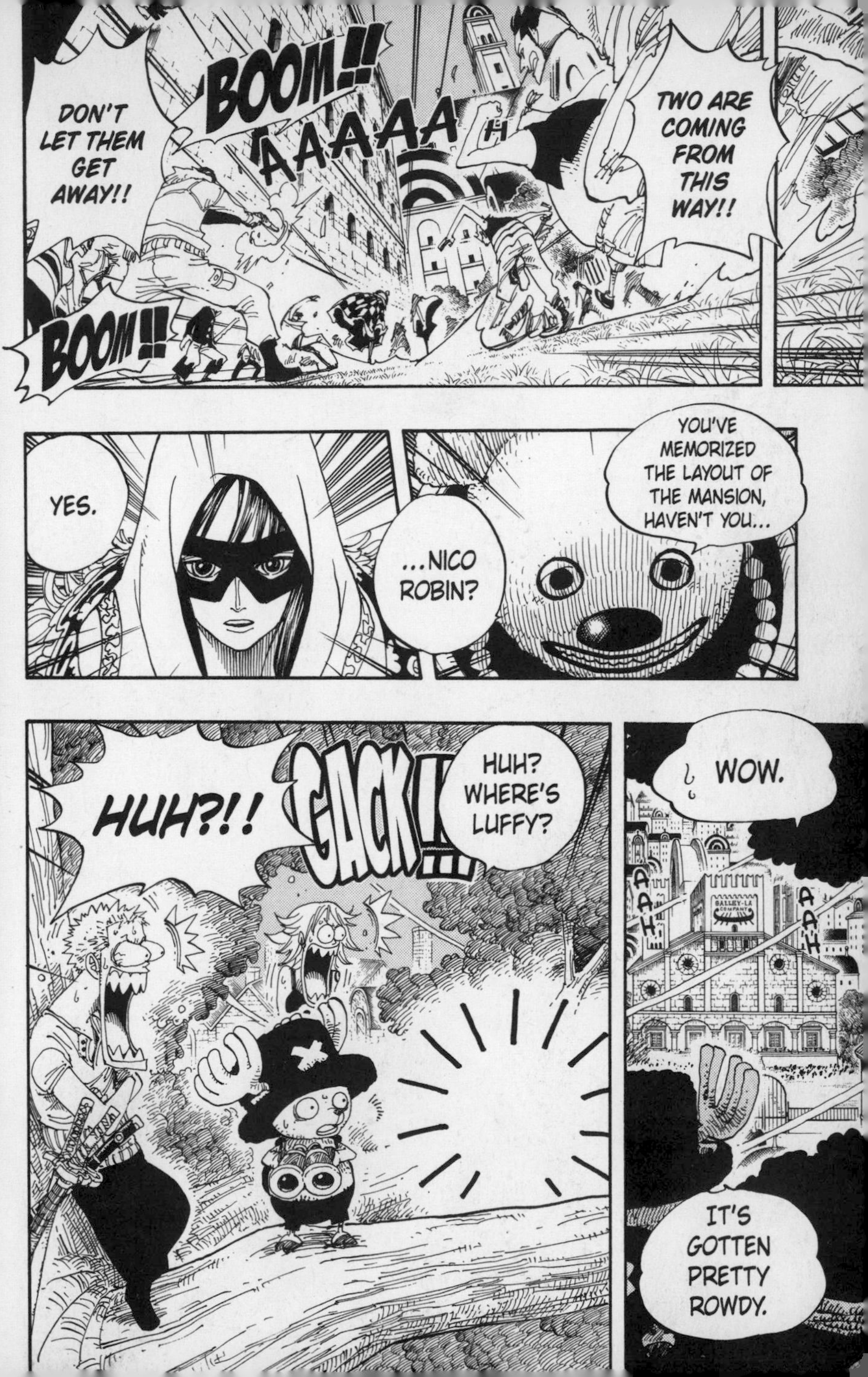
TWO ARE COMING FROM THIS WAY!!
BOOM!!
AAAAAH
DON'T LET THEM GET AWAY!!
BOOM!!
YOU'VE MEMORIZED THE LAYOUT OF THE MANSION, HAVEN'T YOU...
...NICO ROBIN?
YES.
WOW.
GALLEY-LA COMPANY
IT'S GOTTEN PRETTY ROWDY.
HUH? WHERE'S LUFFY?
GACK!!!
HUH?!!

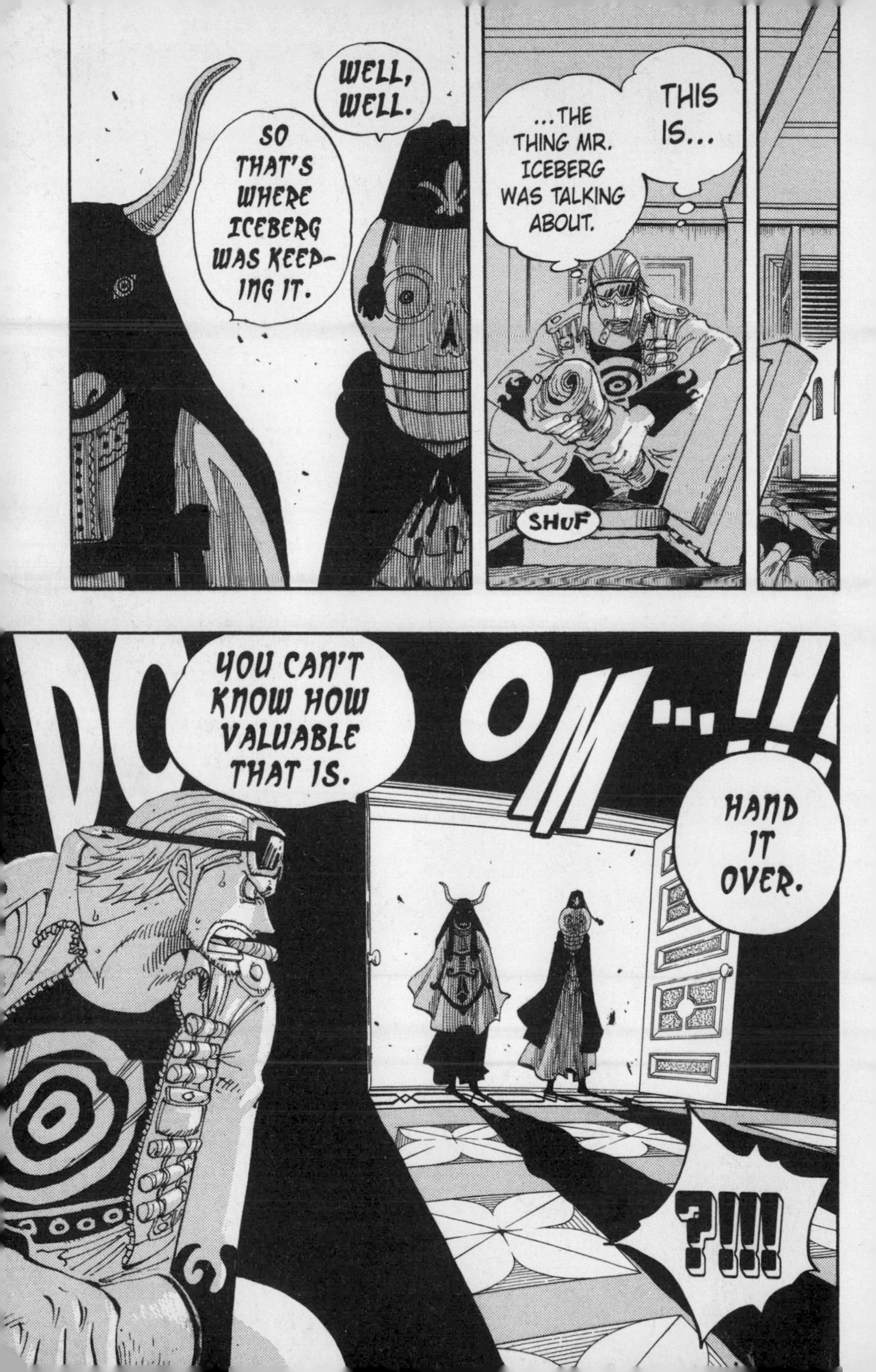
THIS IS...
...THE THING MR. ICEBERG WAS TALKING ABOUT.
SHUF
WELL, WELL.
SO THAT'S WHERE ICEBERG WAS KEEPING IT.
DO
OM..!!
YOU CAN'T KNOW HOW VALUABLE THAT IS.
HAND IT OVER.
?!!!

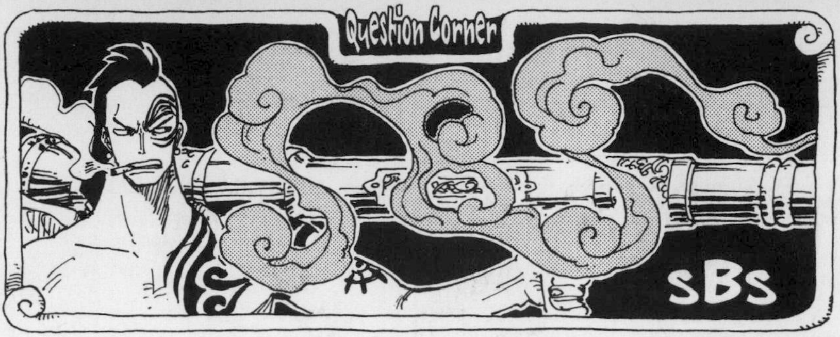
Question Corner
SBS

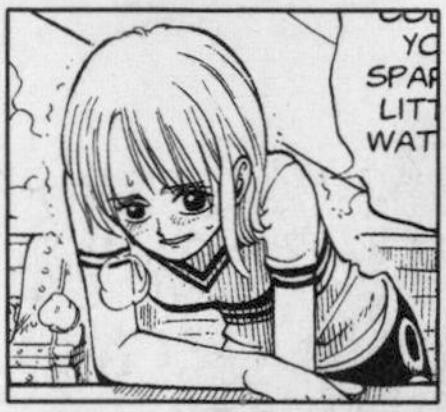

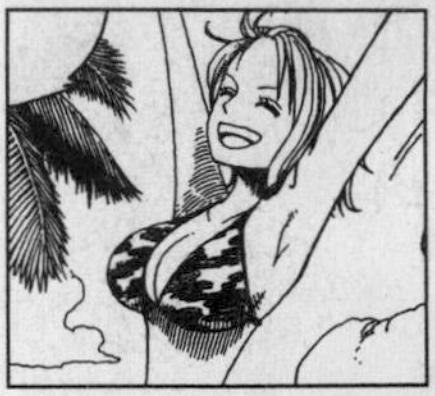

Q: Hello, Oda Sensei. Gosh, Nami is just too cute! That beauty, that figure! I'm just crazy about her. ♡
By the way, hasn't Nami gotten curvier compared to the way she was in volume 1?

--Saori-chan

A: Yeah. I get that question a lot. But Nami's 18; if you think about it, she's still growing. She's not done yet! I'll try my best!! (⬅?)
Robin's still only 28, too! I'll try my best!! (⬅?)

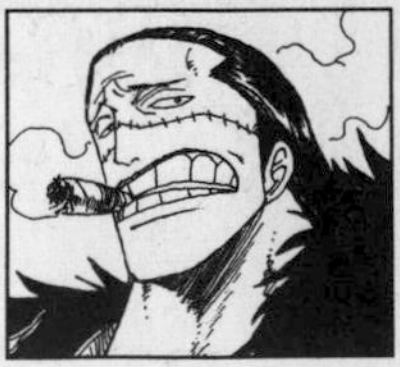

Q: Hello, question for ya. In *One Piece*, what do you base the bounties on? Are they based on strength? If that's the case, then isn't about 80 million berries too low for Crocodile? Or does it get higher the more evil you've done? Or was that a mistake on your part? Because of this matter, a forehead-flicking free-for-all is playing itself out all over my school. Please help me!!

--Master Donuts

A: Yes, if you think hard about this, it's actually a difficult problem. The Seven Warlords of the Sea are allied with the government, and when a pirate joined up, his bounty was cancelled. For this reason, the pirates of the Seven Warlords of the Sea have former bounties of _____ berries recorded, but Baroque Works was secretly formed after Crocodile became one of the Seven Warlords of the Sea, so the added level of danger isn't included into the calculation of the bounty. If we factored all of that in for Crocodile, his bounty would probably jump to at least twice its current 81 million berries.

Chapter 343: CIPHER POL NO. 9

TEXT ABOVE GEDATSU READS "BATHS"--ED.

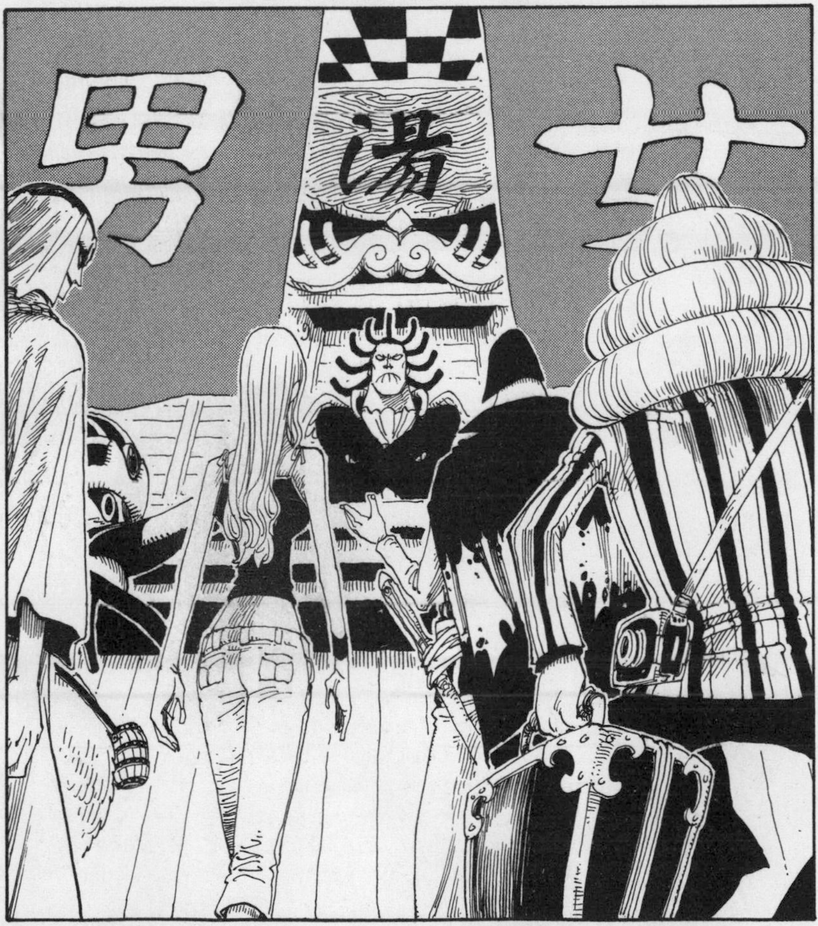
女
湯
男

GEDATSU'S UNEXPECTED LIFE ON THE BLUE SEA, VOL. 27:
"THE PRINCESS AND HER ENTOURAGE PAY A VISIT"

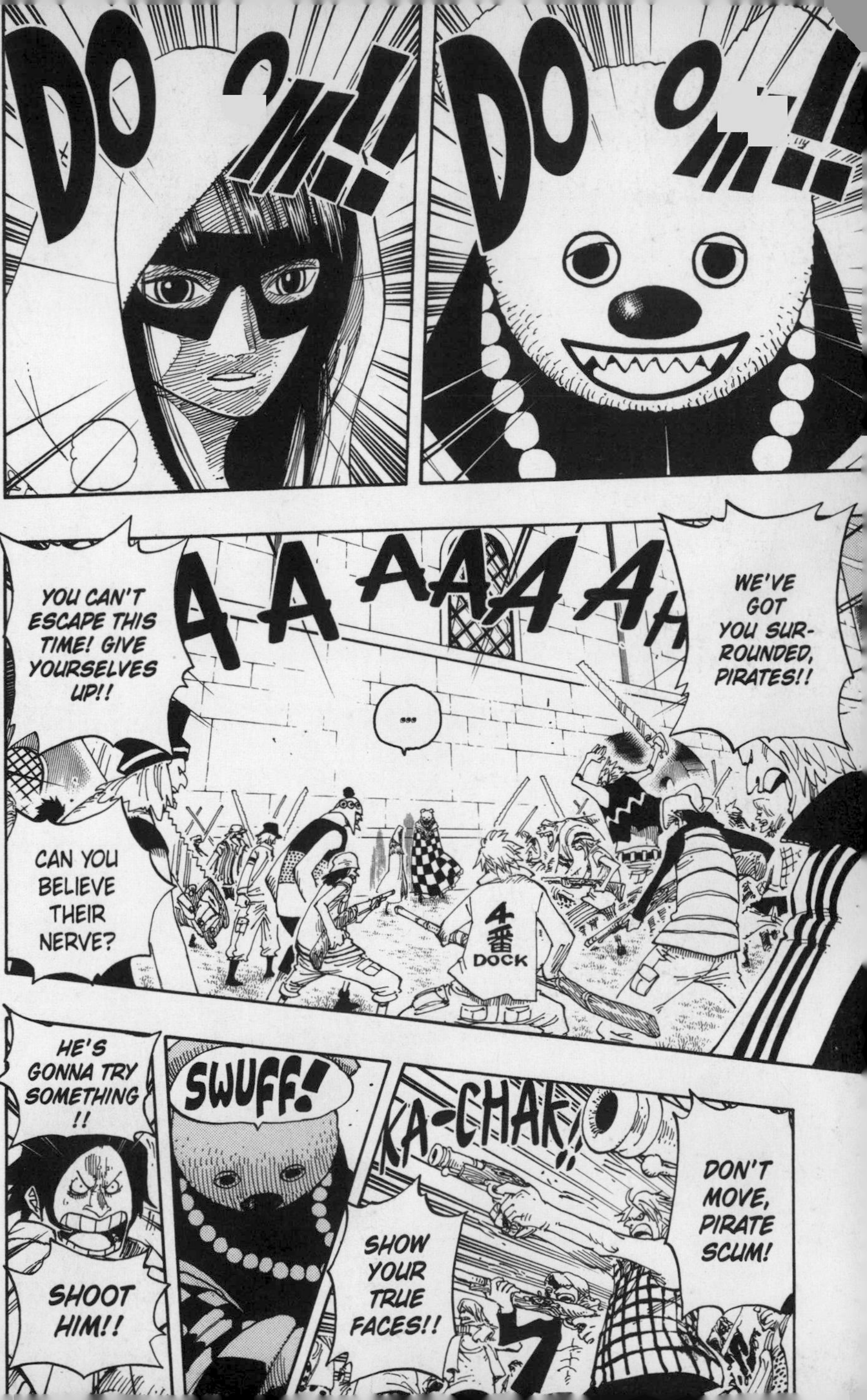
DO O!!
DO ON!!
WE'VE GOT YOU SUR-ROUNDED, PIRATES!!
AAAAAAH
YOU CAN'T ESCAPE THIS TIME! GIVE YOURSELVES UP!!
...
CAN YOU BELIEVE THEIR NERVE?
4番 DOCK
DON'T MOVE, PIRATE SCUM!
KA-CHAK
SHOW YOUR TRUE FACES!!
SWUFF!
HE'S GONNA TRY SOMETHING!!
SHOOT HIM!!

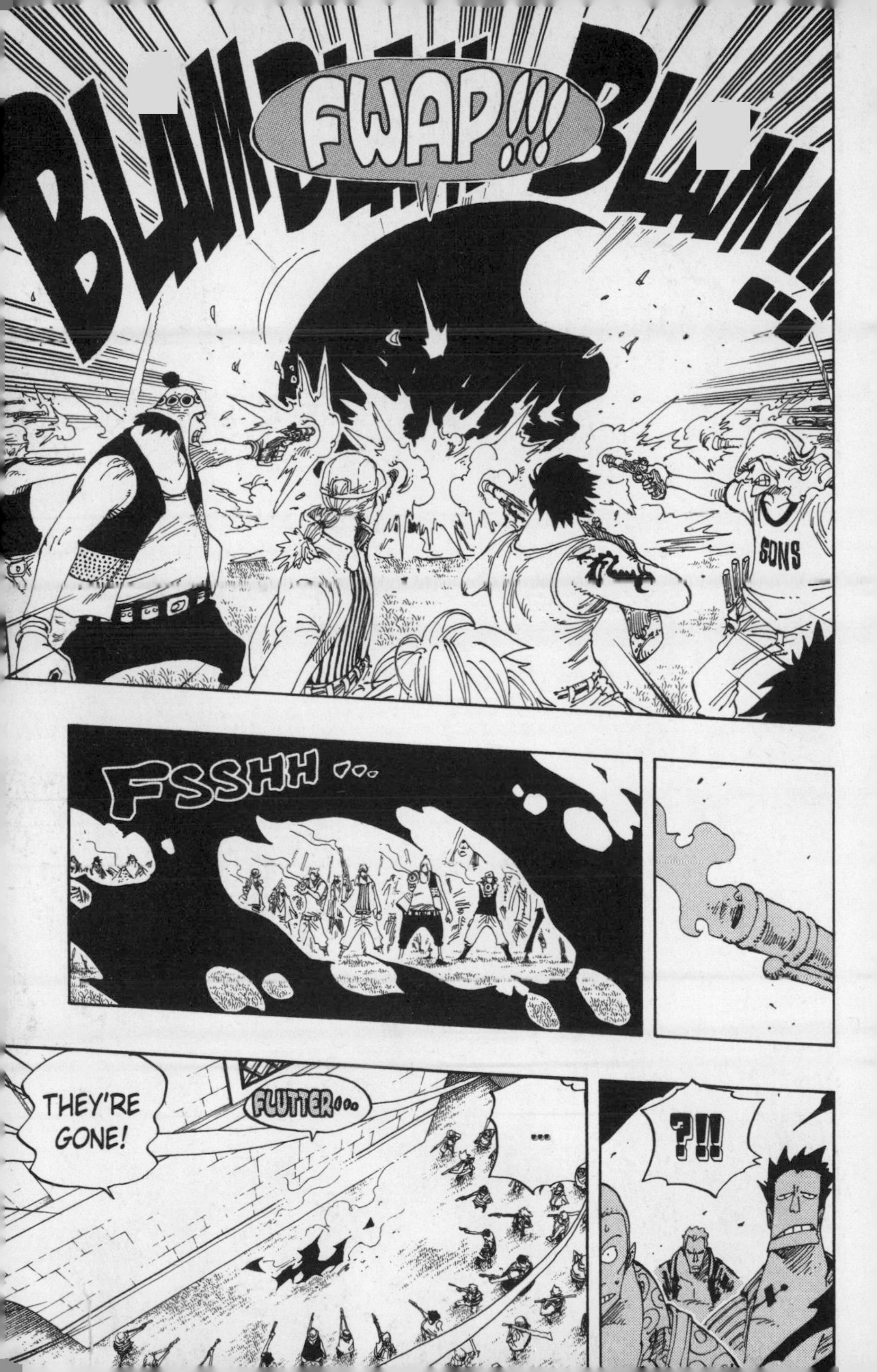
BLAM!!!
FWAP!!!
BLAM
SONS
FSSHH...
?!!
THEY'RE GONE!
FLUTTER...
...

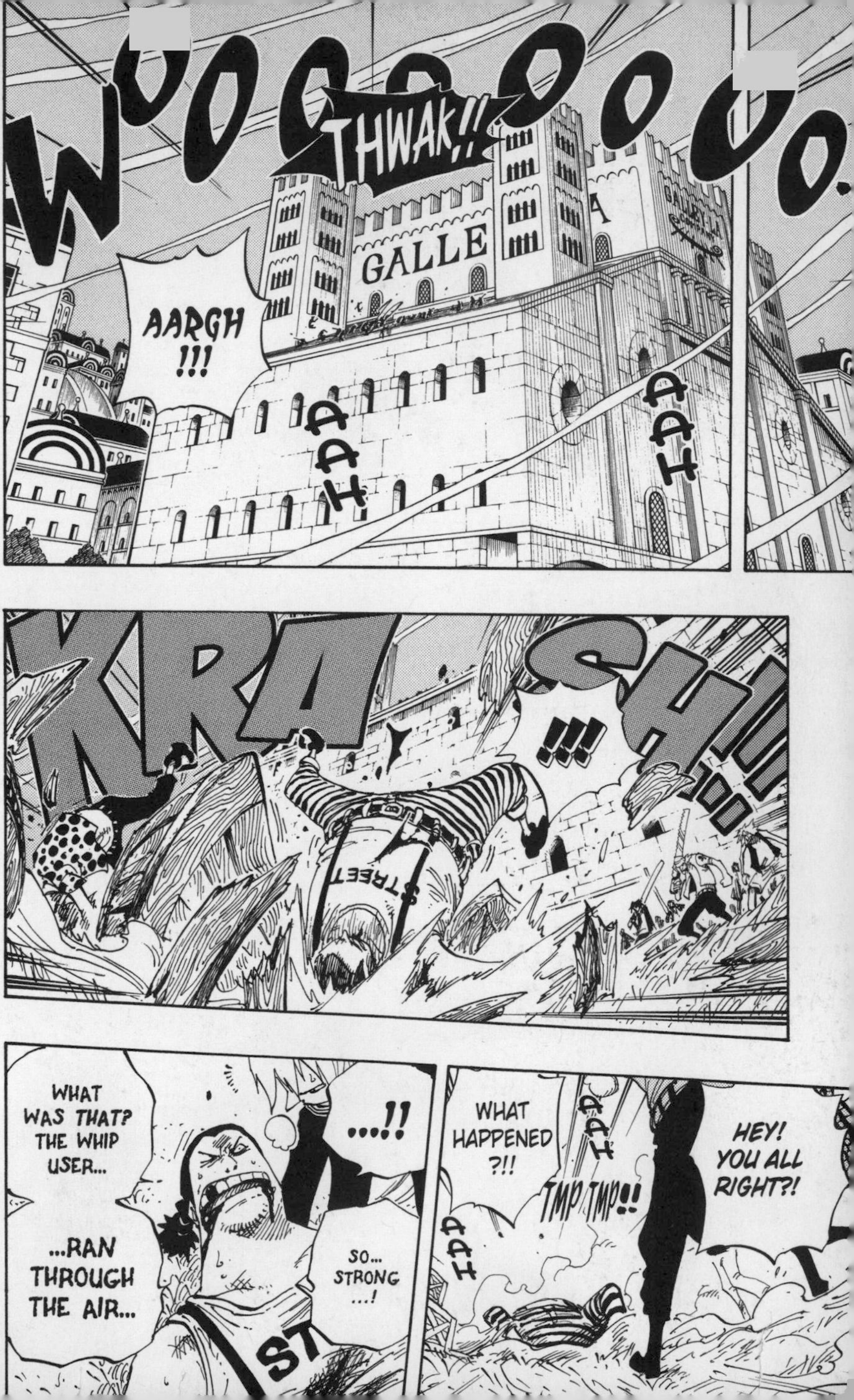

WOOOOOOOOO...
THWAK!!
GALLE
AARGH!!!
AAAH
AAAH
KRA
CH!!
!!!
STREET
HEY! YOU ALL RIGHT?!
WHAT HAPPENED?!!
AAAH
TMP TMP!!
AAAH
...!!
WHAT WAS THAT? THE WHIP USER...
...RAN THROUGH THE AIR...
SO... STRONG...!
ST

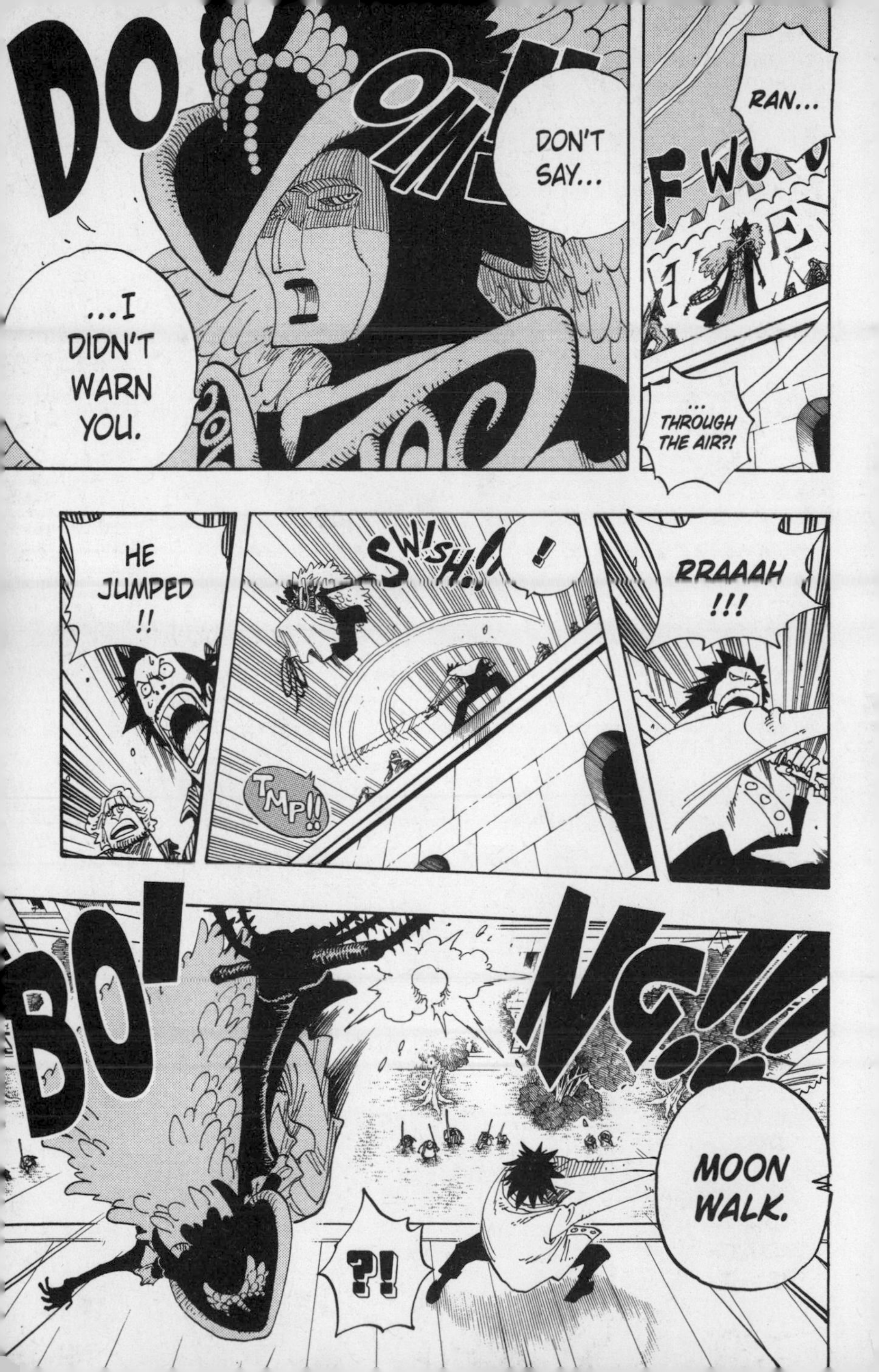
RAN...
F WO
...THROUGH THE AIR?!
DO
OM
DON'T SAY...
...I DIDN'T WARN YOU.
RRAAAH !!!
!
SWISH!!
TMP!!
HE JUMPED !!
MOON WALK.
BO
NG!!
?!

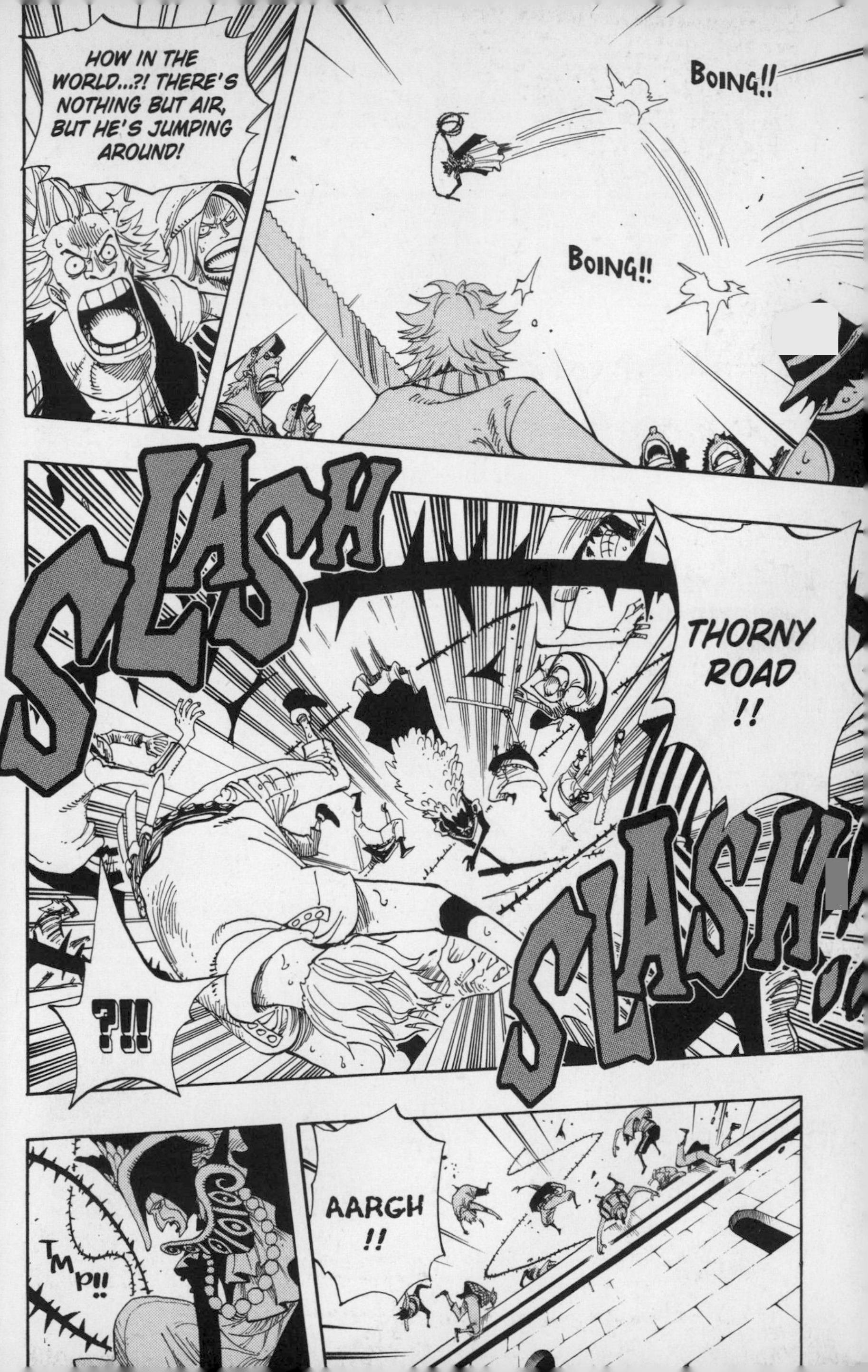
BOING!!
BOING!!
HOW IN THE WORLD...?! THERE'S NOTHING BUT AIR, BUT HE'S JUMPING AROUND!
THORNY ROAD !!
SLASH
SLASH!!
?!!
AARGH !!
TMP!!

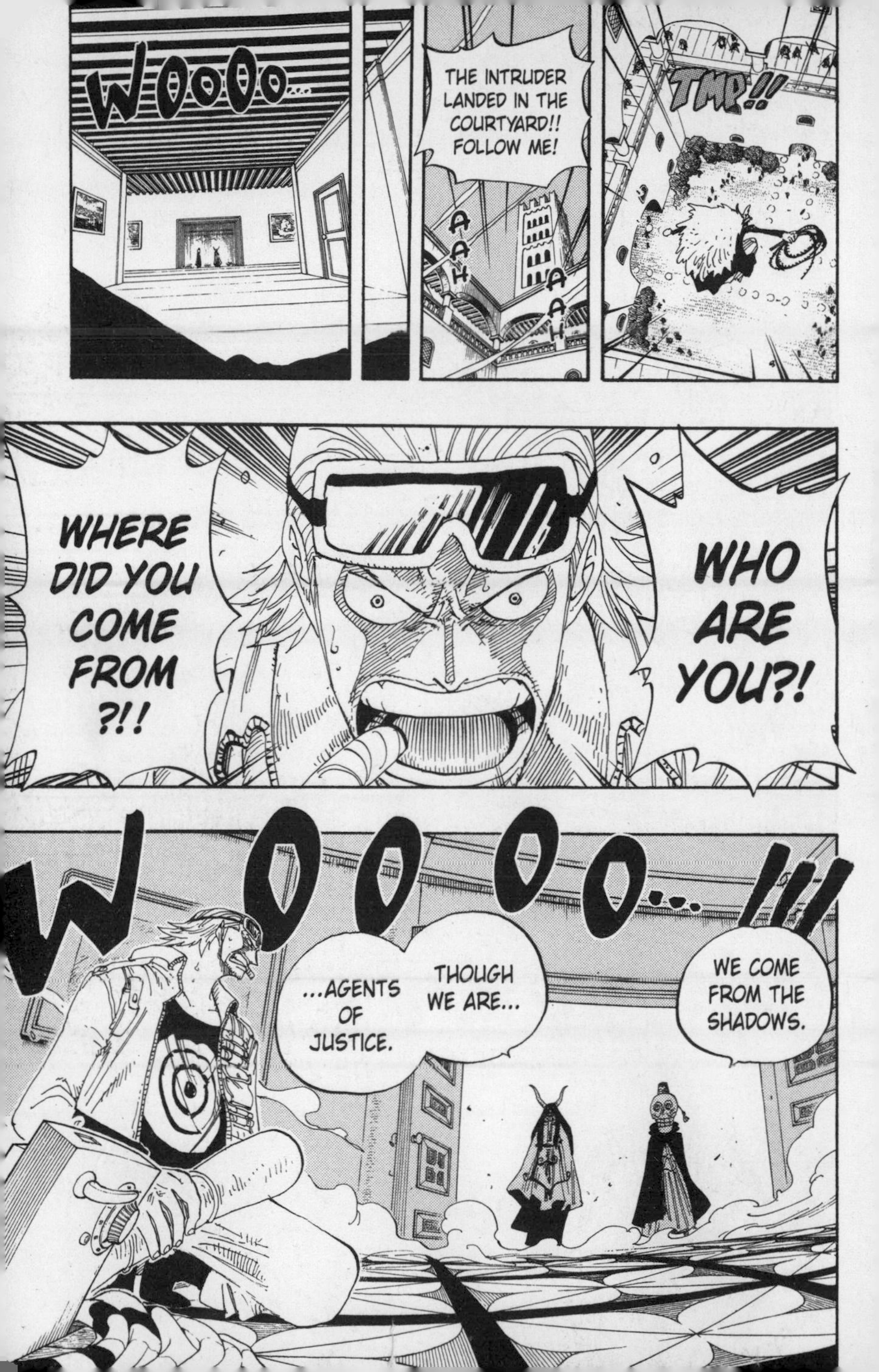
TMP!!
THE INTRUDER LANDED IN THE COURTYARD!! FOLLOW ME!
AAH
AAH
WOOOO...
WHO ARE YOU?!
WHERE DID YOU COME FROM ?!!
WOOOO...!!
WE COME FROM THE SHADOWS.
THOUGH WE ARE...
...AGENTS OF JUSTICE.

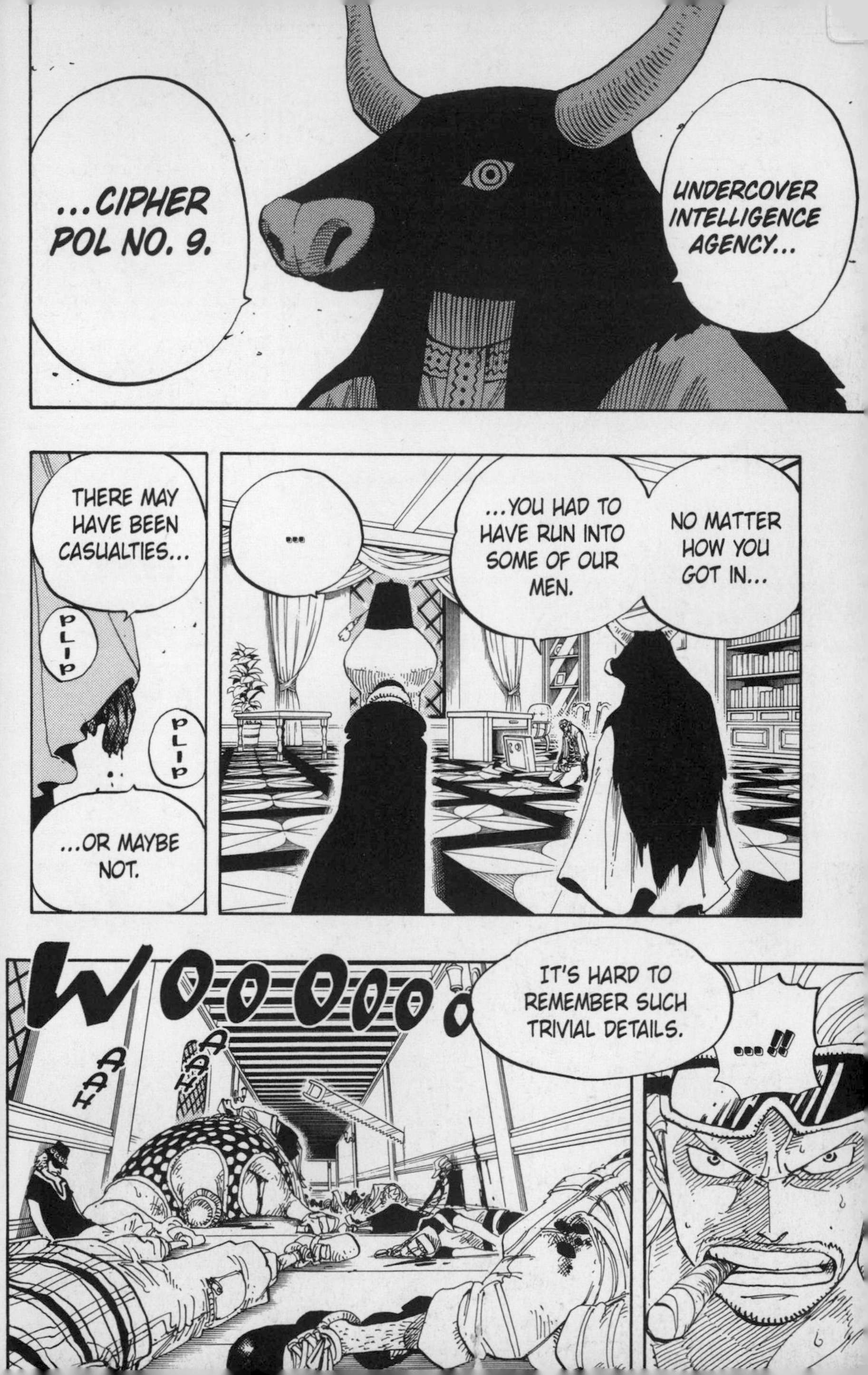
UNDERCOVER INTELLIGENCE AGENCY...
...CIPHER POL NO. 9.
NO MATTER HOW YOU GOT IN...
...YOU HAD TO HAVE RUN INTO SOME OF OUR MEN.
...
THERE MAY HAVE BEEN CASUALTIES...
PLIP
PLIP
...OR MAYBE NOT.
...!!
IT'S HARD TO REMEMBER SUCH TRIVIAL DETAILS.
WOOOOOO
AAAH
AAAH

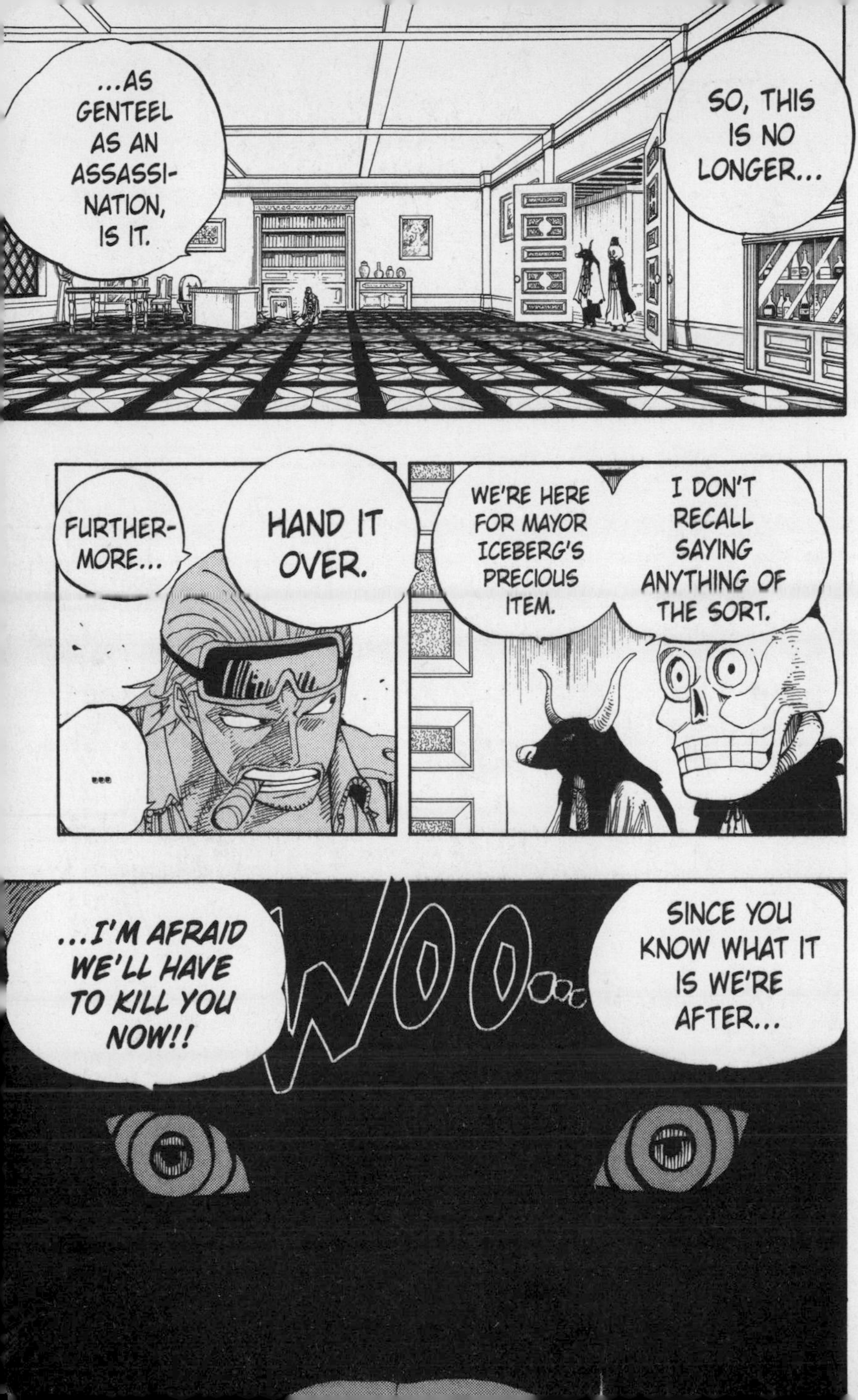
SO, THIS IS NO LONGER...
...AS GENTEEL AS AN ASSASSI-NATION, IS IT.
I DON'T RECALL SAYING ANYTHING OF THE SORT.
WE'RE HERE FOR MAYOR ICEBERG'S PRECIOUS ITEM.
HAND IT OVER.
FURTHER-MORE...
...
SINCE YOU KNOW WHAT IT IS WE'RE AFTER...
WOOO...
...I'M AFRAID WE'LL HAVE TO KILL YOU NOW!!

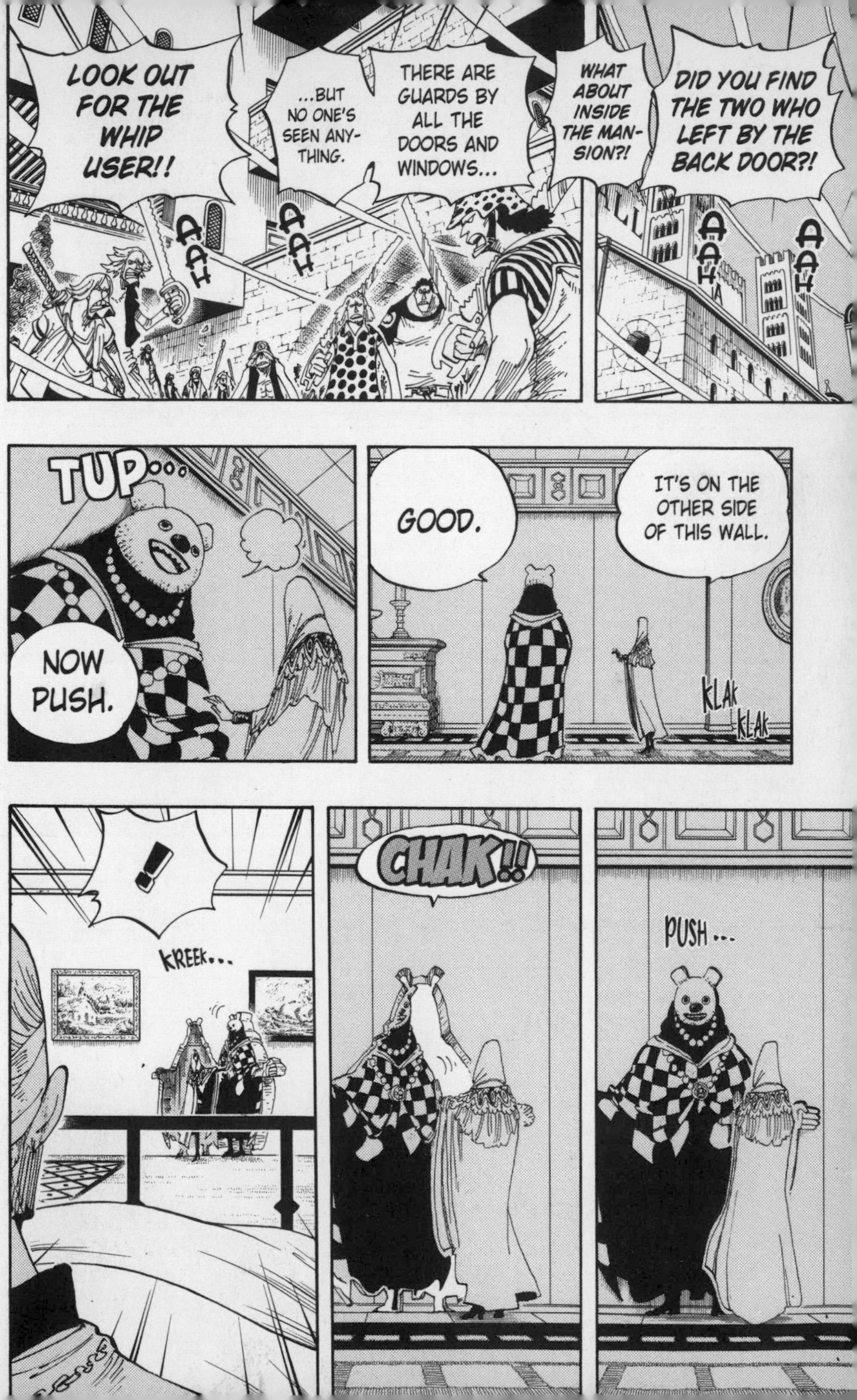
DID YOU FIND THE TWO WHO LEFT BY THE BACK DOOR?!
AAAH
AAAHA
WHAT ABOUT INSIDE THE MANSION?!
THERE ARE GUARDS BY ALL THE DOORS AND WINDOWS...
...BUT NO ONE'S SEEN ANYTHING.
AAAH
LOOK OUT FOR THE WHIP USER!!
AAAH
IT'S ON THE OTHER SIDE OF THIS WALL.
GOOD.
KLAK KLAK
TUP...
NOW PUSH.
PUSH...
CHAK!!
!
KREEK...

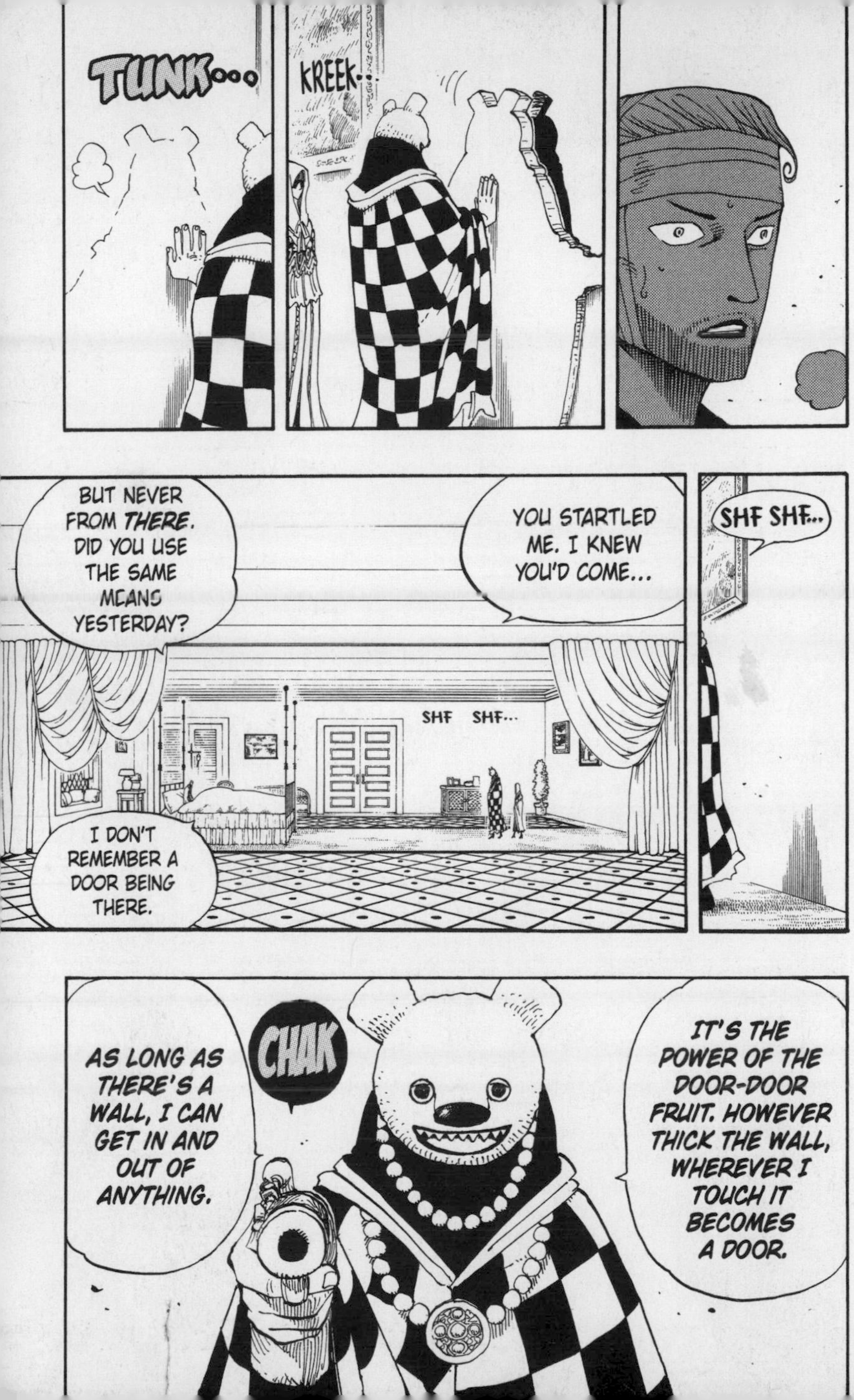
KREEK...
TUNK...
SHF SHF...
YOU STARTLED ME. I KNEW YOU'D COME...
BUT NEVER FROM *THERE*. DID YOU USE THE SAME MEANS YESTERDAY?
SHF SHF...
I DON'T REMEMBER A DOOR BEING THERE.
IT'S THE POWER OF THE DOOR-DOOR FRUIT. HOWEVER THICK THE WALL, WHEREVER I TOUCH IT BECOMES A DOOR.
CHAK
AS LONG AS THERE'S A WALL, I CAN GET IN AND OUT OF ANYTHING.

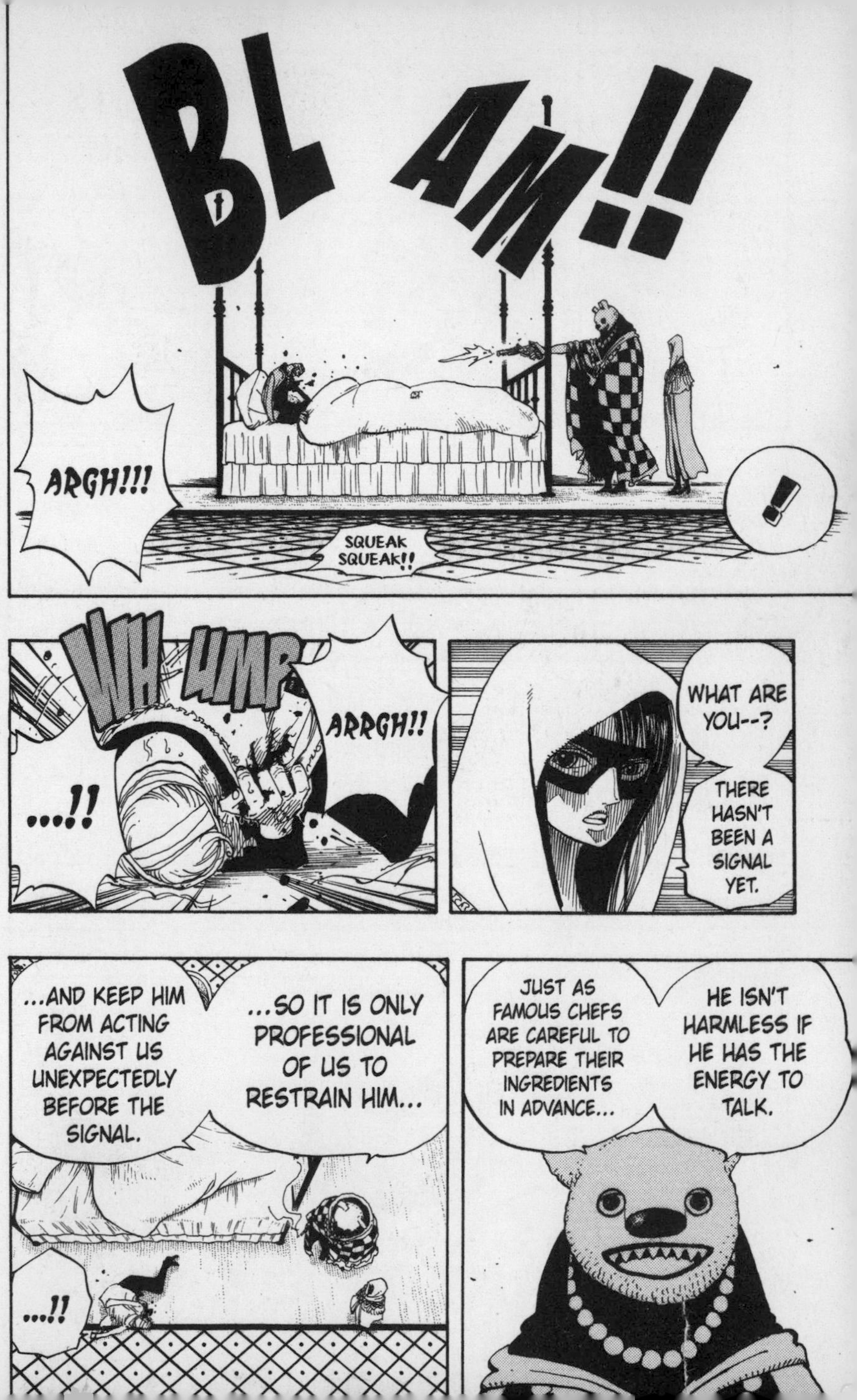
BLAM!!
!
ARGH!!!
SQUEAK SQUEAK!!
WHAT ARE YOU--?
THERE HASN'T BEEN A SIGNAL YET.
WHUMP
ARRGH!!
...!!
HE ISN'T HARMLESS IF HE HAS THE ENERGY TO TALK.
JUST AS FAMOUS CHEFS ARE CAREFUL TO PREPARE THEIR INGREDIENTS IN ADVANCE...
...SO IT IS ONLY PROFESSIONAL OF US TO RESTRAIN HIM...
...AND KEEP HIM FROM ACTING AGAINST US UNEXPECTEDLY BEFORE THE SIGNAL.
...!!

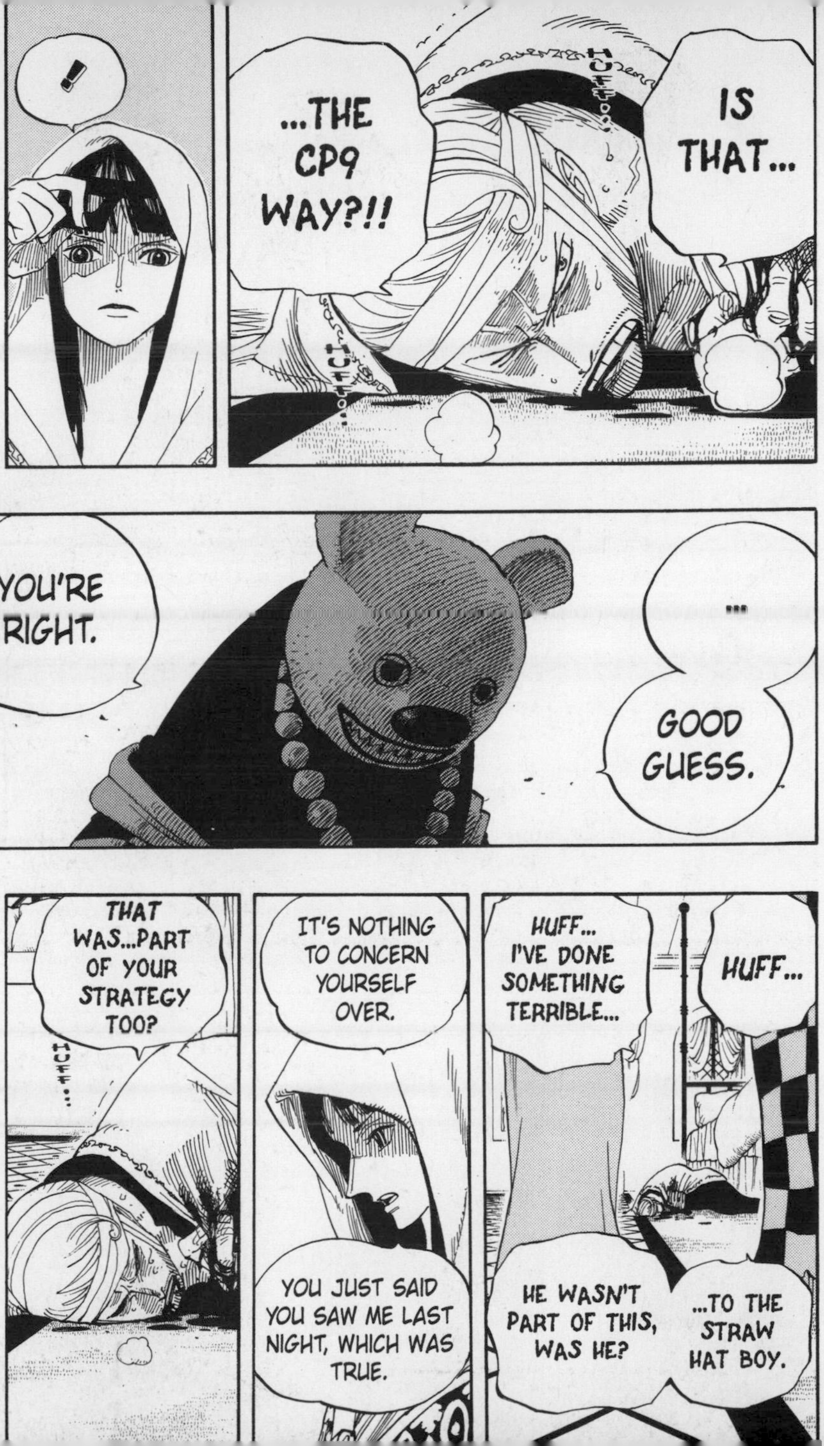
IS THAT...
...THE CP9 WAY?!!
HUFF...
HUFF...
!
...
GOOD GUESS.
YOU'RE RIGHT.
HUFF...
HUFF... I'VE DONE SOMETHING TERRIBLE...
...TO THE STRAW HAT BOY.
HE WASN'T PART OF THIS, WAS HE?
IT'S NOTHING TO CONCERN YOURSELF OVER.
YOU JUST SAID YOU SAW ME LAST NIGHT, WHICH WAS TRUE.
THAT WAS...PART OF YOUR STRATEGY TOO?
HUFF...

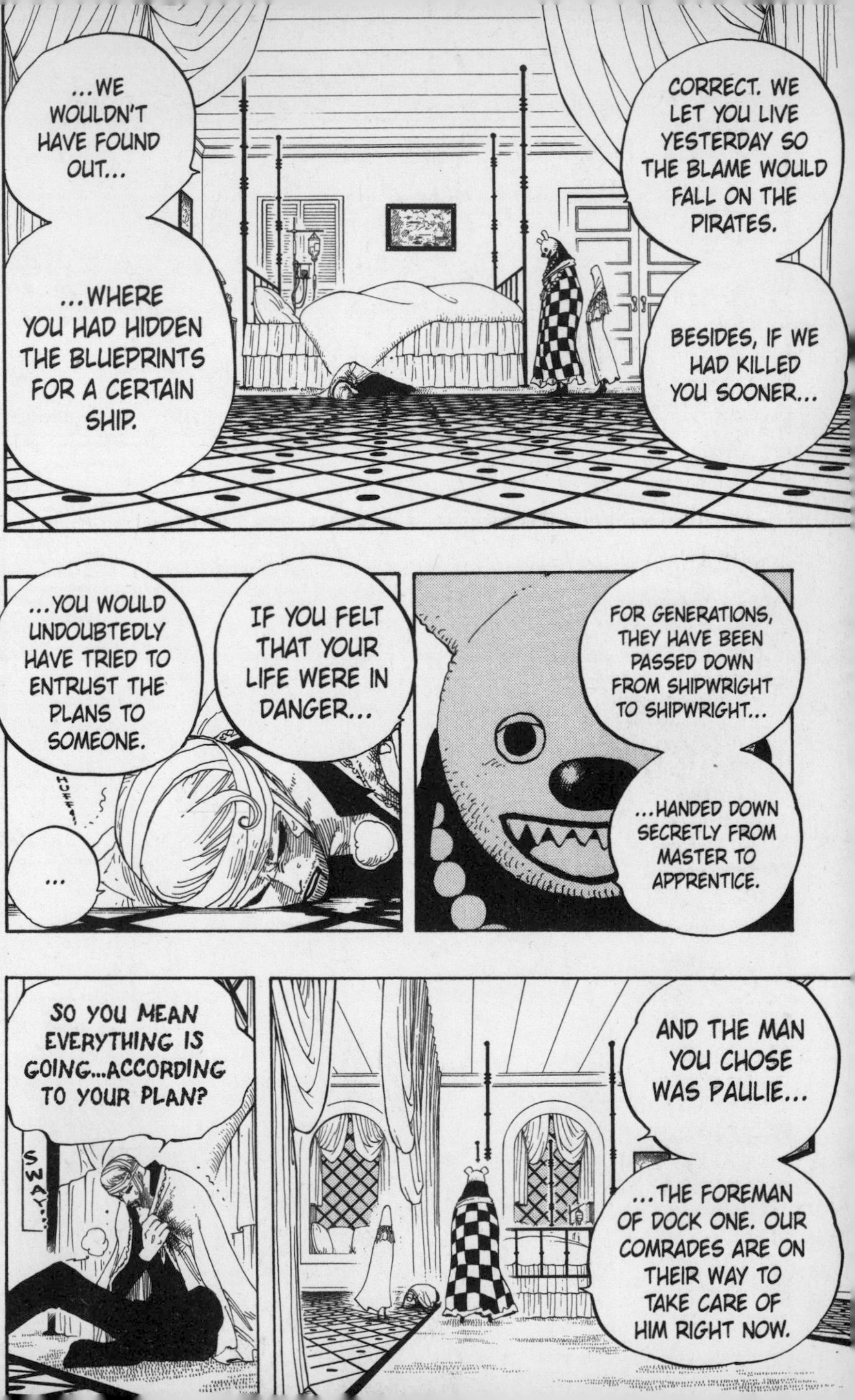
CORRECT. WE LET YOU LIVE YESTERDAY SO THE BLAME WOULD FALL ON THE PIRATES.
BESIDES, IF WE HAD KILLED YOU SOONER...
...WE WOULDN'T HAVE FOUND OUT...
...WHERE YOU HAD HIDDEN THE BLUEPRINTS FOR A CERTAIN SHIP.
FOR GENERATIONS, THEY HAVE BEEN PASSED DOWN FROM SHIPWRIGHT TO SHIPWRIGHT...
...HANDED DOWN SECRETLY FROM MASTER TO APPRENTICE.
IF YOU FELT THAT YOUR LIFE WERE IN DANGER...
...YOU WOULD UNDOUBTEDLY HAVE TRIED TO ENTRUST THE PLANS TO SOMEONE.
HUFF!!
...
AND THE MAN YOU CHOSE WAS PAULIE...
...THE FOREMAN OF DOCK ONE. OUR COMRADES ARE ON THEIR WAY TO TAKE CARE OF HIM RIGHT NOW.
SO YOU MEAN EVERYTHING IS GOING...ACCORDING TO YOUR PLAN?
SWAY...

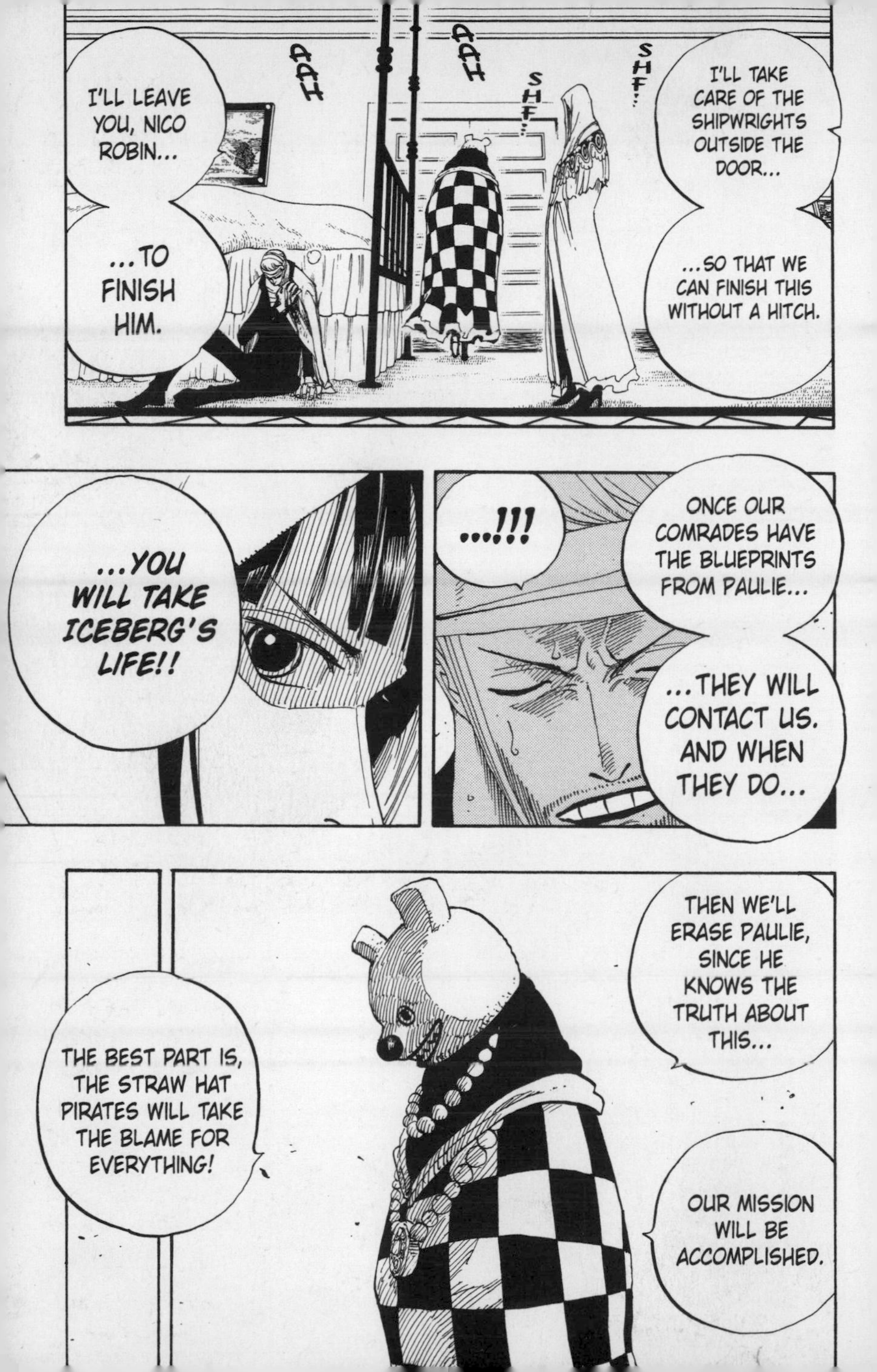
SHF...
I'LL TAKE CARE OF THE SHIPWRIGHTS OUTSIDE THE DOOR...
...SO THAT WE CAN FINISH THIS WITHOUT A HITCH.
SHF...
AAAH
AAAH
I'LL LEAVE YOU, NICO ROBIN...
...TO FINISH HIM.
ONCE OUR COMRADES HAVE THE BLUEPRINTS FROM PAULIE...
...!!!
...THEY WILL CONTACT US. AND WHEN THEY DO...
...YOU WILL TAKE ICEBERG'S LIFE!!
THEN WE'LL ERASE PAULIE, SINCE HE KNOWS THE TRUTH ABOUT THIS...
THE BEST PART IS, THE STRAW HAT PIRATES WILL TAKE THE BLAME FOR EVERYTHING!
OUR MISSION WILL BE ACCOMPLISHED.

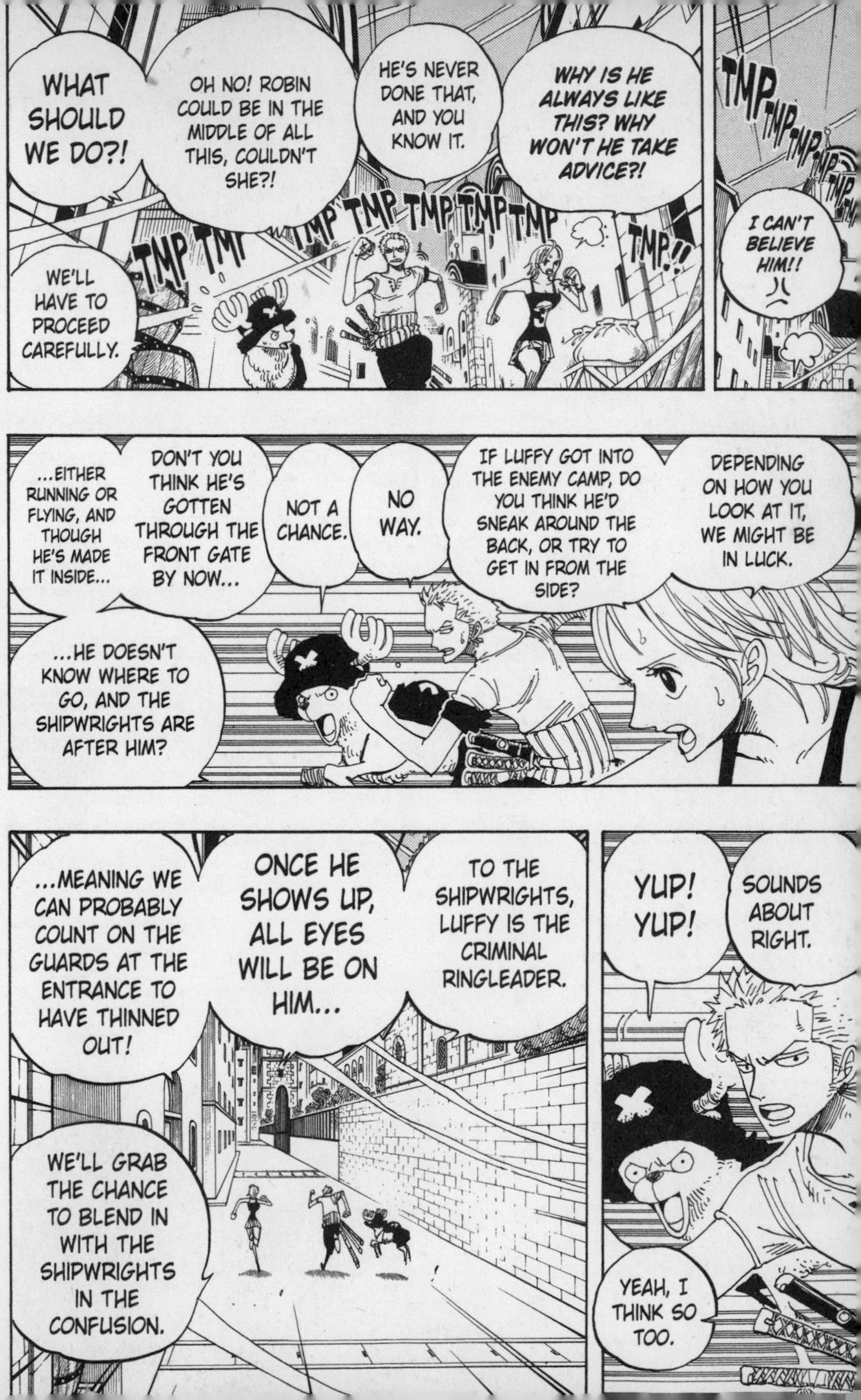
TMP TMP TMP TMP TMP
I CAN'T BELIEVE HIM!!
WHY IS HE ALWAYS LIKE THIS? WHY WON'T HE TAKE ADVICE?!
HE'S NEVER DONE THAT, AND YOU KNOW IT.
OH NO! ROBIN COULD BE IN THE MIDDLE OF ALL THIS, COULDN'T SHE?!
WHAT SHOULD WE DO?!
TMP!!
TMP TMP TMP TMP TMP TMP TMP
WE'LL HAVE TO PROCEED CAREFULLY.
DEPENDING ON HOW YOU LOOK AT IT, WE MIGHT BE IN LUCK.
IF LUFFY GOT INTO THE ENEMY CAMP, DO YOU THINK HE'D SNEAK AROUND THE BACK, OR TRY TO GET IN FROM THE SIDE?
NO WAY.
NOT A CHANCE.
DON'T YOU THINK HE'S GOTTEN THROUGH THE FRONT GATE BY NOW...
...EITHER RUNNING OR FLYING, AND THOUGH HE'S MADE IT INSIDE...
...HE DOESN'T KNOW WHERE TO GO, AND THE SHIPWRIGHTS ARE AFTER HIM?
SOUNDS ABOUT RIGHT.
YUP! YUP!
YEAH, I THINK SO TOO.
TO THE SHIPWRIGHTS, LUFFY IS THE CRIMINAL RINGLEADER.
ONCE HE SHOWS UP, ALL EYES WILL BE ON HIM...
...MEANING WE CAN PROBABLY COUNT ON THE GUARDS AT THE ENTRANCE TO HAVE THINNED OUT!
WE'LL GRAB THE CHANCE TO BLEND IN WITH THE SHIPWRIGHTS IN THE CONFUSION.

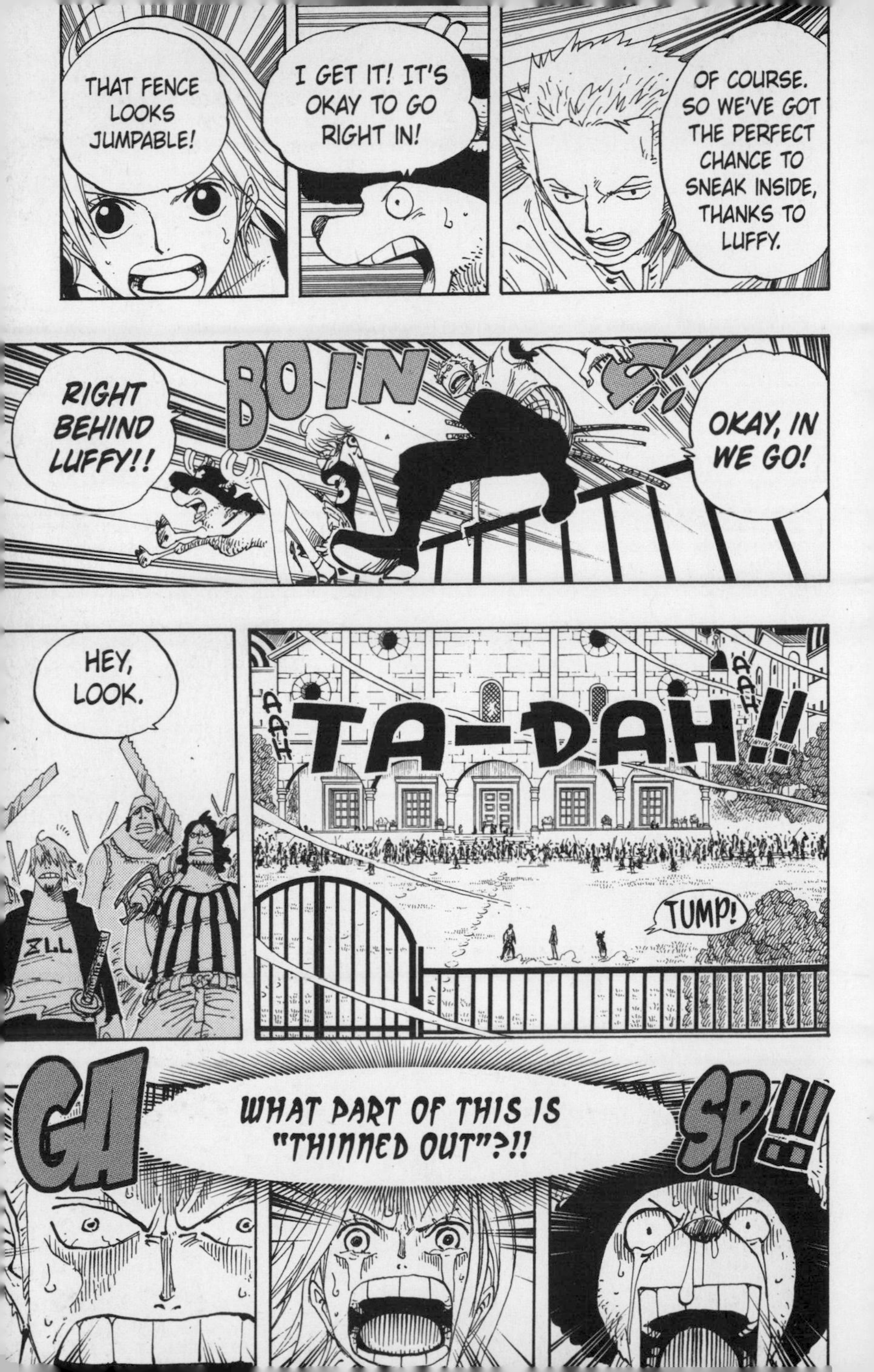

OF COURSE. SO WE'VE GOT THE PERFECT CHANCE TO SNEAK INSIDE, THANKS TO LUFFY.
I GET IT! IT'S OKAY TO GO RIGHT IN!
THAT FENCE LOOKS JUMPABLE!
OKAY, IN WE GO!
BOIN
RIGHT BEHIND LUFFY!!
AAAH
TA-DAH!!
AAAH
TUMP!
HEY, LOOK.
GA
WHAT PART OF THIS IS "THINNED OUT"?!!
SP!!!

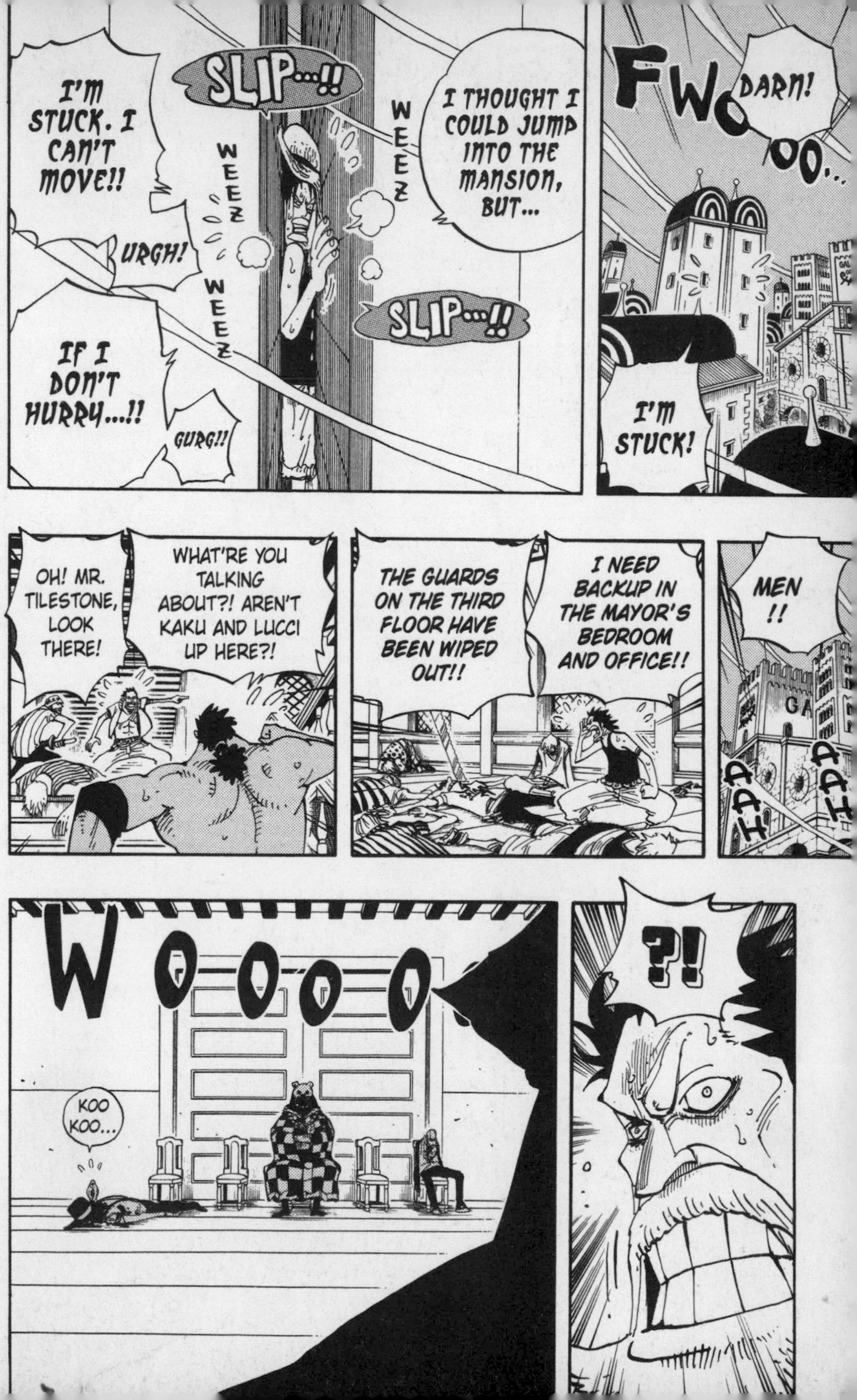
FWOOOO...
DARN!
I'M STUCK!
I THOUGHT I COULD JUMP INTO THE MANSION, BUT...
SLIP...!!
WEEZ
WEEZ
SLIP...!!
I'M STUCK. I CAN'T MOVE!!
URGH!
IF I DON'T HURRY...!!
GURG!!
MEN !!
AAAH
AAAH
I NEED BACKUP IN THE MAYOR'S BEDROOM AND OFFICE!!
THE GUARDS ON THE THIRD FLOOR HAVE BEEN WIPED OUT!!
WHAT'RE YOU TALKING ABOUT?! AREN'T KAKU AND LUCCI UP HERE?!
OH! MR. TILESTONE, LOOK THERE!
?!
WOOOO
KOO KOO...

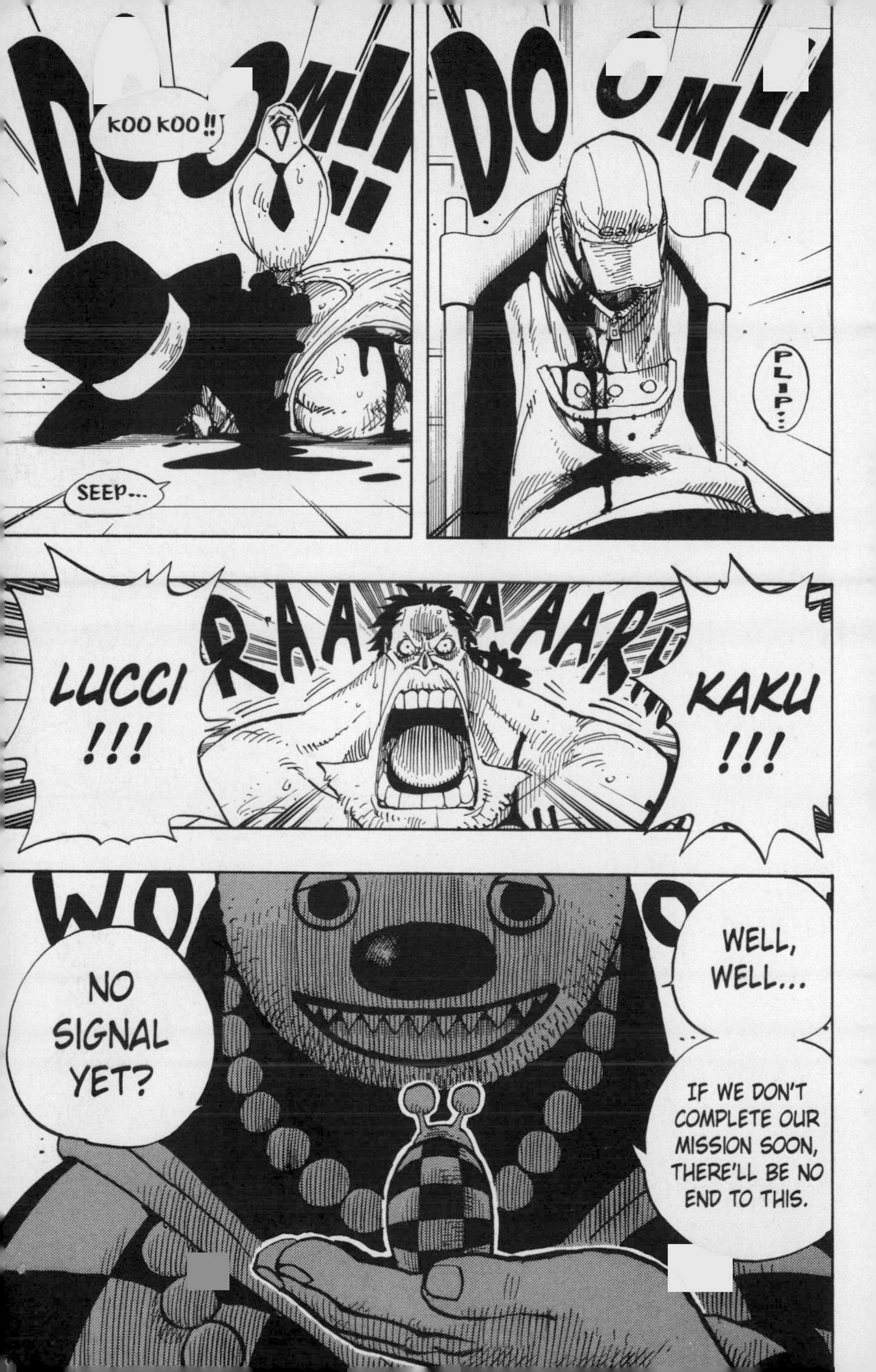
DOOM!!
PLIP...
DOOM!!
KOO KOO!!
SEEP...
KAKU!!!
RAAAAAR!!
LUCCI!!!
WELL, WELL...
IF WE DON'T COMPLETE OUR MISSION SOON, THERE'LL BE NO END TO THIS.
NO SIGNAL YET?

Chapter 344:
OPPOSING FORCE

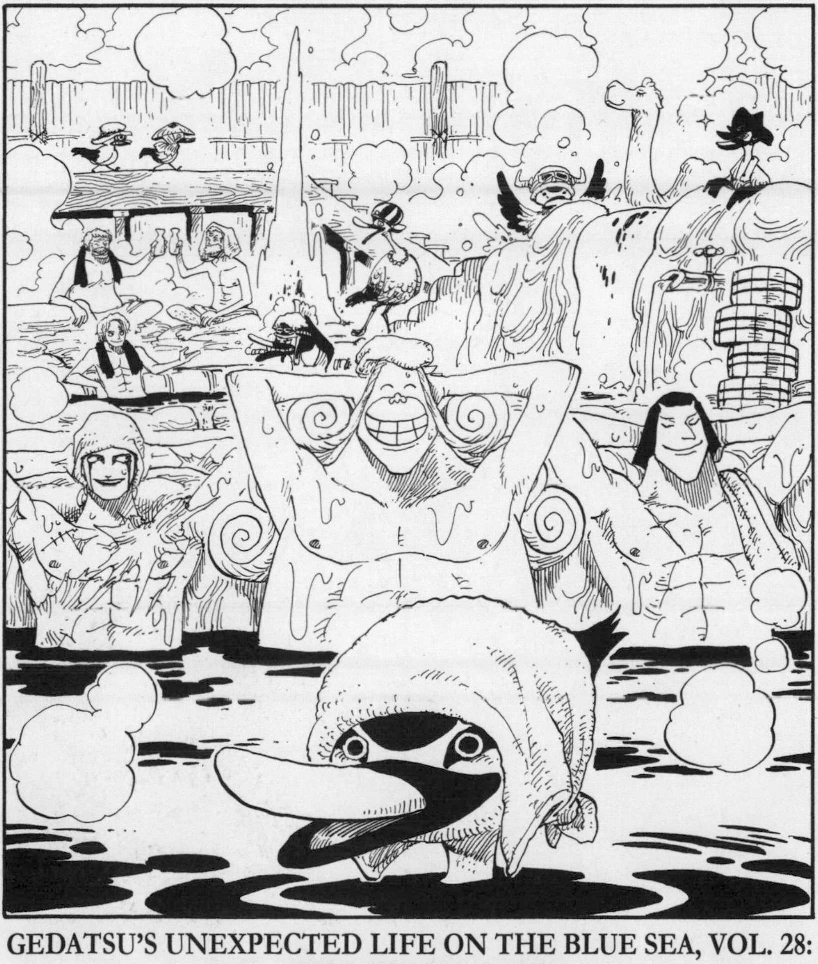

GEDATSU'S UNEXPECTED LIFE ON THE BLUE SEA, VOL. 28:
"THE MEN'S BATH"

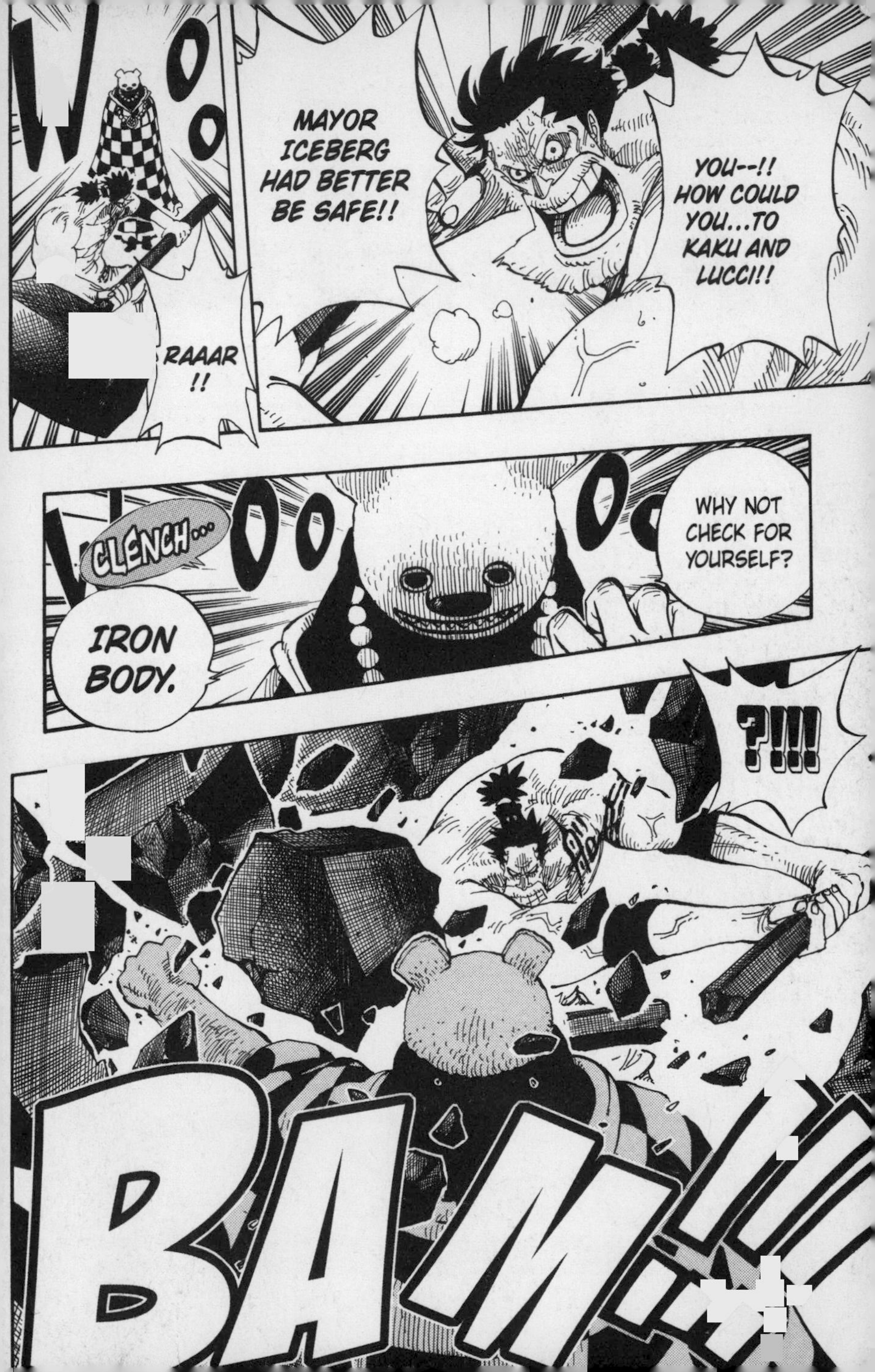
YOU--!! HOW COULD YOU...TO KAKU AND LUCCI!!
MAYOR ICEBERG HAD BETTER BE SAFE!!
RAAAR !!
WHY NOT CHECK FOR YOURSELF?
CLENCH...
IRON BODY.
?!!!
BAM!!

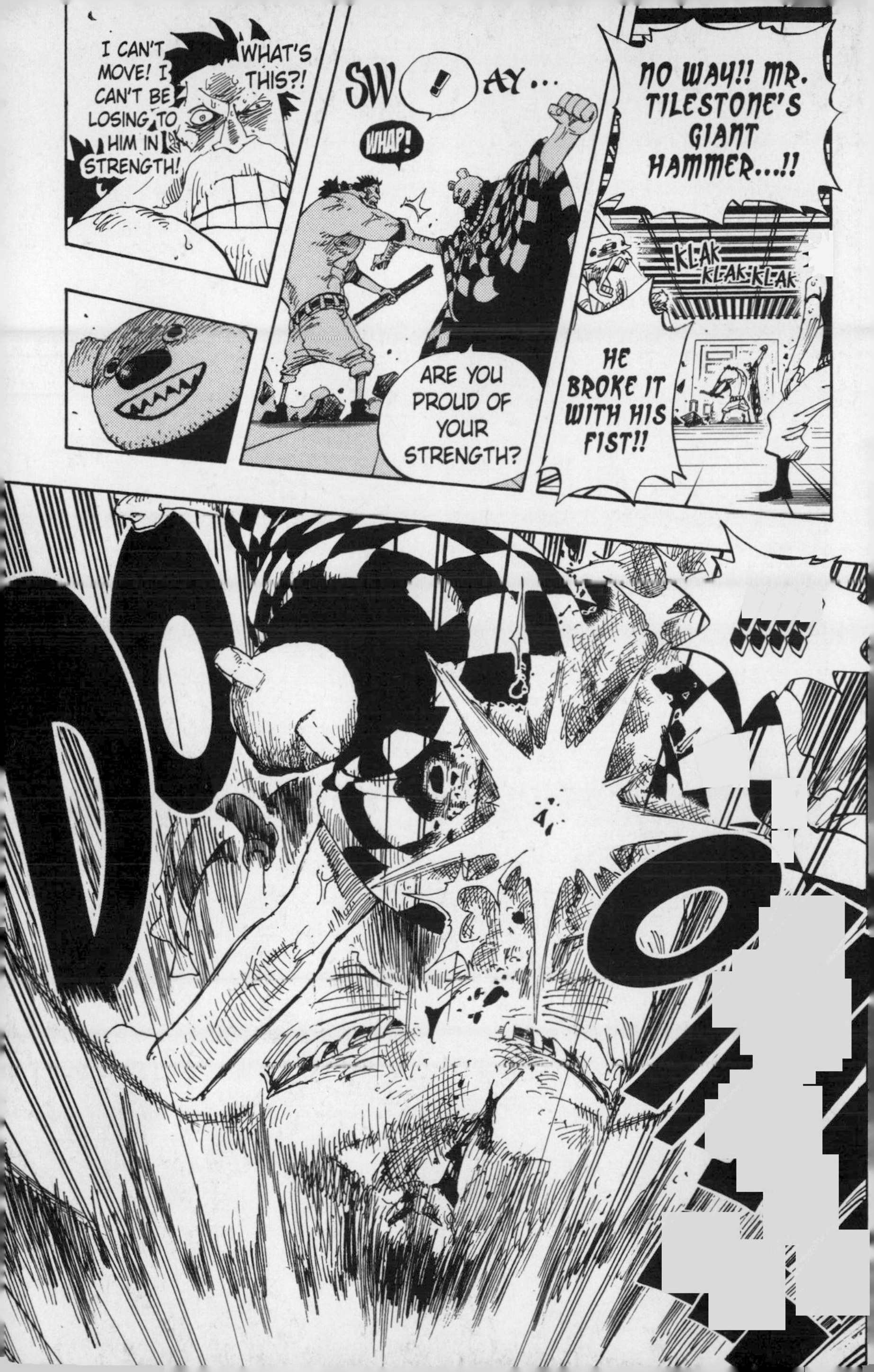
NO WAY!! MR. TILESTONE'S GIANT HAMMER...!!
KLAK KLAK KLAK
HE BROKE IT WITH HIS FIST!!
SW ! AY...
WHAP!
ARE YOU PROUD OF YOUR STRENGTH?
WHAT'S THIS?!
I CAN'T MOVE! I CAN'T BE LOSING TO HIM IN STRENGTH!

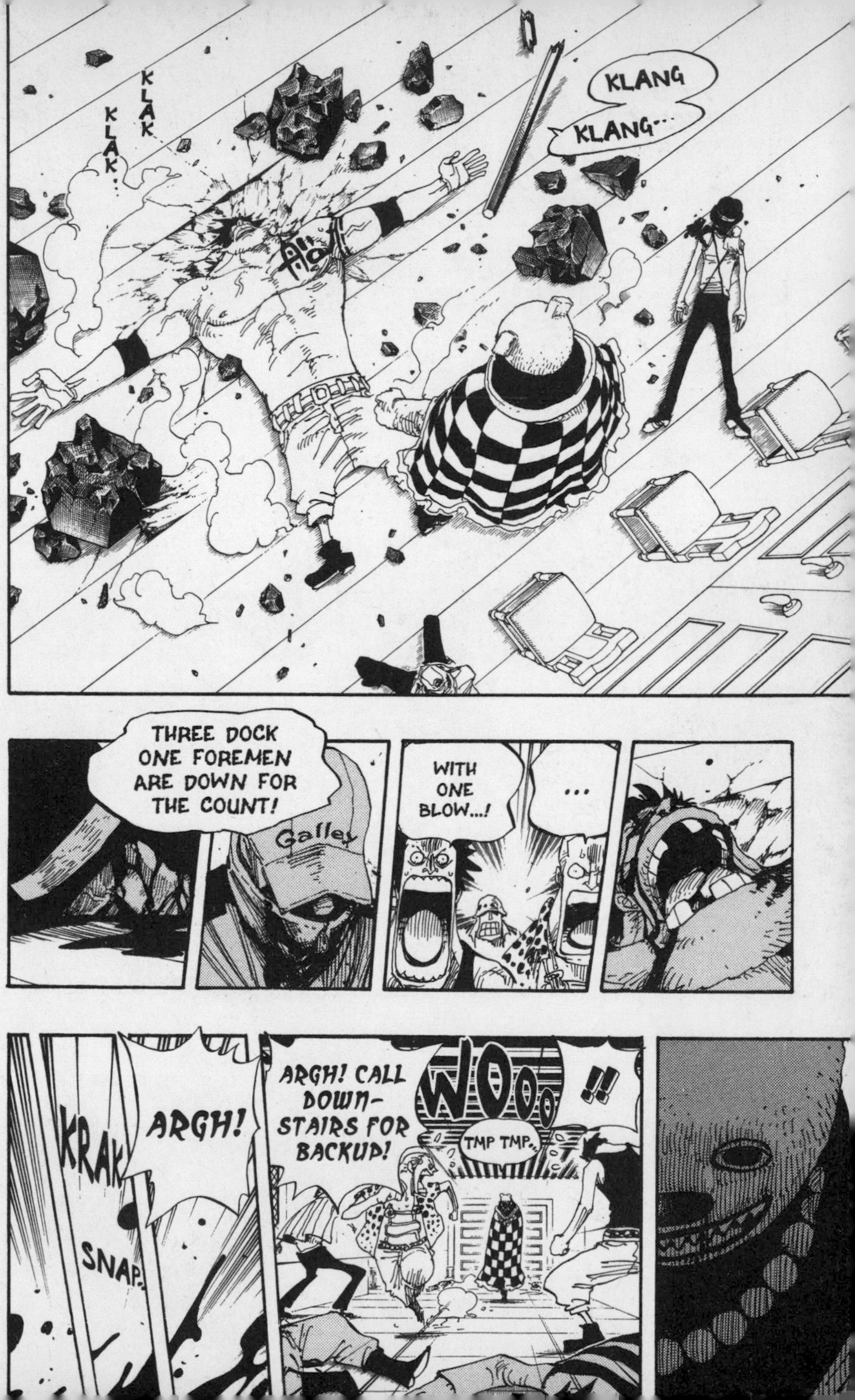
KLANG
KLANG...
KLAK
KLAK...
...
WITH ONE BLOW...!
THREE DOCK ONE FOREMEN ARE DOWN FOR THE COUNT!
Galley
WOOO!!
TMP TMP...
ARGH! CALL DOWN-STAIRS FOR BACKUP!
ARGH!
KRAK
SNAP...

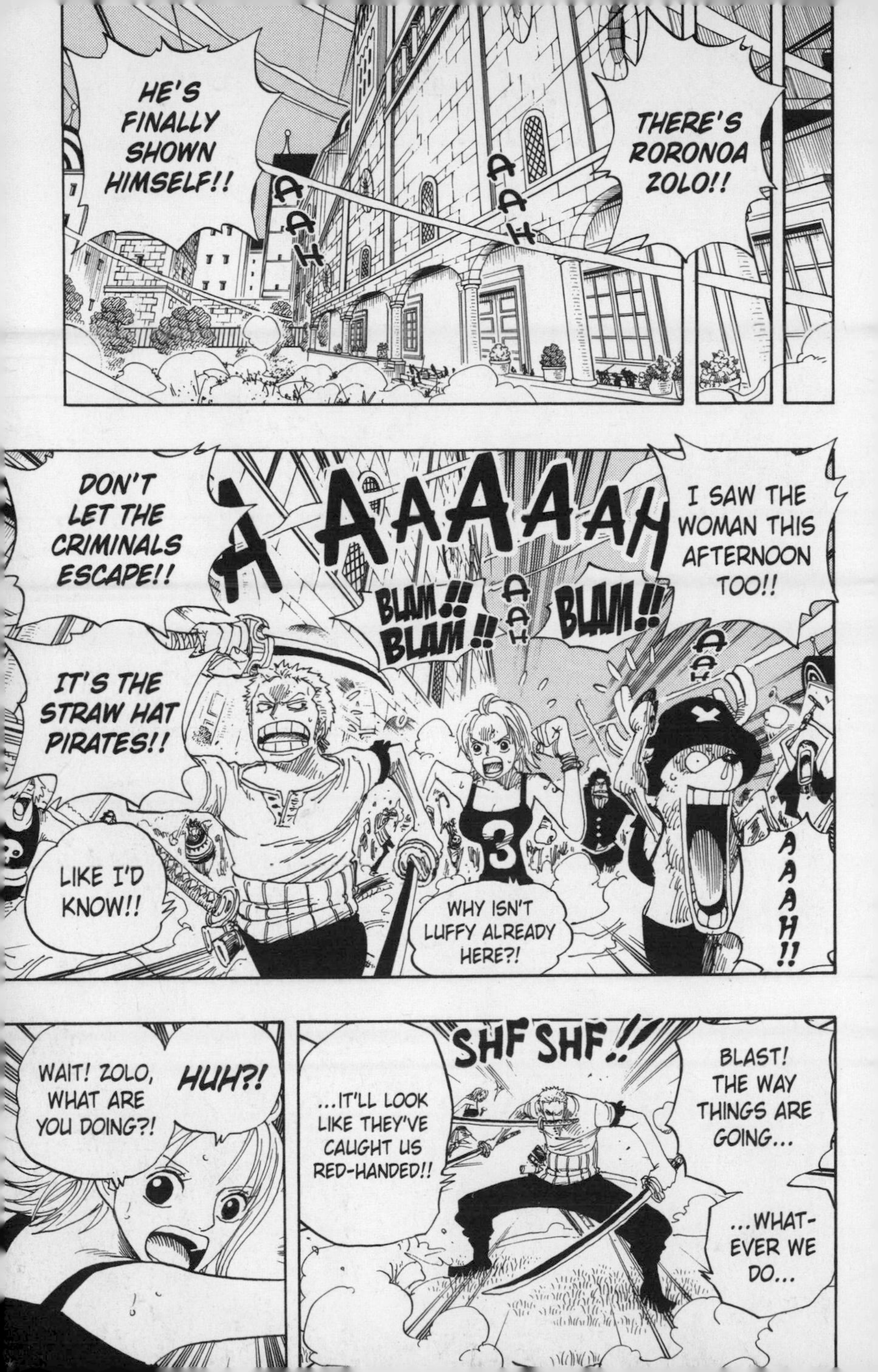
THERE'S RORONOA ZOLO!!
AAH
HE'S FINALLY SHOWN HIMSELF!!
AAH
I SAW THE WOMAN THIS AFTERNOON TOO!!
AAAAAAH
DON'T LET THE CRIMINALS ESCAPE!!
BLAM!!
BLAM!!
AAH
BLAM!!
AAH
IT'S THE STRAW HAT PIRATES!!
AAAAH!!
WHY ISN'T LUFFY ALREADY HERE?!
LIKE I'D KNOW!!
SHF SHF!!
BLAST! THE WAY THINGS ARE GOING...
...IT'LL LOOK LIKE THEY'VE CAUGHT US RED-HANDED!!
...WHAT-EVER WE DO...
HUH?!
WAIT! ZOLO, WHAT ARE YOU DOING?!

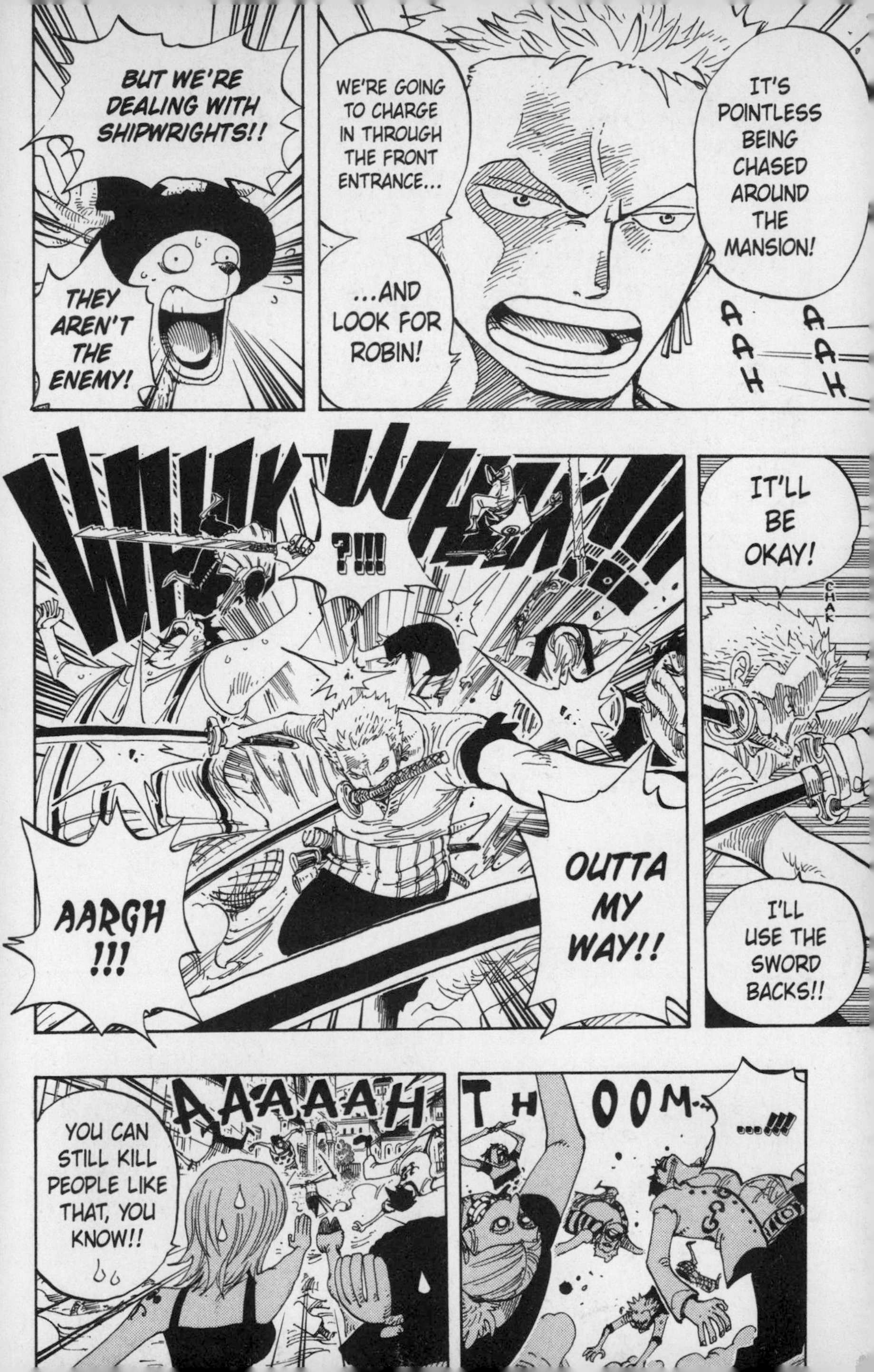
IT'S POINTLESS BEING CHASED AROUND THE MANSION!
WE'RE GOING TO CHARGE IN THROUGH THE FRONT ENTRANCE...
AAH AAH
...AND LOOK FOR ROBIN!
BUT WE'RE DEALING WITH SHIPWRIGHTS!!
THEY AREN'T THE ENEMY!
IT'LL BE OKAY!
CHAK
I'LL USE THE SWORD BACKS!!
WHAK
WHAK!!
?!!!
OUTTA MY WAY!!
AARGH!!!
THOOM
...!!!
AAAAAH
YOU CAN STILL KILL PEOPLE LIKE THAT, YOU KNOW!!

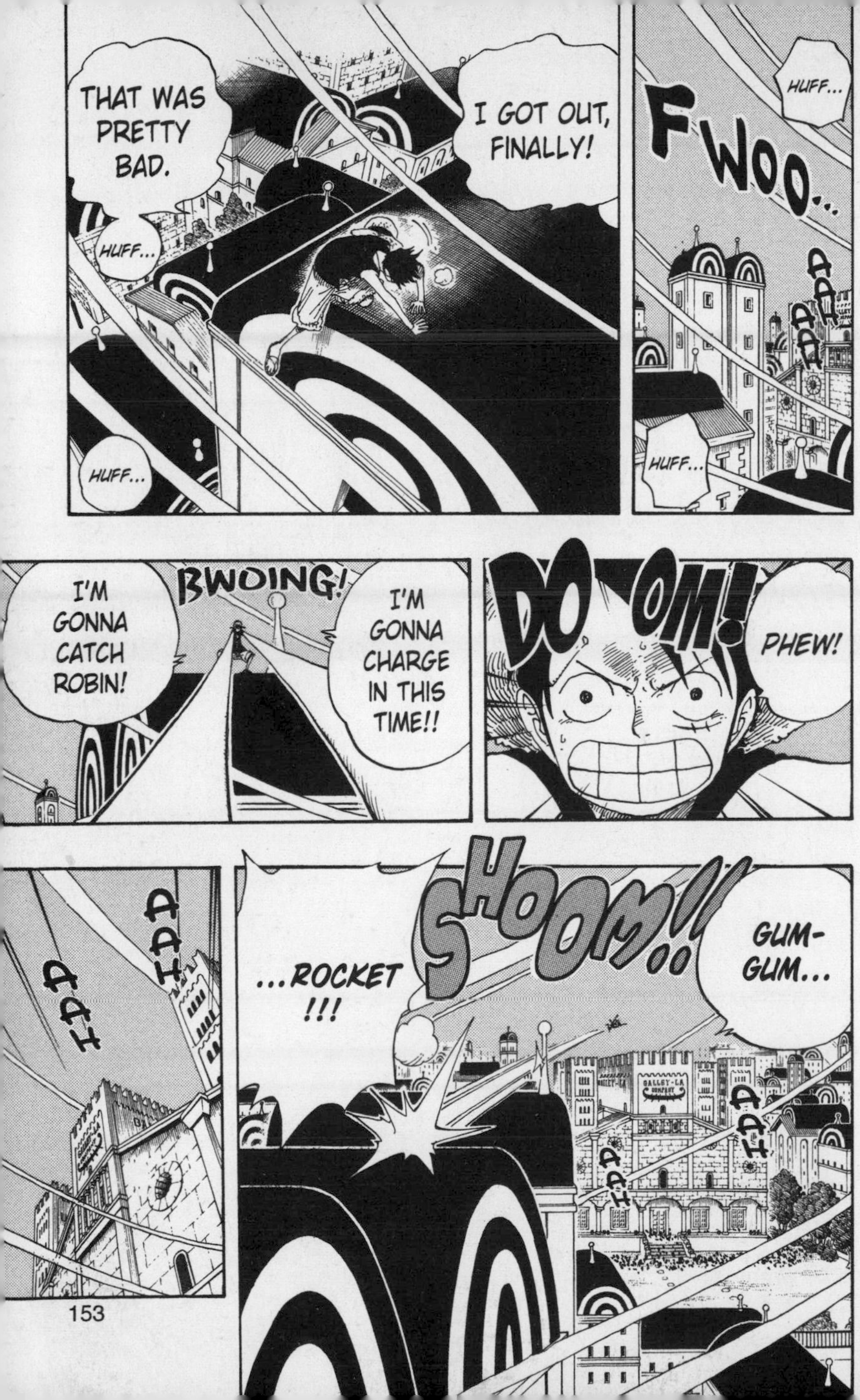
HUFF...
FWOO...
HUFF...
I GOT OUT, FINALLY!
THAT WAS PRETTY BAD.
HUFF...
HUFF...
DOOM!
PHEW!
I'M GONNA CHARGE IN THIS TIME!!
BWOING!
I'M GONNA CATCH ROBIN!
GUM-GUM...
SHOOM!!
...ROCKET !!!
AAAH
AAAH
AAAH
AAAH

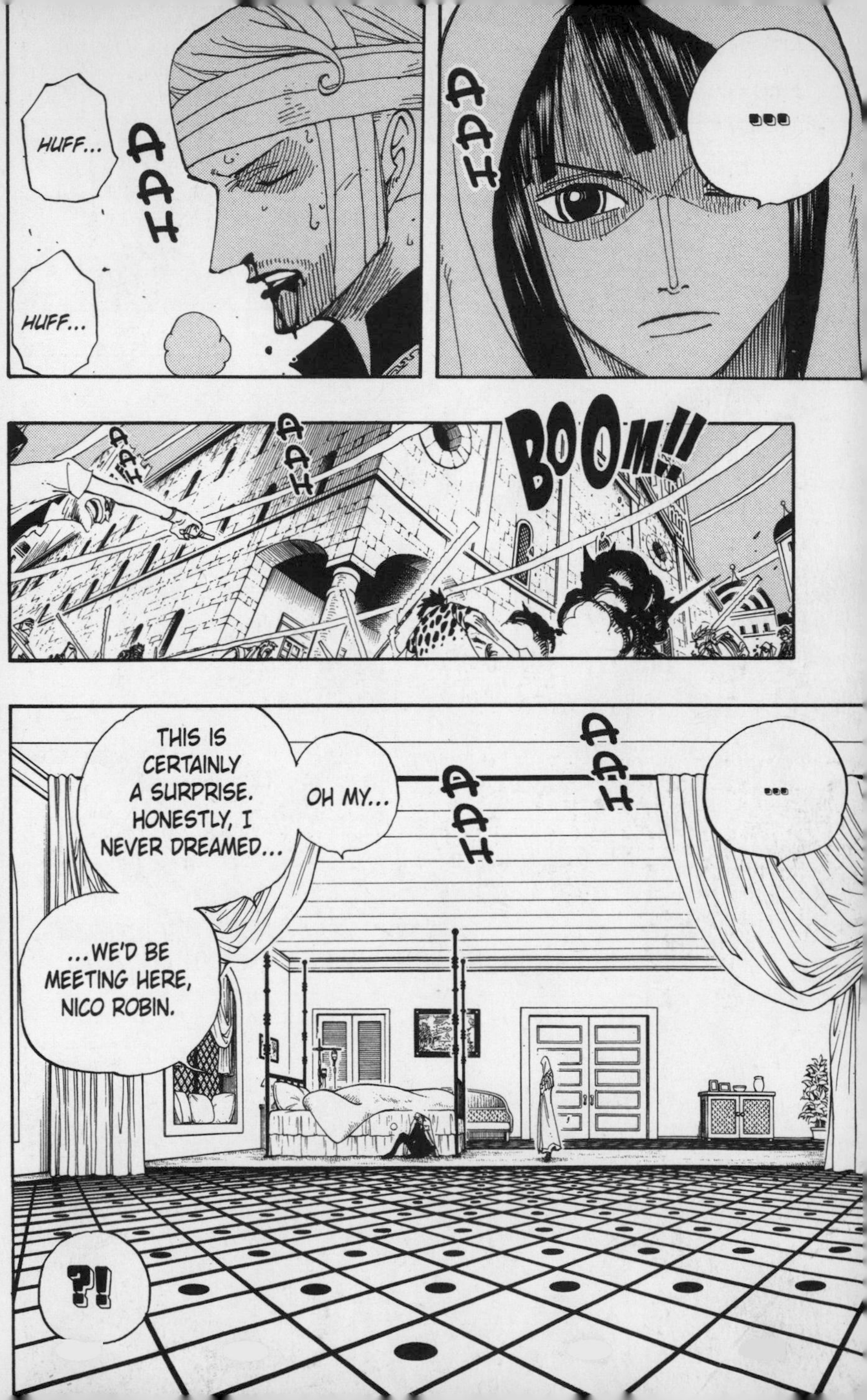
AAH
...
AAH
HUFF...
HUFF...
BOOM!!
AAH
AAH
...
AAH
AAH
OH MY...
THIS IS CERTAINLY A SURPRISE. HONESTLY, I NEVER DREAMED...
...WE'D BE MEETING HERE, NICO ROBIN.
?!

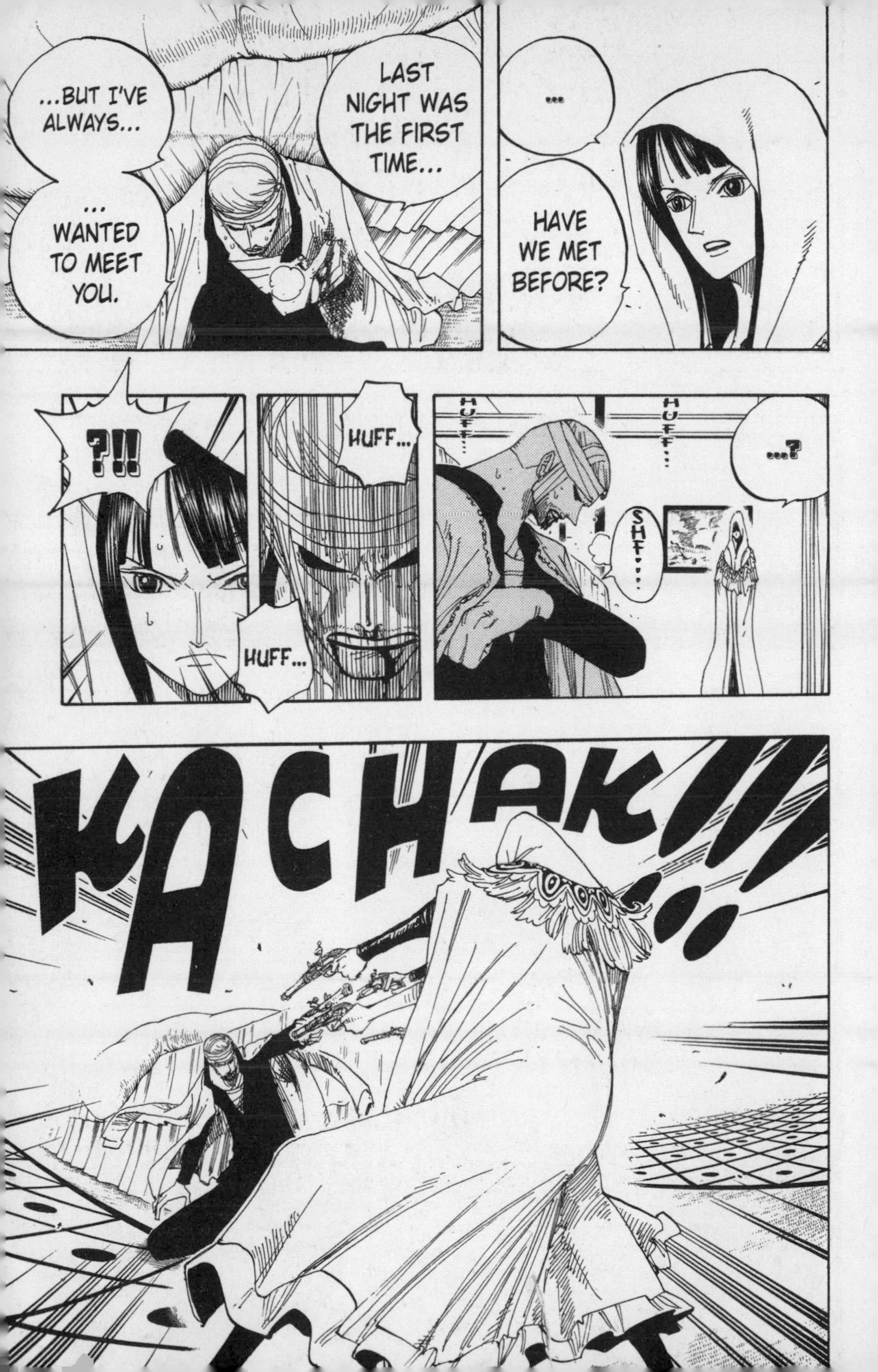
...
HAVE WE MET BEFORE?
LAST NIGHT WAS THE FIRST TIME...
...BUT I'VE ALWAYS...
... WANTED TO MEET YOU.
...?
HUFF...
HUFF...
SHF...
HUFF...
HUFF...
?!!
KACHAK!!

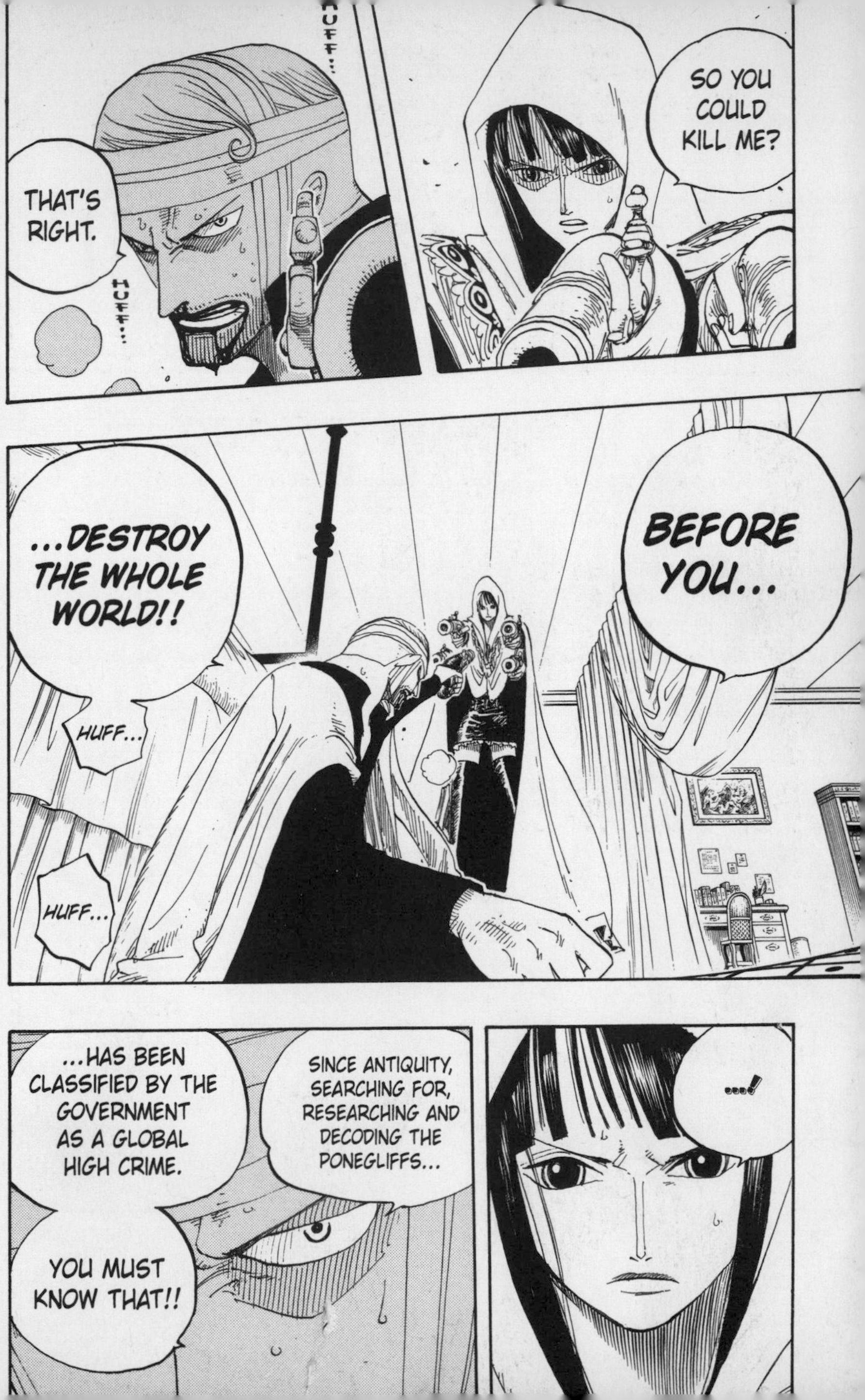
HUFF...
SO YOU COULD KILL ME?
THAT'S RIGHT.
HUFF...
BEFORE YOU...
...DESTROY THE WHOLE WORLD!!
HUFF...
HUFF...
...!
SINCE ANTIQUITY, SEARCHING FOR, RESEARCHING AND DECODING THE PONEGLIFFS...
...HAS BEEN CLASSIFIED BY THE GOVERNMENT AS A GLOBAL HIGH CRIME.
YOU MUST KNOW THAT!!

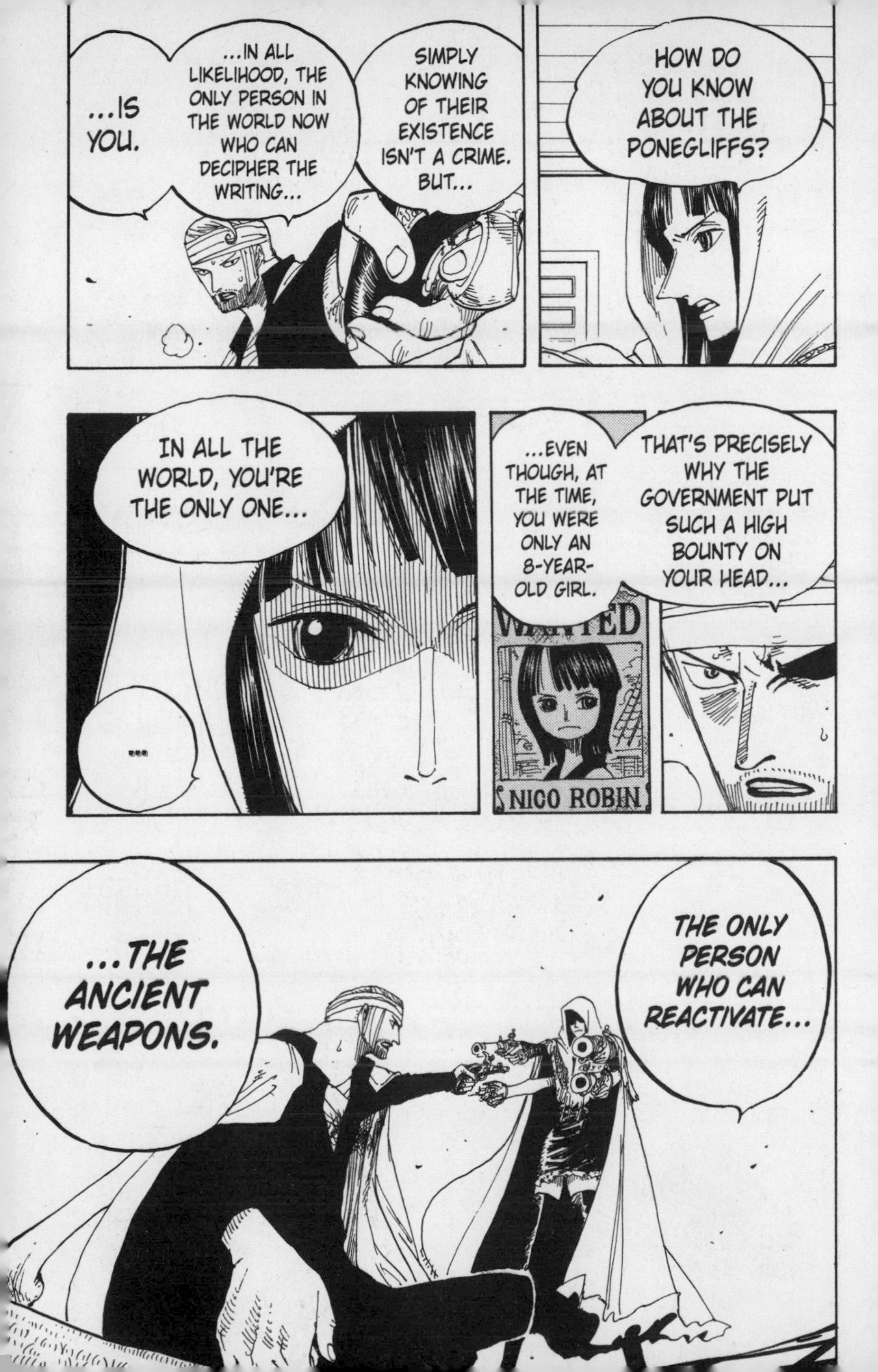
HOW DO YOU KNOW ABOUT THE PONEGLIFFS?
SIMPLY KNOWING OF THEIR EXISTENCE ISN'T A CRIME. BUT...
...IN ALL LIKELIHOOD, THE ONLY PERSON IN THE WORLD NOW WHO CAN DECIPHER THE WRITING...
...IS YOU.
THAT'S PRECISELY WHY THE GOVERNMENT PUT SUCH A HIGH BOUNTY ON YOUR HEAD...
...EVEN THOUGH, AT THE TIME, YOU WERE ONLY AN 8-YEAR-OLD GIRL.
WANTED
NICO ROBIN
IN ALL THE WORLD, YOU'RE THE ONLY ONE...
...
THE ONLY PERSON WHO CAN REACTIVATE...
...THE ANCIENT WEAPONS.

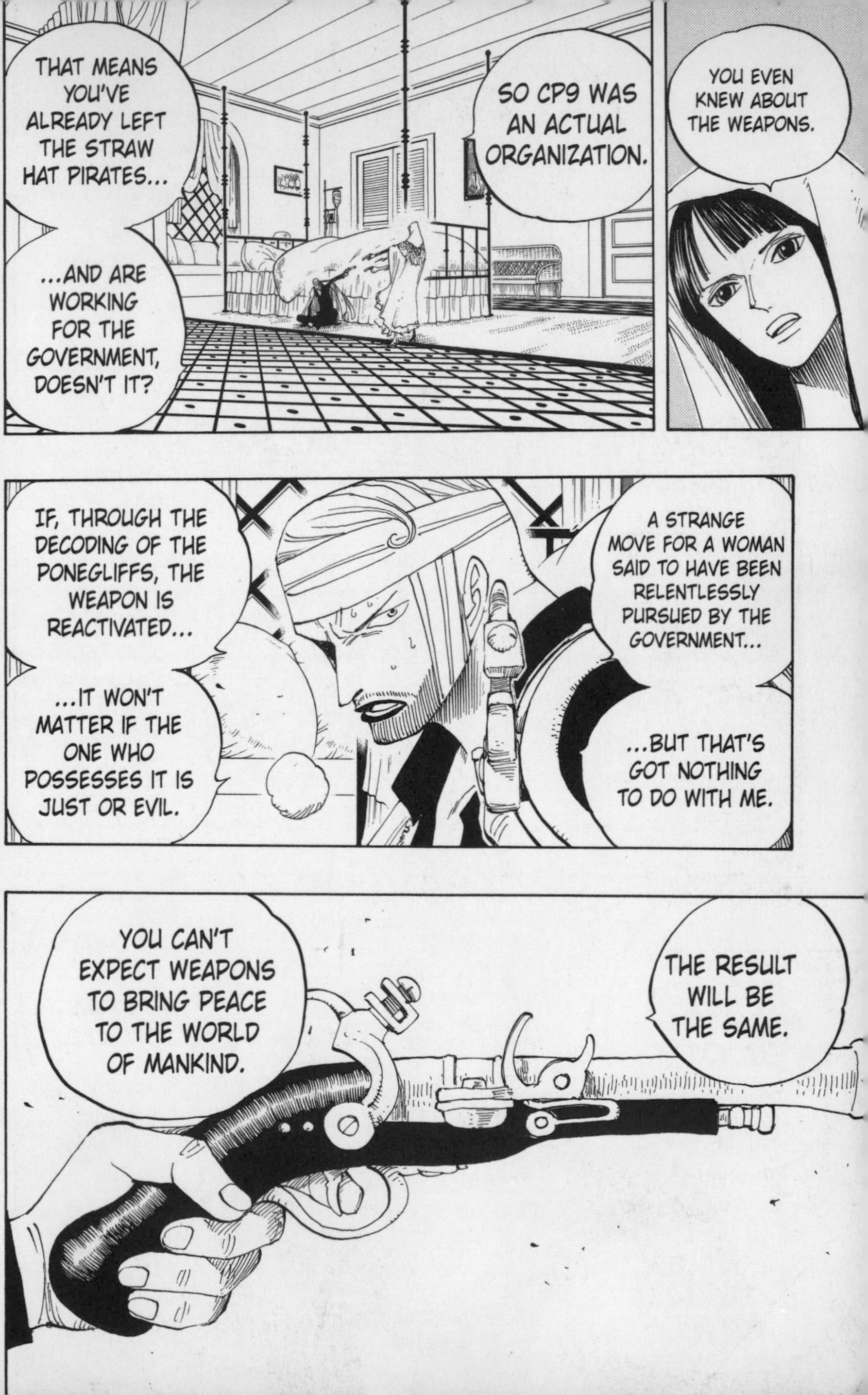
YOU EVEN KNEW ABOUT THE WEAPONS.
SO CP9 WAS AN ACTUAL ORGANIZATION.
THAT MEANS YOU'VE ALREADY LEFT THE STRAW HAT PIRATES...
...AND ARE WORKING FOR THE GOVERNMENT, DOESN'T IT?
A STRANGE MOVE FOR A WOMAN SAID TO HAVE BEEN RELENTLESSLY PURSUED BY THE GOVERNMENT...
...BUT THAT'S GOT NOTHING TO DO WITH ME.
IF, THROUGH THE DECODING OF THE PONEGLIFFS, THE WEAPON IS REACTIVATED...
...IT WON'T MATTER IF THE ONE WHO POSSESSES IT IS JUST OR EVIL.
THE RESULT WILL BE THE SAME.
YOU CAN'T EXPECT WEAPONS TO BRING PEACE TO THE WORLD OF MANKIND.

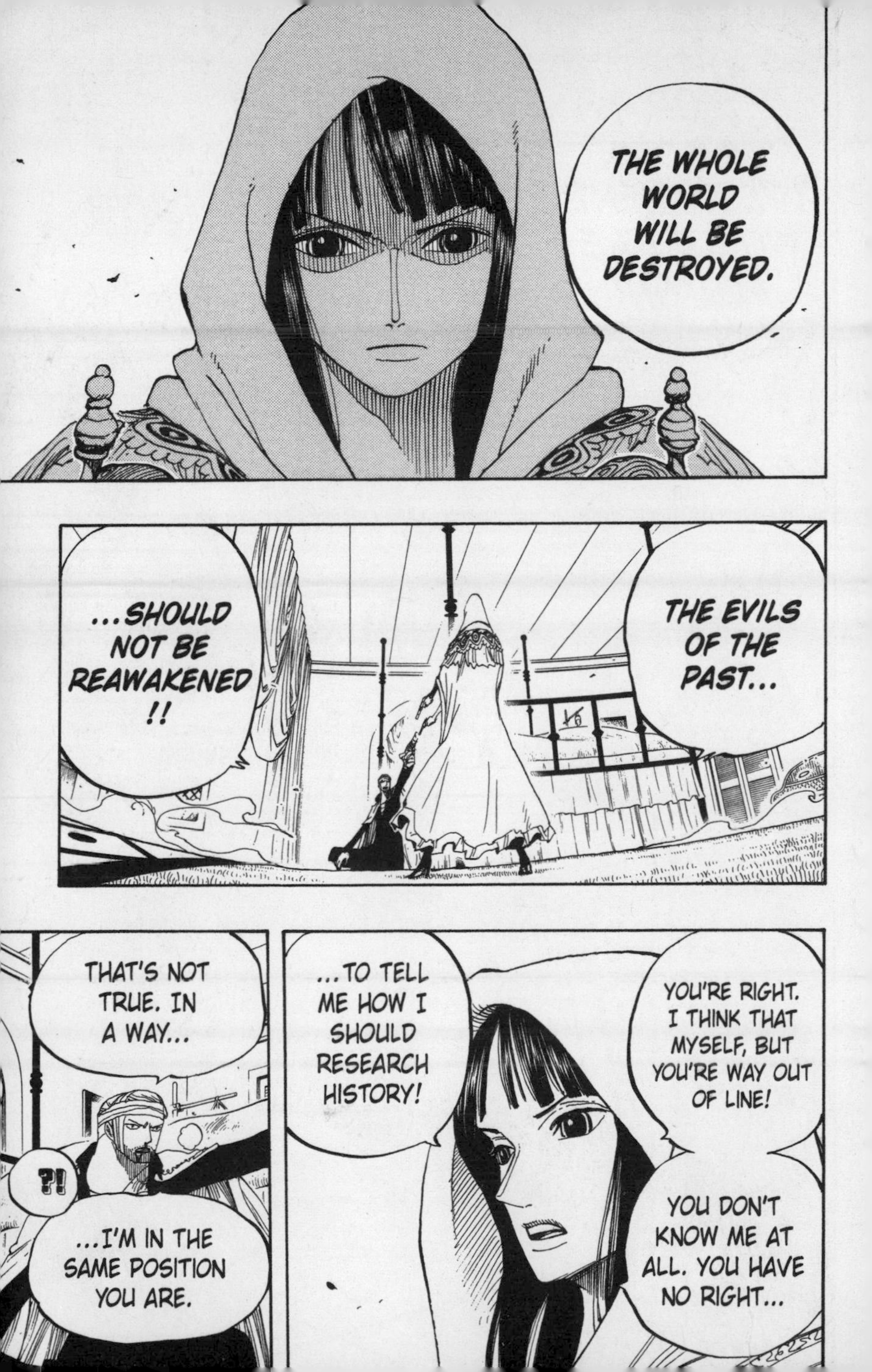
THE WHOLE WORLD WILL BE DESTROYED.
THE EVILS OF THE PAST...
...SHOULD NOT BE REAWAKENED!!
YOU'RE RIGHT. I THINK THAT MYSELF, BUT YOU'RE WAY OUT OF LINE!
YOU DON'T KNOW ME AT ALL. YOU HAVE NO RIGHT...
...TO TELL ME HOW I SHOULD RESEARCH HISTORY!
THAT'S NOT TRUE. IN A WAY...
?!
...I'M IN THE SAME POSITION YOU ARE.

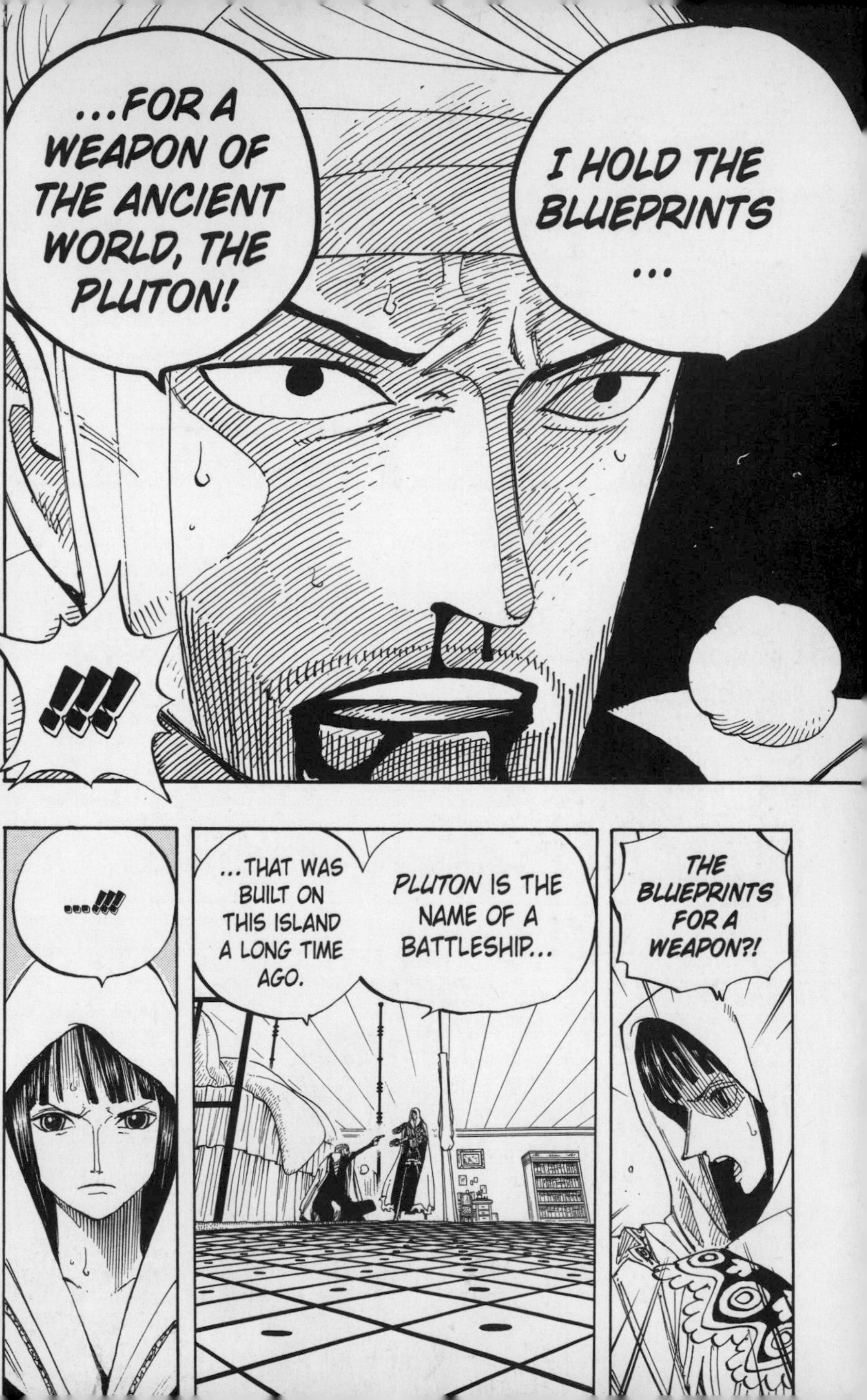
I HOLD THE BLUEPRINTS ...
...FOR A WEAPON OF THE ANCIENT WORLD, THE PLUTON!
!!!
THE BLUEPRINTS FOR A WEAPON?!
PLUTON IS THE NAME OF A BATTLESHIP...
...THAT WAS BUILT ON THIS ISLAND A LONG TIME AGO.
...!!!

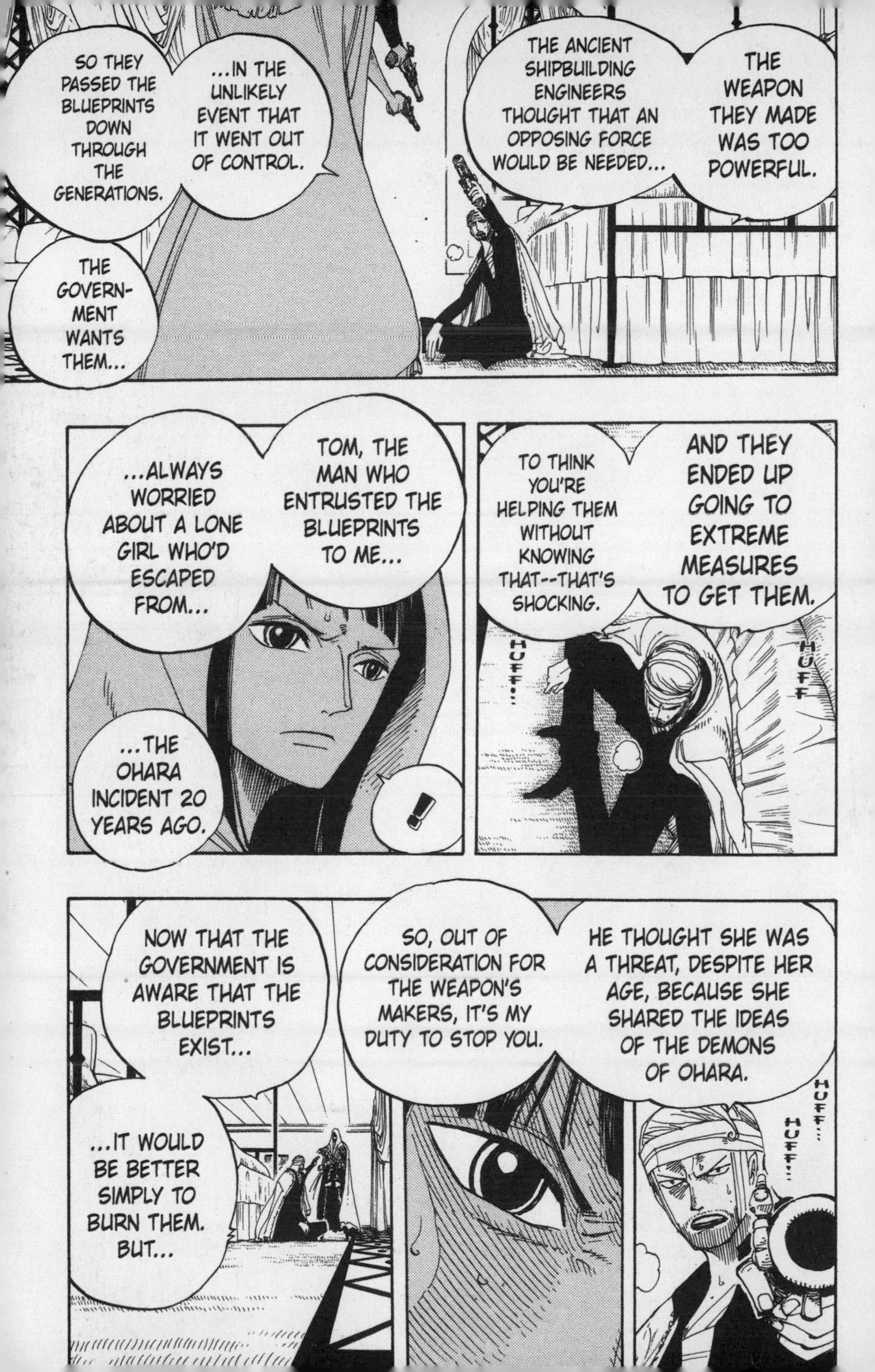
THE WEAPON THEY MADE WAS TOO POWERFUL.
THE ANCIENT SHIPBUILDING ENGINEERS THOUGHT THAT AN OPPOSING FORCE WOULD BE NEEDED...
...IN THE UNLIKELY EVENT THAT IT WENT OUT OF CONTROL.
SO THEY PASSED THE BLUEPRINTS DOWN THROUGH THE GENERATIONS.
THE GOVERN-MENT WANTS THEM...
AND THEY ENDED UP GOING TO EXTREME MEASURES TO GET THEM.
TO THINK YOU'RE HELPING THEM WITHOUT KNOWING THAT--THAT'S SHOCKING.
HUFF
HUFF...
TOM, THE MAN WHO ENTRUSTED THE BLUEPRINTS TO ME...
...ALWAYS WORRIED ABOUT A LONE GIRL WHO'D ESCAPED FROM...
...THE OHARA INCIDENT 20 YEARS AGO.
!
HE THOUGHT SHE WAS A THREAT, DESPITE HER AGE, BECAUSE SHE SHARED THE IDEAS OF THE DEMONS OF OHARA.
SO, OUT OF CONSIDERATION FOR THE WEAPON'S MAKERS, IT'S MY DUTY TO STOP YOU.
NOW THAT THE GOVERNMENT IS AWARE THAT THE BLUEPRINTS EXIST...
...IT WOULD BE BETTER SIMPLY TO BURN THEM. BUT...
HUFF...
HUFF...

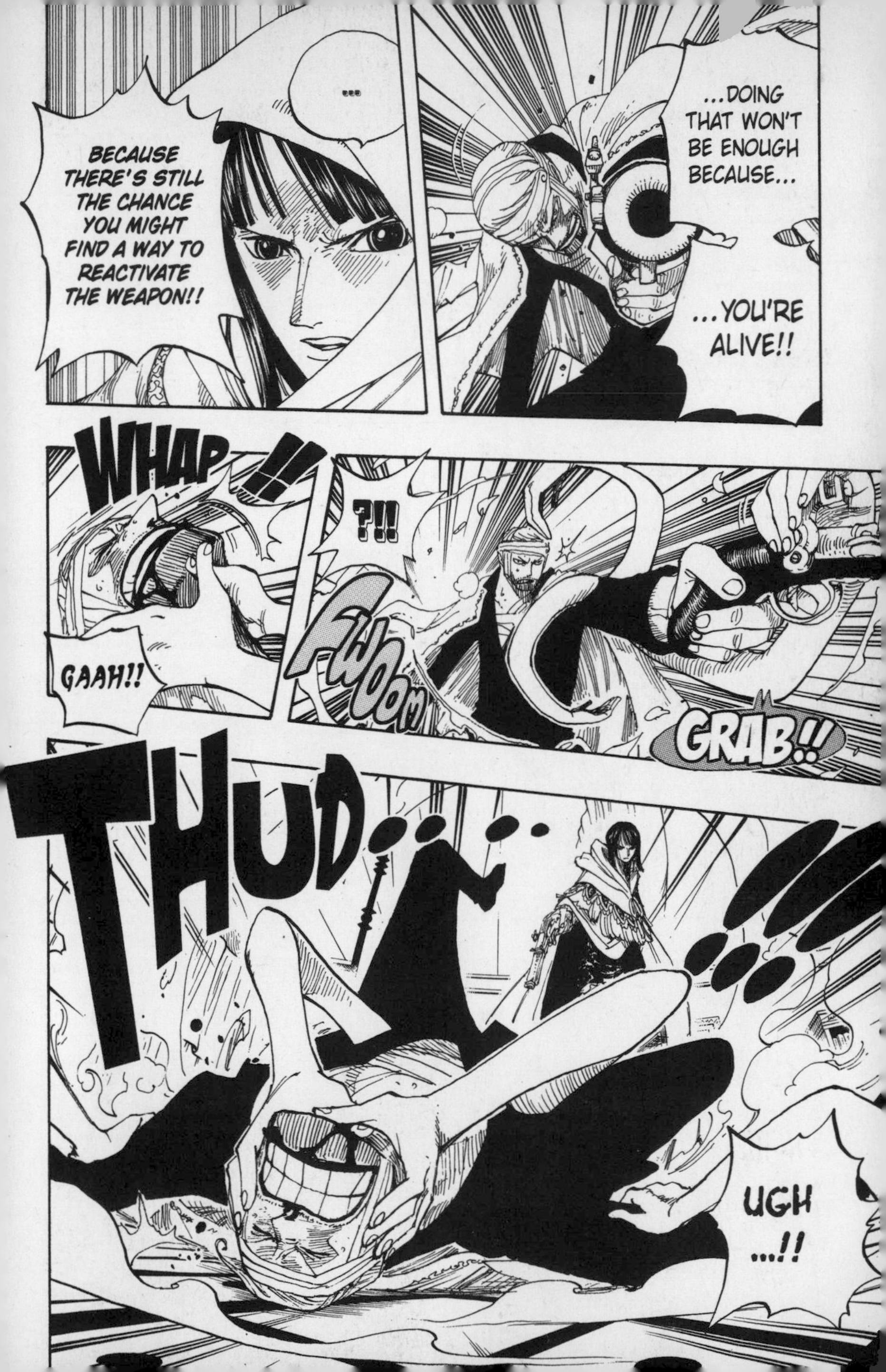
...DOING THAT WON'T BE ENOUGH BECAUSE...
...YOU'RE ALIVE!!
...
BECAUSE THERE'S STILL THE CHANCE YOU MIGHT FIND A WAY TO REACTIVATE THE WEAPON!!
?!!
FWOOM
GRAB!!
WHAP!!
GAAH!!
THUD...!!!
UGH ...!!

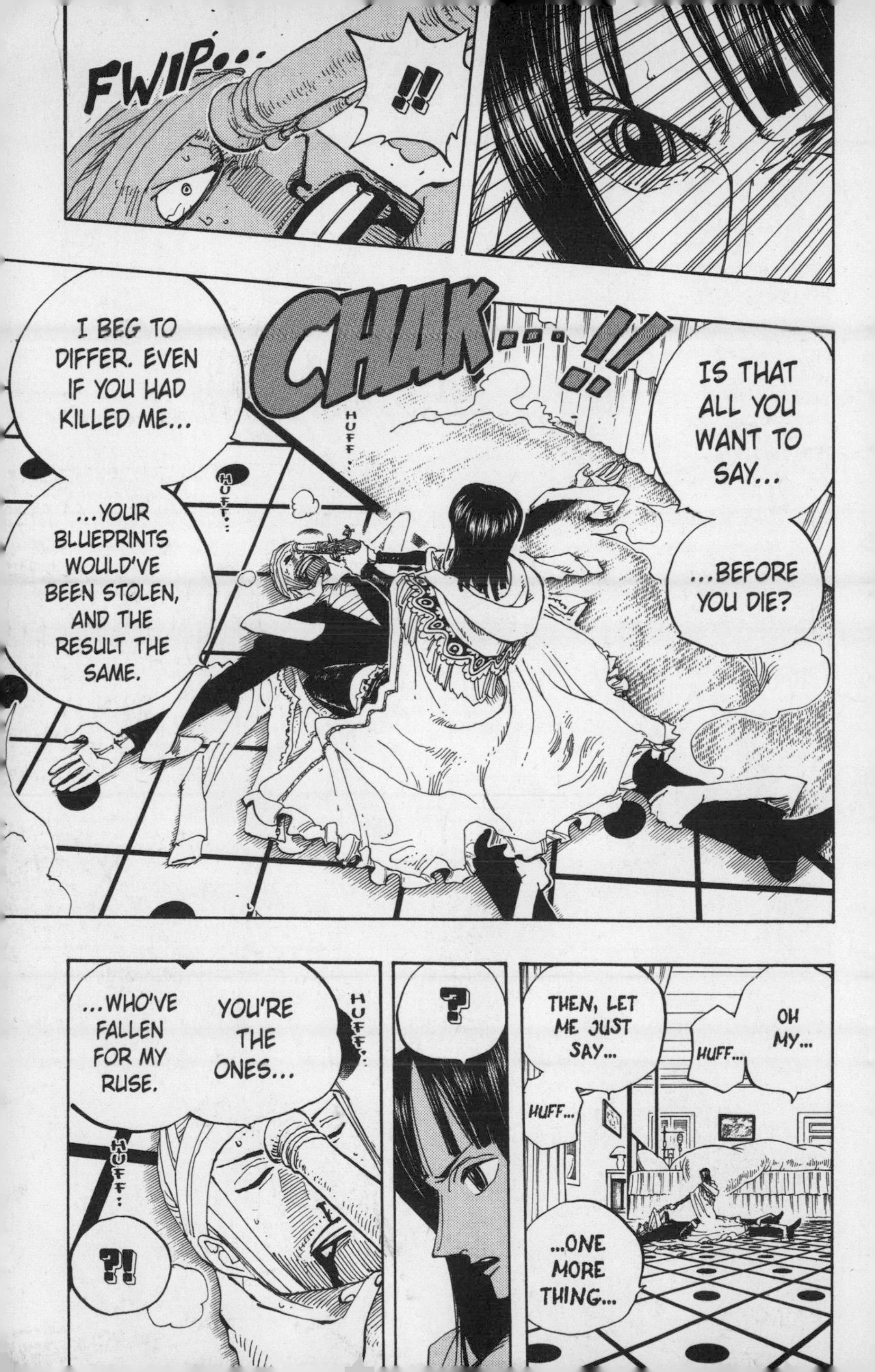
FWIP...
!!
CHAK...!!
IS THAT ALL YOU WANT TO SAY...
...BEFORE YOU DIE?
HUFF...
I BEG TO DIFFER. EVEN IF YOU HAD KILLED ME...
HUFF...
...YOUR BLUEPRINTS WOULD'VE BEEN STOLEN, AND THE RESULT THE SAME.
OH MY...
HUFF...
THEN, LET ME JUST SAY...
HUFF...
...ONE MORE THING...
?
HUFF...
YOU'RE THE ONES...
...WHO'VE FALLEN FOR MY RUSE.
HUFF...
?!

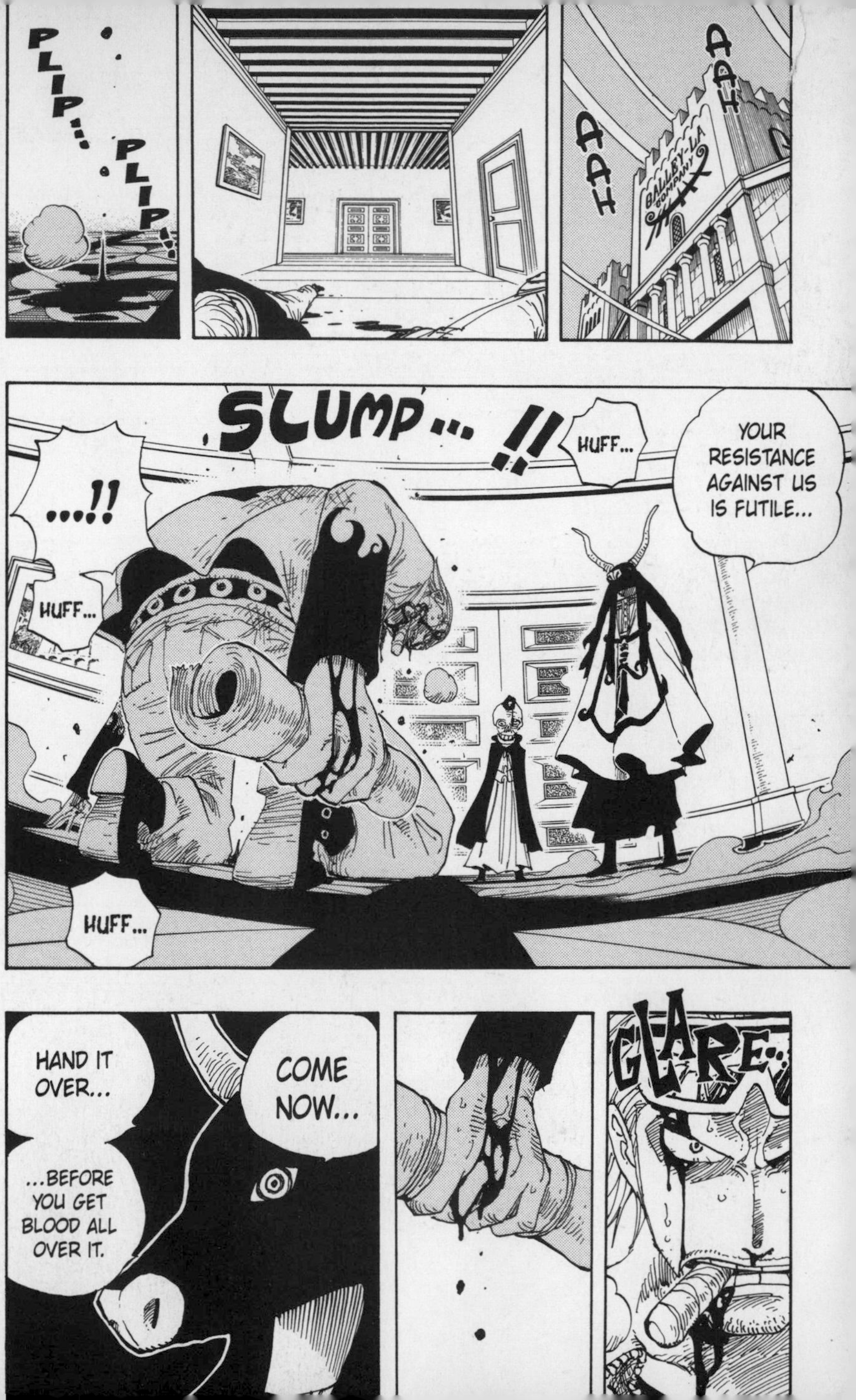
AAH
AAH
GALLEY-LA COMPANY
PLIP... PLIP...
YOUR RESISTANCE AGAINST US IS FUTILE...
HUFF...
SLUMP... !!
...!!
HUFF...
HUFF...
GLARE...
COME NOW...
HAND IT OVER...
...BEFORE YOU GET BLOOD ALL OVER IT.

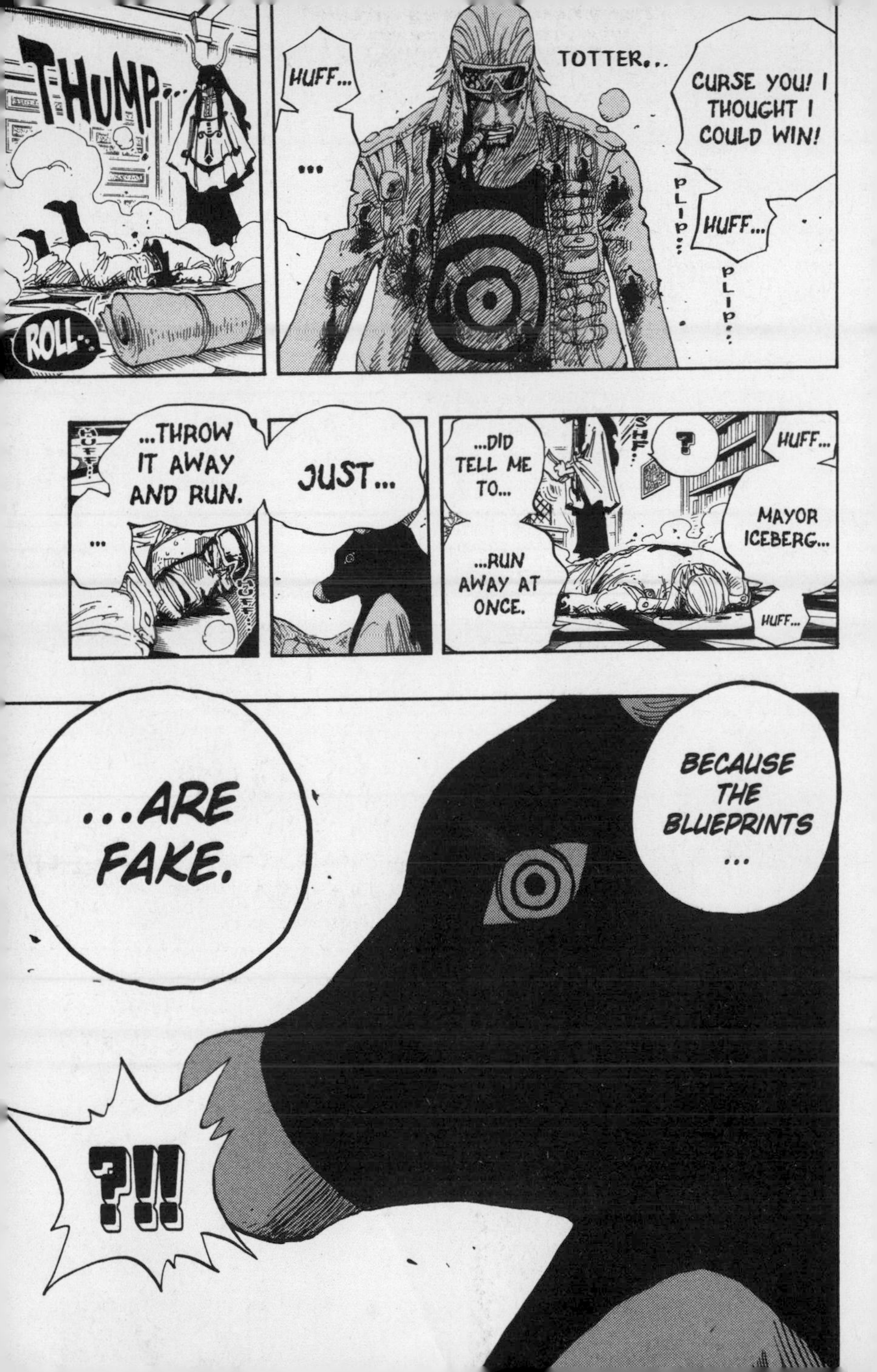
TOTTER...
CURSE YOU! I THOUGHT I COULD WIN!
PLIP...
HUFF...
PLIP...
HUFF...
...
THUMP...
ROLL...
HUFF...
MAYOR ICEBERG...
HUFF...
?
SHF...
...DID TELL ME TO...
...RUN AWAY AT ONCE.
JUST...
...THROW IT AWAY AND RUN.
HUFF...
...
BECAUSE THE BLUEPRINTS ...
...ARE FAKE.
?!!

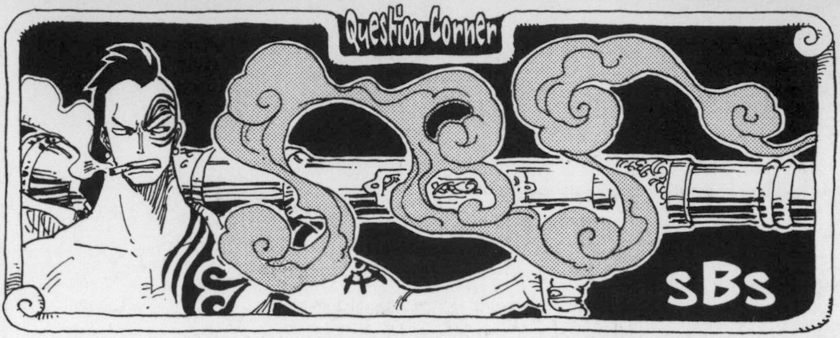
Question Corner
SBS

Q: In chapter 297 of volume 32, how come Luffy could make that big snap-crackle thing (Kingdom Come) disappear? Also, what was the electric discharge that Nami was talking about? I looked into it, but I couldn't figure it out! Please help me out, 'kay?★

--crush

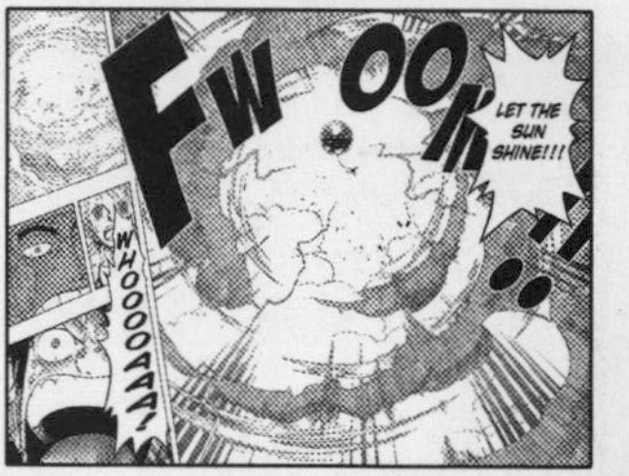
FWOOM!!
LET THE SUN SHINE!!!
WHOOOOAAA!

A: Right. Um... How should I explain this? To begin with, the important thing really is that you felt the power of that scene; if you did, everything's okay. So, first off, Kingdom Come is a cluster of thunderclouds. Think of thunderclouds as clumps of stress with lots of static electricity in them. The thundercloud thinks it wants to take that stress out on something. What comes down at that point is lightning. The kind that people mean when they say, "Hey, a tree just got hit by lightning!" or "Yamada got struck by lightning!" Lightning is an electrical discharge, but electrical discharges aren't limited to occurring outside the cloud. Sometimes that snap-crackle stress is released inside the cloud itself, and then it's called "sheet lightning." Gold conducts electricity. So when Luffy plunged into Kingdom Come with the gold ball, the snap-crackle stress in Kingdom Come discharged inside the cloud and vanished. But you know, it's not like Luffy knew what he was doing either. It's okay. Just be glad the weather cleared up. Skypiea is still peaceful to this day.

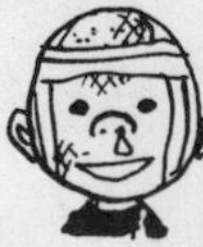
YAMADA

Here ends the Question Corner!!

Chapter 345: SLEEPERS

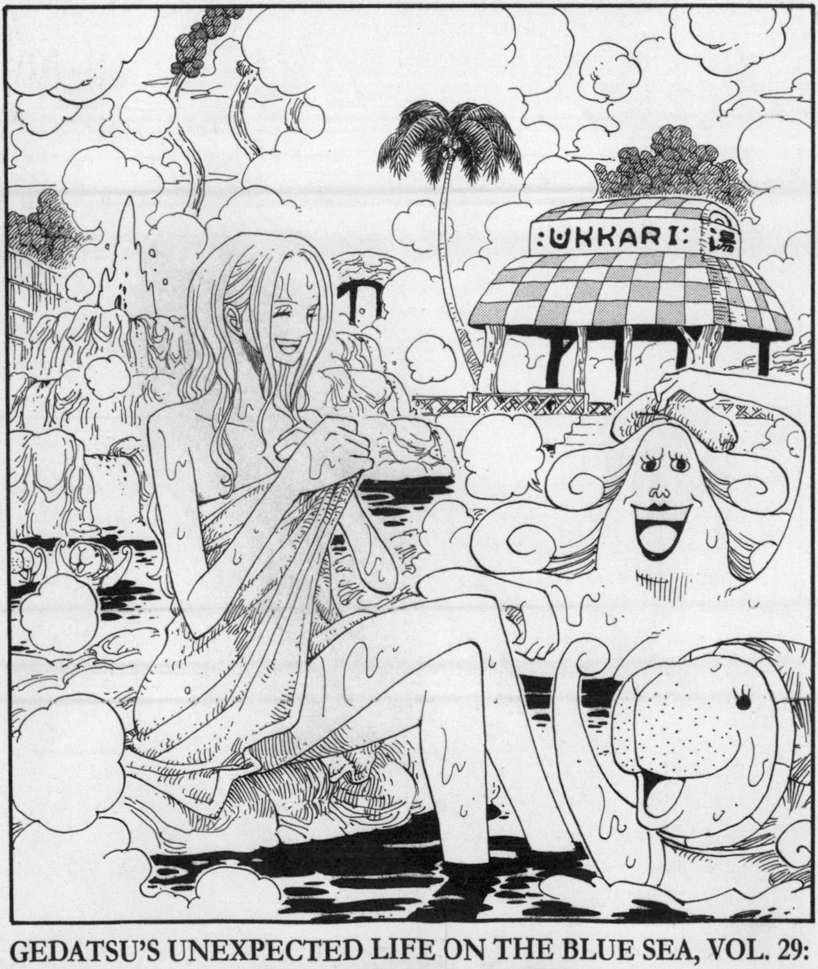
UKKARI

GEDATSU'S UNEXPECTED LIFE ON THE BLUE SEA, VOL. 29:
"THE WOMEN'S BATH"

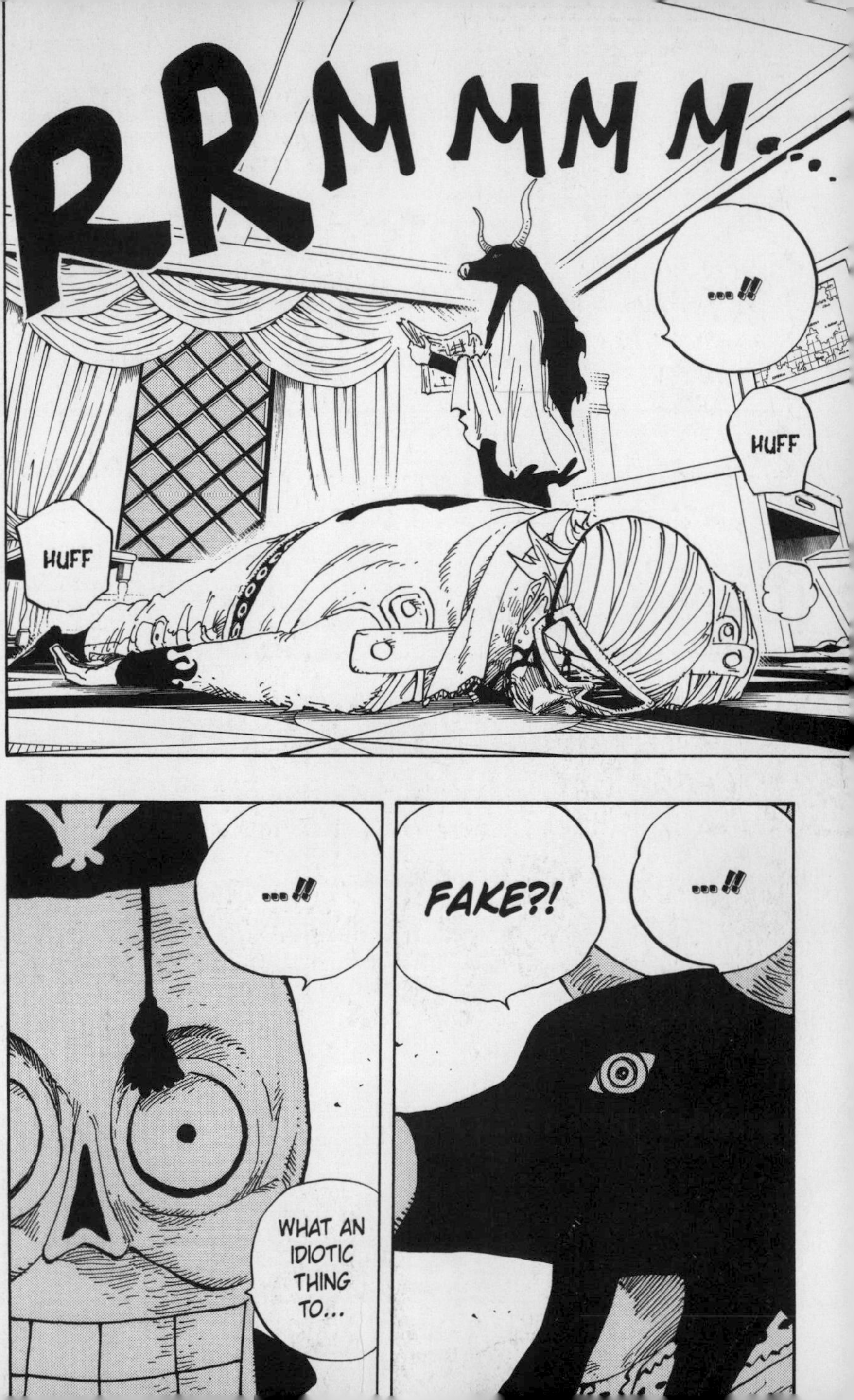
RRMMMM...
...!!
HUFF
HUFF
...!!
FAKE?!
...!!
WHAT AN IDIOTIC THING TO...

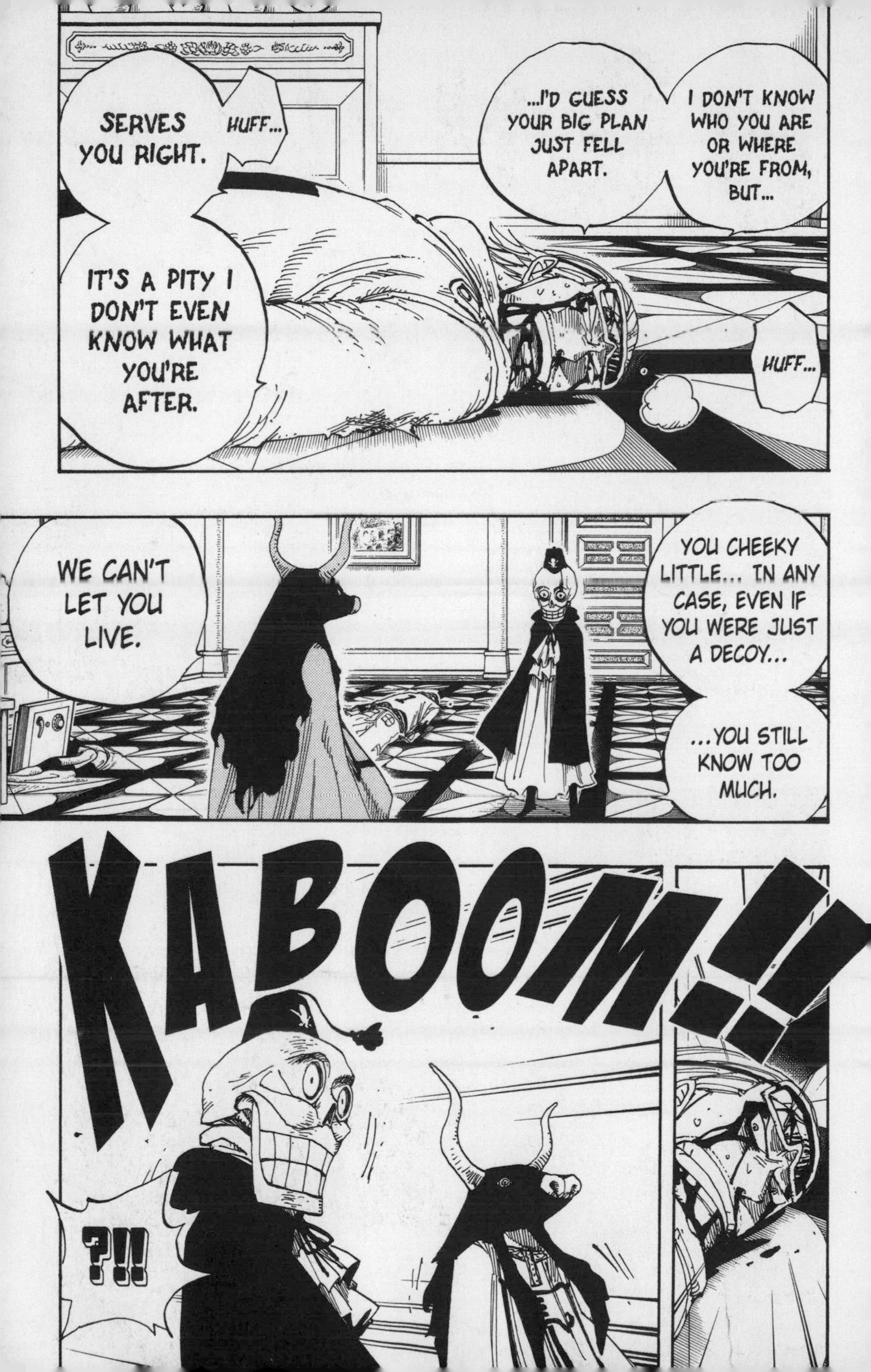
I DON'T KNOW WHO YOU ARE OR WHERE YOU'RE FROM, BUT...
...I'D GUESS YOUR BIG PLAN JUST FELL APART.
HUFF...
SERVES YOU RIGHT.
HUFF...
IT'S A PITY I DON'T EVEN KNOW WHAT YOU'RE AFTER.
YOU CHEEKY LITTLE... IN ANY CASE, EVEN IF YOU WERE JUST A DECOY...
...YOU STILL KNOW TOO MUCH.
WE CAN'T LET YOU LIVE.
KABOOM!!
?!!

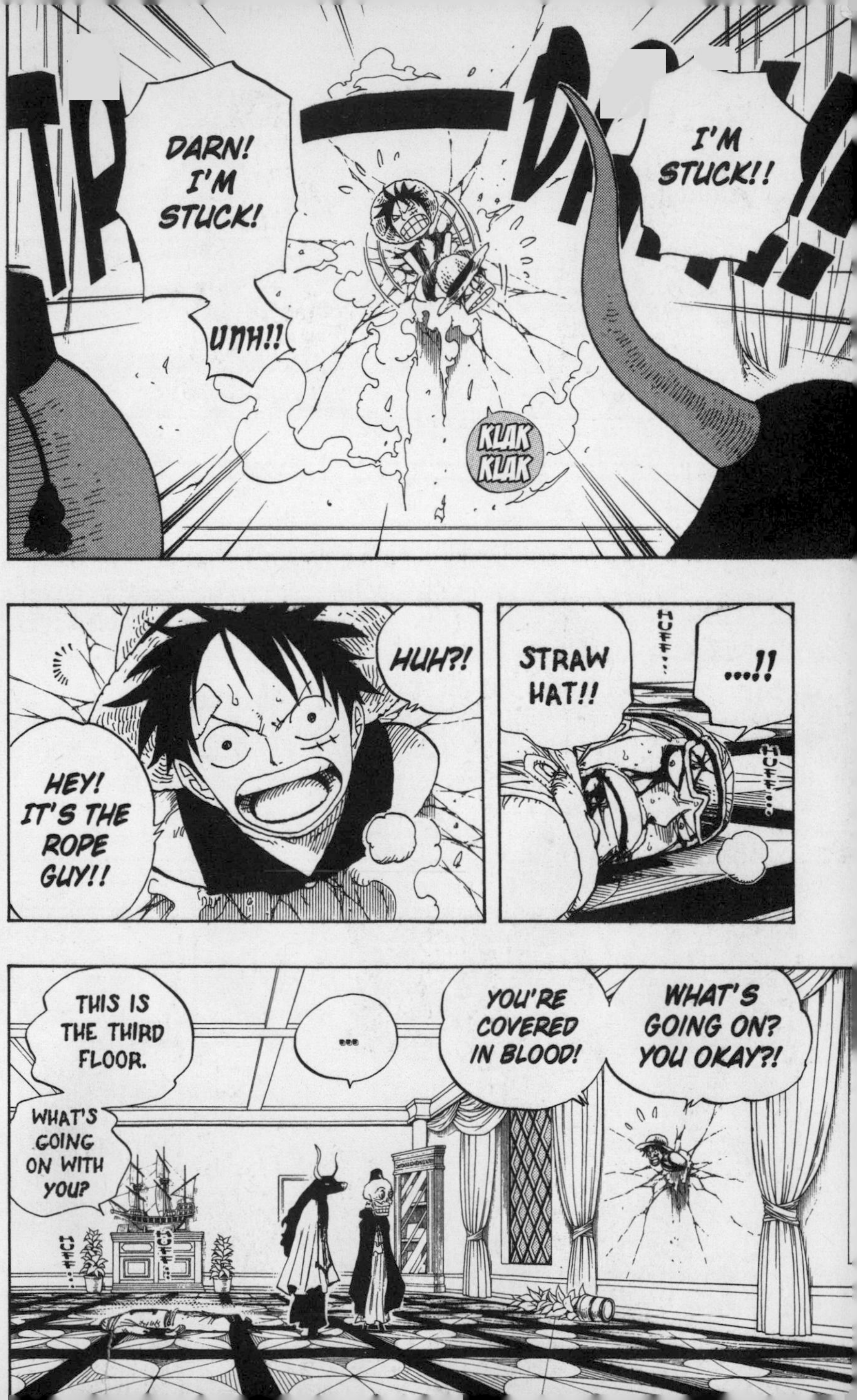
I'M STUCK!!
DARN! I'M STUCK!
UNH!!
KLAK KLAK
...!!
HUFF...
STRAW HAT!!
HUFF...
HUH?!
HEY! IT'S THE ROPE GUY!!
WHAT'S GOING ON? YOU OKAY?!
YOU'RE COVERED IN BLOOD!
...
THIS IS THE THIRD FLOOR.
WHAT'S GOING ON WITH YOU?
HUFF...
HUFF...

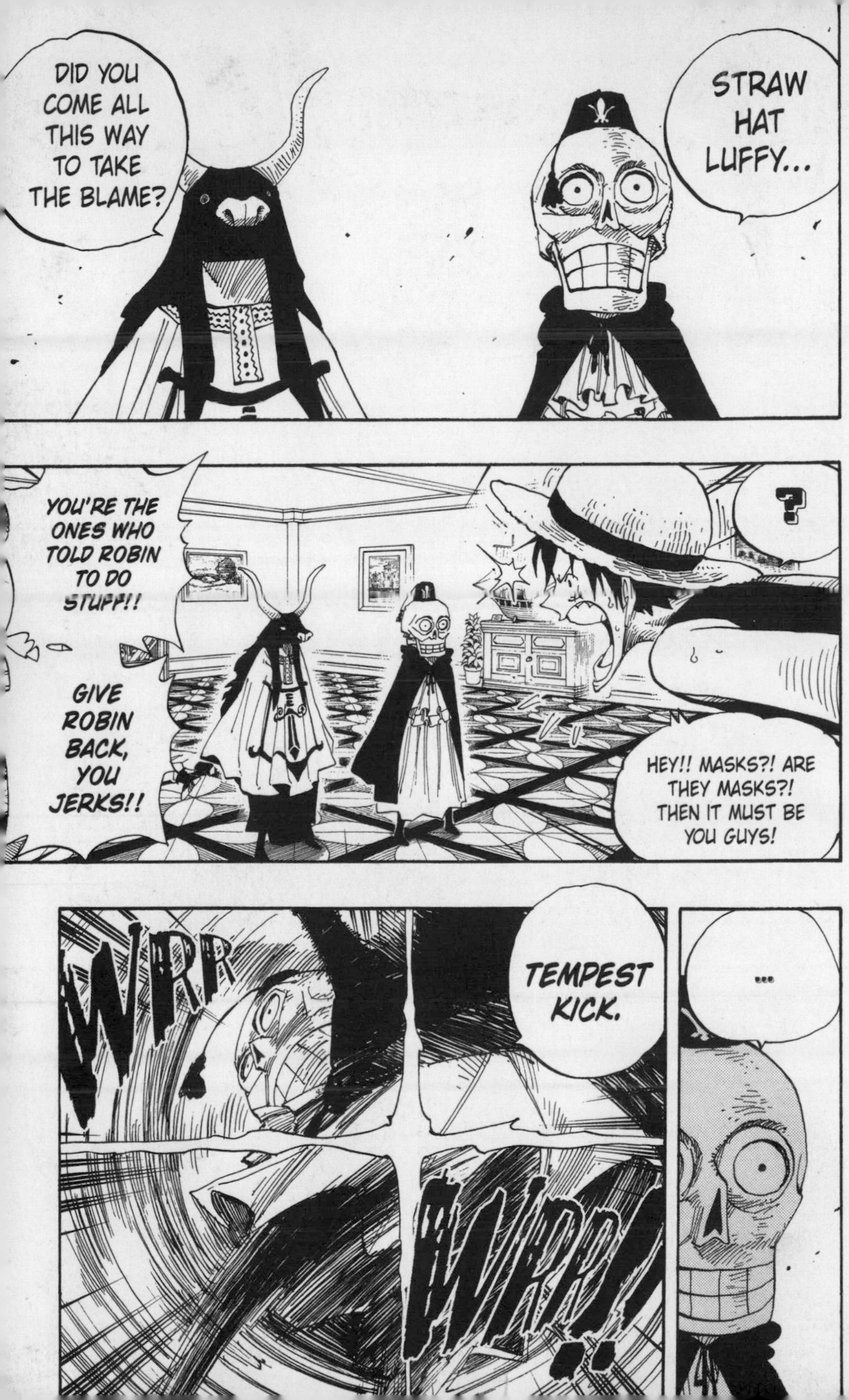
STRAW HAT LUFFY...
DID YOU COME ALL THIS WAY TO TAKE THE BLAME?
?
HEY!! MASKS?! ARE THEY MASKS?! THEN IT MUST BE YOU GUYS!
YOU'RE THE ONES WHO TOLD ROBIN TO DO STUFF!!
GIVE ROBIN BACK, YOU JERKS!!
...
TEMPEST KICK.

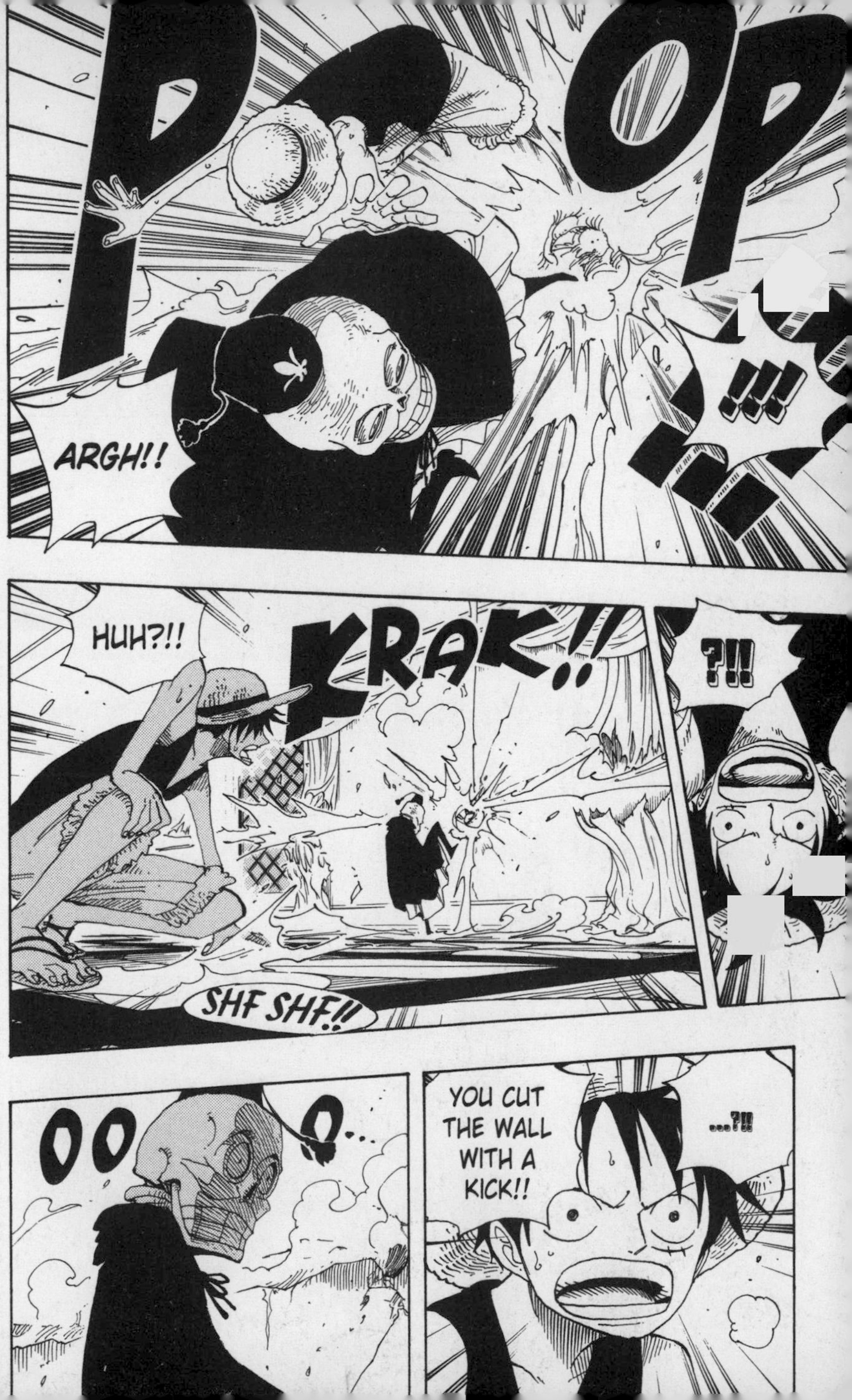
ARGH!!
?!!
KRAK!!
HUH?!!
SHF SHF!!
...?!!
YOU CUT THE WALL WITH A KICK!!
OO O...

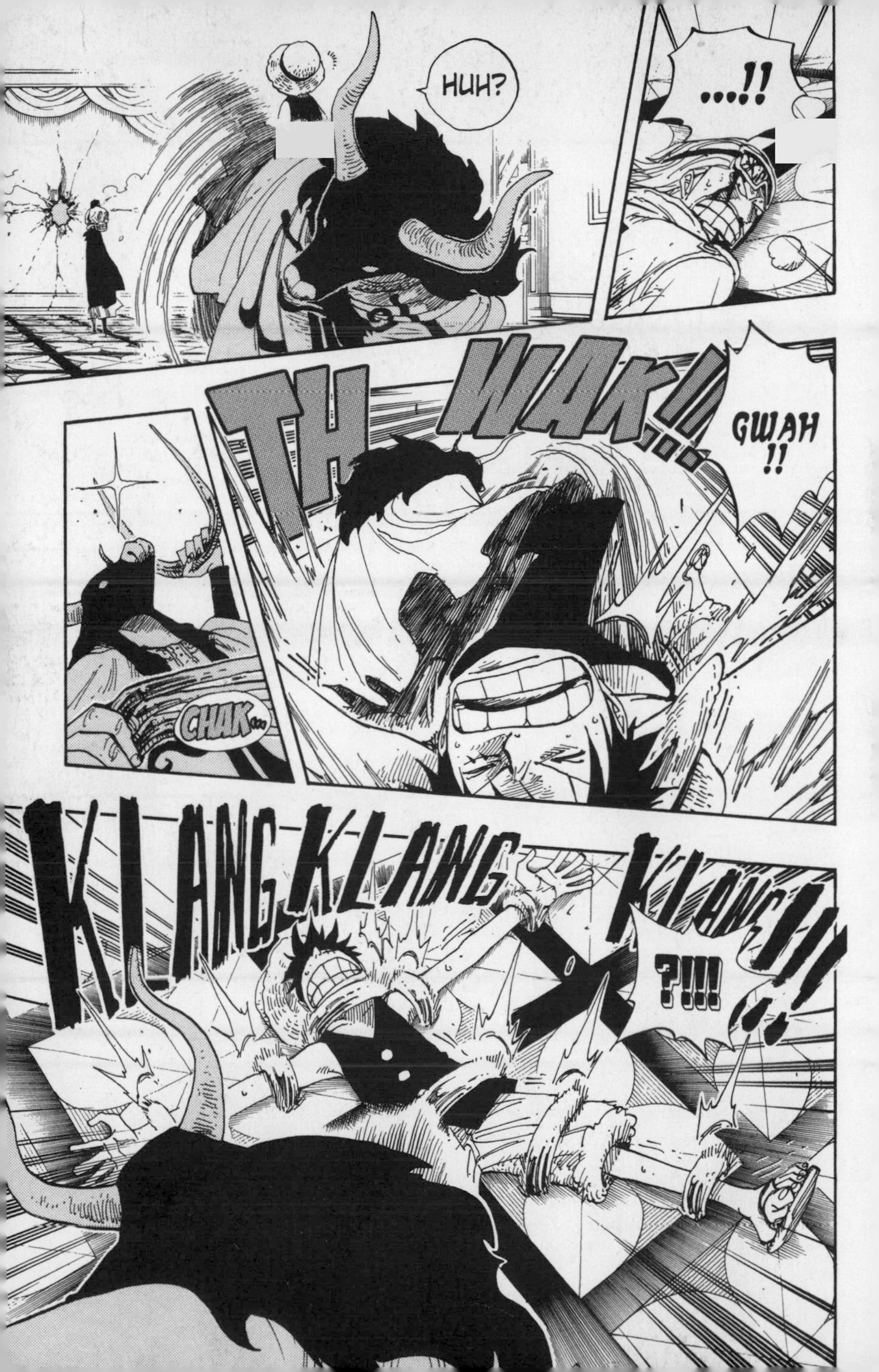

....!!
HUH?
THWAK!!
GWAH!!
CHAK...
KLANG KLANG KLANG!!
?!!!

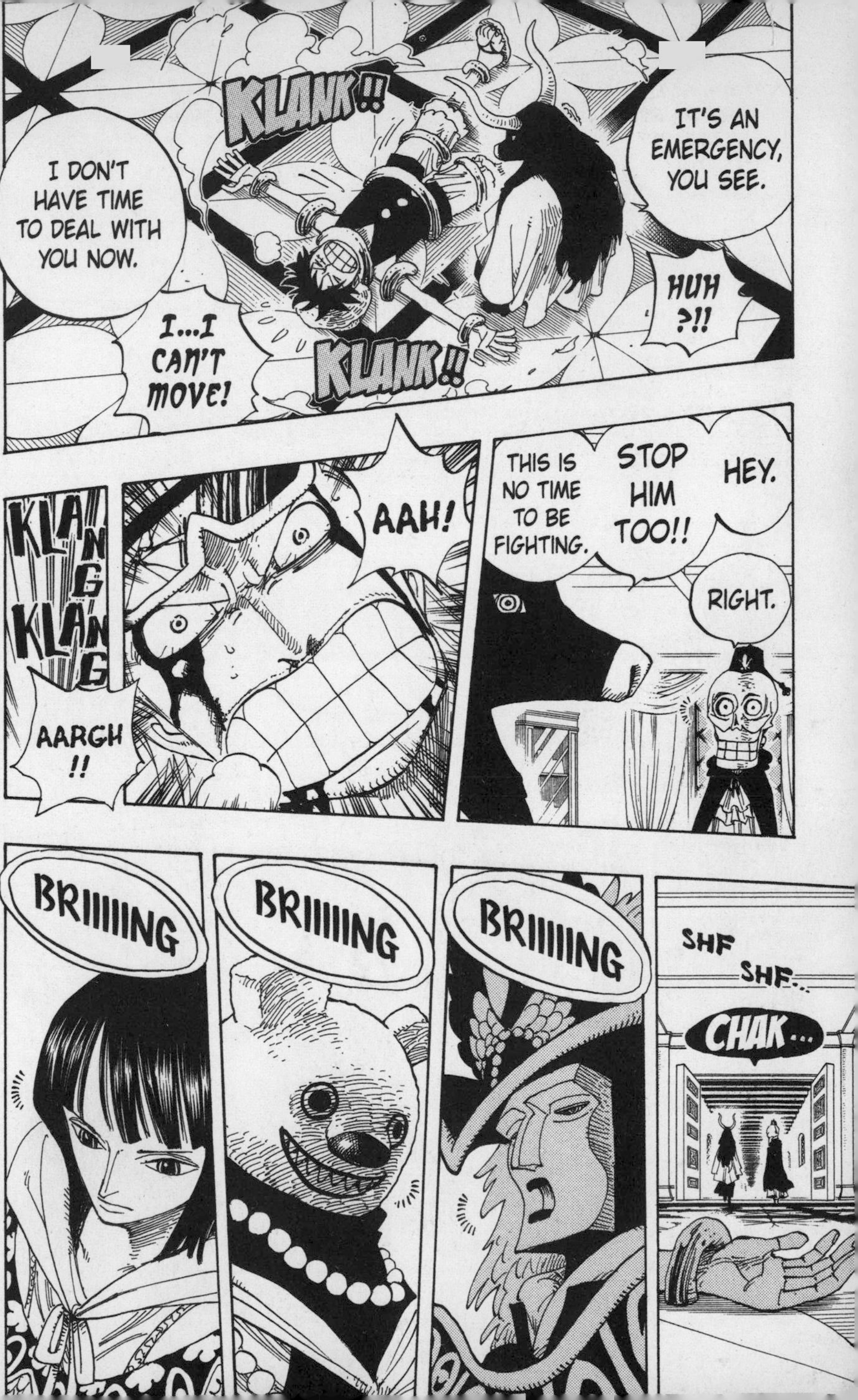
IT'S AN EMERGENCY, YOU SEE.
KLANK!!
I DON'T HAVE TIME TO DEAL WITH YOU NOW.
HUH ?!!
I...I CAN'T MOVE!
KLANK!!
HEY.
STOP HIM TOO!!
THIS IS NO TIME TO BE FIGHTING.
RIGHT.
AAH!
KLANG KLANG
AARGH !!
SHF SHF...
CHAK...
BRIIIIING
BRIIIIING
BRIIIIING

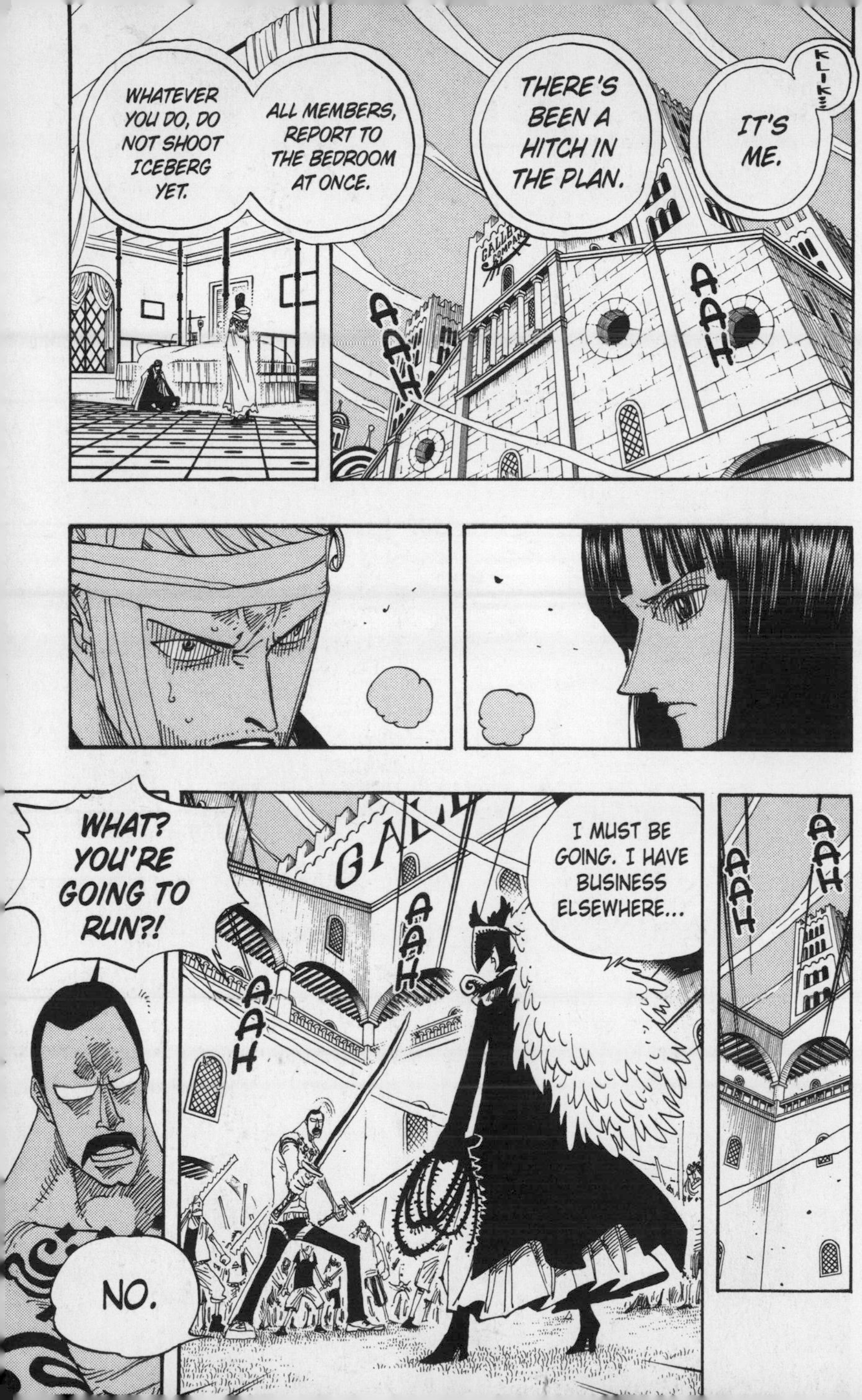
KLIK
IT'S ME.
THERE'S BEEN A HITCH IN THE PLAN.
AAH
AAH
ALL MEMBERS, REPORT TO THE BEDROOM AT ONCE.
WHATEVER YOU DO, DO NOT SHOOT ICEBERG YET.
AAH
AAH
I MUST BE GOING. I HAVE BUSINESS ELSEWHERE...
AAH
AAH
WHAT? YOU'RE GOING TO RUN?!
NO.

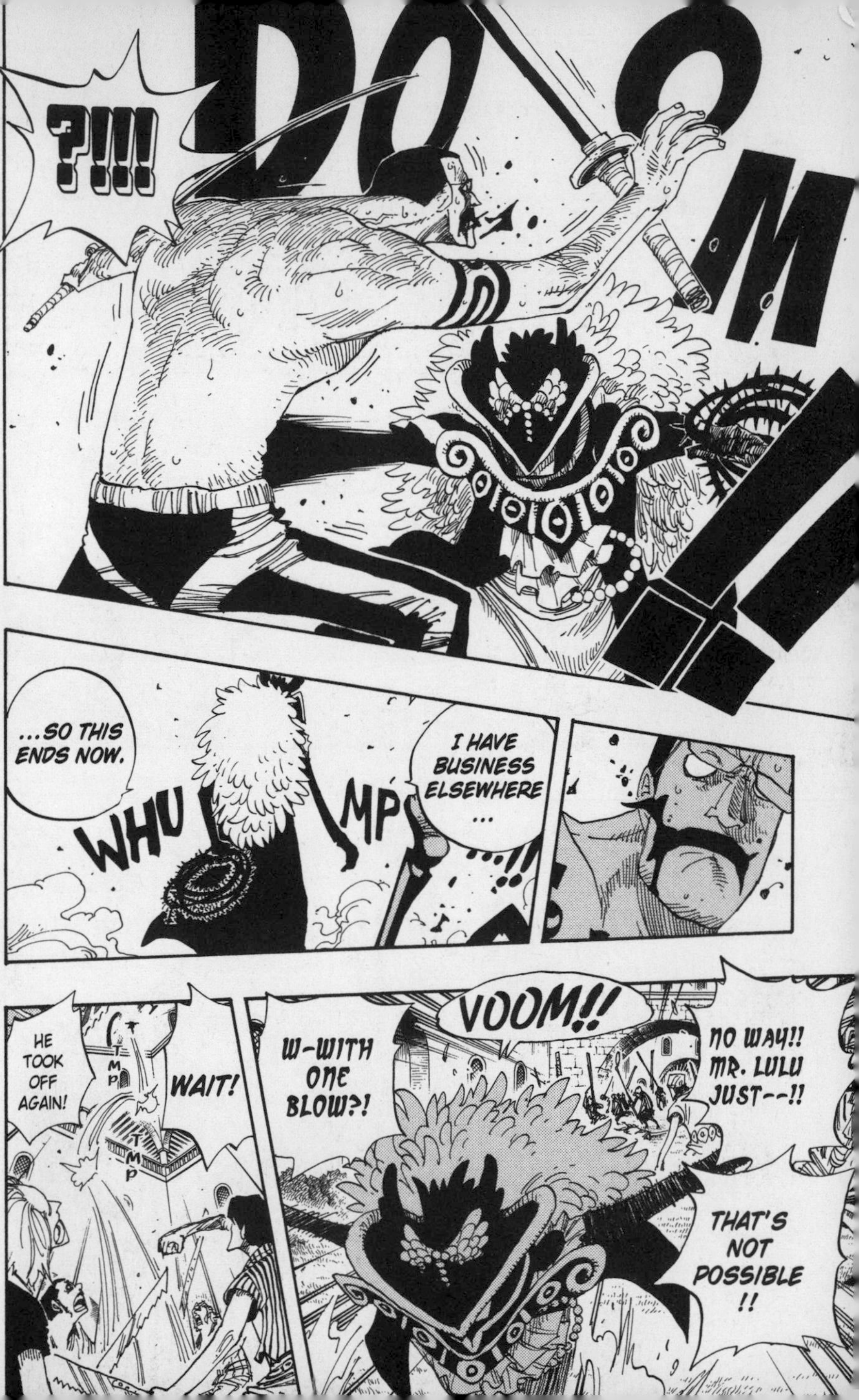
DOOM!!
?!!!
I HAVE BUSINESS ELSEWHERE ...
...SO THIS ENDS NOW.
WHUMP
VOOM!!
NO WAY!! MR. LULU JUST--!!
THAT'S NOT POSSIBLE !!
W-WITH ONE BLOW?!
WAIT!
HE TOOK OFF AGAIN!
TMP
TMP

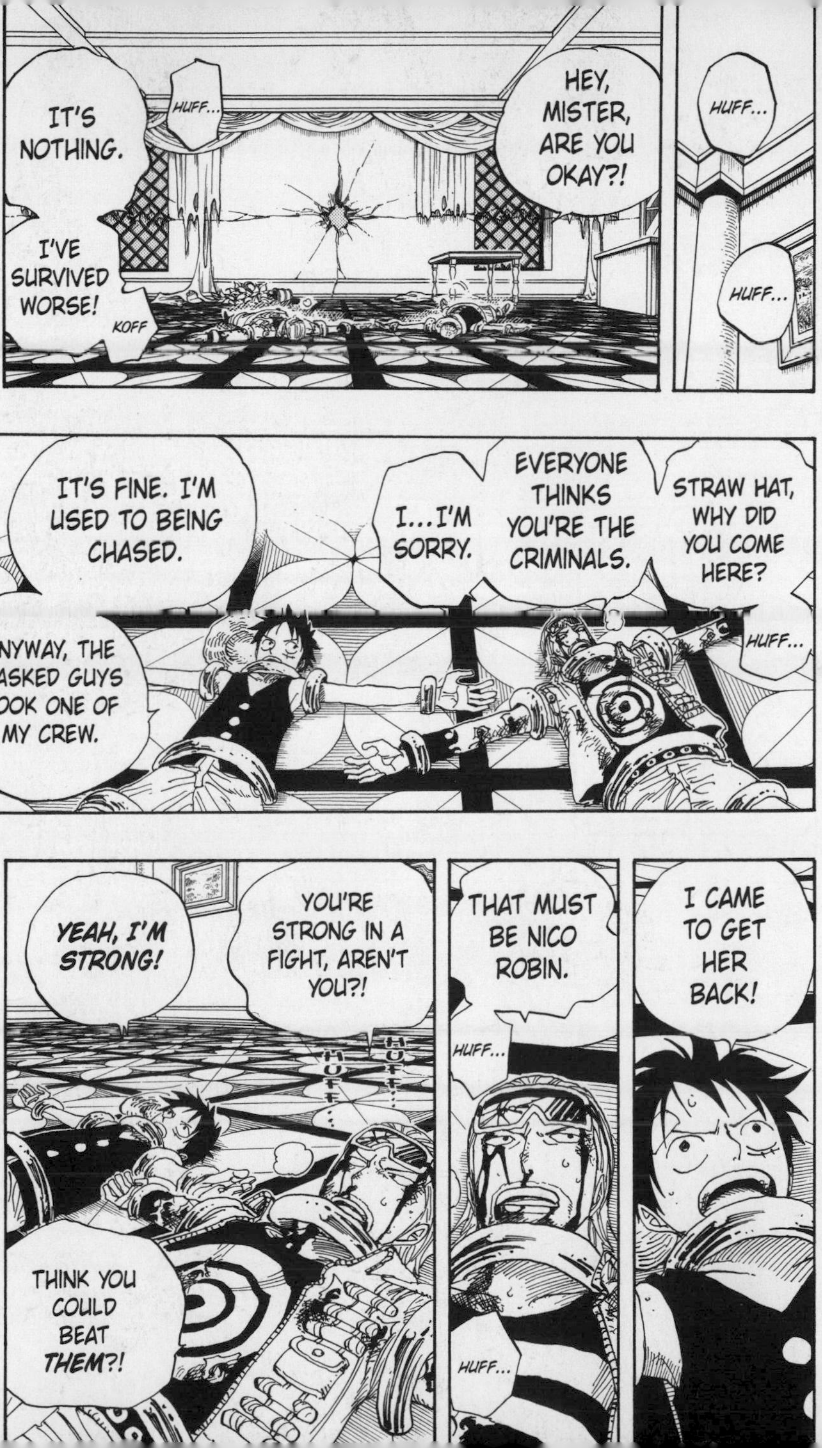
HUFF...
HUFF...
HEY, MISTER, ARE YOU OKAY?!
HUFF...
IT'S NOTHING.
I'VE SURVIVED WORSE!
KOFF
STRAW HAT, WHY DID YOU COME HERE?
HUFF...
EVERYONE THINKS YOU'RE THE CRIMINALS.
I...I'M SORRY.
IT'S FINE. I'M USED TO BEING CHASED.
ANYWAY, THE MASKED GUYS TOOK ONE OF MY CREW.
I CAME TO GET HER BACK!
THAT MUST BE NICO ROBIN.
HUFF...
HUFF...
YOU'RE STRONG IN A FIGHT, AREN'T YOU?!
HUFF...
HUFF...
YEAH, I'M STRONG!
THINK YOU COULD BEAT THEM?!

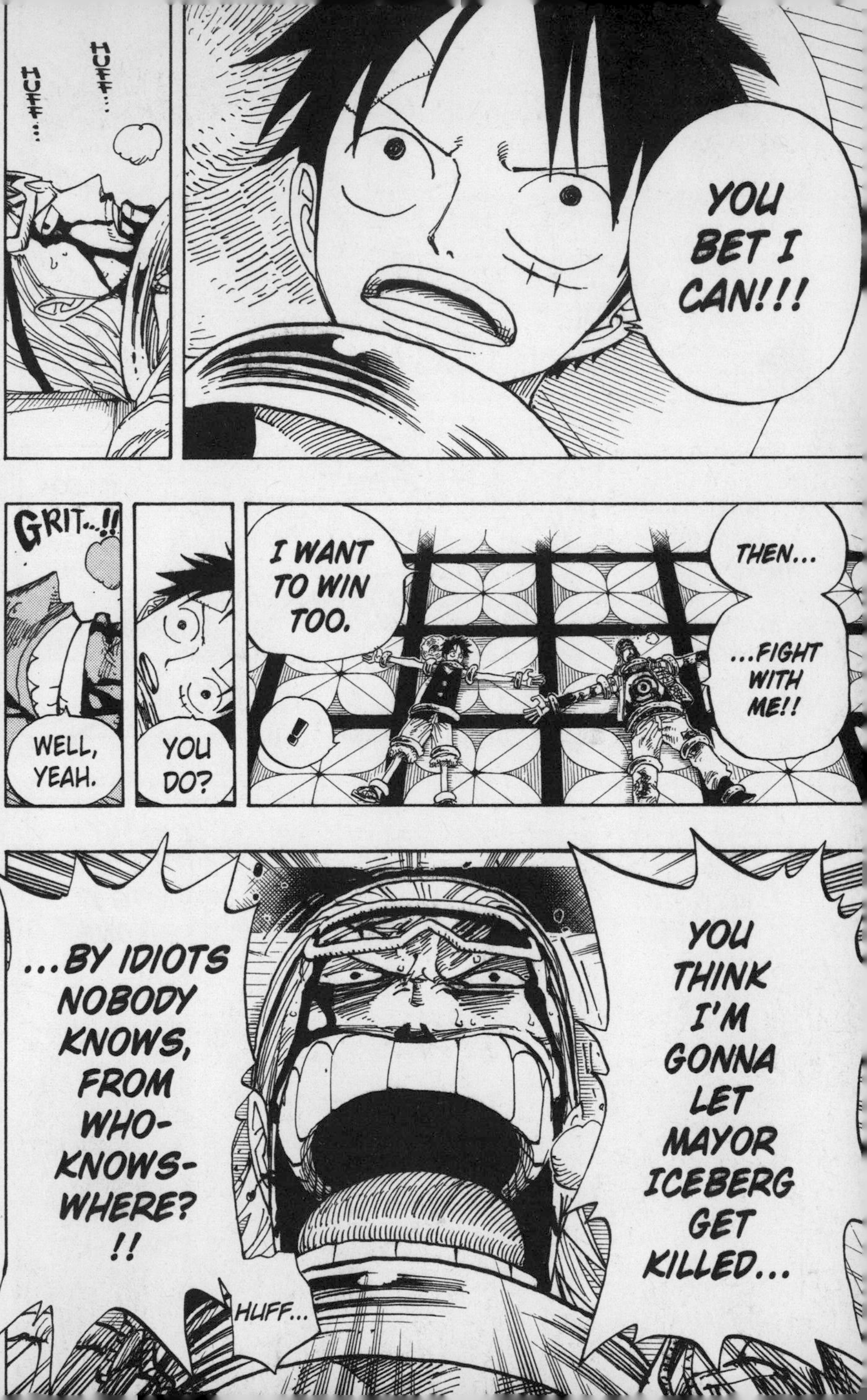
YOU BET I CAN!!!
HUFF...
HUFF...
THEN...
...FIGHT WITH ME!!
I WANT TO WIN TOO.
!
YOU DO?
GRIT...!!
WELL, YEAH.
YOU THINK I'M GONNA LET MAYOR ICEBERG GET KILLED...
...BY IDIOTS NOBODY KNOWS, FROM WHO-KNOWS-WHERE? !!
HUFF...

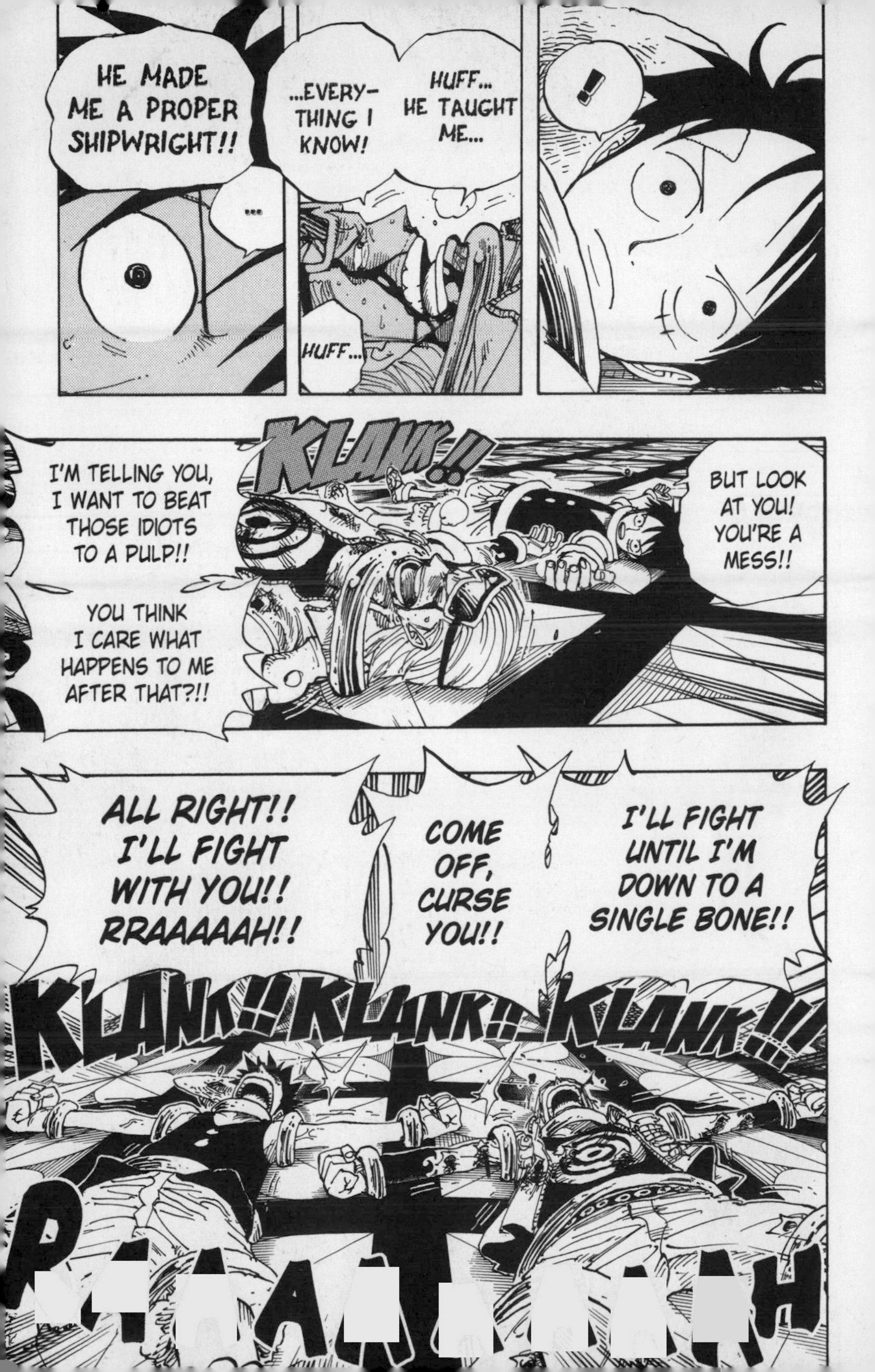
!
HUFF... HE TAUGHT ME...
...EVERY-THING I KNOW!
HUFF...
HE MADE ME A PROPER SHIPWRIGHT!!
...
BUT LOOK AT YOU! YOU'RE A MESS!!
KLANK!!
I'M TELLING YOU, I WANT TO BEAT THOSE IDIOTS TO A PULP!!
YOU THINK I CARE WHAT HAPPENS TO ME AFTER THAT?!!
I'LL FIGHT UNTIL I'M DOWN TO A SINGLE BONE!!
COME OFF, CURSE YOU!!
ALL RIGHT!! I'LL FIGHT WITH YOU!! RRAAAAAH!!
KLANK!! KLANK!! KLANK!!!

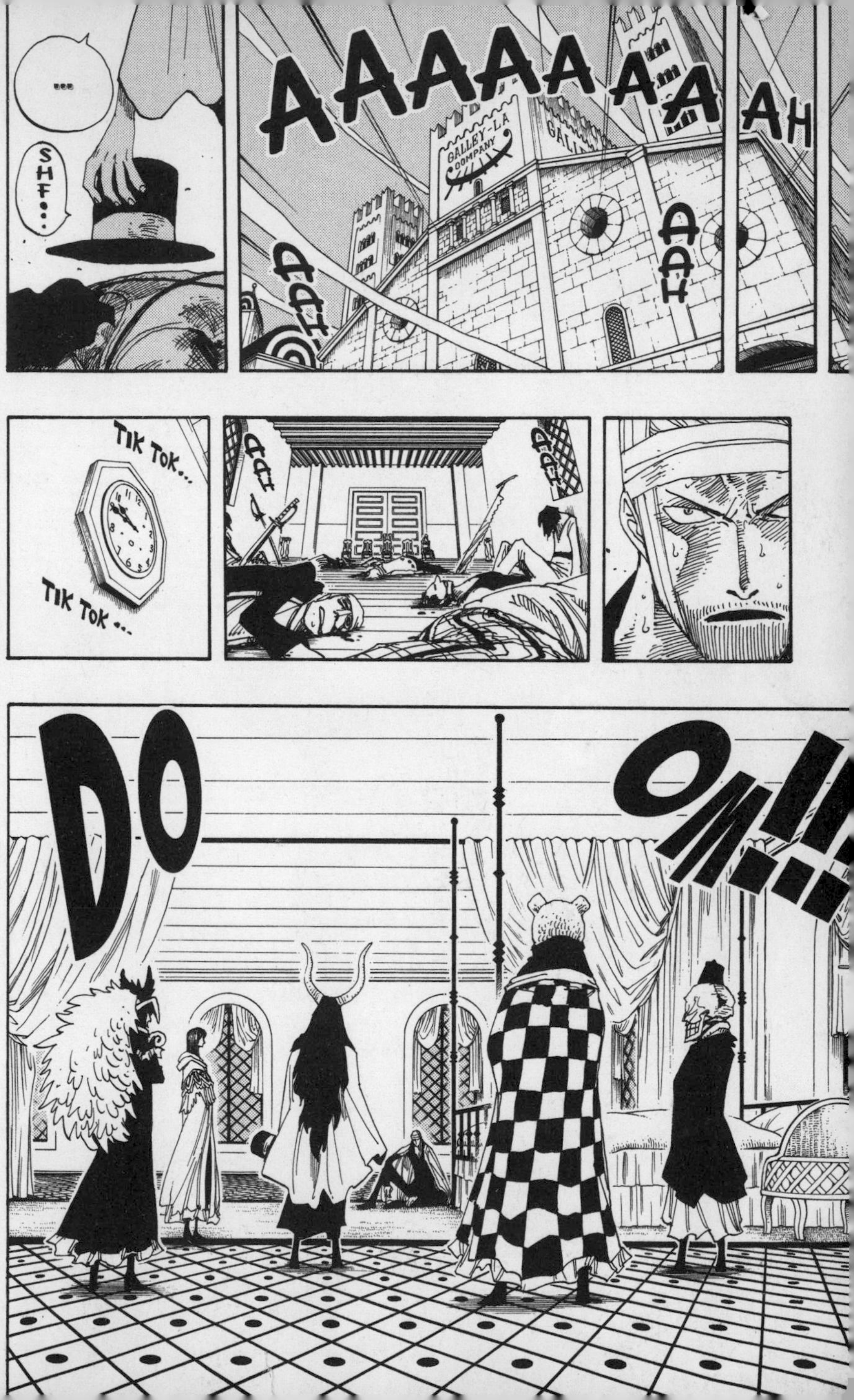
AAAAAAAAH
GALLEY-LA COMPANY
AAH
AAH
...
SHF...
AAH
AAH
TIK TOK...
TIK TOK...
DOON!!!

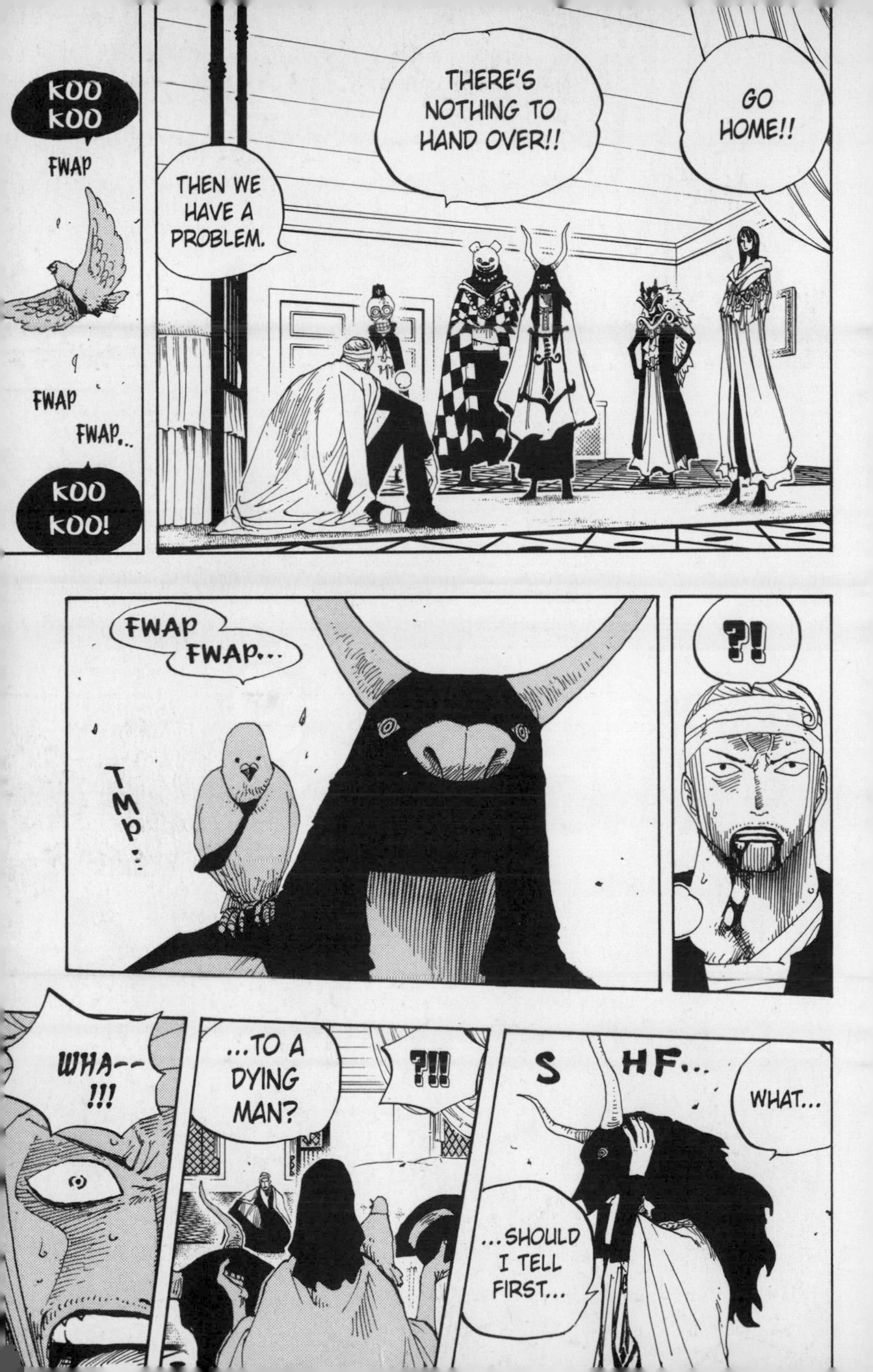
GO HOME!!
THERE'S NOTHING TO HAND OVER!!
THEN WE HAVE A PROBLEM.
KOO KOO
FWAP
FWAP
FWAP...
KOO KOO!
?!
FWAP FWAP...
TMP...
WHAT...
SHF...
...SHOULD I TELL FIRST...
?!!
...TO A DYING MAN?
WHA-- !!!

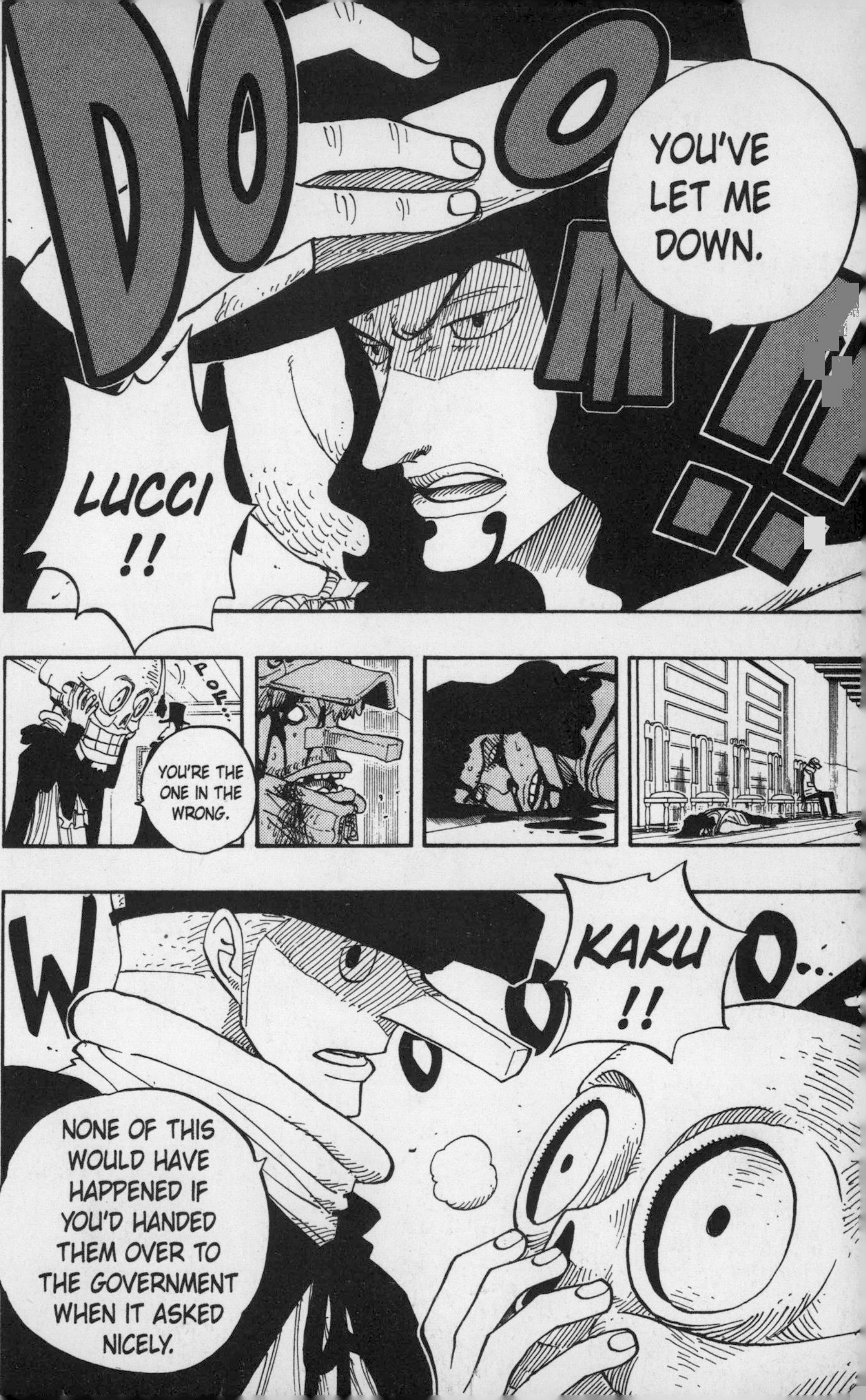
DOOM!!
YOU'VE LET ME DOWN.
LUCCI !!
POF...
YOU'RE THE ONE IN THE WRONG.
KAKU !!
WOO...
NONE OF THIS WOULD HAVE HAPPENED IF YOU'D HANDED THEM OVER TO THE GOVERNMENT WHEN IT ASKED NICELY.

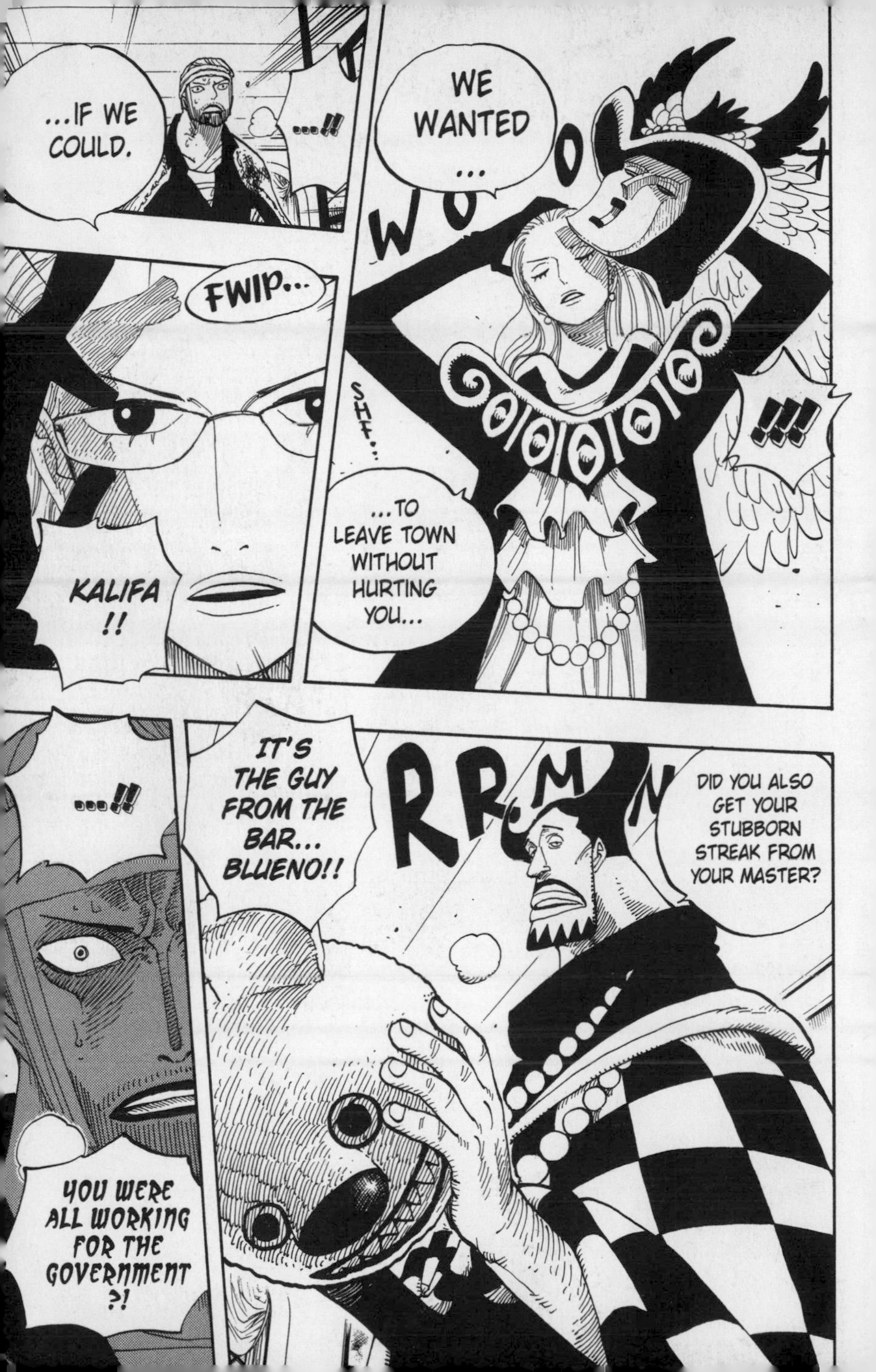
WE WANTED ...
WOO
!!!
SHF...
...TO LEAVE TOWN WITHOUT HURTING YOU...
...IF WE COULD.
...!!
FWIP...
KALIFA !!
RRMN
DID YOU ALSO GET YOUR STUBBORN STREAK FROM YOUR MASTER?
IT'S THE GUY FROM THE BAR... BLUENO!!
...!!
YOU WERE ALL WORKING FOR THE GOVERNMENT ?!

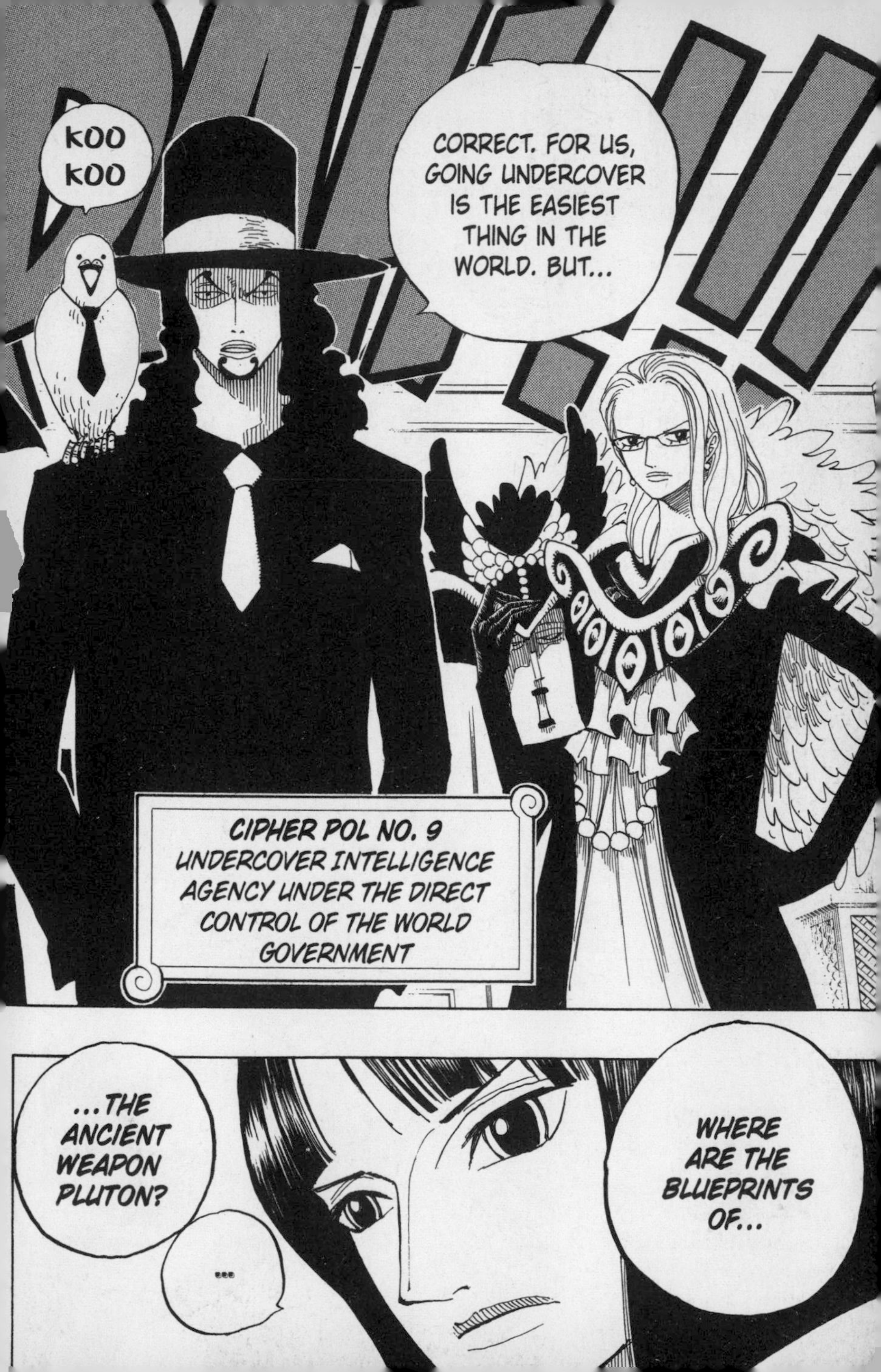
CORRECT. FOR US, GOING UNDERCOVER IS THE EASIEST THING IN THE WORLD. BUT...
KOO KOO
CIPHER POL NO. 9 UNDERCOVER INTELLIGENCE AGENCY UNDER THE DIRECT CONTROL OF THE WORLD GOVERNMENT
WHERE ARE THE BLUEPRINTS OF...
...THE ANCIENT WEAPON PLUTON?
...

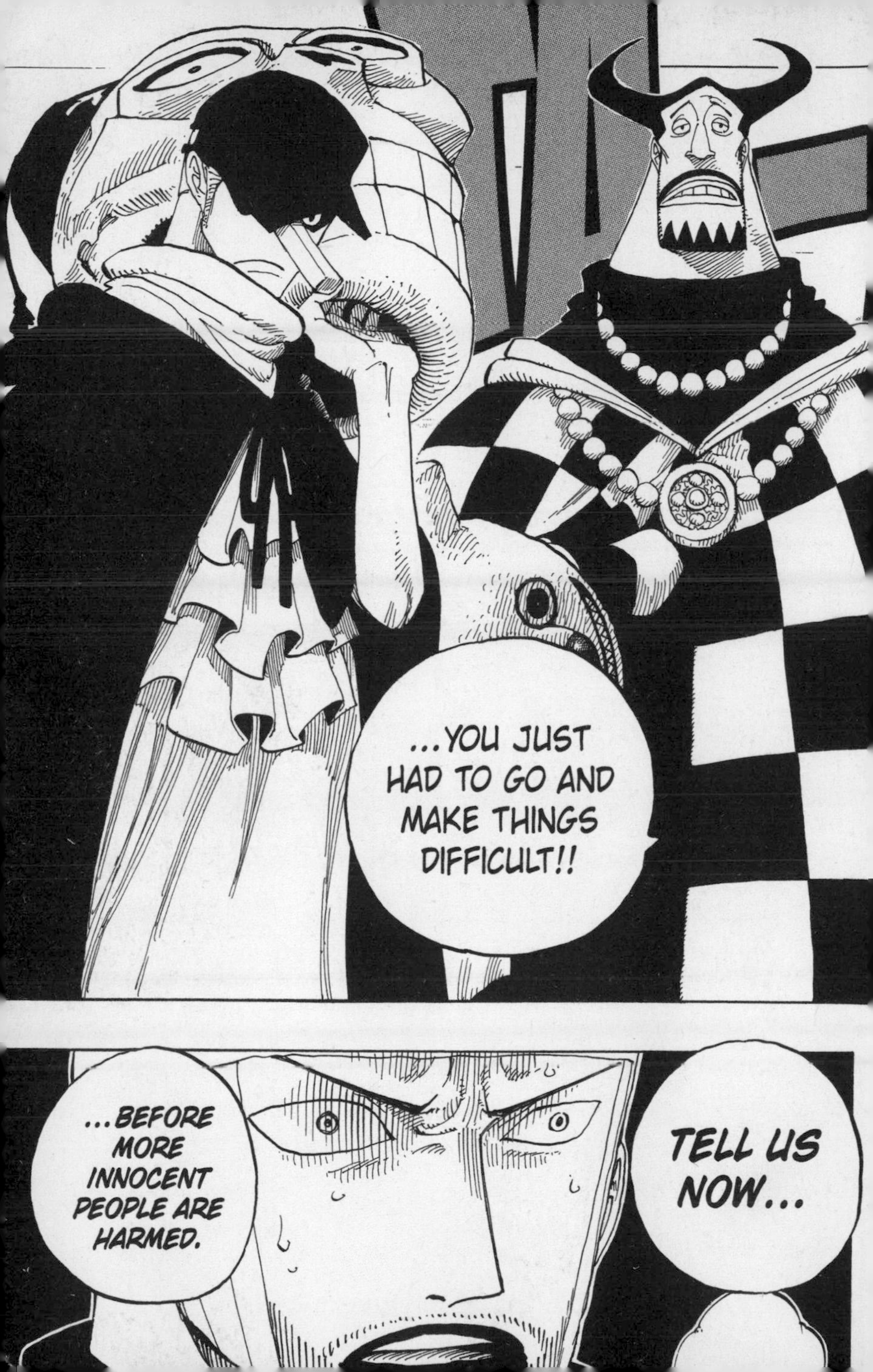
...YOU JUST HAD TO GO AND MAKE THINGS DIFFICULT!!
TELL US NOW...
...BEFORE MORE INNOCENT PEOPLE ARE HARMED.

"There Was No Scene Like This"

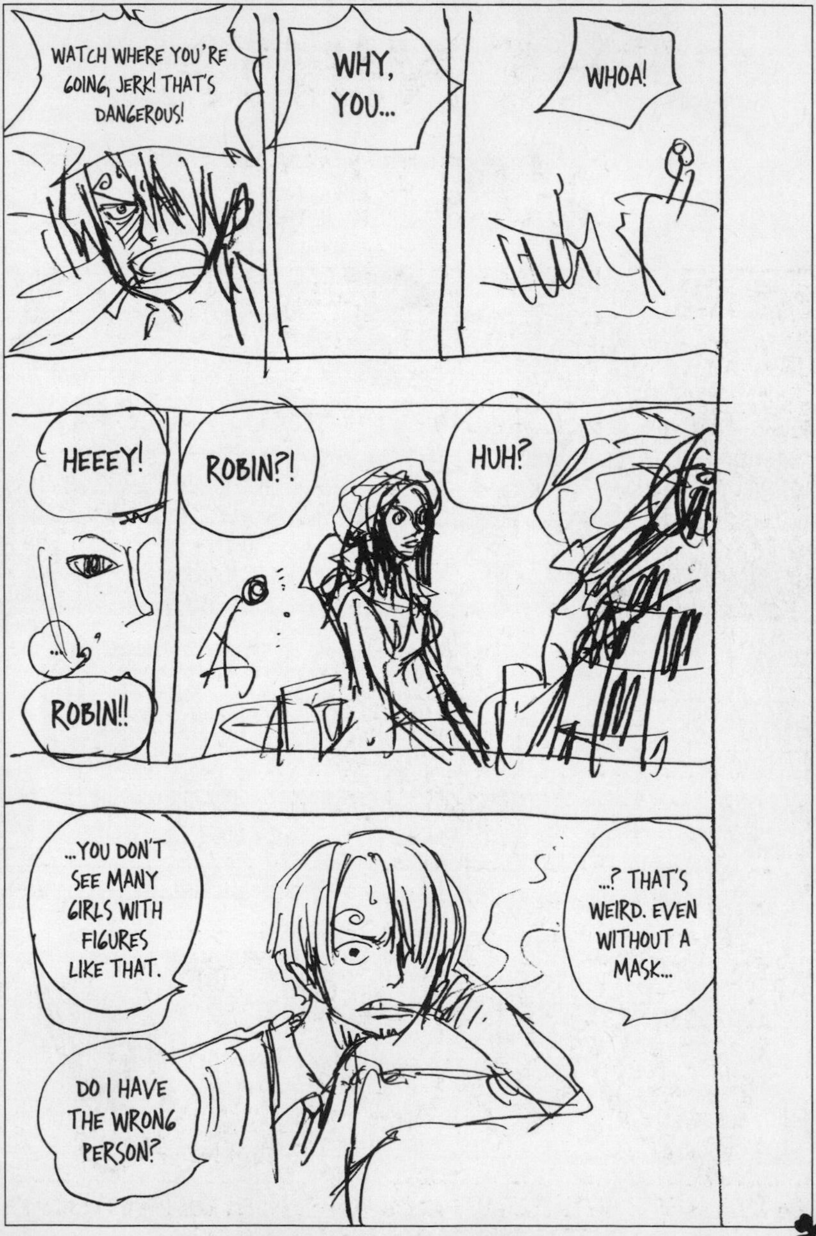
WHOA!
WHY, YOU...
WATCH WHERE YOU'RE GOING, JERK! THAT'S DANGEROUS!
HUH?
ROBIN?!
HEEEY!
...
ROBIN!!
...? THAT'S WEIRD. EVEN WITHOUT A MASK...
...YOU DON'T SEE MANY GIRLS WITH FIGURES LIKE THAT.
DO I HAVE THE WRONG PERSON?

Chapter 346:
THE NINTH JUSTICE

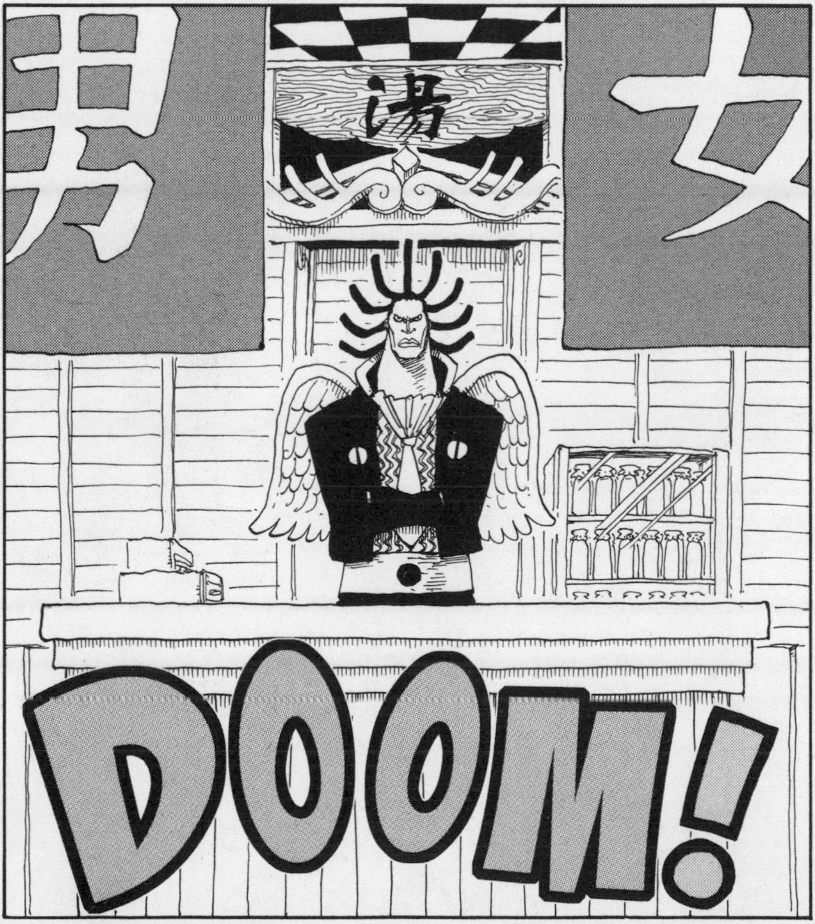
男
湯
女
DOOM!

GEDATSU'S UNEXPECTED LIFE ON THE BLUE SEA, VOL. 30:
"GEDATSU, THE BLUE SEA BOSS"

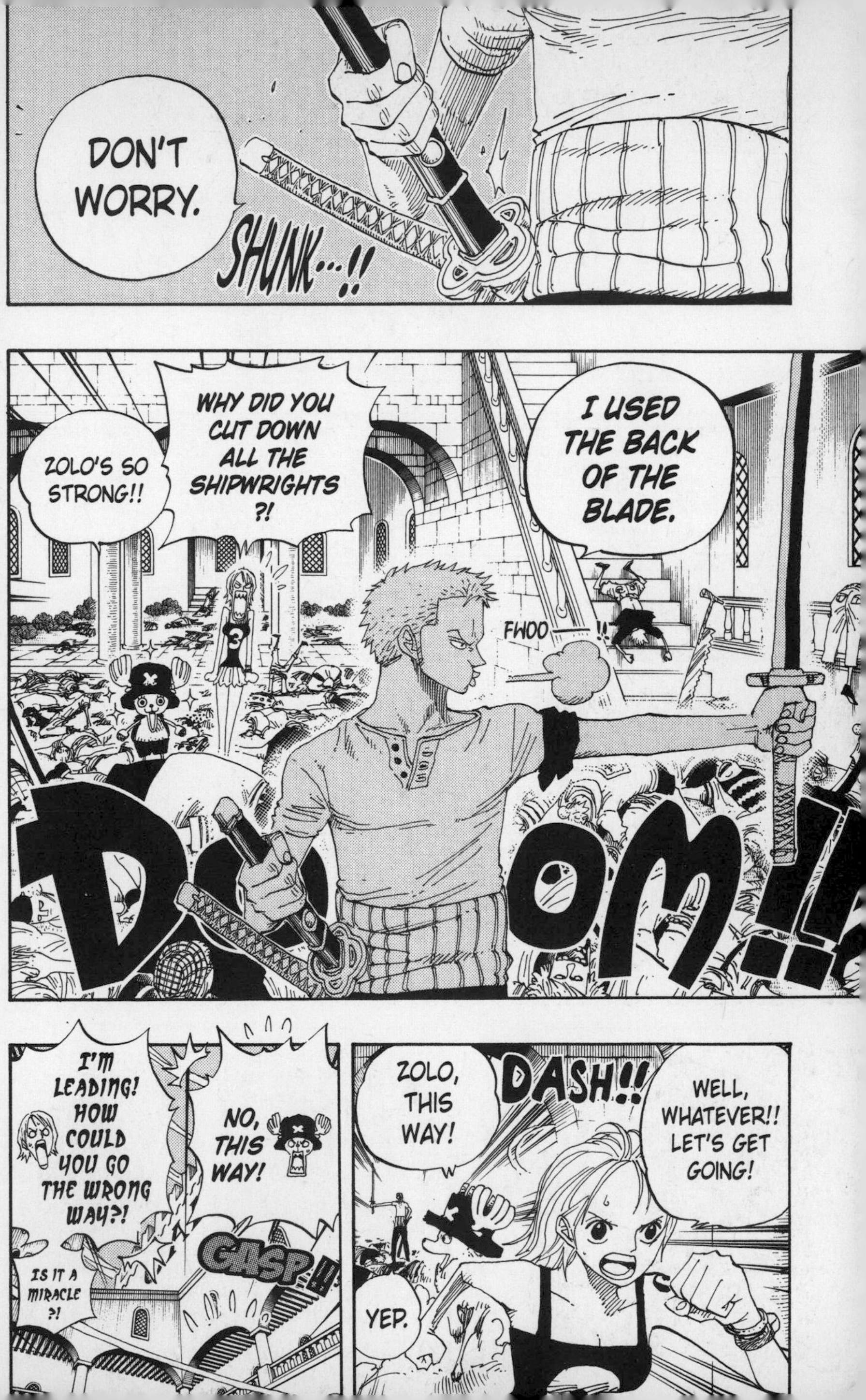
DON'T WORRY.
SHUNK...!!
I USED THE BACK OF THE BLADE.
FWOO—!!
WHY DID YOU CUT DOWN ALL THE SHIPWRIGHTS ?!
ZOLO'S SO STRONG!!
DOOM!!
WELL, WHATEVER!! LET'S GET GOING!
DASH!!
ZOLO, THIS WAY!
YEP.
NO, THIS WAY!
I'M LEADING! HOW COULD YOU GO THE WRONG WAY?!
GASP!!
IS IT A MIRACLE ?!

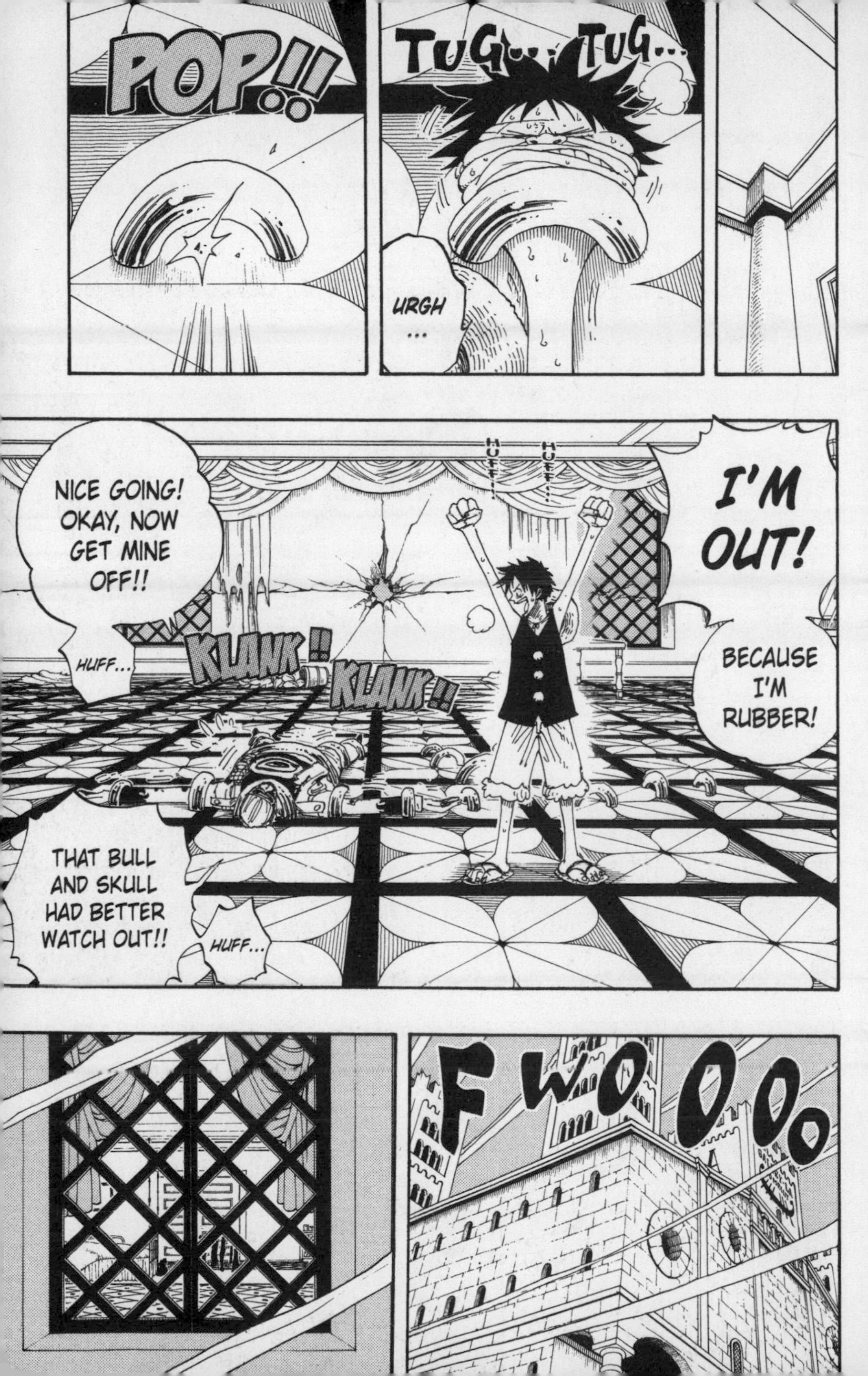
TUG... TUG...
URGH...
POP!!
I'M OUT!
BECAUSE I'M RUBBER!
HUFF... HUFF...
NICE GOING! OKAY, NOW GET MINE OFF!!
HUFF...
KLANK!!
KLANK!!
THAT BULL AND SKULL HAD BETTER WATCH OUT!!
HUFF...
FWOOO

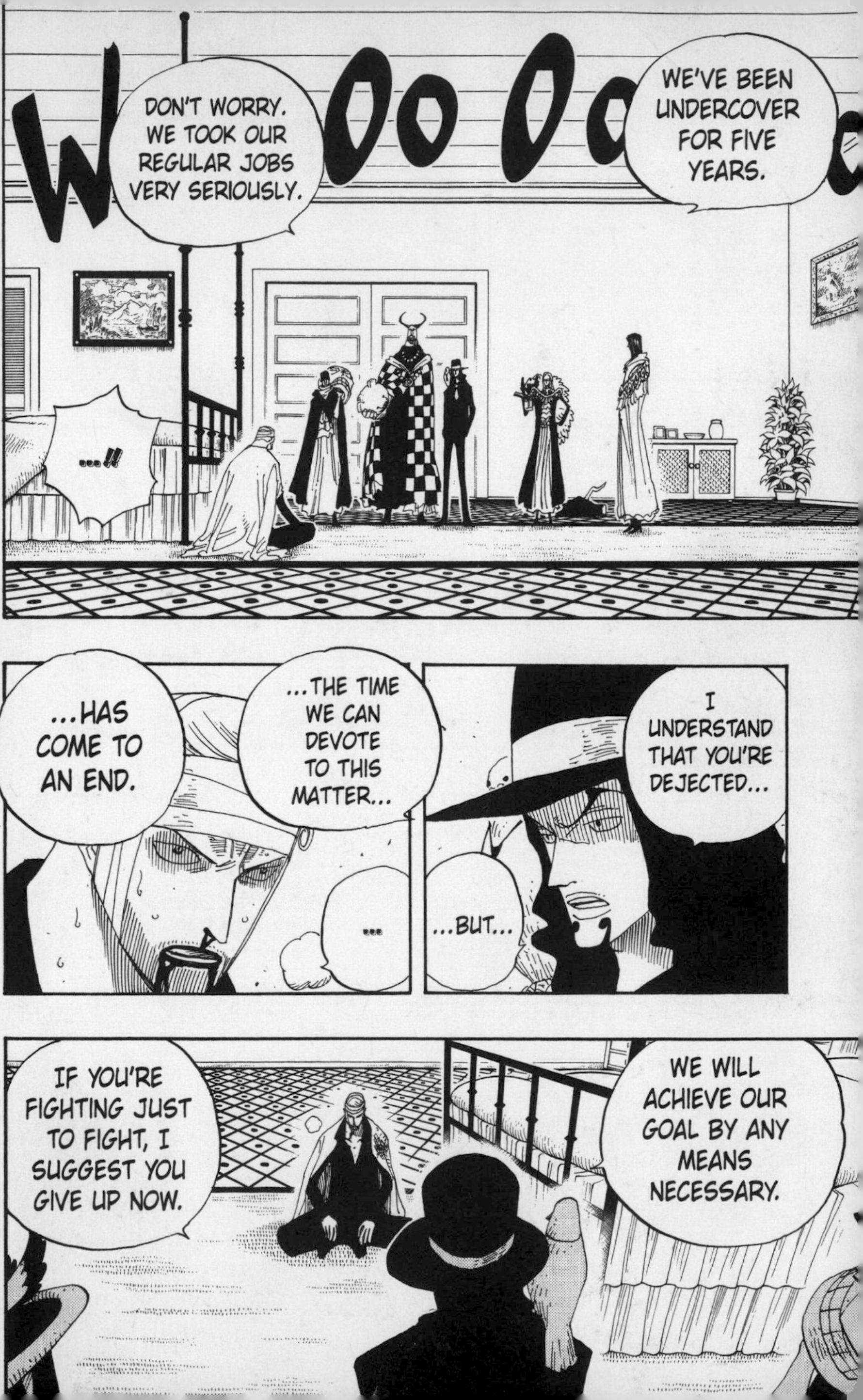
WE'VE BEEN UNDERCOVER FOR FIVE YEARS.
DON'T WORRY. WE TOOK OUR REGULAR JOBS VERY SERIOUSLY.
...!!
I UNDERSTAND THAT YOU'RE DEJECTED...
...BUT...
...THE TIME WE CAN DEVOTE TO THIS MATTER...
...HAS COME TO AN END.
...
WE WILL ACHIEVE OUR GOAL BY ANY MEANS NECESSARY.
IF YOU'RE FIGHTING JUST TO FIGHT, I SUGGEST YOU GIVE UP NOW.

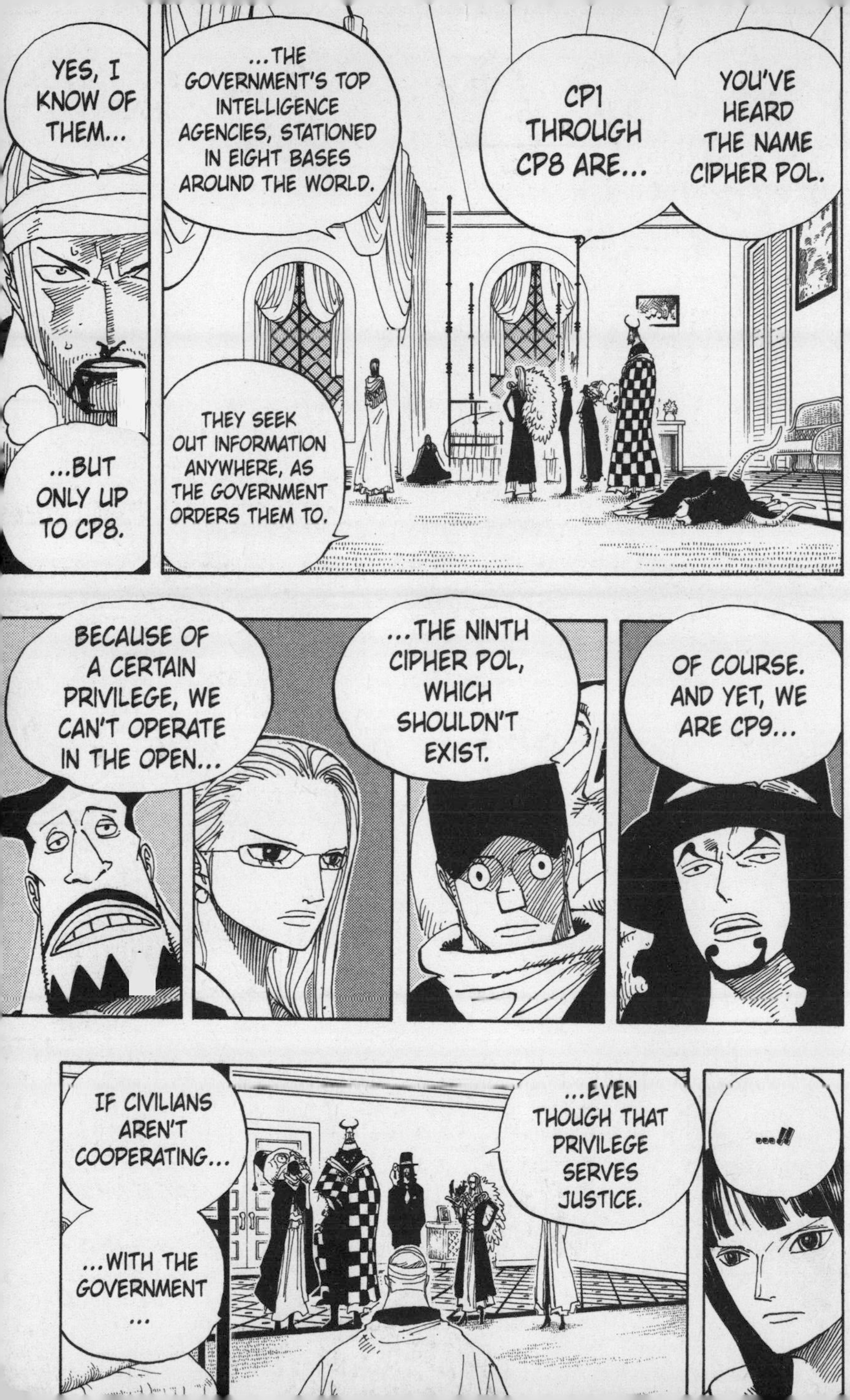
YOU'VE HEARD THE NAME CIPHER POL.
CP1 THROUGH CP8 ARE...
...THE GOVERNMENT'S TOP INTELLIGENCE AGENCIES, STATIONED IN EIGHT BASES AROUND THE WORLD.
THEY SEEK OUT INFORMATION ANYWHERE, AS THE GOVERNMENT ORDERS THEM TO.
YES, I KNOW OF THEM...
...BUT ONLY UP TO CP8.
OF COURSE. AND YET, WE ARE CP9...
...THE NINTH CIPHER POL, WHICH SHOULDN'T EXIST.
BECAUSE OF A CERTAIN PRIVILEGE, WE CAN'T OPERATE IN THE OPEN...
...!!
...EVEN THOUGH THAT PRIVILEGE SERVES JUSTICE.
IF CIVILIANS AREN'T COOPERATING...
...WITH THE GOVERNMENT ...

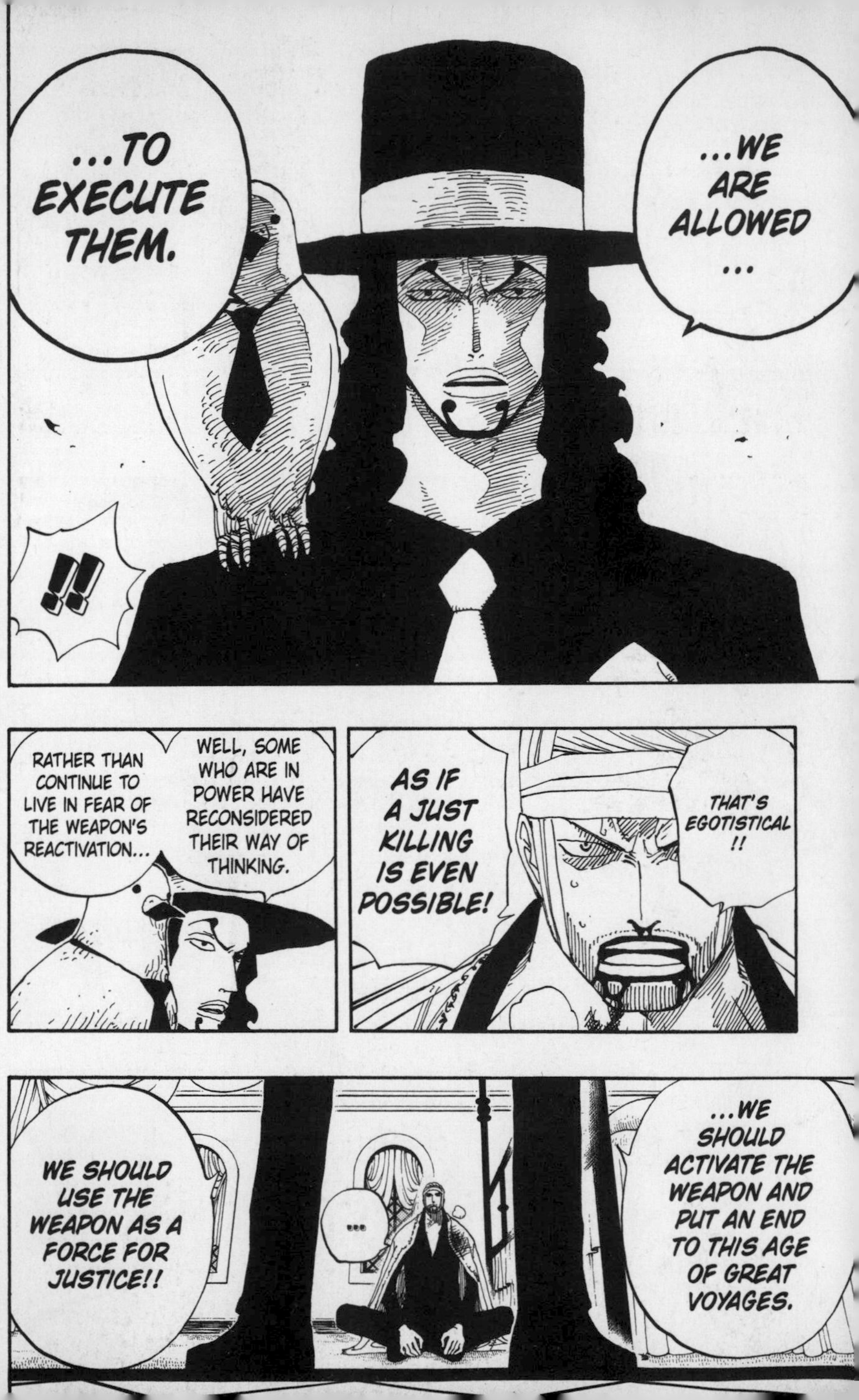
...WE ARE ALLOWED ...
...TO EXECUTE THEM.
!!
THAT'S EGOTISTICAL !!
AS IF A JUST KILLING IS EVEN POSSIBLE!
WELL, SOME WHO ARE IN POWER HAVE RECONSIDERED THEIR WAY OF THINKING.
RATHER THAN CONTINUE TO LIVE IN FEAR OF THE WEAPON'S REACTIVATION...
...WE SHOULD ACTIVATE THE WEAPON AND PUT AN END TO THIS AGE OF GREAT VOYAGES.
...
WE SHOULD USE THE WEAPON AS A FORCE FOR JUSTICE!!

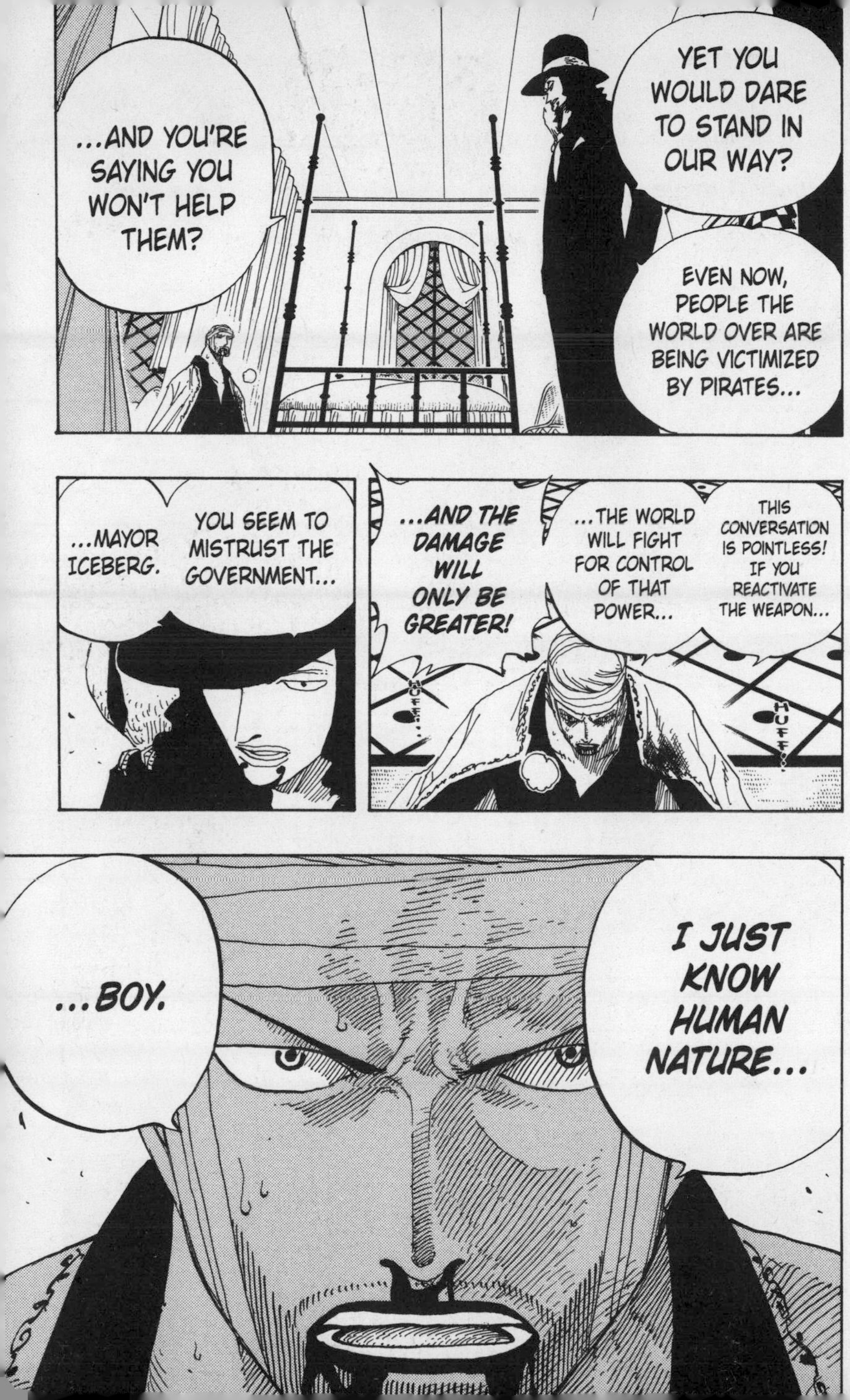
YET YOU WOULD DARE TO STAND IN OUR WAY?
EVEN NOW, PEOPLE THE WORLD OVER ARE BEING VICTIMIZED BY PIRATES...
...AND YOU'RE SAYING YOU WON'T HELP THEM?
THIS CONVERSATION IS POINTLESS! IF YOU REACTIVATE THE WEAPON...
...THE WORLD WILL FIGHT FOR CONTROL OF THAT POWER...
...AND THE DAMAGE WILL ONLY BE GREATER!
HUFF
HUFF
YOU SEEM TO MISTRUST THE GOVERNMENT...
...MAYOR ICEBERG.
I JUST KNOW HUMAN NATURE...
...BOY.

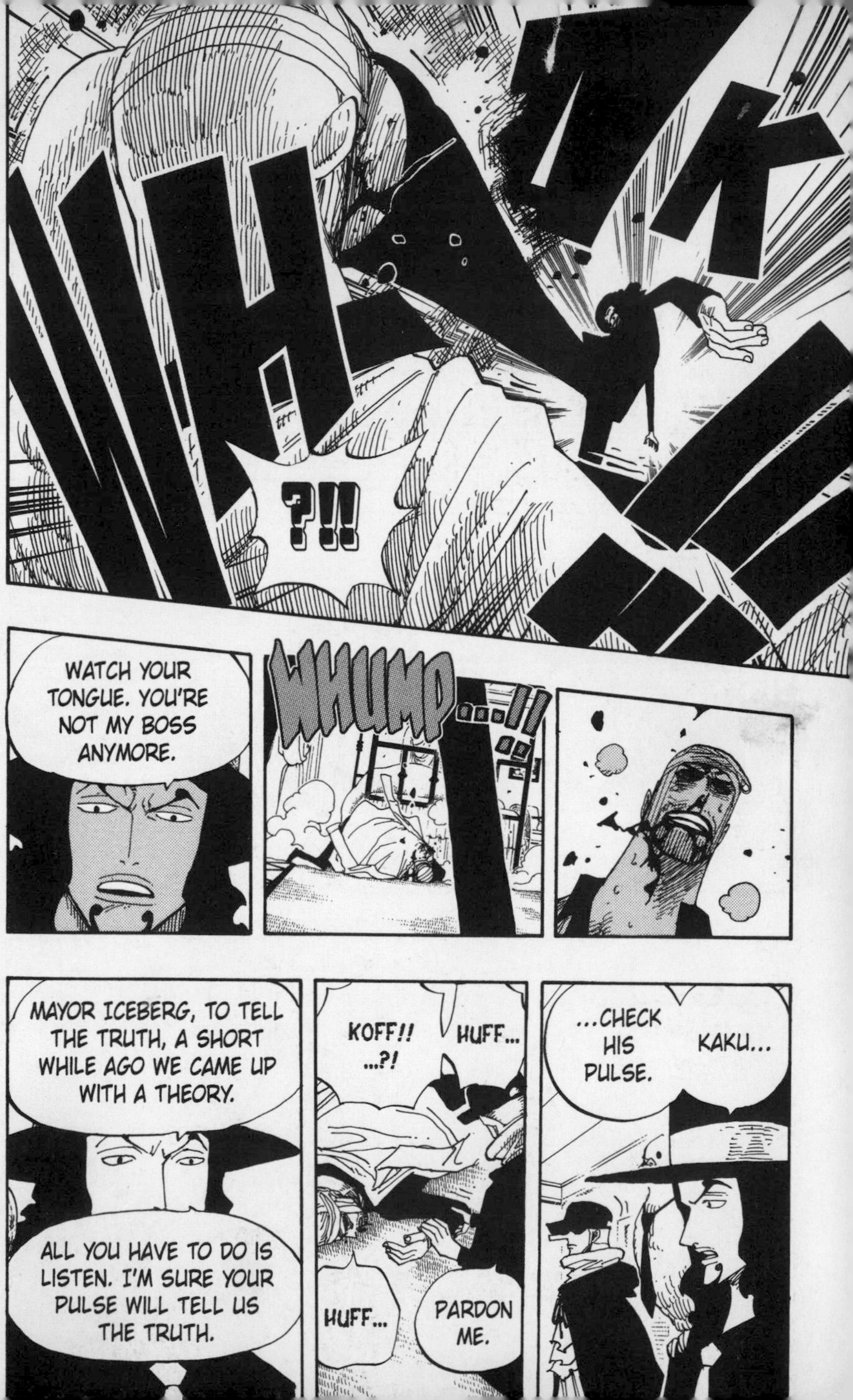
?!!
WHUMP...!!
WATCH YOUR TONGUE. YOU'RE NOT MY BOSS ANYMORE.
KAKU...
...CHECK HIS PULSE.
HUFF...
KOFF!! ...?!
PARDON ME.
HUFF...
MAYOR ICEBERG, TO TELL THE TRUTH, A SHORT WHILE AGO WE CAME UP WITH A THEORY.
ALL YOU HAVE TO DO IS LISTEN. I'M SURE YOUR PULSE WILL TELL US THE TRUTH.

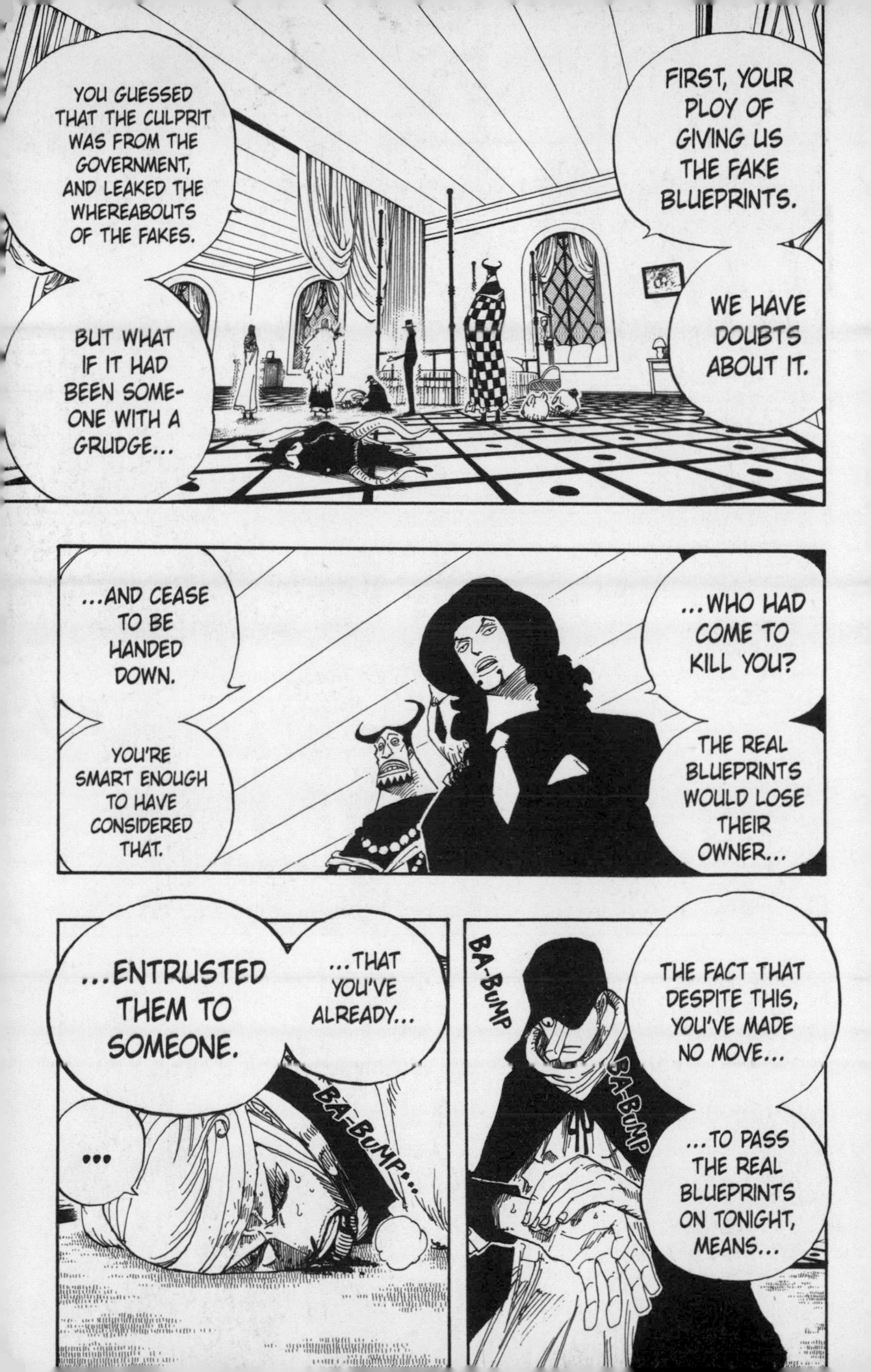
FIRST, YOUR PLOY OF GIVING US THE FAKE BLUEPRINTS.
WE HAVE DOUBTS ABOUT IT.
YOU GUESSED THAT THE CULPRIT WAS FROM THE GOVERNMENT, AND LEAKED THE WHEREABOUTS OF THE FAKES.
BUT WHAT IF IT HAD BEEN SOME-ONE WITH A GRUDGE...
...WHO HAD COME TO KILL YOU?
THE REAL BLUEPRINTS WOULD LOSE THEIR OWNER...
...AND CEASE TO BE HANDED DOWN.
YOU'RE SMART ENOUGH TO HAVE CONSIDERED THAT.
BA-BUMP
THE FACT THAT DESPITE THIS, YOU'VE MADE NO MOVE...
BA-BUMP
...TO PASS THE REAL BLUEPRINTS ON TONIGHT, MEANS...
...THAT YOU'VE ALREADY...
...ENTRUSTED THEM TO SOMEONE.
BA-BUMP...
...

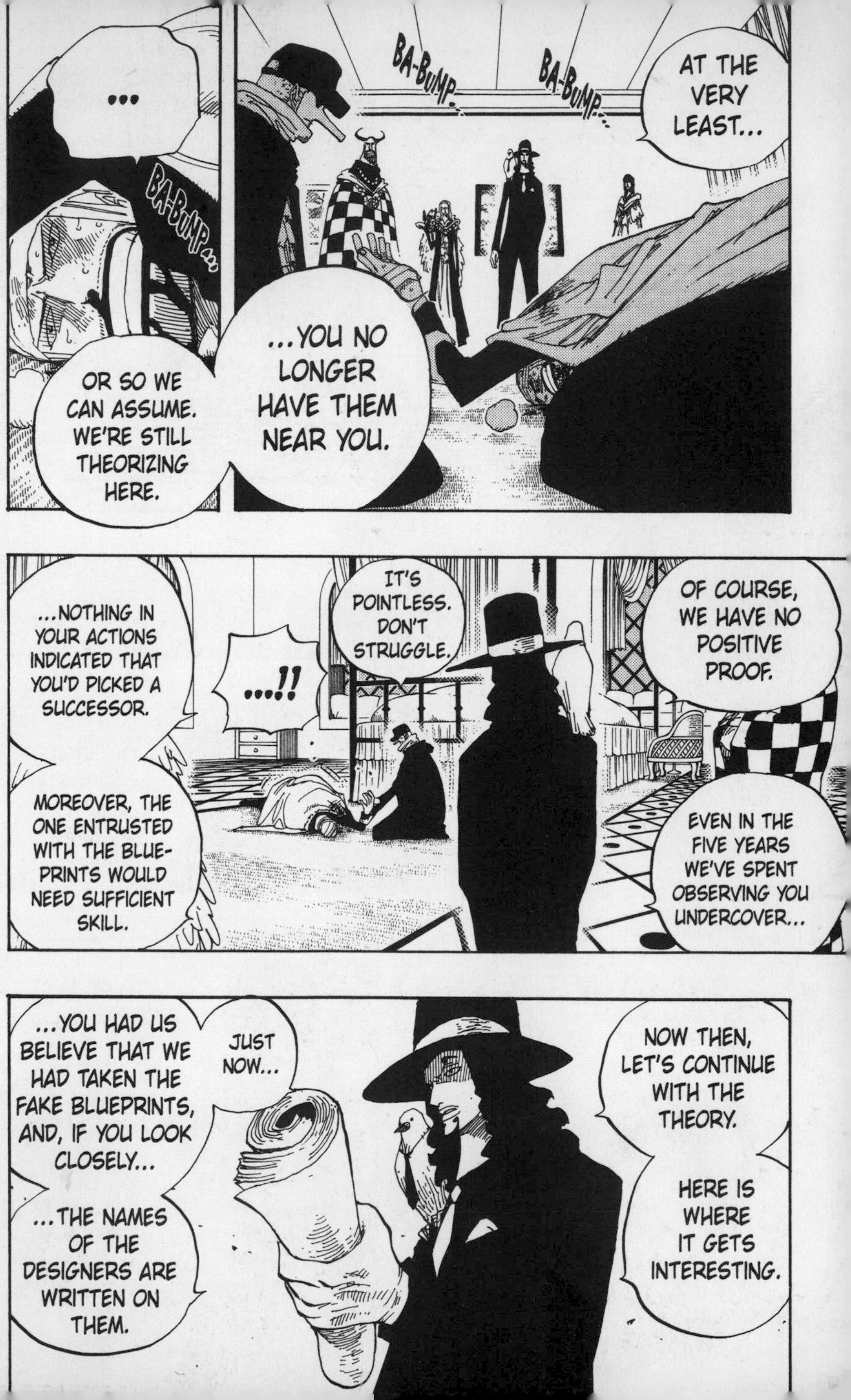
AT THE VERY LEAST...
BA-BUMP...
BA-BUMP...
...YOU NO LONGER HAVE THEM NEAR YOU.
...
BA-BUMP...
OR SO WE CAN ASSUME. WE'RE STILL THEORIZING HERE.
OF COURSE, WE HAVE NO POSITIVE PROOF.
IT'S POINTLESS. DON'T STRUGGLE.
...!!
EVEN IN THE FIVE YEARS WE'VE SPENT OBSERVING YOU UNDERCOVER...
...NOTHING IN YOUR ACTIONS INDICATED THAT YOU'D PICKED A SUCCESSOR.
MOREOVER, THE ONE ENTRUSTED WITH THE BLUE-PRINTS WOULD NEED SUFFICIENT SKILL.
NOW THEN, LET'S CONTINUE WITH THE THEORY.
HERE IS WHERE IT GETS INTERESTING.
JUST NOW...
...YOU HAD US BELIEVE THAT WE HAD TAKEN THE FAKE BLUEPRINTS, AND, IF YOU LOOK CLOSELY...
...THE NAMES OF THE DESIGNERS ARE WRITTEN ON THEM.

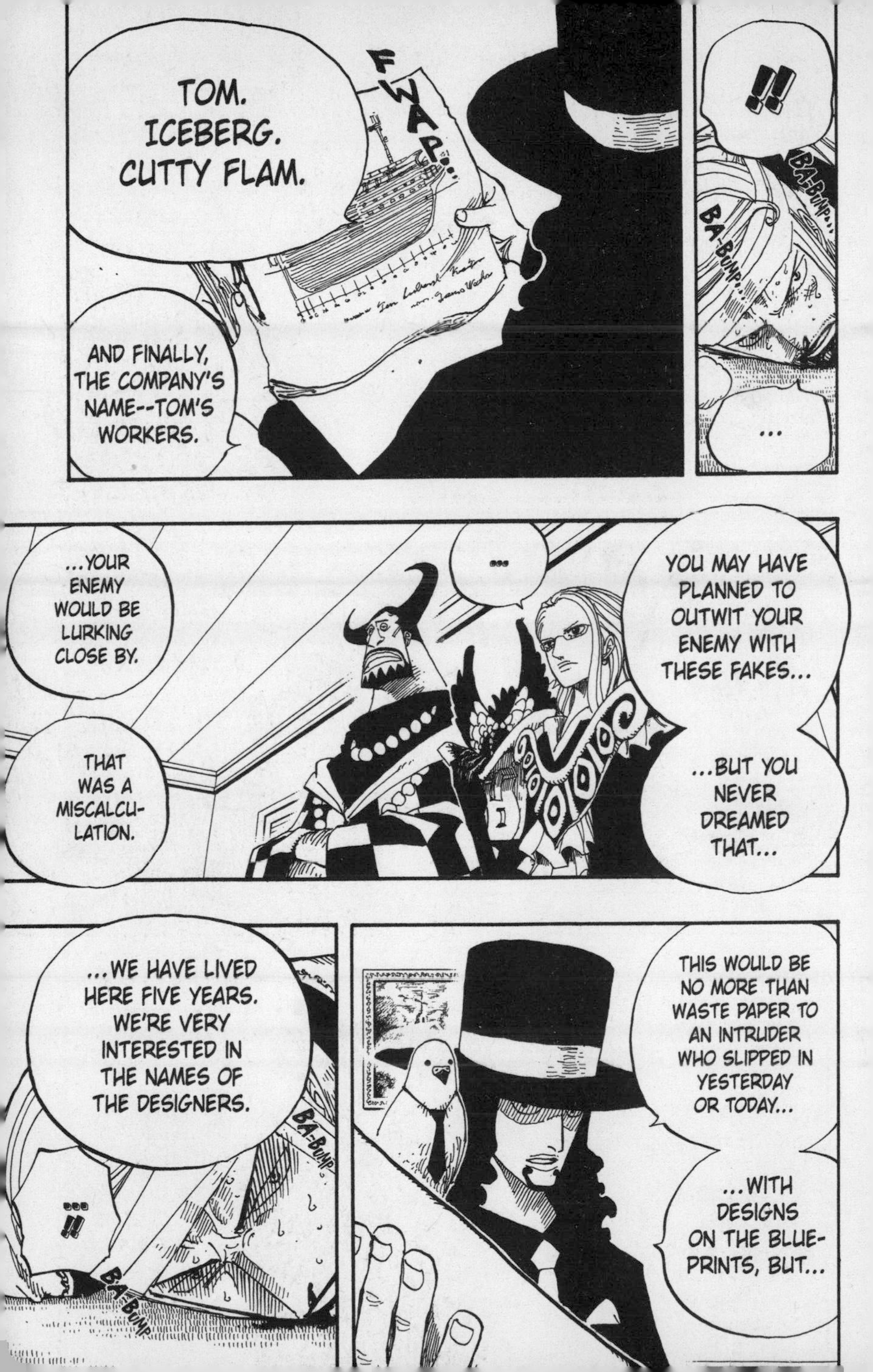
!!
BA-BUMP...
BA-BUMP...
...
FWAP...
TOM.
ICEBERG.
CUTTY FLAM.
AND FINALLY, THE COMPANY'S NAME--TOM'S WORKERS.
YOU MAY HAVE PLANNED TO OUTWIT YOUR ENEMY WITH THESE FAKES...
...BUT YOU NEVER DREAMED THAT...
...
...YOUR ENEMY WOULD BE LURKING CLOSE BY.
THAT WAS A MISCALCU-LATION.
THIS WOULD BE NO MORE THAN WASTE PAPER TO AN INTRUDER WHO SLIPPED IN YESTERDAY OR TODAY...
...WITH DESIGNS ON THE BLUE-PRINTS, BUT...
...WE HAVE LIVED HERE FIVE YEARS. WE'RE VERY INTERESTED IN THE NAMES OF THE DESIGNERS.
BA-BUMP
...!!
BA-BUMP

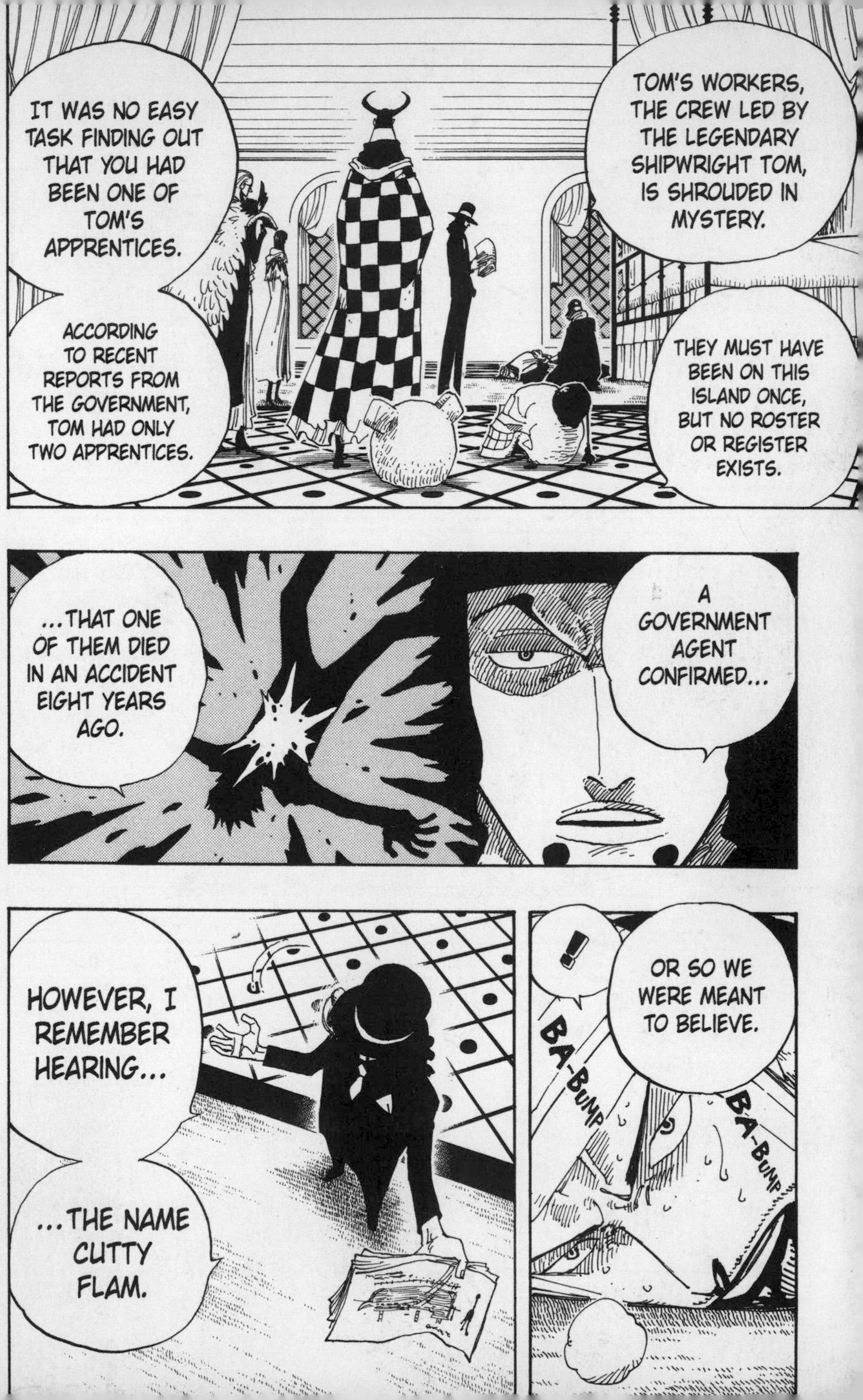
TOM'S WORKERS, THE CREW LED BY THE LEGENDARY SHIPWRIGHT TOM, IS SHROUDED IN MYSTERY.
THEY MUST HAVE BEEN ON THIS ISLAND ONCE, BUT NO ROSTER OR REGISTER EXISTS.
IT WAS NO EASY TASK FINDING OUT THAT YOU HAD BEEN ONE OF TOM'S APPRENTICES.
ACCORDING TO RECENT REPORTS FROM THE GOVERNMENT, TOM HAD ONLY TWO APPRENTICES.
A GOVERNMENT AGENT CONFIRMED...
...THAT ONE OF THEM DIED IN AN ACCIDENT EIGHT YEARS AGO.
!
OR SO WE WERE MEANT TO BELIEVE.
BA-BUMP
BA-BUMP
HOWEVER, I REMEMBER HEARING...
...THE NAME CUTTY FLAM.

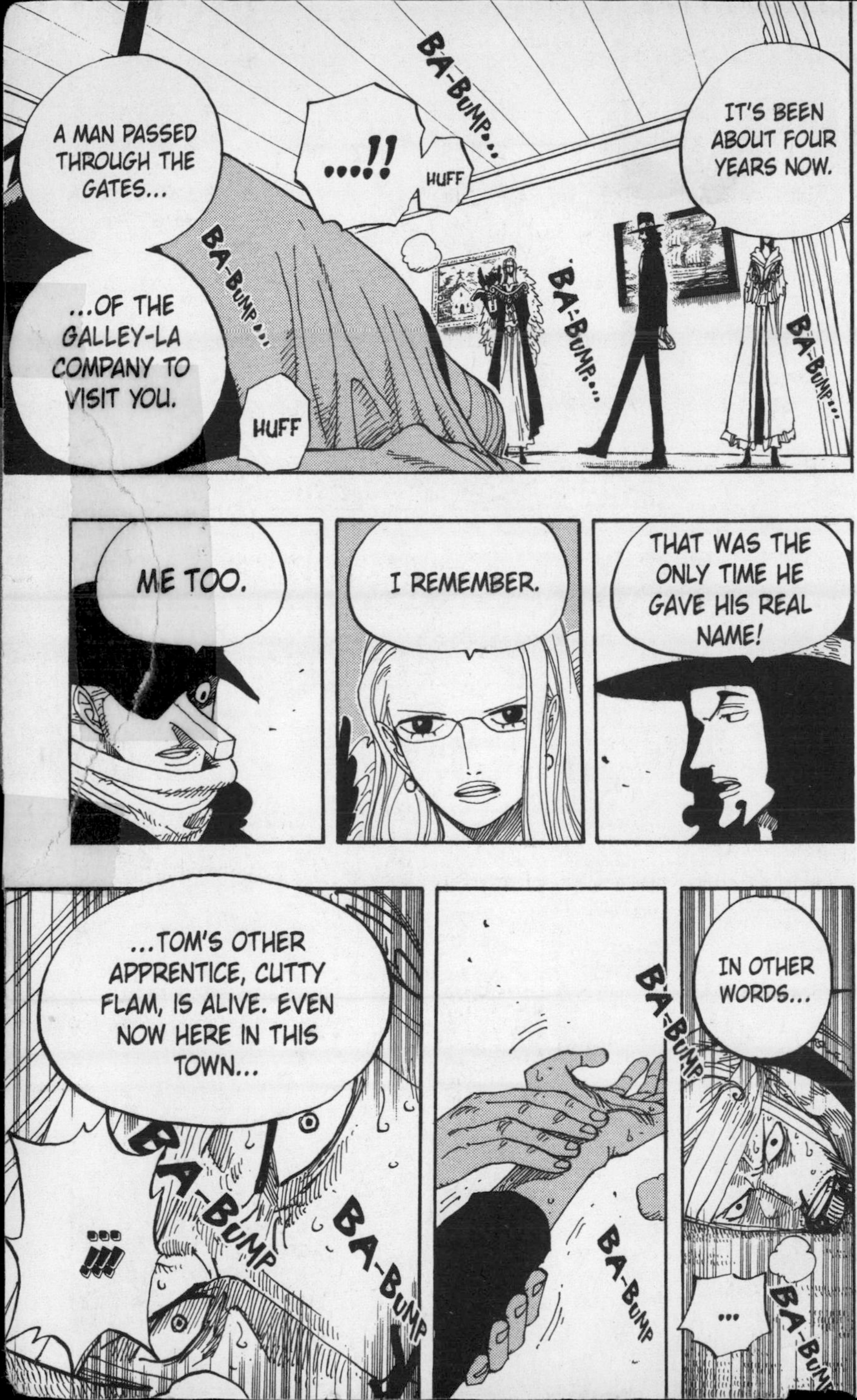
IT'S BEEN ABOUT FOUR YEARS NOW.
BA-BUMP...
BA-BUMP...
...!!
HUFF
BA-BUMP...
BA-BUMP...
A MAN PASSED THROUGH THE GATES...
...OF THE GALLEY-LA COMPANY TO VISIT YOU.
HUFF
THAT WAS THE ONLY TIME HE GAVE HIS REAL NAME!
I REMEMBER.
ME TOO.
IN OTHER WORDS...
BA-BUMP
...
BA-BUMP
BA-BUMP
...TOM'S OTHER APPRENTICE, CUTTY FLAM, IS ALIVE. EVEN NOW HERE IN THIS TOWN...
BA-BUMP
BA-BUMP
BA-BUMP
...!!!

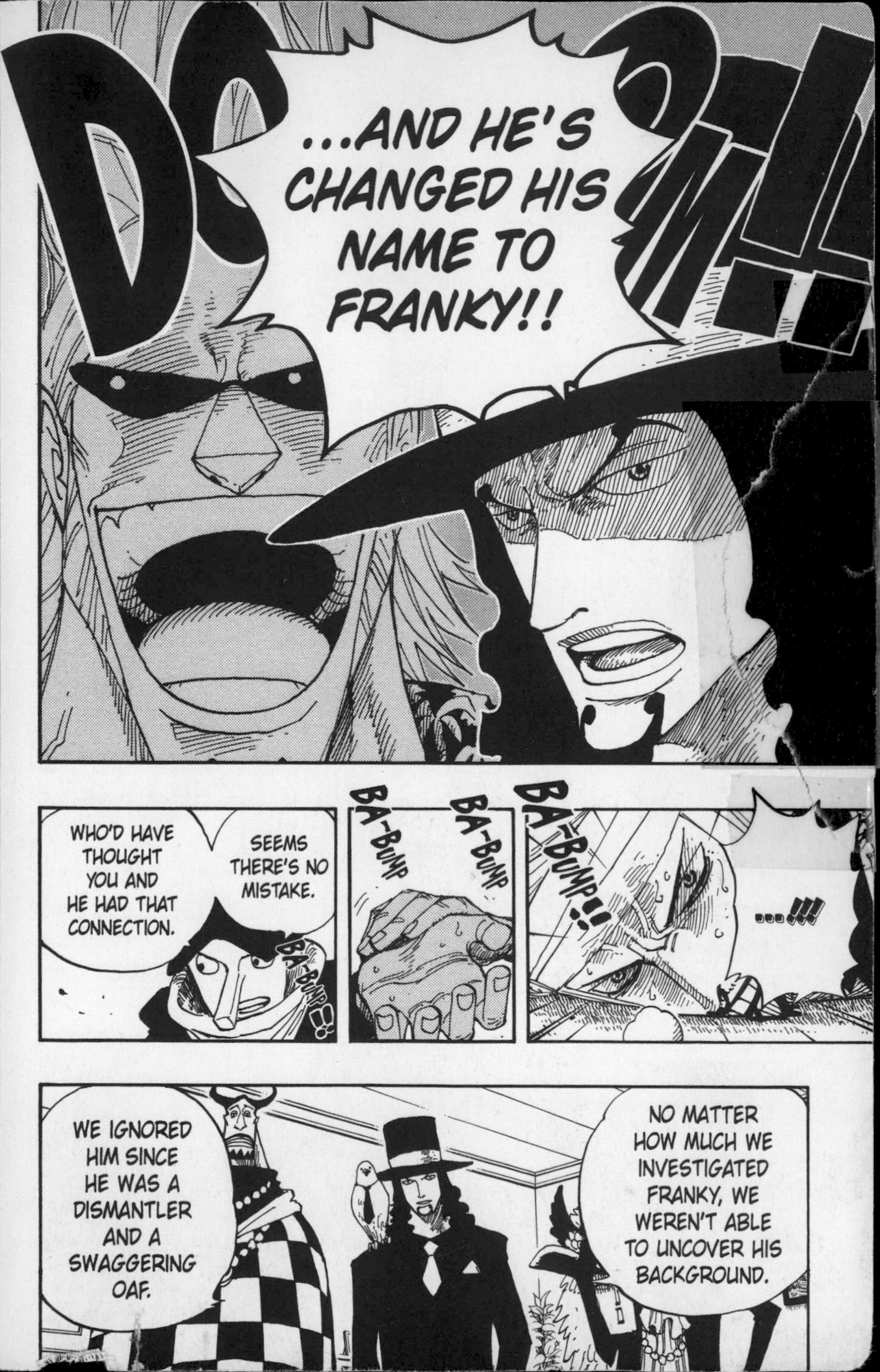
...AND HE'S CHANGED HIS NAME TO FRANKY!!
BA-BUMP!!
...!!!
BA-BUMP
BA-BUMP
SEEMS THERE'S NO MISTAKE.
WHO'D HAVE THOUGHT YOU AND HE HAD THAT CONNECTION.
BA-BUMP!!
NO MATTER HOW MUCH WE INVESTIGATED FRANKY, WE WEREN'T ABLE TO UNCOVER HIS BACKGROUND.
WE IGNORED HIM SINCE HE WAS A DISMANTLER AND A SWAGGERING OAF.

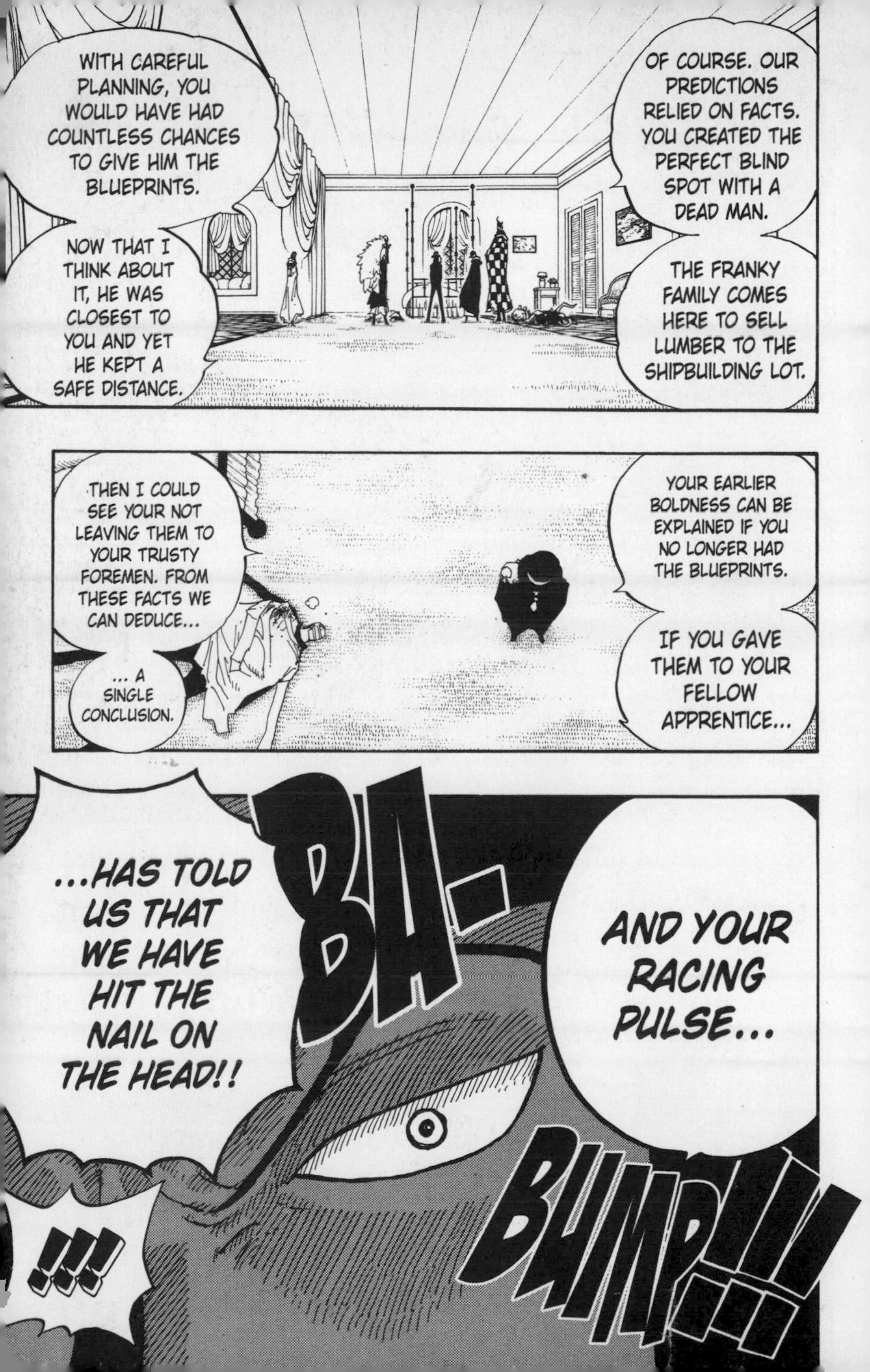
OF COURSE. OUR PREDICTIONS RELIED ON FACTS. YOU CREATED THE PERFECT BLIND SPOT WITH A DEAD MAN.
THE FRANKY FAMILY COMES HERE TO SELL LUMBER TO THE SHIPBUILDING LOT.
WITH CAREFUL PLANNING, YOU WOULD HAVE HAD COUNTLESS CHANCES TO GIVE HIM THE BLUEPRINTS.
NOW THAT I THINK ABOUT IT, HE WAS CLOSEST TO YOU AND YET HE KEPT A SAFE DISTANCE.
YOUR EARLIER BOLDNESS CAN BE EXPLAINED IF YOU NO LONGER HAD THE BLUEPRINTS.
IF YOU GAVE THEM TO YOUR FELLOW APPRENTICE...
THEN I COULD SEE YOUR NOT LEAVING THEM TO YOUR TRUSTY FOREMEN. FROM THESE FACTS WE CAN DEDUCE...
... A SINGLE CONCLUSION.
AND YOUR RACING PULSE...
BA-
...HAS TOLD US THAT WE HAVE HIT THE NAIL ON THE HEAD!!
BUMP!!!
!!!

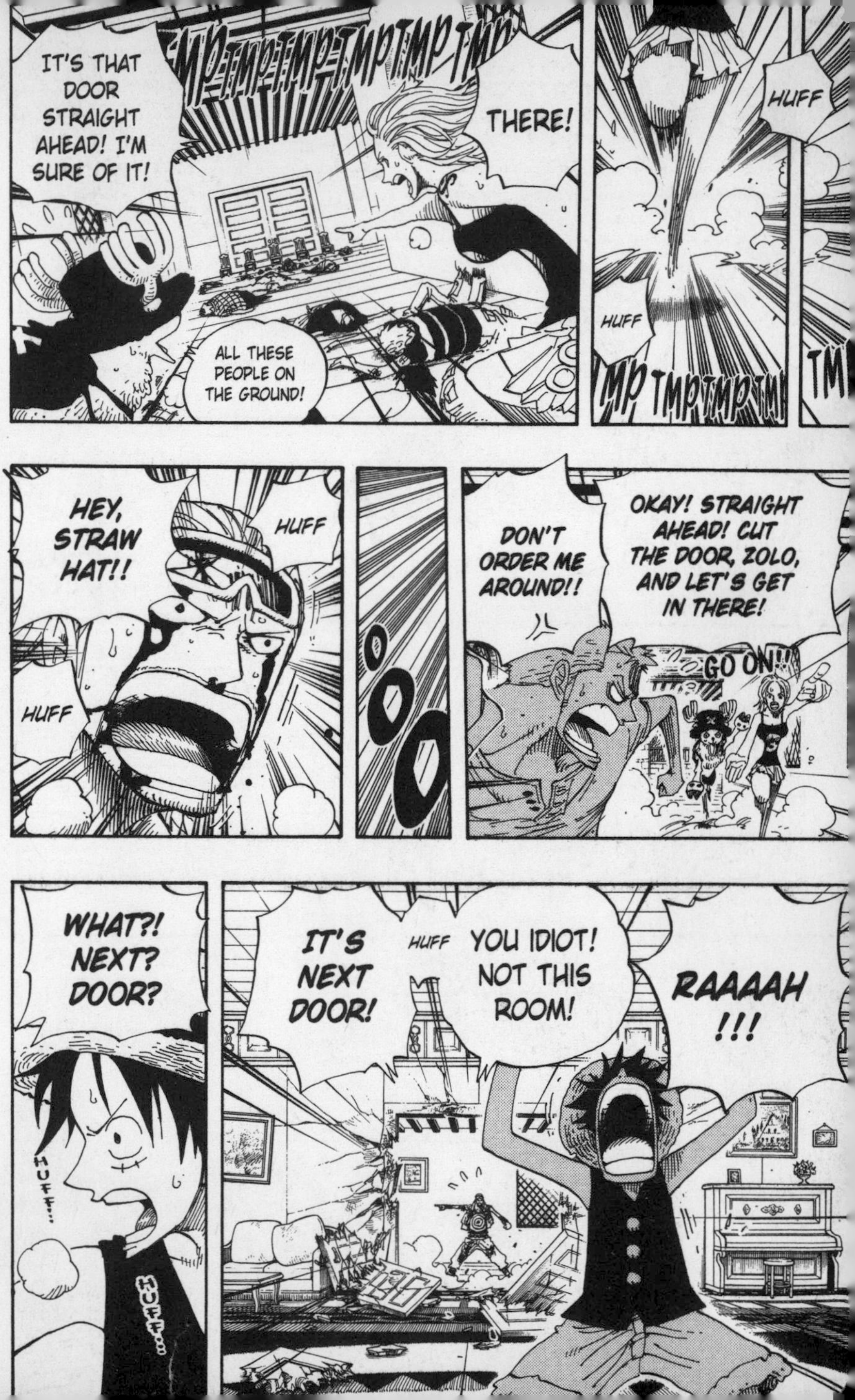
HUFF
HUFF
TMPTMPTMP
THERE!
IT'S THAT DOOR STRAIGHT AHEAD! I'M SURE OF IT!
ALL THESE PEOPLE ON THE GROUND!
OKAY! STRAIGHT AHEAD! CUT THE DOOR, ZOLO, AND LET'S GET IN THERE!
DON'T ORDER ME AROUND!!
GO ON!!
HUFF
HEY, STRAW HAT!!
HUFF
RAAAAH !!!
YOU IDIOT! NOT THIS ROOM!
HUFF
IT'S NEXT DOOR!
WHAT?! NEXT? DOOR?
HUFF...
HUFF...

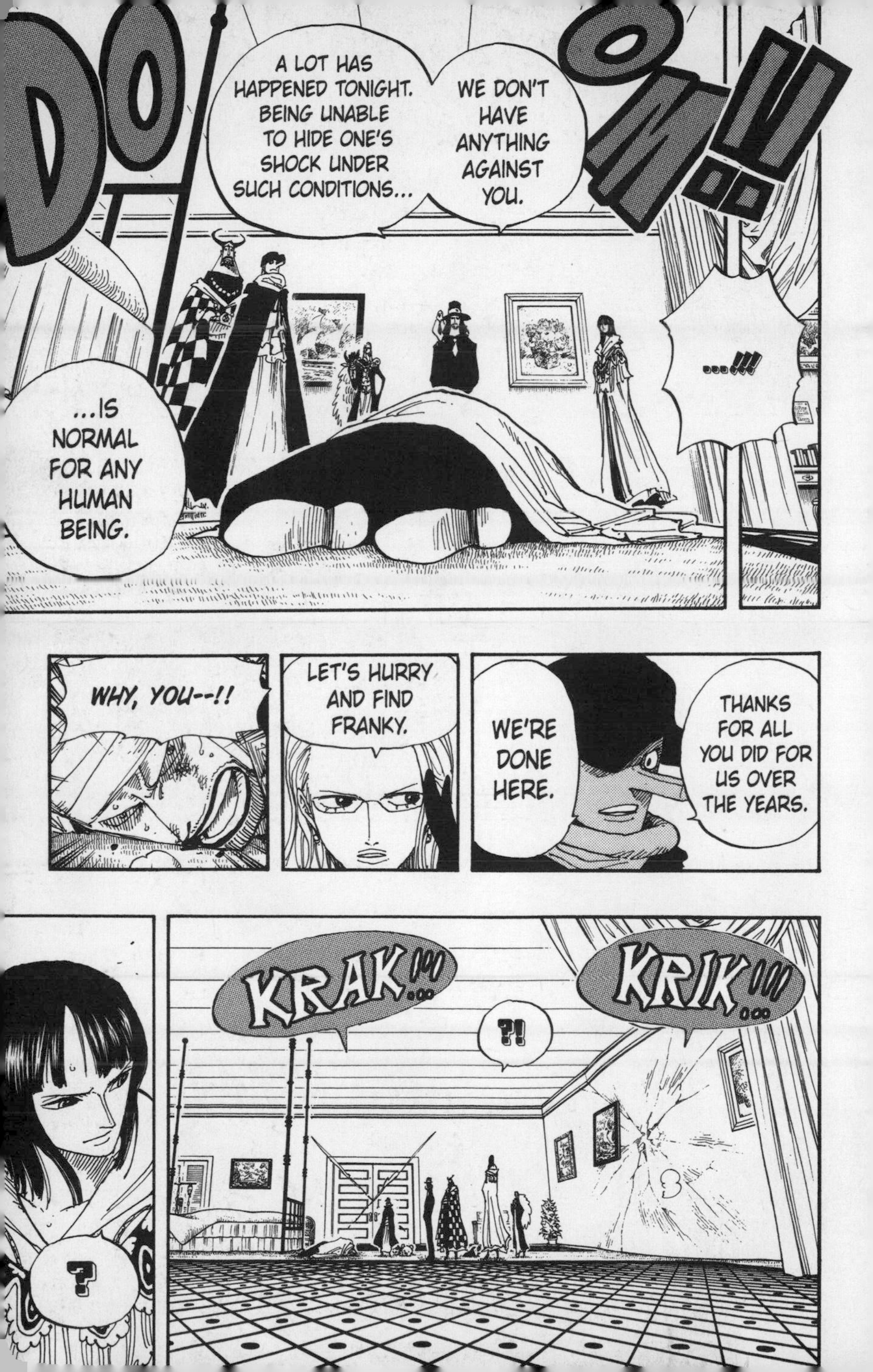
...!!!
WE DON'T HAVE ANYTHING AGAINST YOU.
A LOT HAS HAPPENED TONIGHT. BEING UNABLE TO HIDE ONE'S SHOCK UNDER SUCH CONDITIONS...
...IS NORMAL FOR ANY HUMAN BEING.
DOOM!!
THANKS FOR ALL YOU DID FOR US OVER THE YEARS.
WE'RE DONE HERE.
LET'S HURRY AND FIND FRANKY.
WHY, YOU--!!
KRIK!!
?!
KRAK!!
?

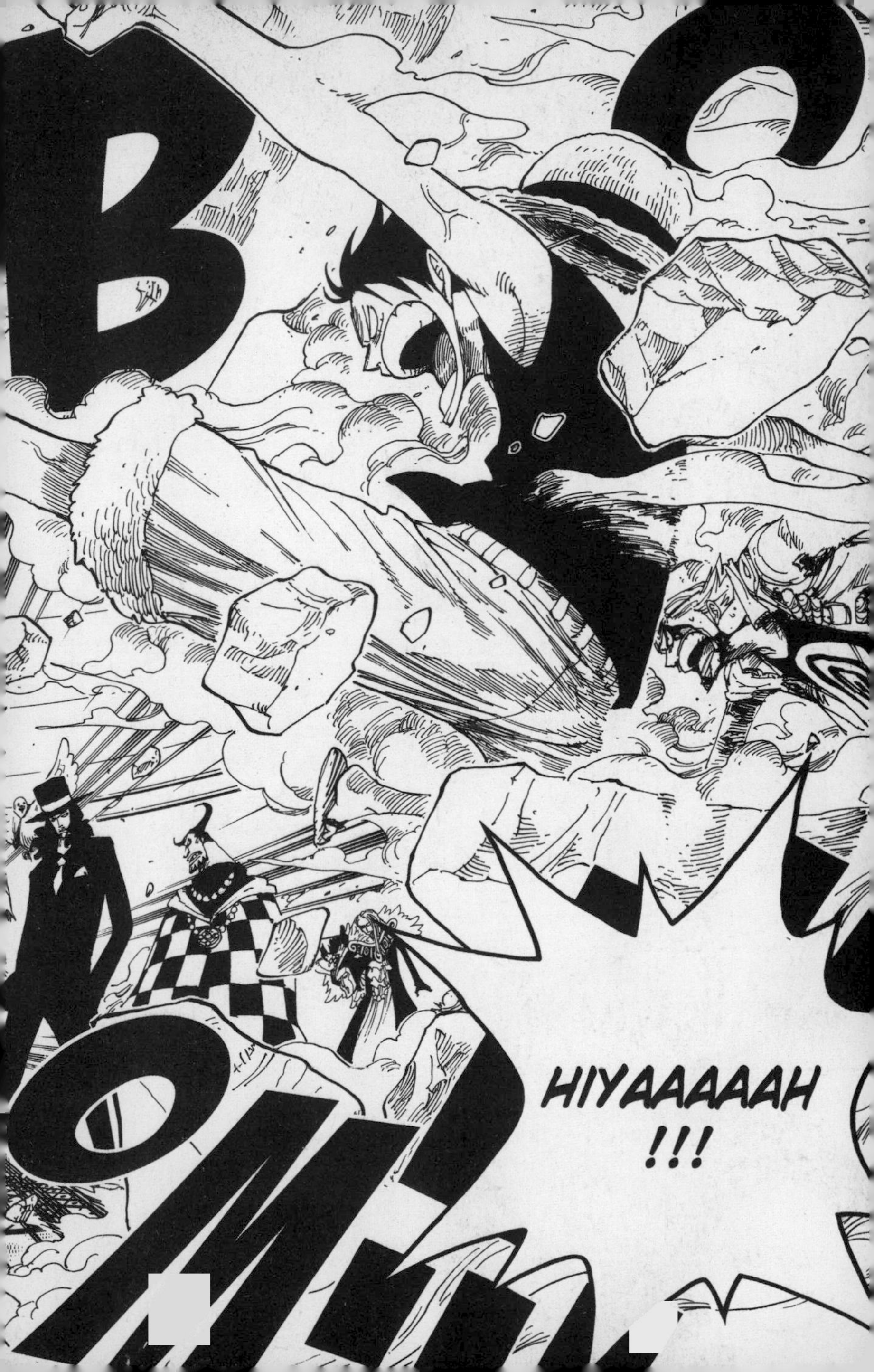
HIYAAAAAH !!!

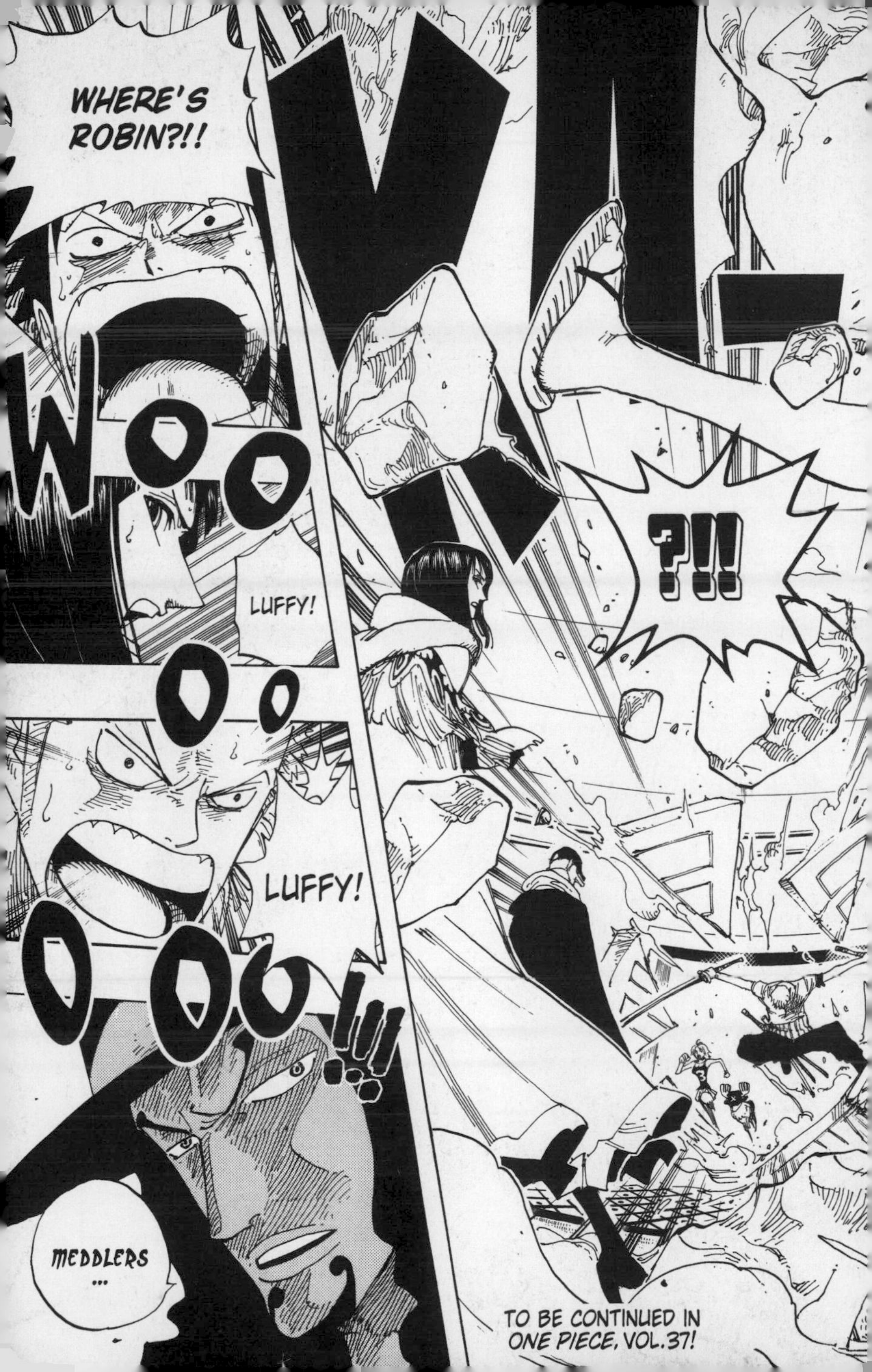
?!!
WHERE'S ROBIN?!!
WOOOOOOO!!
LUFFY!
LUFFY!
MEDDLERS...
TO BE CONTINUED IN ONE PIECE, VOL.37!

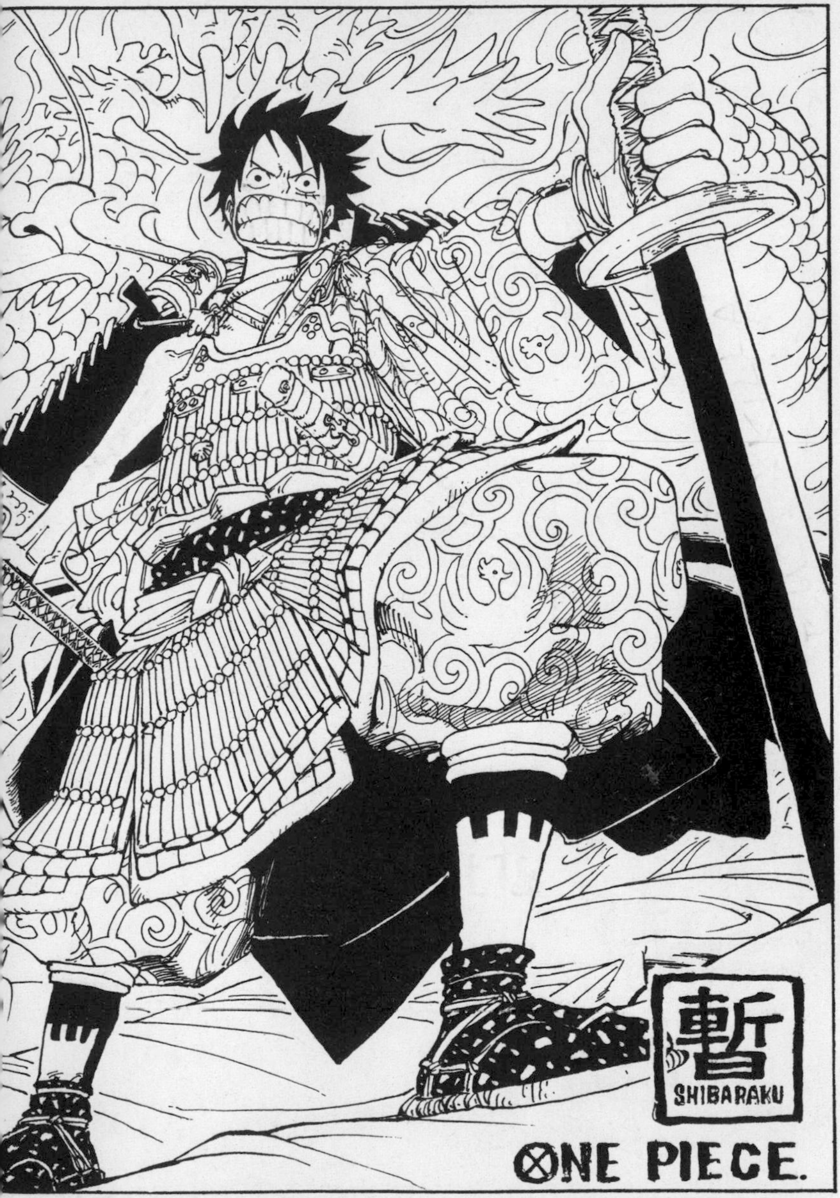
暫
SHIBARAKU
ONE PIECE.

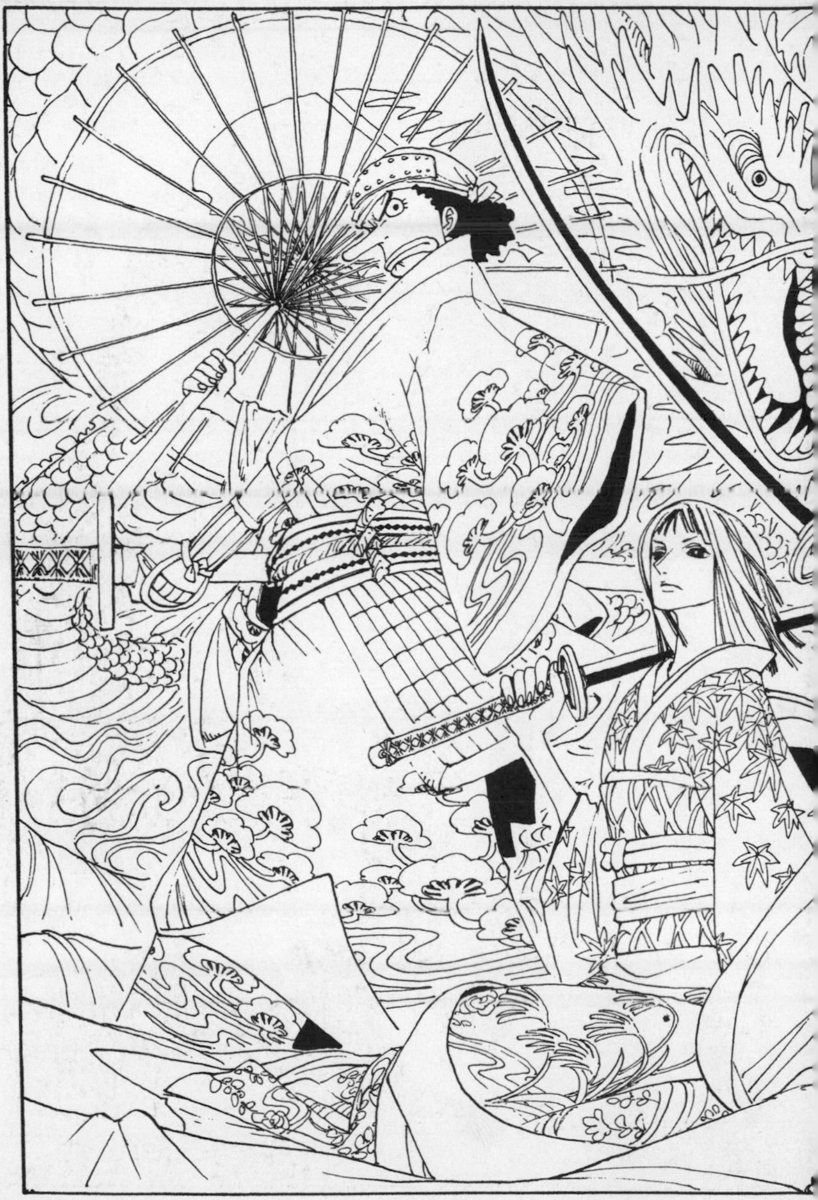

COMING NEXT VOLUME:

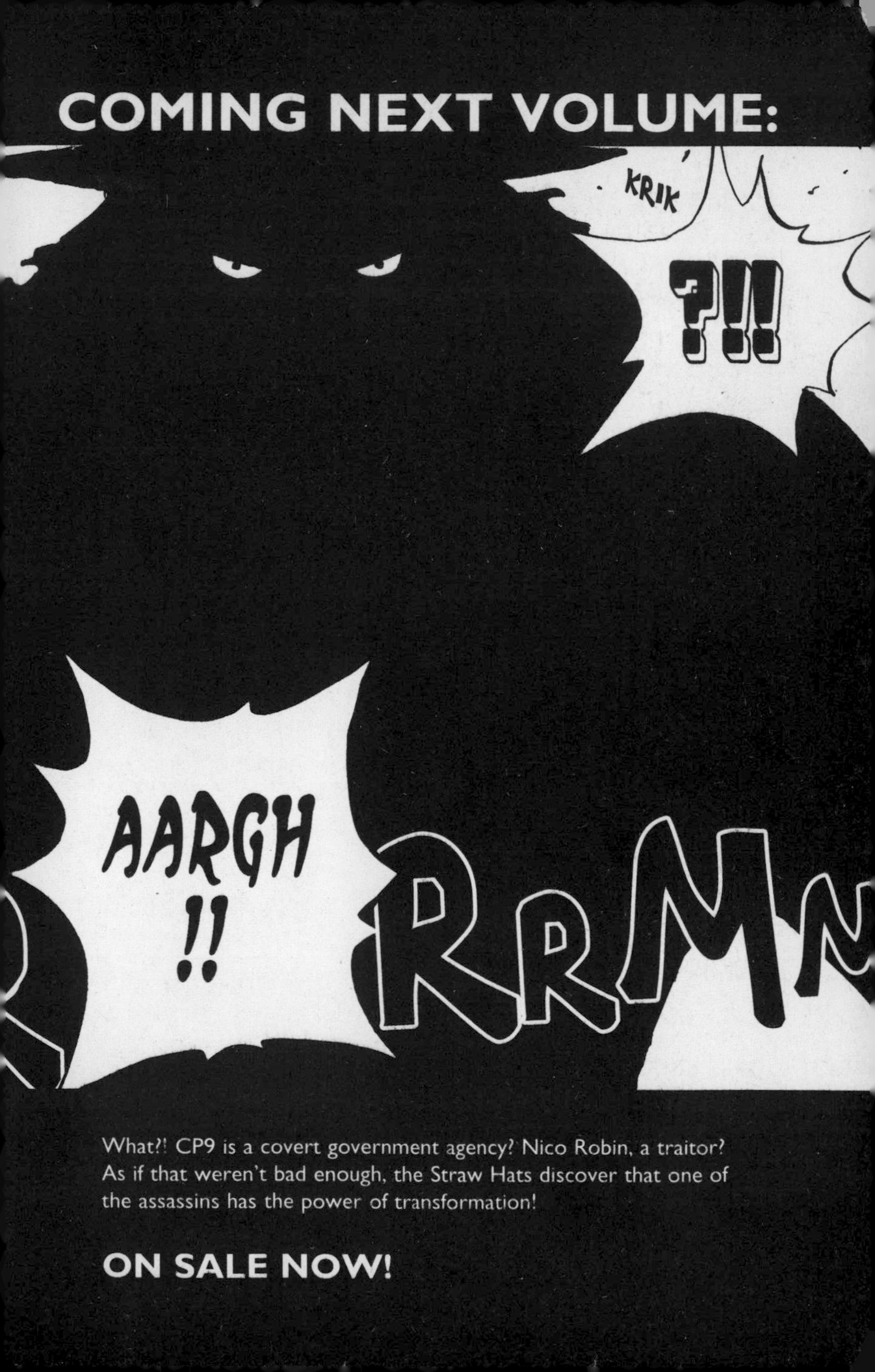
KRIK
?!!
AARGH !!
RRMN

What?! CP9 is a covert government agency? Nico Robin, a traitor? As if that weren't bad enough, the Straw Hats discover that one of the assassins has the power of transformation!

ON SALE NOW!

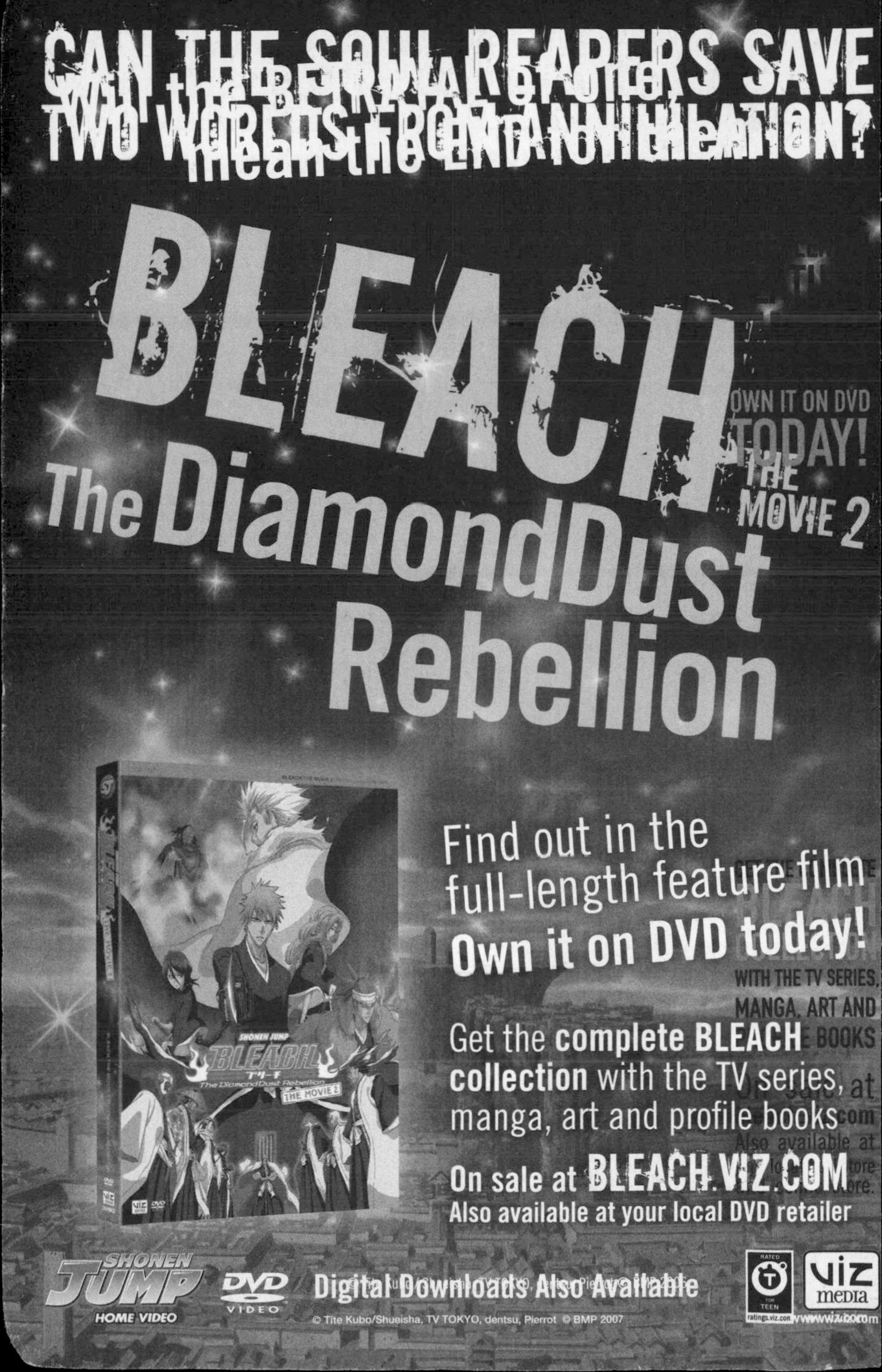
CAN THE SOUL REAPERS SAVE TWO WORLDS FROM ANNIHILATION?
BLEACH
The DiamondDust Rebellion
OWN IT ON DVD TODAY!
THE MOVIE 2
Find out in the full-length feature film
Own it on DVD today!
Get the complete BLEACH collection with the TV series, manga, art and profile books
On sale at BLEACH.VIZ.COM
Also available at your local DVD retailer
SHONEN JUMP HOME VIDEO
DVD VIDEO
Digital Downloads Also Available
© Tite Kubo/Shueisha, TV TOKYO, dentsu, Pierrot © BMP 2007
RATED T FOR TEEN ratings.viz.com
viz media
www.viz.com

Tell us what you think about SHONEN JUMP manga!

Our survey is now available online.
Go to: www.SHONENJUMP.com/mangasurvey

Help us make our product offering better!

THE REAL ACTION STARTS IN...

www.shonenjump.com

ONE PIECE

Story and Art by Eiichiro Oda

Want even MORE?

Visit **onepiece.viz.com/wanted**

and enter the name of the character featured on this sticker for a *One Piece* speed-up bonus!

And DON'T FORGET to check out these other GREAT TITLES from SHONEN JUMP

THE WORLD'S MOST POPULAR MANGA

BLEACH
Tite Kubo
NARUTO
28
Masashi Kishimoto
SHONEN JUMP
THE WORLD'S MOST POPULAR MANGA
$4.99
ON THE DS!
ULTIMO
A HERO IS BORN!
THE ACTION FIGURES ARE HERE!
7
Tegami Bachi

Find more at shonenjump.viz.com

RATED T FOR TEEN ratings.viz.com

RATED T+ FOR OLDER TEEN ratings.viz.com

VIZ MEDIA www.viz.com

Not for sale, resale or auction

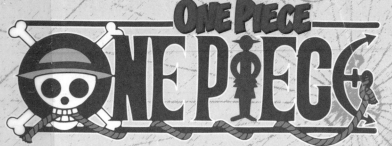

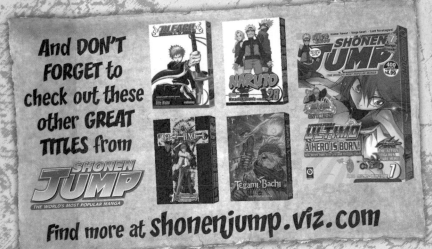

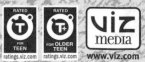